To

with friends

from Nick.

(In memory of the time you
saw me off at King's Cross
Station. See p. 446, note 33.)

Regency Radical

An engraving of William Hone by W. J. Edwards, based on a portrait by George Patten.
By permission of Guildhall Library, Corporation of London.

Regency Radical

Selected Writings of
William Hone

Edited by

DAVID A. KENT AND D. R. EWEN

WAYNE STATE UNIVERSITY PRESS

Copyright ©2003 by Wayne State University Press,
Detroit, Michigan 48201. All rights are reserved.
No part of this book may be reproduced without formal permission.
Manufactured in the United States of America.
Library of Congress Cataloging-in-Publication Data
Hone, William, 1780–1842.
Regency radical : selected writings of William Hone / edited by David
A. Kent and D. R. Ewen.
p. cm.
Includes bibliographical references and index.
ISBN 0-8143-3060-6 (alk. paper)
1. Hone, William, 1780–1842—Correspondence. 2. Radicalism—Great
Britain—History—19th century—Sources. 3. Great
Britain—History—George III, 1760–1820—Sources. 4. Great
Britain—History—George IV, 1820–1830—Sources. 5. Authors,
English—19th century—Correspondence. 6. Journalists—Great
Britain—Correspondence. I. Kent, David A., 1948– II. Ewen, D. R.,
1925– III. Title.
PR4794.H5 A6 2003
828'.709—dc21
2002004799
The paper used in this publication meets the minimum requirements of the Ameri-
can National Standard for Information Sciences—Permanence of Paper for Printed
Library Materials, ANSI Z39.48-1984.

CONTENTS

PART FOUR
SELECTED LETTERS OF HONE

ACKNOWLEDGMENTS

In addition to the more formal acknowledgments below to libraries and other institutions, we wish to express our gratitude to several individuals who have generously helped us with our work on William Hone: Marlene Caplan typed the manuscript over several years and demonstrated her cheerful patience with us on many occasions; John Willoughby, York University, lent us his copies of Hone's prose volumes, though he could hardly have foreseen how long we would keep them, and he read our introduction; Maurice Elliott, chair of the Department of English at York University, Toronto, gave us help in several ways—in supporting grant applications; in giving us access to his copy of *The Queen's Matrimonial Ladder;* and in arranging the co-operative purchase, between the Department of English and York University Libraries, of a substantial number of Hone manuscripts on microfilm from the British Library; Kyle Grimes, University of Alabama, generously gave us his informed advice; Russell McDougall, University of New England, New South Wales, sent us information on Joseph Hone; and Hugh Anson-Cartwright, Toronto antiquarian book dealer, kindly obtained copies of several Hone works we would otherwise have had difficulty consulting. We are also grateful to York University for its program of Minor Research Grants that permitted us to make photo reproductions of the Cruikshank wood engravings so integral to Hone's satires.

We acknowledge with thanks the following libraries who have given their permission to reproduce letters in this volume: the Bath Central Library; the Berg Collection of English and American Literature, the New York Public Library, the Astor, Lenox, and Tilden Foundations; the Bodleian Library, Oxford; the British Library; the

Guildhall Library, Corporation of London; the Director and University Librarian, the John Rylands University Library of Manchester; the National Library of Scotland; the Master and Fellows of Pembroke College, Oxford; and the Principal and Fellows of Somerville College, Oxford. We are also grateful to the Berg Collection of English and American Literature; the New York Public Library; and the Astor, Lenox, and Tilden Foundations for their permission to reproduce George Cruikshank's sketches of Hone and Ellenborough; and to the Guildhall Library, Corporation of London, for permission to reproduce the engraving by W. J. Edwards of George Patten's portrait of Hone.

D. A. K. D. R. E.
Toronto, Ontario

INTRODUCTION

In his annual Christmas letter to William Hone in 1832, besides announcing the imminent arrival of the fifteenth turkey he had given to the Hone family, John Childs expresses continuing admiration for his friend, "a champion against oppression."[1] It was Hone who, fifteen years earlier, had stood up against what the radicals deemed a despotic government:

> it affords me the highest gratification to recur to those days, when you stood before the Wickedst tribunal that ever existed in this Country & were saved by the common sense of a few plain men. The memory of that day ought to be kept fresh in the memory of both old & young,—My Young ones shall not forget it if I can help it, for on every Xmas day I give them the History of your prosecutions, Drink to your Health & prosperity, & sing in full chorus the Carol, *"Lord Castlereagh doth rule this House"* & at five o'clock tomorrow, the Toast *"Mr. Hone & his Jury"* will be drunk by me, & my eight boys with all the noise we can make. . . .
>
> (24 December 1832)[2]

Childs introduced himself to Hone not long after the trials had concluded, and by late January 1818 he was encouraging Hone to have the proceedings published ("you are certain of universal fame"[3]) and to come to the country for a rest (Childs was a printer living in Bungay, in Suffolk). Hone had been put on trial on 18, 19, and 20 December 1817 for publishing parodies of services and prayers in the *Book of Common*

Prayer. On three consecutive days, speaking for about seven hours each day, he conducted his own defense, and on each occasion a jury acquitted him. By the conclusion of the third trial, Hone was exhausted, though a crowd estimated at twenty-five thousand in the streets outside the Guild Hall greeted him as a hero of the radical cause. The "memory of that day" began to fade from the public's memory in subsequent years, however, once reformist principles became accepted political policy (about the time of Childs's letter), and Hone's name was gradually relegated to digressive asides or footnotes in accounts of the period.

As a struggling London bookseller and publisher, Hone was always on the watch for a saleable commodity, and he did publish his *Trials* in 1818 to capitalize on his own notoriety. The trials were not reissued until 1880, by Thomas Tegg, and it is difficult now to appreciate the impact that they had. They have not been reprinted since the late nineteenth century, despite the fact that E. P. Thompson, in his *The Making of the English Working Class*, singled them out as "some of the most hilarious legal proceedings on record."[4] The reactions of both contemporary and nineteenth-century readers are a reliable guide to the trials' importance. The *Times* of London, while deploring some aspects of Hone's parodies as distasteful (their "indecent" qualities blamed on the poor man's lack of education), nevertheless sympathized with Hone and condemned the government's tactics as ill-advised and inhumane. Although the paper had not anticipated "the deep interest" the trials provoked, it was now judged that "Hone's whole defence . . . will be read with interest, and will excite feelings, now and hereafter, which it far exceeds our powers to appreciate."[5] The trials must have caught the public's imagination, since The *Times* printed virtually the full texts of the trials immediately after each concluded.[6] Writing after Hone's death, James Routledge identified Hone's trials as a turning point in the struggle for political reform: "Never in all history had an English, or any government, been more completely defeated. . . . The year 1817 was the beginning of a long series of victories for the nation over mere class."[7] Harriet Martineau placed the trials "amongst the most remarkable in our constitutional history," and claimed that "They produced more distinct effects upon the temper of the country than any public proceedings of that time."[8] Most subsequent commentators have agreed that Hone's legal victory was "a significant mark in the struggle for a free press."[9] In terms of Hone's personal life, the trials made him "a public character," to repeat the phrase used by Charles Knight. Hone the parodist, "the arch-blasphemer" (to use his own words), became indelibly etched in the public's mind.[10] After a few more years of radical activity as a satirist and publisher (until about 1821), he paradoxically spent much of the rest of his life trying to repair his reputation as an infidel and establish his character as a Christian and God-fearing man.

In the past two decades, increasing attention has been paid to Hone. His activities as a radical publisher and writer during the second half of the Regency, often in collaboration with the brilliant visual artist George Cruikshank, are beginning to be rediscovered and recognized.[11] If, as Epstein has recently claimed, Hone is "the greatest radical satirist of the Regency era," then his life and work deserve this increased attention from students of romanticism.[12] This volume intends to introduce readers to Hone through selections from his trials, major satires, and letters. Our selection extends to works beyond the Regency period, and these reveal a much changed man in his later years of recantation. Nevertheless, Hone's career and reputation are identified with Regency radical politics, and the works we have chosen relate primarily to that period.

1

In a letter to his brother Leigh written in 1817, the radical publisher John Hunt listed the issues that he considered synonymous with "reform": "Parliamentary Reform, Catholic Emancipation, Religious *Liberty* (not Toleration), the amelioration of the Penal Laws . . . the cause of the People. . . ."[13] He had been considering whether he would support a new Whig newspaper, the *Guardian,* and these were the bedrock principles that would determine his allegiance. In a period when the term "radical" embraced a wide variety of individuals of different backgrounds and degrees of political involvement, this list—with the addition of freedom of the press—conveniently summarizes the central issues that equally motivated Hone and were the basis of his friendship with John Hunt. Hone, "a representative early nineteenth-century radical," subscribed also to universal suffrage for men and repeatedly attacked the government's system of patronage and corruption as it extended into the church and legal system.[14] So, while it is difficult to define his "politics," it is possible to point to the political principles and issues that drove him to attack the established powers through radical satire.

A concise overview of the reform movement is given by Michael Scrivener in the introduction to his anthology, *Poetry and Reform*.[15] Scrivener identifies its three key phases: the 1790s, post-Waterloo, and 1830. He also names three primary constituencies in the reform movement: the liberal Whigs (led by Charles James Fox until 1806); middle-class reformers, largely Dissenters; and plebeian radicals (initially fostered by the London Corresponding Society). Hone had friends, acquaintances, and admirers in each group. He shared with plebeian radicals the ideal of native English liberty, the veneration of democratic heroes from Alfred the Great to John Hampden, and the goal of restoring ancient rights. However, Hone, together with the aspiring middle-class reformer Francis Place, condemned those radicals who counseled the violent overthrow of the government. At the same time Hone admired Thomas Evans (whom Place, having achieved respectability, later repudiated), and he certainly knew of Thomas Spence. He perhaps adapted techniques used by Spence in his journal, *Pig's Meat*,[16] and he may also have used some of the satiric methods of Daniel Isaac Eaton when he brought out his popular satires in the late Regency period. As Marcus Wood notes, Eaton's *Politics for the People* is "pitted with mock litanies, catechisms, creeds, and hymns."[17] Parody and pastiche were, of course, common practices among radicals, since their effect was to deflate the power and mystique of the ruling class's linguistic systems of control in law and church.[18] Laughter generated by ridicule and mockery erases hierarchical distinctions; it is "profoundly seditious," embodying an "immediate, collective and infectious anti-authoritarianism."[19] It was Hone's brilliance in this mode that, in the government's eyes, made him so dangerous.

Born in 1780 in Bath, Hone moved to London with his family when he was three, and remained there for the rest of his life. He was raised strictly by his devout father, who taught his son to read by studying the Bible. As a young boy, he even met John Wesley, while the latter was visiting Hone's nursery school teacher when she was in her final illness.[20] Hone admired Bunyan's *Pilgrim's Progress* and Foxe's *Book of Martyrs*.[21] He also describes having bought his first "old book" when he was "scarcely eleven years old."[22] This book was *The Trial of John Lilburne*, and it was to exercise a profound effect on Hone's attitudes toward political and legal authority.[23] Hone's early piety did not last. His autobiographical notes describe a gradual loss of religious faith, the discovery of the natural world, and an enthusiastic commitment to the "new philosophy," the political ideals embodied in the French Revolution.[24] Hone's brief membership in the London Corresponding Society (his father sent him out of London to Chatham to eliminate its influence on him) indicates his early reform allegiances and his defiance of his father's religious pietism and political conservatism.[25] In 1800, when he was twenty (and after several years working as a copyist in legal offices), Hone married Sarah Johnson, with whom he had ten children, and started in the bookselling business with the help of money from his mother-in-law.[26] After a series of false starts and several changes of premises, and while still trying to establish his business, in 1805 Hone became involved with John Bone in a scheme to abolish the Poor Rate. They then developed plans for "Tranquillity," an institution that would combine the features of savings bank, insurance office, employment registry, hostel, and bathhouse.[27] By 1808 Hone and Bone were members of a committee supporting the election of Major Cartwright as well as the cause of parliamentary reform. Their partnership in printing political pamphlets and in bookselling came to an end with bankruptcy in late 1810, an all-too-frequent conclusion to Hone's ventures.[28]

Hone next became involved in the movement to reform lunatic asylums. He opposed the prevailing practice of physically restraining the insane and the deranged, and believed that these individuals should be treated as if they were suffering from a "solely intellectual" disease.[29] His allies were Robert Waithman, City radical and alderman, and his friends Edward Wakefield and James Bevans. It was Wakefield who wrote to Hone in late 1813 deploring "the wretched state of the private mad houses near the Metropolis" and indicating that he would propose Hone as secretary of the committee.[30] Having inspected numerous asylums, this small committee produced a report with shocking disclosures and practical recommendations.[31] After this effort, concluding in 1814, Hone became steadily more interested in the legal system and its victims. He was a witness at inquests into the deaths of two rioters in 1815; and he then took up the cause of Eliza Fenning, a young woman, poor and ignorant, sentenced to death by a prejudiced judge on a murder charge supported only by circumstantial evidence. He published *The Maid and the Magpie* in an effort to rouse public attention. Hone wished to expose the corruption of the courts and to present rehabilitation as the proper objective of prisons. He also sought the abolition of the death penalty.[32]

Hone's publications on the Fenning case initiated six years of publications that dealt with a remarkable variety of social and political issues: slavery, income tax, Napoleon, liberty of the press, habeas corpus, parliamentary reform, Peterloo, Queen Caroline, law reform, and corruption in the government and in the Church, among them. As Jonathan Hill summarizes, "Most of his publications were swiftly produced, inexpensive, quick-selling reactions to passing events and current affairs. In format they range from complete books to pamphlets, portraits, broadsides, and caricatures."[33] Although some 500 titles have at one time or another been attributed to Hone, Ann Bowden's doctoral research suggests that a more accurate figure is 228 titles "written, edited and/or published by Hone himself," nearly 90 percent of which were produced in the 1815–21 period.[34] Starting in 1816, Hone's attacks began to focus on key targets, chief among them the Prince Regent, in such pamphlets as *The Regent's Bomb . . . , Saluting the Regent's Bomb,* and *The Yacht for the Regent's Bomb.*[35] Hone also engaged in what we would term piracies, most notably of Byron. Abridgments and continuations of other writers' works were not subject to prosecution, and Hone's own writings were treated similarly once they became popular. When Hone printed Southey's *Wat Tyler* in 1817 to embarrass the now conservative poet laureate with his own youthful republicanism, the judge, Lord Ellenborough, quashed Southey's appeal; as the work was seditious, it was not within the protection of the law.[36] Only a few years later Hone would vigorously object to being associated with the practice of piracy, but by that point he was engaged in an active campaign to redeem his public name.[37]

Early in 1817, perhaps at the urging of Francis Place, Hone undertook to publish a weekly journal commenting on political events. He launched his *Political Register,*[38] in fact, during the massive "burgeoning" of periodicals, many of them reformist, in the post-Napoleonic period. In 1811, for example, there were eight morning and eight evening papers in London; later in the decade, the number of daily papers exceeded 160. Radical publishers avoided the stamp tax on newspapers by publishing informational essays instead of directly presenting news in the form defined as "a newspaper." The circulation of political journals was widespread enough for them to threaten the status quo. Carlile's *Republican* sold fifteen thousand copies at the peak of its popularity; Wooler's *Black Dwarf,* twelve thousand (twice the number of the *Times* newspaper); and Cobbett's twopenny *Political Register* from

forty thousand to sixty thousand in 1816 and 1817. These developments, together with other signs of unrest and opposition, so alarmed
the government that various repressive measures were instituted.
Among these were the so-called Gagging Acts in 1817, and in 1819 the
infamous Six Acts, notably the Newspaper Stamp Duties Act, which put
a temporary end to inexpensive opposition publications since it altered
the definition of "newspaper" to include radical journals.[39] In late
March 1817 Cobbett fled to America to avoid certain arrest after the
suspension of habeas corpus. Meanwhile, Hone published his *Register*
for eight months, in the process again attacking the Regent as well as
rotten boroughs in the House of Commons and effectively using the
publication as the beginning of his self-defense, by addressing directly
the issue of blasphemy. For example, he reprinted (in his 8 March issue) a parody of the *Te Deum* that had originally appeared in the *Times*,
as well as excerpts from both the *Black Dwarf*, in which editor and publisher Thomas Wooler spoke against the charge of blasphemy, and from
the *Guardian*, in which parodies also were seen as essentially political
satires.

Besides starting his political weekly in early 1817, Hone also attracted the government's attention through his publication of four pamphlets in January and one in February that used forms and services
from the *Book of Common Prayer* of the Church of England to create
political satire: *The Political Litany, The Sinecurist's Creed, A Political
Catechism, The Bullet Te Deum,* and *The Late John Wilkes's Catechism*.[40] Hone became aware that the government, using the pretext of
the attack on the Regent's carriage as it returned from the opening of
Parliament on 17 January, was going to strike back at him, so he withdrew all the parodies on 22 February.[41] It was too late. As Kyle Grimes
notes, "Within weeks of their initial publication, at least ten other
printers throughout England were publishing versions of the parodies."[42] A Secret Committee (which included Lord Castlereagh,
William Wilberforce, and George Canning) met during February to consider measures to deal with the radicals (Hone was highly critical of
this committee in his *Register*). Shortly afterward, on 4 March, the
Habeas Corpus Act came into effect, and on 14 March the Seditious
Meetings Act of 1795 was reinstituted. Then Lord Sidmouth, the prime
minister, acting on the legal advice of William Garrow and Samuel
Shepherd (both members of the Secret Committee), issued a circular
letter to the Lords-Lieutenant in England and Wales on 27 March,

stressing the power of magistrates "to arrest the sellers of published material which had been sworn to as seditious and blasphemous."[43] Undoubtedly, the government saw the opportunity to convict Hone by fastening attention on his parodies as blasphemous libels. Hone learned that his parodies had been specifically cited, together with "other dangerous agencies, such as political clubs, secret meetings, and outspoken Radical newspapers," as demanding the vigilance of the authorities.[44]

Hone was arrested 3 May 1817 on an *ex officio* information, one of the special privileges of the prosecution in cases of libel since Sir Vicary Gibbs had introduced an enabling bill in 1807.[45] By employing this legal device, the attorney-general could avoid a preliminary hearing before a Grand Jury. In addition, the defendant paid the costs even if he were acquitted.[46] Two days after his arrest, Hone was called before the Court of King's Bench to plead guilty or not guilty. He refused. As he had not had any opportunity to read the charges or consult legal counsel, he argued that he had been illegally detained. Lord Chief Justice Ellenborough, whom Hone would soon encounter in the courtroom, remanded him into custody for his refusal to plead. In late June the imprisoned Hone wrote to the Crown office protesting the legality of the entire proceedings against him, demanding to be set free, and challenging "special juries," the system of picking juries for state trials such as his. In his aggressive stance, he was following the counsel of Sir Richard Phillips, who had written to Francis Place with legal advice about Hone's predicament.[47] Phillips described informations as "illegal," and believed they constituted "an assault": "It behoves a man therefore who is thus unlawfully proceeded against not to act as a defendant—not to plead or parley—but to consider his assailants as the true culprits, to oblige them to exert force towards him, and thus to proceed against them severally & collectively by actions for damages in the court of Common Pleas, & by indictments in the courts of Session."[48] Hone clearly took this advice to heart. Although he had no opportunity to take action in the Court of Common Pleas, as his trials proceeded his aggressive posture toward his prosecutors was increasingly evident.

The whole question of "special juries" had become an issue in the earlier trial of Hone's fellow prisoner and radical publisher Thomas Wooler.[49] Wooler had also been arrested in May, and in prison the two men developed a close friendship. They were each visited by the government spy Oliver (the *Reformists' Register* of 28 June describes this incident), and Wooler's defense of himself when he was tried in June convinced Hone that he should do the same and prepare his own defense for the December trial.[50] To strike a special jury meant turning to lists furnished by sheriffs of men of significant status, often City merchants sympathetic to government calls to public order. This system effectively allowed the prosecution to "pack" the juries with individuals who would favor their arguments. In July, Charles Pearson, the lawyer advising Wooler, brought this matter before the Common Council of the City of London, of which he was a member. A committee was assigned to investigate, and it issued its damning report in December, just in time for Hone to take advantage of it.[51]

In November, Pearson contacted Hone to offer help.[52] Hone had, by then, been preparing for his trials for months, aided by the advice of a number of sympathetic radicals who put aside their differences over individual policies to rally around one of their own. Besides Place and Phillips, John Hunt had immediately called on Mrs. Hone as soon as he learned of Hone's arrest, offering his help.[53] In any case, Hone wrote to Hunt, seeking his advice about strategy; and, in turn, he himself helped Hunt in 1820 by lending him one hundred pounds—an extraordinary amount for a man so often short of money as Hone was— when Hunt was prosecuted for libels published in the *Examiner*.[54] Another comrade was the Reverend Robert Aspland, who responded to Hone's plea in a letter of 28 June 1817 for "materials" to use in his self-defense, mentioning such sources as a sermon by Latimer and parodies of the Dissenters in Charles II's time. Aspland borrowed these and other authorities from Dr. Williams's Library and was at Hone's side during the first trial, helping to manage the large number of books and to find the appropriate references.[55] Major Cartwright had allowed Wooler to use his library and then helped research "the mountain of references" used in Hone's defense. Cruikshank located caricatures in which Gillray had parodied religious subjects for political purposes; he and Hone discussed the arguments Hone would use; and Hone even rehearsed his presentation in Cruikshank's studio.[56] In subsequent years, Hone reciprocated by helping others, when he could. For example, he went to Birmingham in March 1819 to offer materials used in his own case to help in the defense of a printer by the name of Russell (the charges were eventually withdrawn). He is listed as a subscriber on behalf of Thomas Davison, who was tried 23 October 1820 for a blasphe-

mous libel published in *The Deist's Magazine*.[57] Hone also helped
Carlile at his trial in 1819 for publishing Paine's *Age of Reason*, even
though Hone had been angered by Carlile's republishing of the liturgical parodies before the trials and against Hone's objections.[58]

As late as 23 November 1817, when he wrote a supplicatory letter
to Attorney-General Shepherd (the letter is printed below), a part of
Hone was still hoping to avoid a trial. Another part of him, however, was
spoiling for the confrontation. In his cavalier reply, Shepherd told
Hone, "I think I shall first try the Information for the Catechism," a major error in strategy as it turned out.[59] The government also erred in emphasizing the charge of blasphemy rather than libel on the Prince
Regent, assuming the former would be the more damning charge and
easier to demonstrate. Because the foundations of the nation, its laws,
and public morality were grounded in Scripture, blasphemous parodies
threatened the very basis of British civilization by loosening the re-
straints of religion among the lower classes, or so the government argued and assumed.[60]

In his trying and tiring self-defense, Hone drew upon the help of
friends, certainly, but he also had at his disposal his own considerable
reserves of strength and cunning. He had been a law clerk, he had
read, published, and even parodied trial literature, and he felt himself
to stand in the nonconformist tradition of John Lilburne, Foxe's heroes,
and John Bunyan. As Smith observes, *The Trial of John Lilburne* furnished "a map of strategy and resistance."[61] Like other radicals afforded a public forum in court, Hone knew how to exploit the theatrical
aspects of a state trial and to appeal to the jury, presenting himself initially as a solitary, honest man persecuted by a tyrannous and corrupt
government and then, increasingly, in the persona of a martyr.[62] Crabbe
Robinson was in attendance and reacted to the first trial with the following remarks: "Hone defended himself by a very long and rambling
speech of many hours, in which he uttered a thousand absurdities, but
with a courage and promptitude which completely effected his purpose." Robinson also attended the next two trials and condemned the
government of "inconceivable folly" in trying Hone a third time, "for
an offence of far less magnitude": "He was again acquitted, after having carried his boldness to insolence." The scene that morning in court,
Robinson states, was "without a parallel in the history of the country."[63]

Conscious of the presence of shorthand note takers and of the eventual publication of the trials, Hone vigorously argued that he was being

prosecuted solely for his political ideas and based his defense on a central principle of common law: precedent. Interruptions or objections from the judge or attorney general pointing to the irrelevance of the examples the defendant was citing were treated peremptorily by Hone as impositions on his rights as a plaintiff. Now posing as a novice, now pouncing with agility on some legal point, Hone's impudence undoubtedly reached its rhetorical heights in the third trial when, by then confident of his own position, he confronted the Chief Justice of England, Ellenborough. A much-despised judge, Ellenborough could terrorize defendants. He had once sentenced a man on trial for theft to death in Worcester because he had "counterfeited idiocy" in court, "lolling out his tongue."[64] The son of a bishop, whom Hone had the temerity to use in his testimony as a fellow-parodist, Ellenborough was "deeply offended by Hone's tracts and Republican propaganda."[65] The exchanges between Hone and Ellenborough might often be marked by vituperative energy but there were also flickers of mutual respect, as of enemies who, though joined in battle, acknowledged each other as worthy adversaries.

As Smith has noted, Hone might be the only radical who defended himself by claiming that in his publications he had been attacking the government.[66] He avoided the approach of free-thinkers such as Carlile, which would have played directly into the hands of the prosecution, instead announcing himself a God-fearing Christian and successfully battling to secure the moral high ground.[67] His parodies, he argued, merely used the forms of the Prayer Book to make political points; parody did not ridicule its original, whereas travesty did.[68] Ironically, to demonstrate the criminality of Hone's parodies, the prosecution had to demonstrate their similarity to the originals. That meant reading the parodies out loud for all to hear. Soon Hone was quoting his fellow parodists, including Luther, Boys, Latimer, the Dean of Canterbury, even George Canning, carefully avoiding the quotation of any radical examples.[69] The result was uproar in the courtroom, to the consternation of the government side, and acquittal on all three charges. Ellenborough announced to Lord Sidmouth the following day that he was resigning; he was dead a year later.[70]

Hone's judicial triumph prompted celebrations in the streets and an outpouring of financial aid to help him meet his legal expenses and reestablish himself as a bookseller. Although his supporters managed to raise some three thousand pounds, one thousand went to pay expenses and another thousand was fraudulently stolen.[71] The reaction of contemporary writers divided predictably along party lines. For example, Dorothy Wordsworth told Thomas Monkhouse that the acquittal "is enough to make one out of love with English juries."[72] On the other hand, speaking from the perspective of a liberal reformer, Keats felt "Hone and Wooler have done us an essential service," while Coleridge, as Crabbe Robinson reports, "eloquently expatiated on the necessity of saving Hone, in order to save English law. . . ."[73] In spite of warnings from friends such as Samuel Parr about the possibility of new prosecutions if the parodies were published as part of the trial proceedings, Hone was soon busy preparing his trials for publication in order to exploit his sudden popularity. As with the parodies, Hone's *Trials* did sell briskly; the first went through twenty editions; the second, eighteen; and the third, sixteen.[74] The government, its confidence shaken by defeat, backed away from prosecutions during 1818. This was, however, only a temporary pause, as the repression resumed with increased force in the crucial year of 1819.

2

The Six Acts of 1819 defined the alarm the government felt at the obvious strength of the radical movement. Restrictions were therefore placed on the press (stamp duties were imposed to restrict circulation, effectively ending the radical periodical) and magistrates were given wide powers to search for arms and to control public meetings.[75] The attack by soldiers on a peacefully assembled crowd in Manchester in August 1819, afterward dubbed Peterloo by the reformists, brought Hone back into publishing activity. His first major collaboration with George Cruikshank was *The Political House that Jack Built,* the single most successful pamphlet of political satire in the entire period (100,000 were printed[76]). Between 1819 and 1821, Hone and Cruikshank cooperated in producing sixteen pamphlets that revolutionized popular satire in pamphlet form, many of their publications becoming "the most widely circulated of all illustrated political literature."[77] *The Political House* was so successful that it soon provoked numerous imitations by both reformists and loyalists, though Wood is undoubtedly correct in arguing that the style and format, based on a children's nursery rhyme, were somehow "immune against loyalist satiric appropriation."[78]

Hone's account of the origins of the satire is now thought to be unfair to Cruikshank's contribution (whose notes on the rhyme scheme exist in the Berg Collection of the New York Public Library).[79] At the same time, defenders of Cruikshank in the later nineteenth century tend to be unfair to Hone, overemphasizing the independence of the illustrations from the text and mistakenly accusing Hone of treating his friend badly as far as financial payments are concerned.[80] In fact, Cruikshank and Hone were close friends and highly effective collaborators. Cruikshank was often a guest in the Hone household, and Hone often lent money to his friend when there was little enough available. This long, fruitful friendship, beginning perhaps as early as 1811, unfortunately ended in 1827, over, inevitably, a financial matter, when both were victimized by a business adviser whom Hone had hired, the transaction resulting in Hone's bankruptcy.[81] Only when Hone lay on his death bed in 1842 did the former allies briefly reunite.[82]

The assertion by Olivia Smith that with *The Political House* "Hone reached his mature style and developed the genre for which he was most famous" has been convincingly countered by Marcus Wood, who shows that political satire based on children's literature had been popular since the 1780s and that the use of text and illustration on the same page was not original with Hone and Cruikshank. The possible sources for this satire are multiple, and include, among several others, the use of the rhyme by Lord Erskine in Thomas Hardy's trial of 1794 as well as a satire by Rowlandson appearing at the time of the "O. P." riots in 1809.[83] Despite the emergence of these more qualified assessments in recent scholarship, the work of Hone and Cruikshank still had an enormous influence and led the way to the creation of vast quantities of radical satire that was essentially unprosecutable because no government would risk prosecuting something that assumed the form of children's literature. While *The Political House* takes a moderately reformist position, concentrating on freedom of the press, enlarging the franchise, and reforming the Parliament and the patronage system, its incisive representation of the Prince Regent caused the Prince to consider prosecution until he was talked out of it by Lord Eldon and the solicitor general.[84] Name calling, of course, is part of "childish abuse," and the names Hone attached to certain political targets stuck and were repeated in satires by other writers.[85] What made him so lethal and so influential was his success in reaching so many readers: "Hone's genius lay in his unsurpassed ability to publicize radical interpretations of contemporary social and political events to extremely large audiences."[86]

Among the many satires called forth by the Caroline affair of 1820 were two on which Hone and Cruikshank collaborated, *The Queen's Matrimonial Ladder* and *Non Mi Ricordo*.[87] Utilizing a child's toy as a way of representing the history of the royal relationship and the rise and fall of the Prince Regent, Hone and Cruikshank soon found that *The Matrimonial Ladder* (it went through forty-four editions) was their most successful pamphlet after *The Political House*.[88] The reason for this success was that much of the radical and reform movement coalesced briefly in support of Princess Caroline, as her cause proved an effective means of attacking the Regent and the establishment. Clark believes that the controversy allowed radical writers and caricaturists the chance "to create a new political language that was instrumental in the transition from plebeian to working-class agitation."[89] Even Caroline adopted the instruments of parody and pastiche in asserting her claims. She had a state carriage built for her, and she "held court and received the numerous petitions and addresses of support" at Brandenburg House in Hammersmith.[90] In *Non Mi Ricordo* (which reached thirty-one editions before the end of 1820), Hone transposed the famous remark by the Italian witness Majocchi when asked questions during the Queen's trial (which he preferred not to answer) to the mouth of the Prince Regent, whom Hone called before the bar to answer questions about his own conduct. The idea for the pamphlet came from conversations between Hone and Cruikshank, and probably Hazlitt (whose *Political Essays* Hone had just published), at the Southhampton Coffee House in Chancery Lane.[91] As E. P. Thompson observed, "No British monarch has ever been portrayed in more ridiculous gestures nor in more odious terms than George IV during the Queen Caroline agitation. . . ."[92] The Regent was all too aware of how he was being portrayed in popular satire. Between 1819 and 1822, some 2,600 pounds were spent in an attempt to silence the radical publishers, but to no avail.[93]

The final political satire that Hone and Cruikshank produced, *The Political Showman*, affirmed the power of the press. Hone boldly represented the key members of Liverpool's administration as monsters and freaks. Wood has astutely summarized the technique: "Each politician is turned into an aberrant form which exists outside the natural order. Fascinating, but loathsome and infertile, his creatures are symbolic manifestations of political corruption."[94] Synthesizing the emblematic with a bestiary, Hone again showed his genius in exploiting popular forms to achieve his satiric and partisan ends. The text of the *Showman* was a composite of dozens of other texts, from natural history to poetry, which were brilliantly selected for their apt and unintended comment on the contemporary scene and which linked current politicians "with both wonder and fraud."[95] By not using his own words but rather orchestrating a chorus of other voices from the past and present, Hone could once again elude prosecution.[96]

Yet the Caroline affair was the occasion of Hone's last overt and serious political involvement. Although his interests had begun to move in a different direction, he nonetheless did not escape further controversy. In his researches into the history of parody, both for his trials and after he conceived the topic worthy of research toward an independent study, Hone came upon much arcane, esoteric, and, as it turned out, explosive material in the British Museum. In his compilation of ancient sources, *Apocryphal New Testament* (published in 1820), Hone combined translations of apocryphal texts by two scholars from the eighteenth century, Jeremiah Jones for apocryphal books and William Wake for Apostolic fathers.[97] The introduction discusses probable composition dates for books of the New Testament, as well as the process by which the Apocrypha were excluded from the canon of scripture. In effect, Hone was treating biblical materials as if they were the result of human, rather than divine, composition. One anonymous reviewer in the *Quarterly Review* (October 1821) was particularly harsh in his condemnation of Hone's book, but he was not alone. Marsh observes that the resulting scandal, "anticipated by a generation the storm that would surround reception of the German 'Higher Criticism' in England from the 1840s through the 1880s. Here was a first homegrown threat to the exclusive status and authority of the Holy Scriptures. . . ."[98] *Ancient Mysteries Described* (1823) was Hone's attempt to vindicate himself by demonstrating how influential the apocryphal New Testament texts had been on medieval English society, as reflected in the Coventry mystery plays Hone found in the Harleian MSS and reprinted. Ironically, it had been a remark by Ellenborough during Hone's trials that had "induced" him to investigate the subject.[99] Hone published "Aspersions Answered" to refute the claims of the 1821 review and to respond to the fact that his brother Joseph, a lawyer, was suffering by association with the "imputations of irreligion" aimed at Hone "during the last seven years."[100] When the new book brought yet another critical attack from the *Quarterly Review,* Hone wrote "Another Article for the *Quarterly Review.*"

At the same time that Hone was engaged in acts of polemical self-defense, he was also extending his interest in antiquarian and popular culture into another form of publication and starting to modify his radical stance even further. On 1 January 1825, the first volume of the two-volume *Every-Day Book* was published, "a hybrid of almanac and encyclopedia, popular antiquarian miscellany and literary treasury."[101] One of the innovative aspects of this undertaking was Hone's use of "contributor-correspondents" from around the country who were encouraged to send in articles describing local customs and social and religious practices.[102] Hone's prefatory remarks demonstrate his new anxiety not to offend:

> I may now avow that I have other aims than I deemed it expedient to mention in the prospectus:—to communicate in an agreeable manner, the greatest possible variety of important and diverting facts, without a single sentence to excite an uneasy sensation, or an embarrassing inquiry; and, by not seeming to teach, to cultivate a high moral feeling, and the best affections of the heart.

> (Preface, viii)

Hone's intent to promote "social and benevolent feelings" in an effort to achieve respectability and avoid controversy was a startling reversal of direction. Yet, this shift of priorities reflected the mellowing and fragmenting of the radical movement during the 1820s as the economic climate improved, the repressive Publications Act (1819) exerted its effects, several radicals were imprisoned (including Wooler, Carlile, and Hunt), and government became apparently more receptive to eventual reform legislation, as reflected in such domestic policy changes as the move to Catholic emancipation.[103]

Hone's hefty volumes of largely prose writings on a wide diversity of subjects were the basis for his reputation in the nineteenth century as a respectable antiquarian and collector of popular culture. Originally "published serially in inexpensive weekly numbers and illustrated with woodcuts,"[104] they were widely read, popular, and admired. It was in Hone's volumes, for example, that Christina Rossetti first read Keats's poetry. Although most of the material he published came from contributors from around the country, Hone did occasionally contribute his own pieces; we have tried to identify these and include some of them in this selection. What these essays repeatedly reveal are his attachments to the past and to a London that was being threatened by "developers." His essay on "Canonbury Tower," for example, lamented the incursions of urban development in places where Hone remembered streams and fields. A similar theme emerged after a visit to Hagbush Lane, when Hone complained about the relatively neglected rights of the public against the privileges of a private property owner. A visit to Greenwich brought Hone into contact with the ordinary working man and the lively entertainments of a Sunday afternoon. In "The Newsman" he meditated on the changing world of work in an environment in which speed of communication was changing both the procedures of business and the behavior of working men. Hone visited an exhibition in Oxford Street to see the Clarence Vase, perhaps an almost unconscious allusion to Keats's "Ode on a Grecian Urn," and, on walks to Islington and elsewhere, he nostalgically evoked the history and associations of these places.

By the time Hone brought out *The Table Book*, followed a few years later by *The Year Book*, he had become simply an employee trying to repay debts. Throughout his entire life, Hone experienced financial difficulties as a result of a combination of inattentiveness to the bottom line, bad luck, health problems, and lack of third-party investment.[105] As early as 1814 (and an earlier partnership with Bone had dissolved in 1810), there is evidence that Hone's estimates of patient costs in the scheme to reform asylums were inaccurate, or at least a letter from Edward Wakefield of 9 January expresses such a concern.[106] By the mid-1820s, Hone had exhausted the money raised by subscription following his trials, and so, in spite of "meticulous records and superior illustrations, despite rising sales and commendatory notices," Hone was taken into custody on 4 April 1826 and lived within the Rules of King's Bench Prison for two-and-a-half years until September 1828, when he was declared bankrupt and released.[107] In February 1827 he was forced to sell all the stock and wood blocks from the just-published *Facetiae and Miscellanies;* in October he sold the stereotypes; and during these years and after he was selling autographs to collectors. He had earlier sold the library of books and manuscripts he had collected for the *History of Parody* he had hoped to write.[108] His friends arranged for him to be the manager of a coffeehouse, "The Grasshopper Hotel," but that, too, soon failed. Even in the production of the *Year Book*, Hone's generosity to artists (he habitually commissioned more engravings than had been budgeted for) meant that expenses were "far greater" than the publisher, Tegg, had anticipated.[109] Efforts to secure an annuity from the government for Hone were met with bureaucratic evasion, and Hone spent his final years doing freelance editorial work and acting as subeditor of a weekly newspaper, the *Patriot,* founded to express the views of evangelical nonconformists.[110]

Hone's later years were brightened by his friendship with Charles Lamb, by a reconciliation with Robert Southey, and by his conversion to Christianity, described in an 1834 letter to his brother Joseph.[111] Hone's financial problems were temporarily relieved in 1834 and again in 1840 when his income was supplemented by grants of thirty and forty pounds, respectively, from the Literary Fund.[112] Another major development was his finding of religious faith. As we have seen, Hone had inherited a virulent hatred of "priestcraft" from his father.[113] Together with his early ventures in atheistic radicalism and deism, this prevalent anti-clericalism guaranteed that his religious conversion in the early 1830s was not in the direction of the established church (which he, in any case, found moribund). The Reverend Thomas Binney, minister at the Weigh House Chapel, became Hone's friend and pastor for the last decade of his life. Hone was received into the congregation on New Year's Day of 1832, and his whole family was admitted to membership three years later, on 30 December 1834.[114]

In 1813, Walter Wilson had written to Hone and urged him to commit himself and his family to Christianity. In 1835, Hone, in turn, was admonishing John Childs, then fifty years old, to abandon "the bustle of Politics" and begin "a rigid course of self-examination."[115] In spite of his clear commitment to Christianity, however, Hone never entirely escaped his reputation as a parodist and blasphemer. Even the Reverend Binney, while encouraging Hone to make a public confession of belief, seemed at times to side with his detractors. In a letter of 16 February 1835, for example, Binney told Hone that although his "most notorious political pieces *were* political, & were not direct attacks on Christianity," they nevertheless seemed to promote "ridicule" and "contempt" of religion and were regarded as proceeding "from an infidel."[116] Hone must have found this pronouncement by his pastor ironically and deeply frustrating, as he had been laboring for years to redeem his public reputation.

Hone's letters reveal the complex personality of this largely self-taught man. One of their most endearing qualities is playfulness. He loved to joke with his friends and political allies, such as Francis Place or John and Robert Childs. Legal and financial predicaments, however, produced a very different tone. Hone's stilted appeal to Sir Samuel Shepherd, prior to his trials, is embarrassing for its fawning self-abasement, while numerous letters requesting money show him diminished in dignity. Although he might occasionally seem irresponsible in his pursuit of esoteric and antiquarian interests, he was always conscious of the large family depending on him, and could be driven to write obsequious letters to wealthy patrons to secure food for the table. The letters also reveal Hone as something of a melancholy hypochondriac; at least he was prone to complain about his aches and pains. Yet that was, after all, another part of his candid, plain-spoken manner. It is clear that he was able to make and keep friends for life because he was fundamentally an honest and decent person, sympathetic, compassionate, and humane. He could be kind-hearted to a friend when offering advice, as well as tender to a daughter in anticipation of a visit.[117] How Hone's empathy combined with his discomfort about matters financial may be illustrated by the following anecdote:

> A wealthy London banker told the story of how one day in the City he was waiting in his doorway holding his hat in his hand. A shortsighted stranger, thinking he was begging, benevolently placed a coin in the hat as he passed. It was Hone, characteristically giving away money he could not afford to someone who had no need of it.[118]

Above all, Hone hated the pretentious and the false as much as he hated corruption and sycophancy. Like Keats, he was someone whom most readers feel they could have admired and liked. As a leading radical and as "the most popular and most severe satirist" of the English Regency, he is increasingly being recognized as a central figure of the period.[119]

CHRONOLOGY

1780   Born 3 June in Bath, eldest child of William Hone, legal clerk, and Frances Maria Stawell.

c 1783   Moved to London.

1792   Started work in legal office.

1797   Joined London Corresponding Society.

1800   19 July, married Sarah Johnson. They were to have a large family of ten children. Opened his first business, a circulating library, in Lambeth Walk.

1806   Founded, with John Bone, "Tranquillity," a project to provide financial services for workers. After its failure, their next partnership in book-selling also failed.

1807–14   Series of unsuccessful business ventures.

1814   With James Bevans and Edward Wakefield, campaigned to improve conditions in insane asylums.

1815   Publicized unjust trial and execution of Eliza Fenning. Began collaboration with George Cruikshank.

1817   January–February: Hone publishes five parodies, three of which (*The Late John Wilkes's Catechism of a Ministerial Member, The Political Litany,* and *The Sinecurist's Creed*) became subjects of prosecution the following December.

         February–October: *Hone's Reformists' Register* published weekly.

1817   May–July: Hone arrested and held in custody.

              18, 19, and 20 December: Hone is tried for blasphemous and seditious libel but is acquitted on all three charges.

              29 December: Public meeting held at City of London Tavern to raise funds to meet Hone's legal and other expenses.

1818   *The Three Trials of William Hone:* transcriptions of the proceedings of the trials published.

1819   *The Political House that Jack Built* published in response to the "Peterloo massacre."

              Don Juan, Canto the Third!, parody of Byron published.

1820   *The Queen's Matrimonial Ladder* and *Non Mi Ricordo* published in connection with the trial of Princess Caroline.

              The Apocryphal New Testament

1821   *The Political Showman—At Home!*

              A Slap at Slop and the Bridge-Street Gang

1823   *Ancient Mysteries Described, Especially the English Mystery Plays*

              Begins friendship with Charles Lamb.

1824   "Aspersions Answered" and "Another Article for the *Quarterly Review,*" two pamphlets in response to an attack on *The Apocryphal New Testament* that had appeared in the *Quarterly Review* for July 1821.

              His brother Joseph emigrates to Tasmania.

1825–26   *The Every-Day Book*

1826–28   Imprisoned for debt.

1827   *Facetiae and Miscellanies,* a reprinting of many of his most popular satires. Friendship with George Cruikshank ends over financial problems.

1827–28	*The Table Book*
1830–33	Set up as proprietor of "The Grasshopper," a coffee-house on Gracechurch Street.
1832	New Year's Day conversion experience at Weigh House Chapel.
	Begins friendship with the Reverend Thomas Binney.
1836–37	Subeditor of the *Patriot*, nonconformist newspaper, his last employment.
1841	*The Early Life and Conversion of William Hone*, a memoir of his father.
1842	On his deathbed, Hone was reconciled with George Cruikshank and met Charles Dickens.
	Died 3 November and buried in Abney Park cemetery in Stoke Newington.

PART ONE

———————

THE

TRIALS

AND

OTHER

WRITINGS

In January and February 1817, William Hone published five powerful satires attacking the Prince Regent, the government, and the established church. These satires took the form of parodies of liturgical forms and services from *The Book of Common Prayer* and had an immediate impact both on the reform movement and on an alarmed government. By 22 February 1817, when Hone stopped the sale of the parodies, about three thousand had been sold. Demand increased, however, and for many months they were pirated and circulated throughout the country.

Using "internal evidence from the advertisements printed on the title pages," Ann Bowden ("William Hone's Political Journalism, 1815–1821" Ph. D. diss., University of Texas at Austin, 1975, 1:182 n. 4) gives the order of their publication as follows: 1. *The Political Litany, Diligently Revised* ; 2. *The Sinecurist's Creed, or Belief* ; 3. *A Political Catechism*; 4. *The Bullet Te Deum; with the Canticle of the Stone;* 5. *The Late John Wilkes's Catechism of a Ministerial Member.* The first, second, and fifth parodies were to be the subject of separate trials the following December, and they are reprinted within the following selections from the trials; the first and fifth were adapted by Hone from existing texts, while the second was written by Hone himself. For a summary of the question of authorship for *The Late John Wilkes's Catechism,* see Marcus Wood, *Radical Satire and Print Culture 1790–1822* (Oxford: Clarendon Press, 1994), 115–16. On *The Political Litany,* see our note 40 to the introduction. Of the remaining two, number 3 was not written by Hone (he was the publisher) and is omitted from our text. Number 4 is printed here and was written by Hone.

The immediate occasion for *The Bullet Te Deum; with the Canticle of the Stone* was the attack on the Prince Regent's carriage as he returned from the opening of Parliament on 28 January 1817. The "Te Deum Laudamus" and "Benedicite, Omnia Opera" are both part of the liturgy of Morning Prayer in the *Book of Common Prayer.* The parodies closely follow the original liturgical forms but substitute very different objects of worship.

BULLET

TE DEUM,

WITH THE

CANTICLE

OF

THE STONE [1]

Imprimatur

F. RABELAIS

*There shall be read distinctly, with an audible voice, the Leading Article of the
Courier,[2] (except there be other LESSONS appointed by the Treasury for that
Day:) he that readeth, so standing and turning himself, as he may best be heard
of all such as are present. And after that, shall be said or sung, in English, daily
throughout the week, as followeth:—*

Te Deum Laudamus

WE praise thee O Stone: we acknowledge thee to be a Bullet.

All the Corruptionists doth worship thee: the Placegiver everlasting.

To thee all Placemen cry aloud: the Treasury, and all the Clerks therein.

To thee Pensioners and Sinecurists: continually do cry,

Bullet, Bullet, Bullet: from thee our power floweth.

Borough-mongers and Lords in waiting: are full of thy two holes a quarter of an inch apart.

The glorious company of the Chinese Eating Room: praise thee.

The goodly fellowship of the Pavilion:[3] praise thee.

The noble army of Tax Commissioners: praise thee.

The pure Legitimates throughout all the world: doth acknowledge thee,

The Saviour of an expiring Ministry.

Thou art the Trick of Tricks: O Bullet.

Thou art the everlasting prop: of the Ministry.

When they took upon them to call thee a Bullet: they did not abhor the public shame.

When they had failed to overcome the sharpness of Truth: thou didst open the Kingdom to the leaven of new deceivers.

We believe that thou art a pretext: for rejecting Reform.

We therefore pray thee help the Lord of the Bedchamber: but appear not unto him for his memory's sake.

O Bullet, save the Ministry: for thou alone art their heritage.

Keep them in place: and they will call thee Bullet for ever.

Day by day: the Courier doth magnify thee;

And it worshippeth thy name: every night without end.

Vouchsafe, O Bullet: to keep us this year without Reform.

O Bullet, have mercy upon us: have mercy upon us.

O Bullet, keep Reform afar from us: as our trust is in thee.

O Bullet, in thee have we trusted: let the Reformists for ever be confounded.

[Here endeth the Bullet Te Deum.]

THE

CANTICLE

OF

THE STONE,

Which may, or may not, be sung or said immediately after **Te Deum Laudamus.**

Benedicite omnia, &c.

O ALL ye workers of Corruption, bless ye the Stone: praise it, and *magnify* it as a Bullet for ever.

O most chaste, most pious, most magnificent, and gracious Prince, who alone workest great marvels: magnify it for ever.

O thou Private Secretary, Secretary Extraordinary, and Privy Seal: magnify it for ever.

O thou Chancellor and Keeper of the Great Seal of the Duchy: magnify it for ever.

O thou Vice Admiral, Lord Warden of the Stannaries,[4] and Steward of the Duchy: magnify it for ever.

O ye Lords and Grooms of the Bedchamber: magnify it for ever.

O ye Sticks in waiting: magnify it for ever.

O ye Lords of the Treasury: magnify it for ever.

O ye Solicitors to the Treasury: magnify it for ever.

O ye Tailors and Accoutrement Makers to the Household Troops, whose dress hath not been altered during ten entire days last past: magnify it for ever.

O ye Sword Cutlers, Helmet Makers, Epaulette Makers, Feather Makers, Buttonhole Stitchers, and cunning Workmen in Embroidery: magnify it for ever.

O ye Dames of Hertford and Jersey, and Mother St. Ursula and the Eleven Thousand Virgins: magnify it for ever.[5]

O ye One hundred and Nine Chaplains in Ordinary, whose names are written in the Royal Kalendar: magnify it for ever.

O ye Makers and Manufacturers of Sham Plots: magnify it for ever.

O thou eldest Son of Impudence, George Cunning,[6] who didst transform the foot of an old Stocking with a few Bullets, into a waggon load of Ammunition: magnify it for ever.

O ye Old Cabbage Dog Rose, and the Managers and the Directors of Saving Banks: magnify it for ever.

O thou Old Lady of Threadneedle Street,[7] the Sucking-mother of the Treasury: magnify it for ever.

O ye Borough-brokers, and Money-jobbers: magnify it for ever.

O ye admirers of Louis the Desired, and Ferdinand the Beloved:[8] magnify it for ever.

O ye who believe the People have nothing to do with the Laws but to obey them: magnify it for ever.

O ye who are arrayed in purple and fine linen; who toil not, neither do ye spin: magnify it without end, for ever and ever.

Now to the Right Honourable Lord ELLENBOROUGH, Sir John Silvester, and Mr. Justice Hicks,[9] be committed the entire disposal of the Lives and Liberties of the People of England at this time and for ever hereafter. *Amen.*

[Here endeth the Canticle.]

HONE'S REFORMISTS' REGISTER

Hone published forty numbers of his *Reformists' Register* from 1 February to 25 October 1817. For a week or two it was called *Hone's Weekly Commentary* and sold for sixpence (F. W. Hackwood, *William Hone: His Life and Times* [1912; reprint, New York: Augustus M. Kelley, 1970], 119); Bowden was unable to locate any extant copies ("William Hone's Political Journalism," 1:184 n. 21). Reappearing as a sixteen-page weekly published each Saturday, its tone and stance were virulently antigovernment. Hone was seeking the widest possible audience to support the movement for parliamentary and other reforms. Early numbers contained parliamentary reports and commentary, and very soon Hone was attacking the government's repressive measures against the press, even publishing the text of Sidmouth's circular letter to the Lords Lieutenant (Bowden 1:132). He continued to write, edit, and publish the *Register* while confined in King's Bench Prison from May to early July. Denounced by the *Quarterly* as an "unstamped two-penny farrago" (quoted in Bowden 1:135), Hone's journal made a point of exposing financial patronage and corruption by publishing the names of the system's beneficiaries and the annual amounts they received in pensions and awards. Disappointed in his hope of attracting Cobbett's readers after the latter fled to America, Hone abandoned the paper in October 1817 to focus his attention on defending himself against the charges of blasphemous parody.

What immediately follows in the first extract is Hone's abridged version of the report in the *Times* on Wednesday, 29 January 1817 (all the emphasizing italics and capitalizations are Hone's). The most substantial omissions are remarks condemning Henry Hunt and the inflammatory rhetoric he used to incite the mob "to acts of violence and savage malignity." Hone's strategy is to emphasize that even the *Times* could not accept the fabrication of the bullet. His final stroke is to suggest that the attempted assassination was an aristocratic hallucination.

FROM

HONE'S REFORMISTS' REGISTER (1817)

(1 FEBRUARY 1817)

The CHANCELLOR of the EXCHEQUER asked what situation his Lordship holds in the household of his Royal Highness the Prince Regent?—Lord JAMES MURRAY.[1] That of Lord of the Bedchamber.

The CH. of the EX. Was his Lordship in attendance on his coming to open the Parliament this day?—Lord J. MURRAY. Yes.

The CH. of the EX. Was his Lordship in the carriage with H. R. H. when he returned from the Parliament?—Lord J. M. Yes.

The CH. of the EX. What happened in his Lordship's own sight on that occasion?—Lord J. M. On H. R. H's. return from the House, between Carlton House Gardens and St. James's Gardens, the glass of the carriage on the *left* side of H. R. H. was broken.

The CH. of the EX. In *what manner* did the fracture appear to his Lordship to have been produced?—Lord J. M. It seemed to have been produced by TWO BULLETS of a small size, about a *quarter of an Inch* apart.

The CH. of the EX. Was his Lordship *confident* that the fractures must have been produced by BULLETS or SOME OTHER *substances* thrown with great violence?—Lord J. M. I have *not the slightest doubt* that they were produced by BULLETS.

The CH. of the EX. Would his Lordship make any other observation respecting this proceeding?—Lord J. M. About a minute *after the glass was broken* in the manner I have described, a *large* stone was thrown against the glass of the carriage, which broke it, and *three or four other* small stones were thrown which struck the glass and the *other* parts of the carriage.

The CH. of the EX. Was the glass which was broken by the *large* stone the same which had been perforated by the BULLETS?—Lord J. M. It was the same glass.

The Ch. of the Ex. Had his Lordship TIME to observe the manner in which the glass was perforated, in the interval between the first fracture and the glass being finally broken?—Lord J. M. In *that interval* I observed the part which was first broken minutely.

The Ch. of the Ex. Did the Noble Lord observe whether such a number of persons surrounded the carriage, that a pistol might be discharged, and the person by whom it was fired not immediately recognized?—Lord J. M. The crowd *not being excessive near the carriage,* I conceive that if a *pistol* had been fired *with gunpowder,* the person must have been observed.

The Ch. of the Ex. Does his Lordship conclude that the *first* fracture was produced by a BULLET discharged from SOME OTHER instrument than a pistol SUCH AS AN AIR GUN?—Lord J. M. I suppose, *as I heard no report,* that THE BULLETS must have been discharged *without gunpowder.*

The Speaker then asked whether any other Member wished to put questions to the witness?

Sir B. Hobhouse[2] asked whether any BULLETS had been *found in the carriage? [Hear, hear!]*—Lord J. M. I have not heard that any BULLETS have been found in the carriage; I should observe, that I CONCEIVE, from the manner of the fracture, that the BULLETS must have come from *some height,* perhaps *from one of the* TREES, of which there are many in that part of the Park, in which there were several persons.

A Member asked, Did his Lordship hear any noise, which induced him to suppose that the bullets had passed *through* the carriage?—Lord J. M. I heard no noise but that produced by the fracture of the glass.

Mr. C. W. Wynne[3] asked, Whether the *opposite* glass was up or down?—Lord J. M. It was UP.

Mr. Brougham.[4] Did his Lordship observe similar holes in the *opposite* glass?—Lord J. M. It was NOT BROKEN AT ALL. The reason I supposed the BULLETS to have come from a height was, that *splinters* of the glass were thrown violently to the *lower* part of the opposite side of the carriage.

Mr. Brougham. I would ask whether BULLETS *or any similar substances* were in the *bottom of the carriage?*—Lord J. M. I had *no opportunity* of ascertaining this, as I left the carriage immediately after the Prince Regent.

A Member wished to ask, Whether H. R. H. had given any directions to *search* the carriage?—Lord J. M. I cannot speak to this on my own knowledge.

Mr. BROUGHAM. I wish to ask who was in the carriage besides his Royal Highness and his Lordship, and who sat on the side nearest the glass which was broken?—Lord J. M. The *Master of the Horse* (the Duke of MONTROSE)[5] was in the carriage, and sat on the side where the glass was broken.

Mr. BROUGHAM.—Did his Lordship observe at the bottom of the carriage any thing but the splinters of glass?—Lord J. MURRAY. I only observed the splinters of glass at the bottom of the opposite door of the carriage.

Mr. BROUGHAM. I wish to know whether the large stone which afterwards broke the glass entered the carriage?—Lord J. MURRAY. No; the plate glass is *very thick,* and the stone did not enter.

Lord COCHRANE.[6] Was the window which was broken next his Royal Highness?–Lord J. MURRAY. H. R. H. *sat in the middle* of the carriage.

Lord MILTON.[7] I wish to know whether the stone which was *subsequently* thrown smashed the window, or merely starred the glass?—Lord J. MURRAY. It not only smashed the window, but *pounded* the glass.

Mr. WYNNE (we believe). Was not the glass of an *unusual* thickness?—Lord J. MURRAY. It was *remarkably thick.*

Sir R. HERON.[8] Who were the persons on the *outside* of the carriage nearest the window when thus struck, whether soldiers or others?—Lord J. MURRAY. There was one footman on the side of the door, and one of the Life-Guards immediately behind him, but no soldier opposite the window.

A MEMBER asked whether his Lordship supposed that the BULLETS perforated any other part of the carriage at all?—Lord J. MURRAY. Whether they perforated any other part of the carriage, *I do not know,* but I SUPPOSE they did.

His Lordship was then ordered to withdraw.

The CHAN. of the EX. then moved, that the House do adopt the Address of the House of Lords, which having been again read, it was agreed to—*nemine contradicente.*

The feelings of the House being overpowered by the Examination of Lord J. MURRAY, it adjourned at half-past eight o'clock.

It appears that the PRINCE REGENT left Carlton-house at half-past one o'clock, and repaired to St. James's Palace, from which place it is the etiquette for the royal procession to start. After some formalities usual on these occasions, the REGENT took his seat in the state carriage, accompanied by the Duke of Montrose and Lord James Murray; the other attendants followed in other carriages. The grenadier guards were on duty, and saluted the REGENT with the accustomed honours, except that the band did not play, nor did the trumpets of the life-guards sound, on account of the indisposition of the Duchess of CUMBERLAND,[9] who was delivered the day before of a dead child. From the same motive there was no firing of cannon on the entrance of the REGENT into the House of Lords, nor on his departure from it. In the decorative part of the procession, there was nothing new, except the helmets of the life-guards, which are on the plan of those of the French cuirassiers, and seemed to the unwarlike eyes of the Reporter to the TIMES preposterously *large*. He says, that the procession to the House was not seriously disturbed; nor was there such expression of disapprobation as to excite alarm.—"It is probable, however," he remarks, "that his Royal Highness observed this *unfavourable disposition* of part of the mob; for it appeared to us, that his *manner* of delivering the speech was that of one whose *spirits were somewhat depressed;* at all events, the voice of his Royal Highness was not so strong and distinct as we have been used to hear it."

On the Regent's return, the most offensive epithets were applied to him as he passed along in the State Carriage, guarded on both sides by a strong escort of Guards and Constables. The crowding, clamour, and insults increased, but cries of "God save the King," and huzzas were mixed with the vociferations personally offensive to the Regent. After the cavalcade had entered the Park, at the Horse Guards—and it had proceeded about half way down the Mall, the window was shattered as described by Lord J. Murray.—From the small puncture of the points from which the cracks in the pane radiated, it was at first thought to have happened by the accidental contact of an officer's sword, riding along side, and who might have been pressed by the crowd against the carriage, or that fragments of gravel had been thrown up against the glass by the horses' hoofs, or that it had been done intentionally—but these ideas, says the MORNING CHRONICLE, were *discountenanced: an* ALARM *was therefore excited that it* MIGHT *have proceeded from an* AIR GUN!!!

Lord JAMES MURRAY's evidence goes to show that, between Carlton-House Gardens and the Stable-yard gate, one glass of the State Coach was struck three times and broken, and his Lordship had "*not the least doubt* it was fractured by BULLETS." Some allowance must of course be made for the Noble Lord's being so *confident,* when it is recollected that in answer to the first question put to him in the House, he said, "*I am a* LORD *of the* BEDCHAMBER!*"* In remarking on this *Noble* Lord's conduct, the *Editor* of the TIMES, with great good sense says, "after some consideration, we are inclined to differ from his Lordship. In the first place no gun or pistol was seen, no smoke appeared, no report was heard, NO BULLET *has been* FOUND. It is true, that an air-gun would have emitted no smoke, and that the report from it would be but trifling—*still there would be* A BULLET; *and yet no such substance is found,* though one glass window was *broke,* and the other was *unbroken.* If there had been a bullet fired, it must have been in the coach, for though a stone might rebound from the glass, a *bullet* would not."

The COURIER[10]—in perfect consistency with its character, as the great *Gong* of a desperate faction, who would *dungeon* the best men in the country, and stab the Constitution to its very vitals—this *machine* has been set in motion to ring the *tocsin*[11] of alarm as quickly and as loudly as possible, and in the execution of this insurrectionary duty, it asserts that the REGENT *himself* was aware that he had been FIRED at. The Regent however has not ventured to say any such thing *yet,* but if he *does,* it will very much illustrate the assertion, if the people are indulged with the publication of a Drawing which His Royal Highness is said to have made *with his own hand,* of the perforated glass before it was smashed in: provided, however, that it be a fac-simile of the pane, and not a sketch from memory assisted by the recollection of the *Noble* Lord of the Bedchamber, who, there is "*not the least doubt,*" was very much FRIGHTENED, and who, according to the BRITISH PRESS, "*thrust his* HAT *into the broken window*"—*to prevent the entrance of* ANY MORE BULLETS!!!—"and held it there until the Carriage drove into the Stable Yard." Well done, Lord JAMES MURRAY! Nobody, who reads his Lordship's evidence, and considers the material composing the BULLETS, will think of looking for them beyond his Lordship's *head.*

(1 MARCH 1817)

I should notice the mention in the Reports of the PARODIES entitled the *Political Litany,* &c. at some length; but as I published some of these, I shall not say so much as I intended. I really believe that they would not have found their way into the *Green Bag*,[12] had not certain gentlemen, from motives not necessary for me to talk of at this time, directed an unaccountable attention of His Majesty's Ministers to them. Certainly, prophaneness, as charged in the Report, was no more intended by me in publishing them, than it was intended by the ATTORNEY-GENERAL, in the Court of King's Bench, on Saturday last, when, according to the *Observer* Newspaper, in speaking of some paintings, he said, they were "collected GOD knows where, and painted by GOD knows whom!" a phraseology not perhaps exactly conformable to the third Commandment. *Parodies* of the Church Service have been published as political *squibs* at different periods for nearly a century; and the reader will perhaps excuse me if I tell him how my acquaintance with *parodies* arose. In the year 1793, being very young and inexperienced—little more than 12 years of age—I wrote and composed a small tract, in prose and verse, in praise of the British Constitution, which I caused to be printed, and enclosed a copy thereof to the Chairman of the "Society for preserving Liberty and Property against Republicans and Levellers, at the Crown and Anchor Tavern, in the Strand." This tract furnished the design for a wood-cut or engraving in the said Loyal Association papers, and for the communication I received a letter from the Secretary of the Association, as follows:–

(COPY)

CROWN AND ANCHOR,
April 27th, 1793.
SIR,
I received the favour of your letter, addressed to the Chairman, of the 25th instant; and am requested to make known to you the high opinion the Committee entertain of your abilities, and the good use you make of them. It is with peculiar pleasure they perceive a spirit of loyalty in a person so young as you represent yourself to be, and have no doubt but a continuance in the same sentiments will make you a valuable and useful member of the community.
I have the honour to be,
Your most obedient servant,

J. A. M'DOWALL,
Secretary.

Mr. W. HONE,
Old North St., Red Lion Square.

Being then a purchaser and reader of all the Loyal Association Papers, which contained much varied matter, in a lively style, I went on buying and admiring, until I had the curiosity to read some of the articles which the Association Papers were answers to; when all on a sudden, in spite of my flattering letter from Mr. Secretary M'DOWALL, still in my possession, I began to perceive a rapid "discontinuance of the same sentiments" praised by that gentleman, which I could no more help, than the shining of the sun. But I very well recollect, that a Parody of the Church Catechism was actually published in a penny Political Tract, at the expense of this "Association for preserving Liberty and Property against Republicans and Levellers;" on the Committee of which Association was the celebrated Mr. JOHN BOWLES, and JOHN REEVES, Esq.[13] was the Chairman; which JOHN REEVES, Esq. is one of the Patentees of the Office of King's Printer, and, under and by virtue of his Patent, is the Proprietor of a great number of editions of the Common Prayer, edited by himself, in various forms and sizes, with Introductions written by him in praise of them, and Dedications to the Queen; and all of them containing the Catechism, which he, as Chairman of the said Loyal Association, caused a Political Parody of to be published as aforesaid. This was the first Parody I ever saw; but, about the year 1796, a Parody on the third chapter of Daniel appeared in a daily Newspaper; since when I have seen many, published both before and afterwards, and I have the authority of Earl GREY, for saying that a Parody of the Litany was written even by a Dignitary of the Church! So much for the *Parodies,* and no more—except that, on Saturday last, finding Parliament inclined to adopt the Reports of the Committees, I instantly stopped the sale of them; and since then not a single copy has been parted with by me, either directly or indirectly. It will be seen, therefore, that, though *backed by precedent,* no pertinacity of mine has assisted in abridging the liberties of my country.

WILLIAM HONE.
Friday, 28th February, 1817.

PARODY.

(REPRRINTED VERBATIM.)

Te Deum.

Oh, Emperor of France! we curse thee.

We acknowledge thee to be a Tyrant.

Thou murdering Infidel! all the world detest thee.

To thee all nations cry aloud,

BONEY, BONEY, BONEY!

Thou art universally execrated!

Holland, Russia, Spain, and Portugal, are full of the measure of thy crimes.

To thee, the infernal host of Hell;

To thee, sycophantic, the tribe of Senators,

And the whole army of Sinners and Devils, raise their hideous notes, crying, Thou art the Commander of the *"Legion of Horror."*

The armies of ALEXANDER and FERDINAND contemn thee; the noble Cossacks of the Don despise thee, exclaiming, RUNAWAY, RUNAWAY, RUNAWAY!

The POPE excommunicates thee; saying, RENEGADE! *No Concordat!*

For thou art the parent of infinite sin.

Thy fictitious, and thy true name, are equally accursed,

And thy black spirit maketh mankind to shudder.

Thou art the kernel of infamy, O NAPPY!

Thou art the everlasting son of tyranny and avarice.

Thou hast not scrupled to violate the laws of God, of nature, and of man.

Having, unhappily, escaped the dangers that have awaited thee, thou hast opened thy prison doors, to shut them again on the innocent.

Thou shalt sit at the right hand of Lucifer, ornamented with thy impious spoils, where thou shalt judge in favour of those who shall most flatter thee.

Thou dost not believe that the day of judgment will come.

We recommend thee to have mercy on those whom thou hast robbed of their peace and property.

Let thy Ministers be numbered with thee in eternal damnation.

May the "Lads of Paris" guillotine thee, and thus spare the People whom thou oppressest with thy Corsican yoke; and may thy heritage suffer in a like way!

May they be not simply damned, but damned to all eternity.

Day by day all nations reproach thee, and adjudge thy name to be detested from generation to generation.

Deign, O NAPPY! to leave the world in peace and quiet; and at least spare those who have put their trust in thee.

Thou hast not scrupled to carry fire and sword among the peaceful dwellings of the Russians.

England, testifying her admiration for their glorious resistance to tyranny, her generous sons hasten cheerfully to dry up the tears of that homeless people.

The torrent of thy crimes is stopped; thou sickenest at the punishments that await thee.

Frost, hail, rivers, and all the elements, have waged war against thee, and thy fugitive followers.

Russia has let loose her hardy and patriotic sons: thou, and thy boasting myrmidons, flee; they "bite the dust."[14]

Arise betimes, ye inhabitants of the East and West, to curse the Tyrant.

Curse the name of the Tyrant, at sun-set, ye inhabitants of the North, ye wives and children of the enraged Cossacks (his faithful pursuers); yea, *rise in the night to curse him soundly.*

Let not your curses, though last, be the least, ye inhabitants of the South.

Arouse, ye Sovereigns of Austria, Prussia, Saxony, and Bavaria; shake off the fetters which perfidy hath forged.

Behold the day of settling is at hand; the just God of Armies will confound thy boasted *foresight.*

Behold, now is the appointed time; now is the oppressor sore smitten.

Strike home, that he may fall; let the voice of liberty be heard among the nations, and the murders of ENGHIEN, PALM, and WRIGHT, be revenged.[15]

At the news of thy drubbing and flight, hearest thou not the rejoicing shouts of thy conquerors? *Hourra, Hourra, Hourra!*

Go, roaming tiger, and with a Russian hempen collar adorn thy neck.

But first with some false tale, thou Prince of Liars, thy German blue-eyed, cara sposa's[16] dubious breast compose; and with sweet beet-root sugar-plumbs, thy hopeful URCHIN'S palate please; cram well, and gull thy Parisian slaves with lies.

When thou shalt have reached the Palais Royal *en bas*, thy last and faithful bulletin on earth send forth, signed by his Imperial Majesty, the Commander in Chief of the infernal hosts.

In it thy health; thy Fontainbleau excursion,[17] summers' days, a smiling sky, and snug warm winter-quarters, praise; and let not thy obsequiousness to the supreme commands of the generalissimo be forgotten.

Deign, O Beelzebub, to keep this arch-fiend treble-ironed; and let the *élites de demons* "guard the avenues" of his dungeon.

Oh, Satan, give this "precious despot" a good warm corner in Hell, and take him into thy tender keeping, for he has been thy faithful servant; and, as he has relied on thee, let him partake of thy torments, now, and for evermore.

Thus, the Monster's race being run, return, O BLESSED PEACE! and heal oppressed Europe's bleeding wounds; come at length, long-wished for; and plentifully bestow thy precious gifts.

Long mayest thou dwell among thy cherished BRITONS! ready to conquer, or, in their country's cause, to die.

This *Parody* is quite in the tone and spirit wherein the *Times* was conducted when the above *Parody* was published; and being printed for Mr. JAMES RICHARDSON,[18] whose respectability, as a bookseller, and whose LOYALTY, are undoubted, it must give the *Times* satisfaction, to see the *Parody* again in print. Mr. RICHARDSON, also, will not quarrel with me, perhaps, for giving more extensive publicity to his very *orthodox Parody*. That gentleman is a true Churchman, as well as a Loyalist, and the Parody is right *Loyal*, as well as orthodox. Mr. RICHARDSON reads the *Times*, too, and therefore, the *Times* and Mr. RICHARDSON will not fall out.

Now it seems, that to publish a *Parody* of any part of the Liturgy, is the height of wickedness in *me*—and doubtless, in any publication whatever, to call for People to be *'numbered together in eternal damnation!'* would have been wrong in *me*—to desire that a whole *heritage* might *'be, not simply damned, but, damned to all eternity!'* would have been wrong in *me*—to ask *'Satan'* to provide *'a good warm corner in hell'* for any body, would have been wrong in *me*—and VICE SOCIETIES, and so forth, would have been called on to prosecute *me*. But as to Mr. RICHARDSON, why, he's another man—*he* publishes all this in a *Parody* of the Church Service—but he is another *sort* of man—Mr. RICHARDSON does not write and publish *Reformists' Registers*, not he—and that makes *all* the difference! Surely the *Times* will not fall out with me, for *republishing* this *Parody* of the Church Service, as published by Mr. RICHARDSON, which I shall venture to call, without meaning particular offence, a very Legitimate *Parody:* and I shall also venture to admire it; and to be pleased with it; and to say it is a pretty Parody; and perchance, if I am found fault with—aye, not merely perchance, but for certain, if I am found fault with—I shall publish something further concerning this *Parody*—showing WHO approved of it, HOW they approved of it, what they SAID of it, what they DID with it, WHERE it went to, and various little pieces of curious information concerning this same LEGITIMATE *Parody*, which some People do not dream of.

Now all this the *Times* will not blame me for; particularly if this *Legitimate Parody* should turn out to be a production of the redoubtable DR. SLOP, who, I take to myself the merit of having killed off, to the entire satisfaction of the *Times*, whilst he was in that Office. A little better than a year ago, the DOCTOR was in a violent fit of swearing, and I discharged a shilling squib at him, entitled "BUONAPARTE-PHOBIA, *or Cursing made easy to the meanest capacity.*"[19] It fell on his vitals, and in three days he swore no more!— DR. SLOP'S GHOST, however, has lately appeared in Crane Court, where it walks *"regularly at* SIX O'CLOCK *every morning!"* It talks strangely about "consistent and honourable principle! reputation! unbiassed candour and fairness! unjustifiable calumny! the light of science, of liberty, and of the gospel!"—Alas, poor GHOST!!! It mutters of "proprietors, who have embarked their funds! the *good things* that God has given us! one, and one only directing mind! transplanted fresh and living! and calls the Constitution a *thing* of permanence! and himself a *professional Gentleman*—rather unceremoniously dragged forward!"—Alas, poor GHOST!!! All these 'more last words' are as droll as DR. SLOP'S sayings when alive. Ghost as he now is—an airy nothing—instead of being *'alone,'* as he says, he is all the while accompanied by *certain persons*, who know him to be as mischievous as the 'Spirit of the Chapel,' and watch him narrowly. A *professional* Gentleman?—Poor SLOP!— still hankering, after death, for the GREEN BAG, and a legitimate ERNULPHUS, which rendered his illustrious prototype in STERNE, immortal.[20] He has lately annoyed *me*, by his gibbering in Crane Court; but let his Ghostship remember his fate, when in the body, or I will put my little finger upon him, and sink him a hundred fathom deep, whilst every living soul within hearing, will laugh at his last squeal.

WILLIAM HONE.
Friday, 7th March, 1817.

SATURDAY, 7 JUNE 1817.

TO READERS.

I very earnestly solicit the endeavours of my friends to extend the circulation of the REGISTER wherever they can.
My present confinement renders this appeal necessary.

W. HONE.

King's Bench Prison.

"Here's a pretty kettle of fish," said a fractious old housewife to her husband, who, for want of work, could only bring home half his wages. The cat coming in her way—past services and usefulness being wholly forgotten—she kicked it to the other side of the kitchen; the faithful beseeching dog was cuffed out of doors; she drove the children about and made them cry, and then whipped them for making a noise; and lastly, after frightening and worrying every living thing about her, she began wringing her hands, declared no woman under the sun was every so teazed and worried as *herself*, and that she would not put up with it!

Now who can be more like unto this silly old woman than His Majesty's Ministers? They find the outgoings more than the comings in; that they spend more than they receive; that the People are over-taxed and distressed; that many of them drop down dead in the public streets, for want of food; and that there is no more money to be got from them: they then, in a fit of passion, toss a few poor helpless creatures into jail, who are rather objects of pity than punishment; they thrust *gagging Bills* into the throats of those who cry against their enormities; they suspend the Habeas Corpus Act, to keep in solitary cells, without trial, men whom they suspect of *treasonably* denying their right to do wrong, and of other heinous offences; they, against the sense of the People of England, propose, in the House of Lords, to further suspend the Habeas Corpus Act, on pretences which they refer to a Secret Committee;[21] they the next day, this present 4th of June, set the bells a-ringing, whether for the success of their unconstitutional and outrageous proposition last night, or because yesterday was *my* birthday, or because to-day is the *King's,* the reader may guess; but I do assure him, that between the said bells this morning, and the high wind which blew against my prison window all night, I got no rest; to-morrow they prepare to try Mr. WOOLER, for saying that our ancestors did not *petition* King JOHN for Magna Charta, whom they charge Mr. WOOLER to have libelled by so saying, though I cannot see *how,* inasmuch as it is well known, that the Barons *cudgelled* the Charter out of the said poor dear, dead, and now, it appears, never-enough-to-be-beloved King; on Friday or Saturday they bring up Mr. BUTT for judgment; and on Monday they try the unfortunate WATSON, and the other prisoners in the Tower, on charges of High Treason:[22]—so that, what with the decreasing revenue, the increasing distress, and the number of prisoners and prosecutions, Ministers have, as the old woman said, *"a pretty kettle of fish"* upon their hands. I forgot the three *ex-officio* informations against myself, by the by, which come across their minds rather frequently, I imagine; for my Lord SIDMOUTH[23] takes or makes an opportunity of crying out *blasphemy* in the House of Lords much oftener than there seems occasion for it; and, if I may guess by the report out of doors, full as loudly as foolish Joan, in the puppet show, who unmercifully squalls "murder" at least three times for every blow Punch bestows upon her wooden head. The Noble Secretary of State is extremely welcome to play upon this *chord of blasphemy* as much as he pleases—it will soon cease to vibrate, and like a school-boy with a Jew's harp, he will tire with the *strum.* The new evening paper, the *Guardian,*[24] says, with truth, *"blasphemy* and *treason* are any thing which persons in office do not *like.* The Jews told CHRIST, when he was preaching the doctrines of universal charity and peace, that he was talking *blasphemy;* and we remember, that speakers at public meetings, who have complained that the House of Commons did not represent the People, have been told that they have been talking *treason*." Mr. WOOLER, in the *Black Dwarf*, re-marking on the *ex-officio* informations, charging *blasphemy* upon me, for the parodies, says:—

"The parodies are confessedly *political squibs*; and if they contain any political offence, why are they not treated in a political point of view, and the "front and head of their offending" set fairly before the public? Was it deemed necessary to awaken against Mr. HONE a spirit of *religious animosity*, lest his political offence might be deemed too ve-nial for punishment? In this case, the Crown Prosecutors are acting un-der a masqued battery; they are assailing the politics of the man, under the pretence that the church is in danger, and the interests of society concerned in his punishment. The charge of *blasphemy* is so very in-definite, that no man will venture to abide by a general definition of the term. It is blasphemy at Rome to deny the infallibility of the Pope, or to refuse to kiss his Holiness's toe, or not to worship the Virgin Mary. In Turkey, it is blasphemy to deny the mission of Mahomet; and every sect throughout the world has a blasphemy peculiar to its creed. Thus all are blasphemers, or none are blasphemers. The power who will finally decide upon the merits of his creatures is the only judge of what is blas-phemy, and what is not; and we are not inclined to believe that he ever delegated his authority to an English Attorney-General."

The *Guardian*, in its leading article of yesterday, from which I be-fore quoted, puts the charge of *blasphemy* against me in a light which clearly shows the scandalous falsehood of the allegation. It observes as follows:—

"When we hear the Ministerial prints talk of *blasphemy*, we are nat-urally led to inquire after the prosecutions on this subject. The first prosecution of this kind, was that of Mr. WRIGHT, who was accused of blasphemy, for maintaining the resurrection of the body—a doctrine which has been maintained by some learned Churchmen, and which is laid down in so many words in one of our Creeds. A pretty commentary this, on the propriety of allowing Justices of Peace to commit to prison, on the oath of common informers, persons charged with such offences. The only other case we know of, is that of Mr. HONE, who is charged on *three* several informations with *blasphemous parodies*. It has turned out that these productions are not even alleged to be parodies of any parts of Scripture, but of certain parts of the Form of Prayer, established for the use of the Church of England, and of the Catechism, which is a formula for the examination of young persons, as to the tenets of that church. It will be for the Jury to decide, whether they were intended to ridicule those *formulæ*, and whether such ridicule be allowable,—or whether, on the other hand, they were intended to ridicule certain corruptions in the State; in which case Mr. HONE will be acquitted. It does not necessarily follow that parodies are intended to ridicule the thing parodied. Can any man be absurd enough to suppose, that the exquisite parodies of the Odes of HORACE, which were published in the *"Two-penny Post-bag,"* were intended to ridicule the admirable originals?—There was Mr. CANNING's parody of the 148th Psalm, or of MILTON's noble paraphrase of it—does any one say, that Mr. CANNING intended to ridicule MILTON, or the Psalmist?—He associated the noble ideas of the original with very low and ridiculous ones, merely with the view of impressing more strongly on the mind, the sarcasms which he threw out against his political enemies. But we must here remark, there is a wide difference between parodies of forms of prayer, or creeds, or catechisms, confessed by all to be the productions of mere fallible mortals, and parodies on the Scriptures, such as that of Mr. CANNING. If Mr. HONE were to go north of the Tweed with his Parodies on the Church of England Prayer, even supposing his main object to have been, as the information charges him, to ridicule that form of prayer (which we do not know to be the fact, as the only one of them which we have seen certainly did not to us exhibit any appearance of such an intention), he would be received with open arms by the most pious and zealous of our northern brethren. So far are they from thinking any ridicule too bad for such forms of prayer, that they lavish on them terms which, after the information against Mr. HONE, we hardly feel ourselves safe in repeating. They call them inventions of the Devil—nets for weak souls—idolatrous and popish contrivances. As to Mr. HONE's parodies, we know little of them; but we have thought fit to make these observations on such parodies in general, because we are persuaded, that persons utterly devoid of any religious principle take advantage of the religious spirit which is increasing in the country, to direct the popular indignation against their opponents, and to reconcile the unreflecting to the suspension of their liberties."

It must not be supposed, from my quotations on this subject of *blasphemy*, that I am desirous of shrinking from the charge, or that I am unwilling to refute its calumny. I call it calumny, because it is *false*. There is nothing in an *ex-officio* information which essentially implies that what it charges is true; and these three informations against me, ultimately, I shall have ample opportunity of proving to be *untrue*.

9 August 1817

Suppose a Minister had said to the Prince Regent, "Sir, you have now an opportunity of doing great good; make a progress through the kingdom, show yourself to the people, sift into their complaints, promise to redress their grievances; and where you find distress urgent, relieve it upon the spot. Here is a sum of £80,000 at your disposal; travel in any way most agreeable to your Royal Highness; see things with your own eyes, and we will gladly listen to your recommendations."

How many narratives of distress he would hear, how many poor creatures save from wretchedness and death! He might have recorded, that he could not travel five miles without learning facts he never knew, though he had lived half a century; that not a city, not a village, not a hamlet, but furnished its tale. Here a rich corporation had long outlived the end of its institution; its members were wealthy, and ignorant, and overbearing, and oppressed their fellow-townsmen; they levied contributions, and created jobs for themselves, and fared sumptuously every day; and suffered human beings to drop down and die in their streets for lack of food. There, at *Ilchester,* where all the borough was pulled down, except sixty houses, as related in a former *Register,*[25] in order to limit the number of voters, he might have seen the electors and their families all turned into a large workhouse, which the borough-monger, Sir William Manners, who destroyed their habitations, built on purpose to receive them. Had his Royal Highness heard that the little borough of Gatton, about 20 miles from London, was worth seeing, he might have gone thither, and had an interview with its proprietor, Sir Mark Wood,[26] and held the following

Dialogue.

Q. You are proprietor of this borough, Sir Mark?

A. I am, may it please your Royal Highness.

Q. How many Members does it send to Parliament?

A. *Two,* Sir.

Q. Who are they?

A. Myself and my son.

Q. You are much beloved, then, in the borough, Sir MARK?

A. There are not many tell me otherwise, your Royal Highness.

Q. Were there any opposition candidates?

A. None, Sir.

Q. What is the qualification for an elector?

A. Being an inhabitant, paying scot and lot.[27]

Q. Only *six electors,* then! for I see you have *only six houses* in the place?

A. Only ONE elector, please your Royal Highness.

Q. What, *one* elector, and return *two* members! how is that? But what becomes of the other five householders?

A. By buying the borough, I am the freeholder of the six houses; I let five by the week, pay the taxes myself, live in the other; and thus, being the only elector, return myself and my son as Members, at the election!

And then his Royal Highness might have visited the borough of *Maidstone,*[28] and heard what *I* heard, and what I shall relate at length in my next Register, respecting the *Purples,* as they are called—the *raving distracted Purples.* The name scarcely requires explanation. In the small pox, it denotes disease and death. "The child has a shocking sort," says the nurse; "it has the *Purples,* and if there are too many, it will die." Just so it is with these Maidstone *Purples.* They were too many for the borough; but they have lately dwindled almost into insignificance. Were the Prince REGENT to visit Maidstone, he would see *boroughmongering,* and the *consequences* of boroughmongering, in the appearance of the town. The *Purples* themselves all flat and dull, and low-hearted—beaten, disgraced, and scarcely daring to show their heads; such is the situation of the high-flying, tantivy,[29] church-and-king *Purples;* the BILLY PITT the Tory-*Purples!* I shall have a curious tale respecting them in my next. It's true it is warm weather, and that they are upon the *go;* but they have kept one week, and they'll keep till the next. I wish the REGENT could take a look at them *incog.* and see to what a state of humiliation they have brought the town and trade of Maidstone. This borough is an excellent specimen of the *borough system;* and, as they say amongst the hop-merchants, I will draw a *clean sample* of it. I repeat that I wish the REGENT could see this place, and these *men.* Sure I am that a *patriot Prince* would feel himself disgraced and degraded below a hedge beggar, if, knowing the state of the country, he for one instant consented to rule over its intellect and independence, by such hands as those of the miserable faction, who at Maidstone call themselves *Purples*.

25 OCTOBER 1817

I now take a very unwilling leave of my readers. This is the last *Register* I shall publish. From the period of my arrest, in May last, under Lord ELLENBOROUGH's warrants, I have continued the work under considerable disadvantages. Soon after my liberation in July, my health fluctuated, and I experienced much mortification from the bad conduct of certain of my agents in the country. Some have punctually and honestly paid me. Others have not only not been punctual, but have not paid me, whilst my inability to regulate my accounts when I was in confinement, and the necessity I have been under of attending a little to what business I found when I came out, and to the writing of the *Register*, prevented me from taking such steps as a keen tradesman might have done to enforce payment. One person, by repeated representations of activity and connexion and good will, induced me to send him the *Register* in large quantities every week, besides other goods, agreeable to his orders. I repeatedly wrote him for money, and he always promised, and put off. Being loth to discontinue the sale of the *Register* in a populous district, and he being the only agent I had in the county of *Hants*, I continued to forward them to him regularly. I have never been able to get the money from him for what he has sold, or to get back the publications which remain unsold; he has not paid me a sixpence! This is to be sure the *worst* specimen of my usage, but there are others nearly as bad. These remarks, however, do not apply to the present vendors of the *Register* at Birmingham, Bath, Bury, Maidstone, Norwich, Nottingham, or Oxford; and I would especially except Mr. WROE, of Manchester, whose honourable conduct deserves my most honourable mention. The continuance of the *Register* with decreased sale, and other inconveniences, added to the disadvantages I have mentioned, has become embarrassing to me. I have kept it on as long as I have been able, and longer, perhaps, than prudent persons will think I ought to have done. I shall now return to my business as a publisher; and having brought out last Saturday the first number of *Sermons to Asses*, by the late excellent and *Rev.* JAMES MURRAY, of Newcastle, the second will be published next Saturday; and on the following Saturday I purpose to

publish the first number of Speeches by the late Mr. CURRAN, who, as
an orator, and a champion of Irish freedom, has not left an equal behind
him.[30] My endeavour will be to give to the world, from time to time, publications that will enlighten and amuse. There is a list at the end of this
sheet, which the reader will, perhaps, excuse me for presenting him
with on this occasion, it being the last time we meet in this way.

Before parting, I would say a word or two further, in order to remove
any thing of prejudice against me in the public mind, on account of my
late prosecutions. The Parodies formerly published by me, I may perhaps be allowed to repeat, I always considered as mere *political* squibs,
and nothing else. It is now two years and a half since I commenced to
publish, in the course of which time I have issued upwards of one hundred and thirty pieces, chiefly my own production. Not a week has
elapsed during that period without my having compiled or written
something; but whether it were prose or verse, or

"Grave or gay, or lively or severe,"[31]

I console myself with the reflection that, amidst all I have put on paper,
there is

"Not one immoral, one indecent thought,
One line, which dying, I could wish to blot;"[32]

nor can there be found a single paragraph, or even sentence, of a profane or irreligious tendency, in any of my publications. With a lively
conception of wit, and an irresistible propensity to humour, I have likewise so profound a regard for the well-being of society, and so great a
reverence for public morals, that I know of no temptation capable of in-
ducing me to pen a line injurious to social happiness, or offensive to
private virtue.

I cannot conclude without expressing regret, that somewhat of a
wayward fancy, and, occasionally, too much of strong feeling, excited by
the distractions and cares of a little business, and a large family, and
increased by the consequences of an inexpertness in certain trading
requisites, have been unfavourable to the composition of the *Reformists' Register*. I have found that endeavours at abstraction, amidst
daily regards, stultify the mind. Although, as some modern writer says,
it is disgraceful not to be able to answer with certainty the simple ques-

tions, What will you be? What will you do? yet I am afraid they are questions *I* cannot answer. It is in vain for him who cannot be any thing, to attempt determining to be something. He whose lot has not been cast in pleasant places, cannot expect to walk beside the still waters. He who has fought the billows till he is exhausted, may desire foot-hold; but if he cannot see shore, what rational hope has he of it? Under more favourable circumstances, I should have conducted the *Register* better to my own, and, perhaps, my readers' satisfaction; but I have some-times caught myself, as now, more inclined to skim over morals, than to sail on the ocean of politics; and I incline to think, that greater leisure would have induced further excursions in the same track. Speculation on this head is ended—this is the death-throe of the *Register,* and with pain I bid my readers *farewell!*

WILLIAM HONE.
67, Old Bailey, 23d Oct. 1817.

THE THREE TRIALS OF WILLIAM HONE

Hone was arrested on 3 May 1817 on an *ex officio* information but he refused to enter a plea until he could see the specific charges against him, and consequently he was held in King's Bench Prison. He eventually pleaded not guilty on 19 June, and on 27 June requested to be freed to support his family. After two months' imprisonment, he was released on his own recognizance in early July (Hackwood 150–53). The trials took place on three successive days, 18, 19, and 20 December, at the Guildhall in London.

Hone's key tactic in the trials was to exploit the legal principle of precedent and to insist on the purely political intentions of his parodies. In addition to the larger issues such as freedom of the press, Hone's trials drew attention to two important matters of legal procedure: the status of *ex officio* informations and the questionable methods employed in the selection of jurymen. Well-prepared and strategically acute, the underdog Hone outmaneuvered the leading legal authorities of the crown and secured acquittals on all three charges. Acting as his own lawyer, he was free to call witnesses, to cross-examine, and to review the case in a summarizing final speech (Joss Marsh, *Word Crimes: Blasphemy, Culture, and Literature in Nineteenth-Century England* [Chicago: University of Chicago Press, 1998], 29). Judicial victory brought Hone national attention and made him a hero of the radical cause. William Cobbett captured some of the pride and gratitude many felt when he praised Hone a few months later from America as a "most active and efficient laborer in the cause of Reform generally," and then specifically commended his management of the trials:

> Mr. Hone's trial and his meritorious conduct will long be remembered. . . . Mr. Hone has to thank himself, and the nation have to thank him, for this victory over Corruption, arrayed in her most deadly armour, armed with her prison and her hidden dagger.

> "To the Electors of Westminster, Letter II"
> in *Cobbett's Weekly Political Register*
> 33 (30 May 1818), columns 627, 631

Hone began publishing his *Trials* in late 1817 and throughout 1818, singly and together. The complex bibliographical description of the possible combinations of editions is given by Bowden (1:167–69). Hone did intend eventually to issue a de luxe edition. Like his grandiose scheme to write and publish a history of parody, however, that edition was never completed. *The Three Trials of William Hone* was last reprinted in 1876 by W. Tegg. Following are reprinted selections from the first two trials and the complete third trial.

FIRST TRIAL.

THE KING *against* WILLIAM HONE,

ON AN EX-OFFICIO INFORMATION FOR PUBLISHING THE LATE JOHN WILKES'S CATECHISM.

Tried in Guildhall,[1] London, on Thursday, December 18, 1817, at the *London Sittings after Michaelmas Term.*

BEFORE MR. JUSTICE ABBOTT[2] AND A SPECIAL JURY.

THE Trial of this issue excited considerable interest. So early as eight o'clock the avenues leading to the Court became crowded; the doors were thrown open shortly after, and the Court immediately filled. About twenty minutes after nine o'clock, Mr. Hone entered, attended by a youth, his brother, who placed on the table of the Court several parcels of books and papers, which nearly covered the table. About half-past nine o'clock Mr. Justice ABBOTT took his seat on the Bench, and the following Special Jury were immediately sworn:

THE JURY.

JOHN GODWIN BOWRING, Leadenhall-street
WILLIAM SYME, Fenchurch-buildings
JOHN WOOLLETT, Gould-square
JOHN O'BRIEN, Broad-street-buildings
WILLIAM NOAKES, Little Eastcheap, South-side, wine merchant

JOHN GARDINER, Old Broad-street
NICHOLAS HILTON, Ironmonger-lane
SAMUEL BROOK, Old Jewry
JAMES HUNTER, Barge-yard
WILLIAM THOMPSON, Queen-street
THOMAS LEWIS, Queen-street
THOMAS EDWARDS, Coleman-street.

Mr. SHEPHERD (son to the Attorney-General) stated, that this was an information[3] filed by his Majesty's Attorney-General against the defendant, for printing and publishing a certain impious, profane, and scandalous libel on that part of our church service called the Catechism, with intent to excite impiety and irreligion in the minds of his Majesty's liege subjects, to ridicule and scandalize the Christian religion, and to bring into contempt the Catechism.

The ATTORNEY-GENERAL *(Sir Samuel Shepherd)*[4] addressed the Court as follows:—

My Lord, and Gentlemen of the Jury,—You have understood from my young friend the nature of this cause. It is an information filed by me, as Attorney-General, against the defendant, William Hone, for printing and publishing an impious and profane libel, upon *The Catechism, The Lord's Prayer,* and *The Ten Commandments,* and thereby bringing into contempt the Christian Religion. I won't occupy your time long, Gentlemen, in shewing this to be the effect of the publication, for it seems impossible for me to hear it read without feeling one's-self compelled to apply to it this language. It is charged, and, as I think, justly charged, with being a profane, blasphemous, and impious libel. It has nothing of a political tendency about it, but it is avowedly set off against the religion and worship of the Church of England, as established by Act of Parliament. It has been over and over again said by the most eminent Judges, and particularly by one who was the most learned man that ever adorned the bench—the most even man that ever blessed domestic life—the most eminent man that ever advanced the progress of science—and also one of the best and most purely religious men that ever lived. I speak of Sir Matthew Hale.[5] It was by him in one sentence said, that "the Christian Religion is parcel of the Common Law of England." The service of the Church of England is also part of the statute law of England; for in the reign of Charles the Second, for securing uniformity of public prayer in the Church of England, a book, commonly called *The Book of Common Prayer,* was not composed, but collected, and annexed to an Act of Parliament then framed, as part of the enacted form of the Liturgy of the Church of England. If to revile that—if to bring it into contempt, be not a libel, then Christianity no longer is what Sir Matthew Hale described it—"parcel of the Common Law of England," nor this Sacred Book a part of the Statute Law of the land, because in such an event the law must declare its inability to support its own provisions. In that

book there is a Catechism, the object of which is most important, because it is that part which is peculiarly destined for forming in the
minds of the younger classes of the community that proper foundation
for religious belief which is to influence their future conduct. It is that
part which the Ministers of the Church of England are peculiarly
bound to teach to those between the infant and adult state at certain
periods of time; it is that part which all who are initiated into Christianity through baptism must be confirmed before they come to their
pastor in an adult state. To procure this important object, it consists of
three parts:—1st, The Service of the Church of England; 2nd, The
Apostles Creed (which is professed by every class of Christians, no
matter what be their particular form of worship); and 3d, The Ten
Commandments, which were of divine origin, communicated originally from the mouth of God through Moses to the Jews. These form
the foundation of all our religious and moral duties; they are those
which, if men would but obey, there would be an end to strife; nothing
but peace and happiness could then be found in human society. This
Book (*The Book of Common Prayer*) has also the Lord's Prayer, as in
his sacred and blessed Sermon on the Mount. If these works be not
what ought to be held sacred from ridicule, what is there which can be
called so in the mind of a Christian? I take this to be a proposition of
law, that he who attempts to parody these three sacred parts of Christian belief, and presents them to the mind in a ridiculous shape, does
that which is calculated to bring them into contempt, and is therefore,
by the law of the land, guilty of a libel. It cannot be necessary to Christian minds to reason on the baneful effect of such a publication as the
Defendant's. If any of you, Gentlemen, be fathers, and wish your children to hold in reverence the sacred subjects of Christian belief, read
these publications of the Defendant, and say if you would put them
into the hands of those children you love. If you would not put them
into their hands, would you into those of the lower classes of society,
which are not fit to cope with the sort of topics which are artfully raised
for them? I ask you, if it be possible, that after such publications are
thus cheaply thrown among this class of people, they can, with the
same degree of reverence that becomes the subject, look at the contents of the Sacred Book of our belief? Nay, even in better cultivated
minds, the firmness of moral rectitude is shaken, and it often becomes
necessary to make great mental exertion to shake off the influence of
these productions, and recall the mind to a true feeling towards sacred

truths. They are inevitably calculated to weaken the reverence felt for the Christian faith. It may be said that the Defendant's object was not to produce this effect—I believe that he meant it, in one sense, as a political squib, but his responsibility is not the less, for he has parodied *The Catechism* in terms which it is impossible to believe can have any other effect than that of bringing it into contempt. The publication is called "*A Catechism;* that is to say, an Instruction to be learned of every person before he be brought to be confirmed a Placeman or Pensioner by the Minister." The Jury will see these are the very words of the original in parody. Again, *The Apostles Creed* is also in complete parody. We say, "I believe in God," &c. &c.; here he says, "I believe in George, the Regent Almighty, Maker of New Streets, and Knights of the Bath; and in the present Ministry, his only choice, who were conceived of Toryism, brought forth of Wm. Pitt, suffered loss of place under Charles James Fox; were execrated, dead, and buried. In a few months they rose again from their Minority; they re-ascended the Treasury Benches, and sit at the right hand of a little man in a large wig; from whence they laugh at the petitions of the people who pray for Reform, and that the sweat of their brow may procure them bread." The *Ten Commandments* are also parodied, and divided precisely in the same manner as the rest of the publication, for the purpose of keeping the whole resemblance more complete. The child is supposed to be examined precisely as it is laid down in the 2d chapter of *Exodus*, of course parodied. He answers, as to the promise of belief his sponsors made for him—

"The same to which the Minister for the time being always obliges all his creatures to swear. I, the Minister, am the Lord thy liege, who brought thee out of want and beggary into the House of Commons."

[Here an expression of feeling was manifested by some individuals of the crowd in the Hall of the Court.]

Mr. Justice ABBOTT—If there is any body present of so light a disposition as to think that a matter of this kind should be made a subject of laughter, at least he shall learn that he shall not come here to interrupt those who are of a graver disposition, and in the discharge of an important duty.

The ATTORNEY-GENERAL—My Lord, if there be any persons here who can raise a smile at the reading of the Defendant's publication, it is the fullest proof of the baneful effect it has had, and with which I charge it. It is for that very reason I charge it as a libel on the Law of

England. I am not sorry for the faint smile just uttered in Court. It establishes the baneful tendency of the work. If there be any here who are not Christians of some sect or other, God forbid that I should have their applauding support. Their approbation or disapprobation is alike indifferent to me. When I allude thus to Christians, let me be supposed as only alluding to those who have had the opportunity of having the light of Christianity shed upon them—God forbid I should be supposed to denounce those who had not had that opportunity. The next Commandment in this Parody is, 'Thou shalt have no other Patron but me.' At last comes that part where a young man is desired to recite the Lord's Prayer, and this is parodied in the same manner. I know, Gentlemen of the Jury, that by the Law of England, it is your province to decide on the matter of the libel, and to say if it be such or no. I am not sorry that this is the case, for I think it impossible that any twelve men who understand the Law of England, and the precepts of Christianity, which are part and parcel of that Law, can read this production of the Defendant's without being decidedly of opinion that it is impossible to read it without seeing that its necessary and obvious consequence must be to bring into contempt the Liturgy of the Church of England. I forbear, Gentlemen, from reading any more of this production, as it will shortly be read by the Clerk. I shall now go to prove the publication by the Defendant; it will be for you to take it fairly and fully under your investigation, and, according to the solemn obligation you have taken—that obligation of an oath which is founded on religion, or it is no oath at all—decide upon it; and so help you God.

The ATTORNEY- GENERAL then called witnesses to prove the publication of the Parodies by the Defendant.

Griffin Swanson, *examined by* Mr. TOPPING.

He held in his hand a pamphlet, called *Wilkes's Catechism*, which he bought on the 17th of February last, at Mr. Hone's shop, No. 55, Fleet-street. He bought it from a boy or a girl in this shop, which then had Mr. Hone's name over the door. The girl, he believed, said she was Mr. Hone's daughter. Two-pence was the price of it. He bought pamphlets afterwards at the same place, and marked them at the time. He observed bills in the window, that a publication by the name of this Catechism was sold there, but he could not recollect whether there were posting bills advertising it.

Henry Hutchings, *examined by* Mr. RICHARDSON.

On the 7th of February last, he was the landlord of a shop, No. 55, Fleet street, and Mr. Hone, now in Court, was then his tenant, and up to Midsummer. He used to sell books and pamphlets. The parish was situate in St. Dunstan's in the West, and he believed in the City of London.

Thomas White, *examined by* Mr. SHEPHERD.

Was Clerk of the Inner Treasury at the King's Bench, and produced *The Book of Common Prayer* and the Seal. He pointed out in the Book the Church Catechism, signed by the Commissioners, and exemplified by the Great Seal. It corresponded to the publications by the King's Printers and the Universities.

Mr. Justice ABBOTT. It would be a highly penal offence to publish as from authority any other than the real authenticated form.

Mr. Thomas White.—Certainly, my Lord.

Here the printed Catechism, with the publication of which the Defendant stood charged, was put in, and read by the Clerk. It was as follows:—

The late John Wilkes's[6] Catechism of a Ministerial Member; taken from an Original manuscript in Mr. Wilkes's Handwriting, never before printed, and adapted to the Present Occasion.—With Permission.—London: Printed for one of the Candidates for the Office of Printer to the King's Most Excellent Majesty, and Sold by William Hone, 55, Fleet Street, and 67, Old Bailey, Three Doors from Ludgate Hill. 1817. Price Two-pence.

A Catechism, that is to say, An Instruction, to be learned of every person before he be brought to be confirmed a Placeman or Pensioner by the Minister.

Question. What is your name?

Answer. Lick Spittle.

Q. Who gave you this name?

A. My Sureties[7] to the Ministry, in my Political Change, wherein I was made a Member of the Majority, the Child of Corruption, and a Locust to devour the good Things of this Kingdom.

Q. What did your Sureties then for you?

A. They did promise and vow three things in my Name. First, that I should renounce the Reformists and all their Works, the pomps and vanity of Popular Favour, and all the sinful lusts of Independence. Secondly, that I should believe all the Articles of the Court Faith. And thirdly, that I should keep the Minister's sole Will and Commandments, and walk in the same, all the days of my life.

Q. Dost thou not think that thou art bound to believe and to do as they have promised for thee?

A. Yes, verily, and for my own sake, so I will; and I heartily thank our heaven-born Ministry, that they have called me to this state of elevation, through my own flattery, cringing, and bribery; and I shall pray to their successors to give me their assistance, that I may continue the same unto my life's end.

Q. Rehearse the Articles of thy Belief.

A. I believe in GEORGE, the Regent Almighty, Maker of New Streets, and Knights of the Bath,[8]

And in the present Ministry, his only choice, who were conceived of Toryism, brought forth of WILLIAM PITT, suffered loss of Place under CHARLES JAMES FOX,[9] were execrated, dead, and buried. In a few months they rose again from their minority; they re-ascended to the Treasury benches, and sit at the right hand of a little man with a large wig; from whence they laugh at the Petitions of the People who may pray for Reform, and that the sweat of their brow may procure them Bread.

I believe that King James the Second was a legitimate Sovereign, and that King William the Third was not; that the Pretender was of the right line; and George the Third's grandfather was not; that the dynasty of Bourbon is immortal; and that the glass in the eye of Lord James Murray was not Betty Martin.[10] I believe in the immaculate purity of the Committee of Finance, in the independence of the Committee of Secresy, and that the Pitt System is everlasting. Amen.

Q. What dost thou chiefly learn in these Articles of thy Belief?

A. First, I learn to forswear all conscience, which was never meant to trouble me, nor the rest of the tribe of Courtiers. Secondly, to swear black is white, or white black, according to the good pleasure of the Ministers. Thirdly, to put on the helmet of Impudence, the only armour against the shafts of Patriotism.

Q. You said that your Sureties did promise for you, that you should keep the Minister's Commandments: tell me how many there be?

A. Ten.

Q. Which be they?

A. The same to which the Minister for the time being always obliges all his creatures to swear, I the Minister am the Lord thy liege, who brought thee out of Want and Beggary, into the House of Commons.

   I. Thou shalt have no other Patron but me.

  II. Thou shalt not support any measure but mine, nor shalt thou frame clauses of any bill in its progress to the House above, or in the Committee beneath, or when the mace is under the table, except it be mine. Thou shalt not bow to Lord COCHRANE, nor shake hands with him, nor any other of my real opponents; for I thy Lord am a jealous Minister, and forbid familiarity of the Majority, with the Friends of the People, unto the third and fourth cousins of them that divide[11] against me; and give places, and thousands and tens of thousands, to them that divide with me, and keep my Commandments.

  III. Thou shalt not take the Pension of thy Lord the Minister in vain; for I the Minister will force him to accept the Chilterns[12] that taketh my Pension in vain.

  IV. Remember that thou attend the Minister's Levee[13] day; on other days thou shalt speak for him in the House, and fetch and carry, and do all that he commandeth thee to do; but the Levee day is for the glorification of the Minister thy Lord: In it thou shalt do no work in the House, but shalt wait upon him, thou, and thy daughter, and thy wife, and the members that are within his influence; for on other days the Minister is inaccessible, but delighteth in the Levee day; wherefore the Minister appointed the Levee day, and chatteth thereon familiarly, and is amused with it.

  V. Honour the Regent and the helmets of the Life Guards, that thy stay may be long in the Place, which the Lord thy Minister giveth thee.

  VI. Thou shalt not call starving to death murder.

  VII. Thou shalt not call Royal gallivanting adultery.

  VIII. Thou shalt not say, that to rob the Public is to steal.

  IX. Thou shalt bear false witness against the people.

  X. Thou shalt not covet the People's applause, thou shalt not covet the People's praise, nor their good name, nor their esteem, nor their reverence, nor any reward that is theirs.

Q. What dost thou chiefly learn by these Commandments?

A. I learn two things—my duty towards the Minister, and my duty towards myself.

Q. What is thy duty towards the Minister?

A. My duty towards the Minister is, to trust him as much as I can; to fear him; to honour him with all my words, with all my bows, with all my scrapes, and all my cringes; to flatter him; to give him thanks; to give up my whole soul to him; to idolize his name, and obey his word; and serve him blindly all the days of his political life.

Q. What is thy duty towards thyself?

A. My duty towards myself is to love nobody but myself, and to do unto most men what I would not that they should do unto me; to sacrifice unto my own interest even my father and mother; to pay little reverence to the King, but to compensate that omission by my servility to all that are put in authority under him; to lick the dust under the feet of my superiors, and to shake a rod of iron over the backs of my inferiors; to spare the People by neither word nor deed; to observe neither truth nor justice in my dealings with them; to bear them malice and hatred in my heart; and where their wives and properties are concerned, to keep my body neither in temperance, soberness, nor chastity, but to give my hands to picking and stealing, and my tongue to evil speaking and lying, and slander of their efforts to defend their liberties and recover their rights; never failing to envy their privileges, and to learn to get the Pensions of myself and my colleagues out of the People's labour, and to do my duty in that department of public plunder unto which it shall please the Minister to call me.

Q. My good Courtier, know this, that thou art not able of thyself to preserve the Minister's favour, nor to walk in his Commandments, nor to serve him, without his special protection; which thou must at all times learn to obtain by diligent application. Let me hear, therefore, if thou canst rehearse the Minister's Memorial.

Answer.

Our Lord who art in the Treasury, whatsoever be thy name, thy power be prolonged, thy will be done throughout the empire, as it is in each session. Give us our usual sops, and forgive us our occasional absences on divisions; as we promise not to forgive them that divide against thee. Turn us not out of our places; but keep us in the House of

Commons, the land of Pensions and Plenty; and deliver us from the People. Amen.

Q. What desirest thou of the Minister in this Memorial?

A. I desire the Minister, our Patron, who is the disposer of the Nation's overstrained Taxation, to give his protection unto me and to all Pensioners and Placemen, that we may vote for him, serve him, and obey him, as far as we find it convenient; and I beseech the Minister that he will give us all things that be needful, both for our reputation and appearance in the House and out of it; that he will be favourable to us, and forgive us our negligences; that it will please him to save and defend us, in all dangers of life and limb, from the People, our natural enemies; and that he will help us in fleecing and grinding them; and this I trust he will do out of care for himself, and our support of him through our corruption and influence; and therefore I say Amen. So be it.

Q. How many Tests hath the Minister ordained?

A. Two only, as generally necessary to elevation; (that is to say) Passive Obedience and Bribery.

Q. What meanest thou by this word Test?

A. I mean an outward visible sign of an inward intellectual meanness, ordained by the Minister himself as a pledge to assure him thereof.

Q. How many parts are there in this Test?

A. Two; the outward visible sign, and the intellectual meanness.

Q. What is the outward visible sign or form of Passive Obedience?

A. Dangling at the Minister's heels, whereby the person is degraded beneath the baseness of a slave, in the character of a Pensioner, Placeman, Expectant Parasite, Toadeater, or Lord of the Bedchamber.

Q. What is the inward intellectual meanness?

A. A death unto Freedom, a subjection unto perpetual Thraldom: for being by nature born free, and the children of Independence, we are hereby made children of Slavery.

Q. What is required of persons submitting to the Test of Passive Obedience?

A. Apostacy, whereby they forsake Liberty; and faith, whereby they stedfastly believe the promises of the Minister, made to them upon submitting to that Test.

Q. Why was the Test of Bribery ordained?

A. For the continual support of the Minister's influence, and the feeding of us, his needy creatures and sycophants.

Q. What is the outward part or sign in the Test of Bribery?

A. Bank notes, which the Minister hath commanded to be offered by his dependants.

Q. Why then are beggars submitted to this Test, when by reason of their poverty they are not able to go through the necessary forms?

A. Because they promise them by their Sureties; which promise, when they come to lucrative offices, they themselves are bound to perform.

Q. What is the inward part, or thing signified?

A. The industry and wealth of the People, which are verily and indeed taken and had by Pensioners and Sinecurists, in their Corruption.

Q. What are the benefits whereof you are partakers thereby?

A. The weakening and impoverishing the People, through the loss of their Liberty and Property, while our wealth becomes enormous, and our pride intolerable.

Q. What is required of them who submit to the Test of Bribery and Corruption?

A. To examine themselves, whether they repent them truly of any signs of former honour and patriotism, stedfastly purposing henceforward to be faithful towards the Minister; to draw on and off like his glove; to crouch to him like a spaniel; to purvey for him like a jackall; to be as supple to him as Alderman Sir WILLIAM TURTLE; to have the most lively faith in the Funds, especially in the Sinking Fund;[14] to believe the words of Lord CASTLEREAGH alone; to have remembrance of nothing but what is in the Courier; to hate MATTHEW WOOD, the present Lord Mayor, and his second Mayoralty; with all our heart, with all our mind, with all our soul, and with all our strength; to admire Sir JOHN SILVESTER, the Recorder, and Mr. JOHN LANGLEY;[15] and to be in charity with those only who have something to give.

[Here endeth the Catechism.]

This being the whole of the case on the part of the prosecution,

Mr. HONE rose, and addressed the Court to the following purport:—
He called upon the jury, as earnestly and as solemnly as the Attorney-General had done, to decide upon this case according to their oaths. If he felt any embarrassment on this occasion, and he felt a great deal, it was because he was not in the habit of addressing an assembly like

that: he had never, indeed, addressed any assembly whatever; and, therefore, he hoped that they and the Court would show their indulgence to him, standing there as he did, unassisted by counsel, to make his own defence. If he were really guilty of this libel, as the Attorney-General had called it, he should not have stood there this day. So far back as May, he was arrested under a warrant by the Lord Chief Justice of that Court, Lord Ellenborough, and brought suddenly to plead to informations filed against him. He did not plead, because he conceived the proceeding by information to be unconstitutional, and he thought so still. However ancient this mode of proceeding might be, he was satisfied that it was never intended to be exercised in the way that it had been of late years. By this process, every man in the kingdom, however innocent he might be, was entirely at the mercy of the Attorney-General, and of the Government. There was no security for honour, integrity, and virtue; no presentment to a jury, no previous inquiry; the victim was taken in a summary way by warrants, and brought to answer suddenly to informations of which he was wholly ignorant. Another objection which he had to plead on that occasion was, the enormous expense that must have been incurred. He had been given to understand, that making his defence in the usual way, by solicitor and counsel, would cost £100, which would have been utter ruin to him. He applied to the Court for copies of the informations, but the Court did not grant him those copies. He was sorry for this, because if they had been granted, he should have known what he was specifically charged with. On Friday last, he applied for copies at the Crown-office, and upon paying the customary charges, he procured them. When he was placed on the floor of the Court of King's Bench, the late Attorney-General, Sir William Garrow,[16] stated, that the informations charged him with blasphemous publications. Now he found, that this information did not charge him with blasphemous publications; it charged, that he, being an impious and wickedly disposed person, and intending to excite impiety and irreligion, did publish that which was stated in the information. And here he must beg leave to call to their attention the great prejudice which had been raised against him throughout the country by this circumstance, and the injury which he had sustained by misrepresentations coming from the highest authorities in the country. The late Attorney-General had charged him with a second information, and he then observed, that whether he were charged with one information, or 300 informations, he would not plead unless copies were given to him.

The Attorney-General in reply observed, that the number of informations depended on the number of publications. He did not, however, mean to charge Sir William Garrow with any intention to produce an unfavourable impression in the public mind against him. But he must say, and he would say it boldly, because he said it truly, that no man was ever treated with greater injustice than he was by Lord Ellenborough. Previous to his arrest, under a warrant issued by his Lordship, he had not been out of the house all the week: he had been engaged in writing, and no application had been made by any one to see him of which he did not hear. Two officers seized him near his own door upon the warrant of Lord Ellenborough and refused to let him go home, without stating any reason why they made that refusal. He was taken to Sergeant's-inn coffee-house, and afterwards carried to a lock-up house in Shire-lane, where he remained till half-past five, anxiously expecting Mr. Gibbon, the tipstaff,[17] (who, he was told, was coming), in order that he might learn from him the charge, and send for friends to bail him. Gibbon did not come, and he remained ignorant of the charge. On the Monday following, at a moment when he was retiring for the purposes of nature he was put into a coach, and ordered to be taken to Westminster-hall[18] to plead; but even then the officer could not tell him to what he was to plead. While in the coach, he found it almost impossible to keep himself from fainting: but he was told, that when he arrived at Westminster, sufficient time would be allowed him. He was, however, taken into Court, and whilst one of the informations was being read, a mist came before his eyes, he felt giddy, and applied for leave to sit. The answer of Lord Ellenborough was "No;" and it was pronounced with an intonation that might have been heard at the further end of the hall.[19] This refusal, instead of making him sink on the floor, as he had before expected to do, had the effect that a glass of water on being thrown into his face would have had, and he felt perfectly relieved. At the same time, however, he could not help feeling contempt for the inhumanity of the Judge. He was then taken to the King's-Bench, and was afterwards found senseless in his room there, not having performed an office of nature for several days. That arose out of the inhumanity of Lord Ellenborough.

Here Mr. Justice ABBOTT interrupted the defendant, stating, that he had better apply himself to the charge against him. He was unwilling to interrupt any person who was making his defence; but where, as in this case, it became absolutely necessary, he could not refrain. It was the duty of Lord Ellenborough to pursue the course of the Court, and it was customary for defendants to stand while the informations filed against them were being read.

The defendant proceeded—He should be sorry to be out of order, but he believed instances had been known in which defendants were permitted to sit. He thought that such cases might be found in the state trials. But whether so or not, such was the feeling of Sir William Garrow, that he leaned over and whispered to him, "If you wish to retire for any purpose of nature, you can." He thanked him, and replied, that the purpose had gone by. He stated this because he should never forget the humanity which Sir William had shown on that occasion, and which formed a strong contrast to the behaviour of the Judge whom he had mentioned. Having stated these facts, he would not take up their time in detailing what he endured for two months in the King's Bench; suffice it to say, that he had suffered the utmost distress in a domestic way, and very considerable loss in a pecuniary way. He had gained nothing there but a severe lesson. He learned that, however honourable a man's intention might be, they might be construed into guilt, and the whole nation might be raised against him, except, indeed, the few cool, dispassionate, and sober persons who would read such publications as the present calmly, and determine upon the motives of the writer. It was upon this intention that they (the jury) were to decide. The Attorney-General, Sir Samuel Shepherd, had stated, that his publication was issued for a political squib. He quite agreed with the Attorney-General; he joined issue with him upon this interpretation of the work; it was published for a political squib, and if they found it a political squib, they would deliver a verdict of acquittal. If they found it an impious and blasphemous libel, they would consign him to that punishment from which he should ask no mercy. This was the question which they were to try, and they had nothing to try but that. They had nothing to do with the tendency which his work might have out of doors, or the effect which it might produce in that Court, or, at least, they had so little to do with it, as not to suffer it to weigh a feather in their minds in returning their verdict to the Court. They would remember, that he was not standing there as a defendant in an action brought by a private individual. In that case, they would not have to look at the intention of the party; they would have to assess the amount of the damages; but here they had every thing to do with the intention of the party, and if they did not find that this political catechism was published with an impious and profane intention, they would give him a verdict of acquittal. The Attorney-General had stated, that the very smile of a person was an evidence of the tendency of this publication. He denied that. The smile might arise from something wholly different from the feeling of the person who wrote that publication. But he would now proceed to call their attention to a very important branch of this question. In 1771, it was the intention of certain intelligent persons, Members of the House of Commons, to explain the powers of juries relating to libels. Mr. Dowdeswell moved to bring in a bill for that purpose; and Mr. Burke,[20] than whom he could not quote a man whose authority would be greater in that Court, delivered a most eloquent and impressive speech on that occasion. He said, "It was the ancient privilege of Englishmen that they should be tried by a jury of their equals; but that, by the proceeding by information, the whole virtue of juries was taken away. The spirit of the Star-chamber[21] had transmigrated, and lived again in the Courts of Westminster-hall, who borrowed from the Star-chamber what that Court had taken from the Roman law. A timid jury will give way to an awful Judge, delivering oracularly the law, and charging them to beware of their oaths. They would do so; they had done so; nay, a respectable member of their own house had told them, that on the authority of a judge, he found a man guilty in whom he could find no guilt." Mr. Dowdeswell's bill was brought in, but it did not pass into a law. Mr. Burke persevered in the same cause for a number of years, without success; but in 1790, the late Mr. Fox brought in a bill, which was now called the Libel Bill,[22] and it was under the authority of that solemn Act of Parliament that they now sat to try this information. This bill had fixed the powers of juries in cases of libel, and made it imperative on them to determine on the whole of matters charged in the information. Now he was charged— with what? With intending to excite impiety and irreligion, not with having excited it; so that, as the law stood before, if there had been but one copy printed, they would have been told to find him guilty, if it could be proved that the work was published by him; but now, if he had sold 100,000 copies, it was the intention with which they had to do. As to blasphemy and profaneness, he spurned the charge; and when he said he spurned it, he could assure them they should not hear him say one word to-day which he did not utter from his heart, and from the most perfect conviction. They were not to inquire whether he was a member of the Established Church or a Dissenter; it was enough that he professed himself to be a Christian: and he would be bold to say, that he made that profession with a reverence for the doctrines of Christianity which could not be exceeded by any person in that Court. He had, however, been held up as a man unfit to live, as a blasphemer, a monster, a wretch; he had been called a wretch who had kept body and soul together by the sale of blasphemous publications. If any man knew any one act of his life to which profaneness and impiety might be applied, he would ask and defy that man to stand forward and contradict him at that moment. He was innocent of that charge; and it was the proudest day of his life to stand there, because he was not putting in a plea of not guilty against a charge of infamous and blasphemous libel; for if he were guilty of blasphemy, he would go to the stake and burn as a blasphemer, at the same time avowing the blasphemy. He said this, because he considered nothing was dearer to man than sincerity. It had been the misfortune of his life to have his actions misinterpreted by the papers, by the lookers on—the mere every-day observers; but there were a few individuals of the Established Church who knew every thing alledged against him to be a foul and base calumny. It was impossible for a man so humble in life as himself to wage war with opinions broached by a Secretary of State; but when he heard Lord Sidmouth,[23] in the House of Lords, rising every night and calling these little publications blasphemous, he had felt disposed to interrupt him. The odds were terribly against him in a prosecution of this kind, for he had to contend with the Secretary of State—a man whose opinions were adopted by a great number of persons of the first rank and consideration, and whose private life was, he believed, unimpeachable. This eminent character was, however, like other men, liable to error, else he would not have denounced this publication as blasphemous in his place in the House of Lords. Even if it were so, was it justice to pronounce so decided an opinion, one which must necessarily carry so much weight and influence, before the proper course of inquiry and decision were had upon it? It was by these means that a war-whoop and yell were sent forth against him throughout the country. But, friendless and unprotected as he was, he was obliged to submit, and hence his conduct had been held up to the amusement of the ill-thinking throughout the country. He did not desire, for he did not know how, to obtain popularity; he never went all lengths with any description of persons whatever. He was as independent in mind as any gentleman in that Court was independent in property: he had made to himself many enemies, because it is in human nature that the persons with whom we are intimate scarcely ever forgive one dereliction from what they consider duty. He always endeavoured to make up his mind as coolly as possible: sure he was, that if he ever did a man injury in his life, it was from mistake, and not from intention. And he asked the jury, if they had ever seen any of his publications before, whether they had observed in them any thing that would induce them to think that he was desirous of exciting impiety or profaneness? No man in the country had a greater respect than himself for the constituted authorities; if he differed from some public men in opinion, it was not at all times that he differed; it was not because there was a common cry against a measure that he joined in it. He had told them it was the intention of which they were to judge; and he would sit down immediately, if the Attorney-General could lay his hand on any publication in which in any one passage or sentence, he could point out any thing tending to degrade or vilify the Christian religion. He stated this, not in bravado, but in the sincerity of his heart. If he were a man of a blasphemous turn of mind, it was scarcely possible, amongst the numerous works which he had published, and the greater part of them written by himself, that something of this kind should not have appeared; but whatever opinions the Attorney-General might form respecting his notions of religion, he knew that he could not produce any blasphemous writings against him. He came now to another part of this subject. It was his fate, when he was taken to the King's-Bench, although it might be an advantage to the country, to differ with the Master of the Crown-office, as to the way in which the special juries were returned. After the juries in his case were struck—

Here Mr. Justice ABBOTT again interrupted the defendant, observing, that he did not think this had any bearing on the question. He was sorry, he repeated, to interfere with his defence, but he had better confine himself to the point at issue.[24]

* * * * *

He now came to his trial, and it was perfectly immaterial to him of what opinion the jury were, satisfied as he was that they would return a true verdict. He had a very serious impression upon his mind of what his situation would be if a verdict went against him. In that case he firmly believed that he should never return to his family from that court. The Attorney-General was entitled to a reply; and though the learned gentleman had shewn great courtesy, he could not expect him to wave that right. If he would, the defendant would engage to conclude in 20 minutes. He did not see any disposition of that kind, and he would therefore proceed. He should state nothing that was new, because he knew nothing that was new. He had his books about him, and it was from them that he must draw his defence. They had been the solace of his life; and as to one of Mr. Jones's little rooms in the Bench, where he had enjoyed a delightful view of the Surrey hills, they would afford him great consolation there, but his mind must be much distracted by the sufferings of his family. He knew no distinction between public and private life. Men should be consistent in their conduct; and he had endeavoured so to school his mind that he might give an explanation of every act of his life. If he had ever done an injury to any one, it was by accident, and not by design; and, though some persons had lost money by him, there was not one who would say that he did not entertain a respect for him [the defendant]. From being a book-dealer he became a bookseller; and what was very unfortunate, he was too much attached to his books to part with them. He had a wife and seven children, and had latterly employed himself in writing for their support. As to parodies, they were as old, at least, as the invention of printing; and he never heard of a prosecution for a parody, either religious or any other. There were two kinds of parodies; one in which a man might convey ludicrous or ridiculous ideas relative to some other subject; the other, where it was meant to ridicule the thing parodied. The latter was not the case here, and therefore he had not brought religion into contempt. It was remarkable that in October last a most singular parody was inserted in the Edinburgh Magazine, which was published by Mr. Blackwood.[25] The parody was written with a great deal of ability, and it was impossible but that the authors must have heard of this prosecution. The parody was made on a certain chapter of Ezekiel, and was introduced by a preface, stating that it was a translation of a Chaldee manuscript preserved in a great library at Paris. There was a key to the parody which furnished the names of the persons described in it. The key was not published, but he had obtained a copy of it. Mr. Blackwood is telling his own story; and the two cherubims were Mr. Cleghorn, a farmer, and Mr. Pringle, a schoolmaster, who had been engaged with him as editor of a former magazine; the "crafty man" was Mr. Constable; and the work that "ruled the nation" was the "Edinburgh Review."[26] The defendant then read a long extract from the parody, of which the following is a specimen:—

"Now, in those days, there lived also a man who was crafty in counsel, and cunning in all manner of working: and I beheld the man, and he was comely and well favoured, and he had a notable horn in his forehead wherewith he ruled the nations. And I saw the horn, that it had eyes, and a mouth speaking great things, and it magnified itself even to the Prince of the Host, and it cast down the truth to the ground, and it grew and prospered. And when this man saw the book, and beheld the things that were in the book, he was troubled in spirit and much cast down. And he said unto himself, why stand I idle here, and why do I not bestir myself? Lo! this book shall become a devouring sword in the hand of my adversary, and with it will he root up or loosen the horn that is in my forehead, and the hope of my gains shall perish from the face of the earth. And he hated the book, and the two beasts that had put words into the book, for he judged according to the reports of men; nevertheless, the man was crafty in counsel, and more cunning than his fellows. And he said unto the two beasts, come ye and put your trust under the shadow of my wings, and we will destroy the man whose name is as ebony, and his book."

He observed, that Mr. Blackwood was much respected by a great number of persons.

Mr. Justice ABBOTT said, he could not think their respect could be increased by such a publication. He must express his disapprobation of it; and at the same time observed, that the defendant, by citing it, was only defending one offence by another.

The ATTORNEY-GENERAL said, he had been thinking for the last few minutes where a person in his situation could interrupt a defendant. He now rose to make an objection in point of law. The defendant was stating certain facts of previous publications, and a question might arise as to the proof of them. The same objection applied to the legality of his statement. The defendant had no more right to state any previous libel by way of parody, than a person charged with obscenity had of bringing volumes on the table and exhibiting them in his defence. The defendant had no right to be stating, and so to be publishing, things which had better remain on the shelves in a bookseller's shop than be in the hands of the public.

Mr. HONE said, that the Attorney-General called this parody a libel, but it was not a libel till a jury had found it to be so. His was not a libel, or why did he stand there to defend it? In taking this course of defence, he did not take it as a selection of modes; it was his only mode.

He had no intention to send forth any offensive publication to the world, but merely to defend himself. When he heard that his own parodies had given pain to some minds, he was sorry for it. This sort of writing was familiar to him from his course of reading. This parody, called Wilkes's Catechism, was published by him on the 14th of February, and on the 22d he stopt the sale of the other pamphlets. He should adduce evidence to show that this sort of writing had never been prosecuted. He then held in his hand a little publication drawn up by the late Dr. Lettsom,[27] shewing the effects of temperance and intemperance, by diverging lines, as a man gets from water to strong beer, and from strong beer to spirituous liquors and habits of brutal intoxication. He took this as a popular mode of conveying instruction with preservation of health, and had no intention to ridicule the thermometer on the plan on which it was framed.

He (the defendant) knew there were some most excellent persons who occasionally made applications of the Scripture in a way which they would not do in the pulpit. In 1518, a parody of the first verse of the first psalm was written by a man whom every individual in this Court would esteem—a man to whom we were indebted for liberty of conscience, and finally for all the blessings of the Reformation itself— he meant Martin Luther. In the first volume of Jortin's Life of Erasmus, page 117, the following parody, on the first verse of the first psalm, to which he had alluded, appeared: "Blessed is the man that hath not walked in the way of the Sacramentarians, nor sat in the seat of the Zwinglians, or followed the counsel of the Zurichers."[28] Would any man say that Martin Luther was a blasphemer? and he was a parodist as well as William Hone. But parodies had been published even in the pulpit. He had then in his hand a parody on the Lord's Prayer, delivered in the pulpit by Dr. John Boys, Dean of Canterbury,[29] in 1613, and which was afterwards inserted in a folio volume of his works which he published. He stated, that he gained great applause by preaching on that occasion, which occurred on the 5th of November, 1600. The parody ran in these words: "Our Pope, which art in Rome, hellish be thy name, give us this day our cup in the Lord's supper," and so on.

Mr. Justice Abbott thought it better that the defendant should not read any more of this parody; it could only shock the ears of well-disposed and religious persons; and he must again repeat, that the law did not allow one offence to be vindicated by another. He wished the defendant would not read such things.

Mr. HONE.—My Lord, your Lordship's observation is in the very spirit of what Pope Leo X. said to Martin Luther—"For God's sake don't say a word about the indulgences and the monasteries, and I'll give you a living," thus precluding him from mentioning the very thing in dispute. I must go on with these parodies, said Mr. Hone, or I cannot go on with my defence.[30]

* * * * *

He next came to "a copy of a letter written by our Lord and Saviour Jesus Christ, and found under a stone, eighteen miles from Judea, now transmitted from the Holy City. Translated from the original copy, now in the possession of the family of the Lady Cuba in Mesopotamia. Blessed are those who find this letter and make it known. Many persons attempted to remove the stone under which it lay—but none could force it from its place, till a young child appeared and wrought the miracle."

The ATTORNEY-GENERAL.—The misguided or mistaken feelings which can induce such publications by any man, do not form a ground of defence for others. I, therefore, submit, that publications of this kind ought not to be read in Court.

Mr. Justice ABBOTT.—It is no use to interrupt the defendant. I have repeatedly stated, that it cannot avail him, as a matter of defence, to quote a variety of profane publications. It is for him to shew that his publication is not profane—and this cannot be done by quoting the example of others.

Mr. HONE—The publication which he had last noticed, was a *Christmas Carol.* It had been before the public upwards of thirty years—and he should be very sorry to read it, if it were likely to bring the publisher of it into any danger. He was sure it was far from that individual's intention to do any thing wrong, that person printed various publications of the same nature which went through the country—and, in fact, they were of that description, which the common people had been accustomed to for centuries.

Mr. Justice ABBOTT.—I don't care what the common people have had for centuries. If the publication be profane, it ought not to be tolerated.

Mr. HONE—It was most evident that this practice worked its own remedy. Publications of this kind could not have any effect, except amongst persons of the most ignorant description. Millions of these Carols had been sold—and he had never heard that religion was brought into contempt by them.

The Christmas Carol attached to this publication began in the usual way—

> God rest you merry gentlemen,
>   Let nothing you dismay;
> Remember Christ our Saviour
>   Was born on Christmas day.

It contained verses which, to a person of the least cultivated intellect, were ridiculous; but to the lowest class of the community, who purchased these, the lowest species of literary ware, such compositions, and the ideas they conveyed, were familiar, and were not of ludicrous construction. For instance, there was a verse in this very carol which he remembered to have heard sung in the streets every Christmas since he was a child, which described the pleasure of the Virgin Mary in tending on her infant in these homely words:—

> The first good joy our Mary had,
>   It was the joy of one;
> To see her own child Jesus
>   To suck at her breast bone.

And so it went on.—*[The Attorney-General here manifested great uneasiness.]*—The Attorney-General need not be alarmed. It could have no effect even upon the most ignorant, and millions of copies had been circulated long before he came into office.

But he would now call the attention of the jury to a parody differing very much from any of those he had hitherto noticed. He alluded to the celebrated parody of Mr. Canning—yes, of Mr. Canning, who ought, at that moment, to be standing in his place, but who had been raised to the rank of a Cabinet Minister, and was one of those very men who were now persecuting him——for he could not give any milder appellation to the treatment he had received. He was dragged before the Court, from behind his counter—and for what? For doing that which a Cabinet Minister had been suffered to do with impunity. He would assert that the Attorney-General would act wrong—that he would proceed partially and unfairly—if he did not bring Mr. Canning forward. "If I," said Mr. Hone, "am convicted, he ought to follow me to my cell—if my family is ruined, his family ought to be made to feel a little—if I am injured by this indecent, this unjust prosecution, he ought not to be suffered to escape unpunished."—This parody, after being first printed in the Anti-Jacobin newspaper, was re-published in a splendid work, which he now held in his hand, entitled *The Poetry of the Anti-Jacobin;* the expense of printing was defrayed by the late Mr. Pitt, by Mr. Canning, nearly all the Cabinet Ministers, and many other persons connected with that party. The parody was also ornamented by a masterly engraving by Mr. Gilray.[31] Was it not enough to have written the parody to which he alluded, without proceeding to have it illustrated by the talents of an artist? Yet it was so illustrated.—

(*A number of persons in Court here applauded.*)

Mr. Justice ABBOTT declared, if such indecent interruptions were persisted in, he would order the Court to be cleared—and he directed the officer to bring before him any person he saw misconducting himself.

Mr. HONE.—The parody he alluded to was entitled *"The New Morality; or, The Installation of the High Priest."* He understood it was levelled at a man named Lepaux, who was well known at the commencement of the Revolution, and was, he understood, an avowed Atheist. Mr. Hone said, his attention was directed to the parody by a speech of Earl Grey's.[32] His Lordship had noticed this parody in his place in Parliament, and had well observed—"With respect to blasphemous parodies, he thought, in common with others, that such productions should be restrained, but by the ordinary course of justice. But this disposition to profane parodies had been used for certain purposes on former occasions; and improper and profane as they were, they were pretended by some to be made in support of religion. He would recommend the Noble Lord, and the friends who surround him, to consider well the case of sending persons before a magistrate on charges of this nature. He held then in his hand a publication called the *Anti-Jacobin,* which contained a parody of this description, and which he would take the opportunity of reading to their Lordships." His Lordship then repeated the verses. Thus the jury would see that he was supported in his opinion by Earl Grey, and the report from which he had read the extract might be safely relied on. It was from the reports lately published by Mr. Harding Evans,[33] a most correct, and, in every respect, excellent reporter. Indeed, the authority of his reports was unquestionable. Mr. Hone said, it appeared from Mr. Evans's volume, which he used in Court, and quoted from, that Earl Grey said, if Lord Sidmouth was determined to suppress the practice of parodying, he should not confine his efforts to the prosecution of Mr. Hone, but should seek out the authors of the Anti-Jacobin, *whether in the Cabinet or elsewhere.* Mr. Hone said, his intention being thus pointed to the subject, he soon after saw this same parody in the Courier newspaper, with the blanks filled up, and he should read it to the Jury. It was in ridicule of certain persons in this country, who were said by the writer to be followers of Lepaux, one of the men who had made themselves famous in the French Revolution, and who was said to have publicly professed Atheism: such at least, seemed to be the assertion of the parody. It began thus—

> Last of the anointed five behold, and least
> The directorial Lama, sovereign priest—
> Lepaux—whom Atheists worship—at whose nod
> Bow their meek heads—*the men without a God.*

> Ere long, perhaps to this astonished isle,
> Fresh from the shores of subjugated Nile,
> Shall Bonaparte's victor fleet protect
> The genuine Theo-philanthropic sect—
> The sect of Marat, Mirabeau, Voltaire,[34]
> Led by their pontiff, good La Reveillere.
> Rejoic'd our CLUES shall greet him, and instal,
> The holy hunch-back in thy dome, St. Paul,
> While countless votaries thronging in his train
> Wave their red caps, and hymn this jocund strain:

> "Couriers and Stars, sedition's evening host,
> "Thou Morning Chronicle and Morning Post,
> "Whether ye make the Rights of Man your theme,
> "Your country libel, and your God blaspheme,
> "Or dirt on private worth and virtue throw,
> "Still, blasphemous or blackguard, praise Lepaux!

"And ye five other wandering bards that move
"In sweet accord of harmony and love,
"Coleridge and Southey, Lloyd and Lamb, and Co.
"Tune all your mystic harps to praise Lepaux!

Priestley and Wakefield, humble, holy men,
"Give praises to his name with tongue and pen

"Thelwall,[35] and ye that lecture as ye go,
"And for your pains get pelted, praise Lepaux!

"Praise him each Jacobin, or fool, or knave,
"And your cropp'd heads in sign of worship wave.

"All creeping creatures, venomous and low,
"Paine, Williams, Godwin, Holcroft,[36] praise Lepaux!

"And thou Leviathan!* on ocean's brim
"Hugest of living things that sleep and swim;
"Thou in whose nose, by Burke's gigantic hand,
"The hook was fixt to drag thee to the land;
"With Coke, Colquhoun, and Anson, in thy train,
"And Whitbread wallowing in the yeasty main—
"Still as ye snort, and puff, and spout, and blow,
"In puffing, and in spouting, praise Lepaux!"

* The Duke of Bedford.[37]

Mr. Justice ABBOTT—Of what use is this to you, as a matter of defence?

Mr. HONE—The Parody was written by Mr. Canning, who has not been molested.

Mr. Justice ABBOTT—How do you know that he is the author of it? It does not appear to be a Parody on any part of the Sacred Writings.

Mr. HONE—I will shew that it was written by Mr. Canning—but I know it is unpleasant that his name should be mentioned here.

Mr. Justice ABBOTT—It is unjust that any person's name should be mentioned otherwise than properly. It is my duty to take care that no man shall be improperly noticed here. Whether a man be Ministerial or

Anti-Ministerial has nothing to do with it.

Mr. HONE—It is my duty, though your Lordship says this is not a Parody on the Sacred Writings, to endeavour to shew, with due deference, that it is.

Mr. Justice ABBOTT—As far as you have gone, it does not appear to be a parody on any thing sacred. It seems to be a parody on passages in Milton and Pope. But, if you ask my opinion, I distinctly state, I do not approve of it—nor of any parody on serious works.

Mr. HONE said, he should prove that it was a parody on Scripture; and there were two lines which that contemptible newspaper The Courier—the proprietors of which had been abused in that production, the authors of which it now eulogized—had omitted. It was—

"And—and—with—join'd,
And every other beast after its kind."

This last line was a parody from the account of the Creation in the book of Genesis; this parody had alluded to Milton, who himself was a parodist on the Scripture; but this by Mr. Canning directly parodied certain parts of Scripture. The passage representing the Leviathan referred to the celebrated passage in the Book of Job. The rest contained the turn of expression and some of the very words of the 148th Psalm, as well as the general turn of the expression of other parts.

"Praise ye him all his angels; praise ye him all his hosts.
"Praise ye him, sun and moon; praise ye him all ye stars of light.
"Beasts and all cattle; creeping things and flying fowl."

—Psalm 148, verses 2, 3, and 10.

This publication was accompanied by a plate by Gilray, a most admirable caricaturist, since dead, who, to the day of his death, enjoyed a pension from his Majesty. In that print, which he held in his hand, the late Duke of Bedford was represented as the Leviathan of Job, with a hook in his nose, and with Mr. Fox and Mr. Tierney[38] on his back. The passage in Job was, "Canst thou draw out Leviathan with an hook; or his tongue with a cord which thou lettest down?"—Chap. 41, verse 1. He had been advised to subpœna Mr. Canning as a witness, but he had really abstained from a regard to Mr. Canning's feelings. He had reflected what an awkward figure Mr. Canning would cut if he were placed in the witness box, to answer questions which he should put to him. He did not wish unnecessarily to hurt any man's feelings, and he had not thought such a course necessary to his defence. The work which contained this, was, as he said, published by a general subscription of the Ministers of the Pitt and Canning school, and the notoriety of the nature of that publication was sufficient for his purpose. Now it was plain that the object of Mr. Canning's parody was the same as that of his own: it was political; and it proved that the ridicule which the authors of the parodies attempted to excite, was not always intended to fix on the production parodied.

He had not exhausted the subject, but he was afraid of exhausting the patience of the Jury. He must, however, mention one thing which, in addition to those he had already stated, proved that persons of the most strictly religious character did not regard the mixing up of profane and sacred subjects with the same sort of horror which the Attorney-General appeared to do. Mr. Rowland Hill[39] had remarked in his chapel, that the devil had some great beauties, and had followed up the remark by appropriating secular tunes to hymns: one hymn was sang, at Surrey Chapel, to the air of *God save the King*, having an appropriate burden—another was adapted to the tune of *Rule Britannia*, the chorus to which was—

"Hail Immanuel! Immanuel We adore,
"And sound his praise from shore to shore."

He could not recollect all the tunes he had heard there—but one of them, that of *"Lullaby,"* was a peculiar favourite. There was also a selection of tunes adapted to the Psalms and Hymns of Dr. Watts, and others. These tunes were selected by a respectable Baptist minister, now living, the Rev. John Rippon, Doctor of Divinity.[40] Amongst these was a hymn, commencing—

"There is a land of pure delight,
"Where saints immortal dwell;"

which was set to the tune of

"Drink to me only with thine eyes,
"And I will pledge with mine."

There was also one to the tune of *"Tell me, babbling Echo, why,"*—another, commencing

"How blest are they whose sins are covered o'er,"

was to a tune in one of Mr. Corri's operas.[41] There were, indeed, several similar instances in this, and other books of melodies for Divine worship. This book of Hymn Tunes contained *"When war's alarms called my Willy from me,"* and one hymn was set to *"Bonaparte's March."* These different instances proved that those who had the most decided religious feelings might make use of profane or secular means for the purpose, not of bringing religion into contempt, but of supporting it. It was the intention that constituted the libel, and not the mere act of publication. They all knew very well how guarded the Jewish Law was with respect to homicide. If a man committed homicide, he was put on his trial for it—but whether it was justifiable, or unjustifiable, or accidental homicide, depended on the circumstances under which it was committed. If a man striking a blow with an axe at a tree, caused the head of the axe to fly off, and a man was thereby slain, though the circumstance was to be deplored, yet it was but accidental homicide, and the person who committed the deed, not having intended it, would not be punished. But, if a person stabbed another with a knife, designedly, it was murder.—The same distinction should be taken in this case—and he utterly denied that he had the slightest idea of offending or injuring any person when he published the parody. He had thus shown that there was no practice in the annals of literature more common than that of parodies on sacred or devotional writings; that they had been written by the highest and most dignified Members of the Church—by the Father of the Reformation—by the Martyrs of the Church of England—by men to whose motives not a shadow of suspicion could attach—in all times—in all manners—in defence of the Government and the Church itself—that at no time had it been condemned by Courts of Justice—and now for the first time a friendless, and, as his persecutors hoped, a defenceless man, was fixed on to be made a sacrifice for this sin, which had been cherished and applauded for centuries. He was told that these productions of Reformers, of Martyrs, of Dignitaries, of Clergymen, of Ministers, and Pensioners, had been illegal. The Judge told him so. He denied it. What proof did the Judge produce—in what instance had one of those productions which he had read, or of coach loads of others which he might have read, been condemned or even prosecuted. He should now attempt to prove that he had not that intention which was charged in the indictment, to create impiety and irreligion. From the beginning to the end of the production in question, the subject and the object was political. It was intended to ridicule a certain set of men, whose only religion was blind servility, and who subjected their wills and their understandings to persons who, they thought, would best promote their sinister interest. The principles which he ascribed to these persons were so enumerated as to contrast with the duty which Christianity enjoined; and the Christian principles shone more bright as contrasted with infamous time-servingness. Was it to be supposed that the Ten Commandments, which contained all the great principles of morality, as well as religion, could be debased by a comparison with another set of Commandments, framed in somewhat the same form, but the principles of which were as detestable and noxious as those of the first were respectable and beneficial?—Was the Lord's Prayer to be ridiculed by placing in contrast with it the Prayer of a Ministerial Member? It was evidently impossible that such could have been his intention. As an honest man, speaking before those whose esteem he valued, he declared that it was not his intention. The Political Catechism was charged as an impious and wicked publication, tending to excite irreligion in the minds of his Majesty's subjects. But he would prove to the Jury, that it had not been disseminated with any intent to bring religion into contempt, for it was a matter purely political. If they could find a passage in it, that, in any way, tended to turn any thing sacred into ridicule, he called on them to find him guilty; but, if they could not discover such a passage, he demanded an acquittal at their hands. Let the Jury look to the Catechism. It commenced thus—

Q. What is your name?—A. Lick Spittle.

Q. Who gave you that name?—A. My Sureties to the Ministry, in my Political Change, wherein I was made a Member of the Majority, the Child of Corruption, and a Locust to devour the good things of this Kingdom.

The majority meant those who were always ready at the beck of the Minister—the corruption was that which was known to exist in the

House of Commons, and was as notorious as the sun at noon day.

Q. What did your Sureties then for you?—A. They did promise and vow three things in my name. First, that I should renounce the Reformists and all their Works, the pomps and vanity of Popular Favour, and all the sinful lusts of Independence. Secondly, that I should believe all the Articles of the Court Faith. And Thirdly, that I should keep the Minister's sole Will and Commandments, and walk in the same, all the days of my life.

Surely it could not be denied that the friends of the Minister did renounce the Reformists—they could not be his friends else. If Mr. Canning were here he would admit this. Mr. Hone said if he went through the whole of the *Catechism,* it would be found, like the extracts he had quoted, entirely political, and not at all intended to bring religion into contempt. But it was said, that the publication of similar parodies, during two centuries, did not justify the act. It might be so—but it would be a most cruel hardship if he, who, from the long continuance of the system had been induced to adopt it, should be punished for that which his predecessors and contemporaries did with impunity. In his opinion the existence of such publications for so long a time, proved that they were not libellous—for, if they were, they would have been prosecuted. But they had not been prosecuted—not even in times when Judges on the Bench told the Jury that they had only to find the fact of publication, but that they were not to decide the questions of libel or no libel. His Majesty's Secretaries of State, who ought to be the conservators of the public morals, had committed high treason against the peace and happiness of society, if, believing such publications to be libellous, they had suffered them so long to exist unnoticed. They had now, however, selected him for punishment—but, he was sure, the good sense and excellent understanding of Mr. Attorney-General, must have led him to think that the selection was not a just one. Whether he went home to his distressed family, or retired in the custody of Mr. Jones's gentlemen, [Mr. Jones is the Marshal of the King's Bench Prison, was present in Court with his tipstaves] he should leave the Court conscious that he was innocent of any intention to bring the religion of his country into contempt. If suffering the sentence he was sure to receive, should he be found guilty, and he were placed within the walls of a dungeon, with a certainty that he should never see his family again, still he should, to his dying moment, deny that he had ever published those tracts in order to ridicule religion.—[*Loud cheering.*]—The Attorney-General, and every man with whom laws originated, would do well, to render them so clear, that they could be easily understood by all—that no person could be mistaken. Was it to be supposed that he, with a wife and a family of seven children, would, if his mind were ever so depraved, have sat down and written a libel, if he were aware that it was one? None but a *maniac* would act so indiscreetly. There were, however, very few men who understood the law of libel. It was, in fact, a shadow—it was undefinable. His Lordship called this publication a libel—but he would say, with all due deference, that his Lordship was mistaken. That only could be called a libel, which twelve men, sworn well and truly to try the cause, declared to be one. He would not occupy their time much further. It was an important feature of his defence, to shew that parodies might be written, in order to excite certain ideas, without any desire to turn the original production into ridicule. He thought he had already shewn that this was not the case; he thought it was pretty clear that Martin Luther did not mean to ridicule the Psalms; that Dr. Boys, the Dean of Canterbury, did not mean to ridicule the Lord's Prayer; that the Author of the "Visitation Service for a sick Parliament," published by a zealous partizan of Charles I. did not mean to ridicule the service of the Church of England; that Mr. Canning did not mean to ridicule the Scripture nor Milton. Why, then, should it be presumed that he had such an intention? In *The Spirit of the Journals* was to be found the following parody on *Black-eyed Susan*. It was well-known to have been written by Mr. Jekyll, now a Master in Chancery, and certainly no man could say, that that gentleman meant to turn Gay's beautiful poem[42] into ridicule:—

"All in the Downs the fleet was moor'd,[43]
The streamers waving in the wind,
When Castlereagh appeared on board,
"Ah, where shall I my Curtis find![44]
"Tell me, ye jovial sailors, tell me true,
"Does my fat William sail among your crew?"
William, who high upon the poop—

Mr. Justice ABBOTT—You need not go on with that parody. It is no defence for you. How can a parody, ridiculing any person, be material to your defence?

Mr. HONE—I will prove that it is.

Mr. Justice ABBOTT—Prove that it is, first, and then read it. It is my duty to prevent the reading, in a Court of Justice, of productions ridiculing public or private characters.

Mr. HONE—May I ask your Lordship whether, in your judicial character, you have a right to demand the nature of the defence I mean to make?

Mr. Justice ABBOTT—Certainly not; but, when you quote, that which is apparently irrelevant, you are bound, if called on to shew its relevancy.

Mr. HONE—This is a whimsical Parody, and my object is to shew, that the humour of it does not tend to bring the original into contempt. It is a case in point—and no person can suppose Mr. Jekyll intended to ridicule the original.

Mr. Justice ABBOTT—You have read enough of it for your purpose, which is to shew, that the Parody is not intended to turn the original into ridicule.

Mr. HONE.—Your Lordship and I understand each other, and we have gone on so good humouredly hitherto, that I will not break in upon our harmony by insisting on the reading the remainder of this humorous Parody. He was sorry he had occasion to detain them so long, though for his own part he was not half exhausted. He was, however, obliged to mention some publications which he had before omitted, and which would strongly shew the impunity which publishers of works of a description similar to his own had enjoyed. These were *graphic* Parodies by way of parody on Mr. Fuseli's celebrated picture of *The Night Mare.*[45] The Parody was intended, not to ridicule the work of that celebrated artist, but to create a laugh at the expence of a late very respectable Chief Magistrate of London, whom he would not name, remarkable for his exertions to clear the streets of women of the town. He now called their attention to another caricature, entitled *"Boney's Meditations in the Island of St. Helena; or, The Devil addressing the Sun."* This was a parody on Milton, not turning the passage from that part into ridicule, but meant to ridicule Bonaparte. The Prince Regent was the *Sun*, whom Bonaparte was supposed to address:—

"To thee I call, but with no friendly mind,
To tell thee, George, Prince Regent, how I hate,
Whene'er I think from what a height I fell."

He next produced a parody, by Mr. Gilray, entitled, "Would you know Men's Hearts, look in their Faces." In this Mr. Fox was depicted as the arch-fiend—Mr. Sheridan as Judas Iscariot—Sir Francis Burdett as Sixteen-string Jack,[46] &c. &c. In another of those graphic Parodies, Lord Moira[47] was represented endeavouring to blow out a candle, in allusion to a story which he related in the course of his speech on the Watch and Ward Bill, relative to a poor woman who was ill-treated, because, after a certain hour, she continued to keep a candle lighted in order to attend on her sick child. Another of those Parodies was called *The Reconciliation,* the inscription to which was taken from *The New Testament;* and the print itself was a Parody on the parable of the Prodigal Son: "And he rose, and came to his father's servants, and he fell on his father's neck, and kissed him, (who was represented falling on his father's neck) saying, 'I have sinned against Heaven, and am no longer worthy to be called thy son.'" Who was meant by either father or son, he would not say, but the Gentlemen of the Jury might satisfy themselves on that point. It was engraved by Mr. Gilray. He would now advert to another Parody. It was denominated *"The Impious Feast of Belshazzar."* It was a complete Parody—but no man could suppose that Mr. Gilray, who engraved it, meant to ridicule the Scriptures: it was designed to ridicule Napoleon. At the time he published it, Mr. Gilray was pensioned by his Majesty's Ministers.

Mr. Justice ABBOTT—You must not make these assertions.

Mr. HONE—I can prove it.

Mr. Justice ABBOTT—But, if you can prove that he, being pensioned, published those things, will that form a defence for you?

Mr. HONE—My Lord, I have no pension.[48]

* * * * *

The Jury then withdrew, and returned to the box in less than a quarter of an hour. Their names were called over, and Mr. Law, in the usual manner, inquired whom they had appointed to speak for them as foreman?

It being signified that Mr. Bowring had been directed by his fellows to deliver the verdict, Mr. Law asked him whether the Jury found the defendant, William Hone, guilty or not guilty.

Mr. BOWRING replied, in a firm voice,—NOT GUILTY.

The loudest acclamations were instantly heard in all parts of the

Court; *Long live the honest Jury,* and *an honest Jury for ever,* were exclaimed by many voices: the waving of hats, handkerchiefs, and applauses continued for several minutes. When order had been somewhat restored, Mr. Justice ABBOTT interposed, and desired that those who felt inclined to rejoice at the decision, would reserve the expressions of their satisfaction for a fitter place and opportunity. The people accordingly left the Court, and as they proceeded along the streets, the language of joy was most loudly and unequivocally expressed; every one with whom they met, and to whom they communicated the event, being forward to swell the peal.

The Trial of the Information against Mr. Hone, for a Parody on the Litany, was ordered by the Court to come on the next morning at half-past nine o'clock.

SECOND TRIAL.

THE KING *against* WILLIAM HONE,

ON AN EX-OFFICIO INFORMATION FOR PUBLISHING A PARODY

ENTITLED

"THE POLITICAL LITANY."

Tried in Guildhall, London, on Friday, December 19, 1817, at the *London Sittings after Michaelmas Term*.

BEFORE LORD ELLENBOROUGH[49] AND A SPECIAL JURY.

It having been announced by the Attorney-General, at the close of the first day's proceedings, that he intended to persevere in the trial of the second information against Mr. Hone, the curiosity of the public became so intense this morning, as well on account of the importance of the case, as of the triumphant defence of Mr. Hone the former day, that at a very early hour all the avenues of the Court were literally blocked up by a multitude of spectators, anxious to become auditors of the proceedings; and when the doors of the Court were opened, not one-twentieth part of the multitude could find standing accommodation.

It was generally supposed, as indeed might naturally have been expected, that Mr. Hone having been acquitted on one of the informations, the Attorney-General would not proceed against him on any of the others. It appeared, however, that this was a supposition unfounded in fact; and at a quarter after nine Mr. Hone entered the court, followed by several large bundles of books, regularly tied up. He took his station at the end of the court table, and having untied them, he ranged them before him, covering nearly a fourth of the table.

At twenty minutes before ten Lord Ellenborough entered the court,

Sketches of Lord Ellenborough by George Cruikshank.
By permission of Berg Collection of English and American Literature,
The New York Public Library, Astor, Lenox and Tilden Foundations

and took his seat on the bench. His Lordship's appearance was unexpected, Mr. Justice Abbott having presided on Mr. Hone's trial the day before. The Attorney-General, and other Counsel for the prosecution, next entered, and took their places.

Lord ELLENBOROUGH.—Are the Sheriffs in court?

The UNDER SHERIFF.—They are not, my Lord.

Lord ELLENBOROUGH.—Then let them be immediately sent for.

The Sheriffs were then sent for.

The Hon. Mr. LAW, Clerk at *Nisi Prius,*[50] then called on the case of the KING *v.* WILLIAM HONE, and desired the gentlemen on the Special Jury pannel to answer to their names. Six of these gentlemen only appeared; when the officers of the Crown were asked, if they would pray a *tales?*[51]

The ATTORNEY-GENERAL remained for some minutes in doubt; and, after consulting with the other Counsel for the Crown, nodded assent to the question; and, accordingly, six common Jurymen were put into the box. JOHN AUSTEN, shoemaker, of Aldgate, answered to his name, and was challenged by the Crown. The Jury, which was composed of twelve of the most respectable and independent men in the city of London, were then sworn.

THE JURY.

RICHARD WILSON, Great Eastcheap	TALESMEN.
JOHN LINDSAY, Lawrence-Pountney Lane	JAMES JONES
RICHARD THORNTON, Old Swan Passage	JAMES SMITH
WILLIAM GILLMAN, 54, Bread Street	JOSHUA THORNE
JOHN MACKIE, 12, Watling Street	JAMES DONALDSON
NEIL BLACK, 11, Bread Street	WILLIAM HALE
	WILLIAM GREEN.

Mr. SHEPHERD opened the pleadings, and stated, that this was an information filed by his Majesty's Attorney-General against William Hone, for printing and publishing a certain *impious and profane* libel upon a part of the Church Service in the Common Prayer Book, called *"The Litany, or General Supplication."* There was a second count, charging the said publication to be a wicked and *seditious* libel of and concerning the Prince Regent, and the Houses of Lords and Commons. To this information the defendant had pleaded Not Guilty.

The ATTORNEY-GENERAL then addressed the Jury.—The question

they were assembled to try was one of the utmost importance to the constitution of society. The information charged the offence committed by
the defendant in two ways:—in the first count it was alleged to be a profane and impious libel, and in the second a seditious libel. He should
call the attention of the Jury particularly to the first. The libel was a
parody upon that part of the Divine service established by law, called
"The Litany, or General Supplication." After the authority of Sir
Matthew Hale, and of other great lawyers, no man could dispute that
Christianity was part or parcel of the law of the land: it had been held
to be so in all times, and all the rights we enjoyed more or less depended upon that principle; the very oaths which the Jury had so
solemnly taken were founded upon it. In all Christian countries it was
necessary that some form of public worship to the Creator should exist:
in England it had been established by statute in the reign of Charles II;
and if any man in writing should revile, scoff at, or ridicule it, by the
law of the land he was guilty of a libel: no man could venture to contradict that position. The information charged that the defendant, devising and intending to excite impiety and irreligion, and to scandalize
and defame, and bring into contempt in the minds of the King's subjects, that part of the public and divine service called *"The Litany, or
General Supplication,"* and to apply the style and form of expression
there used to scandalous purposes, published the libel in question. It
was not necessary to remind the Jury that the Litany was a most solemn
prayer to the Almighty, to the Redeemer of the World, and to the Holy
Ghost, and had justly been considered the most sublime part of the
public service of the Church; and it was impossible to make the most
distant approach to its style and form in a parody, without exciting in
the most pious mind ideas that would have never have otherwise entered it; and the taint of profaneness and ridicule, even of the most sacred subjects, was rapidly disseminated. The Litany, after the
supplication to God, the Redeemer, the Holy Ghost, and the Trinity,
went on to pray deliverance in the hour of death and in the day of judgment. It was succeeded by a most devout and impressive reiteration:
"Son of God, we beseech thee to hear us! O Lamb of God, that takest
away the sins of the world, have mercy upon us!" He would not proceed; it seemed too solemn even for the solemnity of a court of justice;
yet (would the Jury believe it?) the defendant had turned it to ridicule
by making an impious parody of it. It began, "O Prince, Ruler of the
people, have mercy upon us, miserable subjects. O House of Lords,

hereditary Legislators, have mercy upon us, pension-paying subjects. O House of Commons, proceeding from corrupt borough-mongers, have mercy upon us, miserable subjects." It was too disgusting to read the whole, but he would turn to that part which was substituted for the devout reiteration at the end of the Litany of the Church; instead of "Son of God, we beseech thee to hear us," &c. the defendant had said, "Son of George, we beseech thee to hear us. O House of Lords, that takest away so many thousands of pounds in pensions, have mercy upon us."

[These parts of the parody produced an involuntary burst of laughter from the auditory, which evidently proceeded, not from a wish to disturb the Court, but was really the irresistible impulse arising from the matter of the parody.]

Lord ELLENBOROUGH.—Where are the Sheriffs? I desired their attendance, and they shall attend.

The UNDER-SHERIFF.—My Lord, I have sent for them; but they live a great distance from this, and they have not yet arrived.

Lord ELLENBOROUGH.—Very well.

Mr. HONE joined the Court in reprehending in strong terms this interruption of the order of the proceedings.

The ATTORNEY-GENERAL resumed as follows:—Will any one now say that the dangerous, the impious and profane publication before you, has not been the means of raising scoffing among the scoffers? I will ask, if there can possibly be a stronger proof of its dangerous effects?—If the social bonds of society are to be burst asunder by the indecent conduct of a rabble, the Court may as well discontinue its proceedings. But, Gentlemen, if any man supposes that an interruption of this description can have the effect of intimidating me, or of making me swerve for a moment in the execution of my duty—my sacred duty to the public and to the cause of God, he is perfectly mistaken. That shall never be the case with me, while I stand in an English court of justice, whether as the law officer of the crown, or as a private advocate; and while God gives me strength and understanding to perform that duty, I will never be deterred by any thing of this description which can possibly pass. Gentlemen, in calling your attention to the parody upon this most sacred prayer, I shall have little occasion to guide you in your verdict. You will, I doubt not, read every word of it before you give in that verdict, and you will compare it with the sacred book (the Prayer-Book) which I now hold in my hand, and which is an exact duplicate of the legal Book of the Common Prayer which will be produced to you in evidence. If there be any among you, which is doubtless the case, who is the father of children, and the master of a household, I will ask him, if he would suffer that publication to be perused by his servants, who are not so well educated as himself? or if he would suffer his children for one moment to read it? I will ask him, if he does not believe that it would have the effect I have described? What man is there, even though he is not a Christian himself, but as a father, must wish his child to be a Christian? Gentlemen, the express purpose of the book is clear, from its being circulated at a cheap rate, so as to be within the reach of the common and ordinary people. This is the object of the publication; and it is because this is the object that I have thought it to be my duty to bring it before you. There may be many writings which sensible men may read in their closets; some of them may be highly improper for general circulation, although some may be properly open to a free discussion: but the subject of the present question is not to be looked at in this point of view, for the mode of publication plainly shews what the real object is, and fully proves that it was intended that it should find its way among the ignorant and uninformed, where it was calculated to have a gross effect. It may be, that the defendant will produce, as heretofore, books which have been at different times published, and which, if they had not now been taken down from their shelves, would have been forgotten; they were written at different periods of time, and principally, if not entirely, when the persons so writing were engaged in all the vehemence and rancour of political disputes. But it never can be offered as a justification or excuse by an individual offending at the present period, that he had followed a bad example. If that observation could be made as an answer to offences, it might be pleaded as an excuse in other cases, of a nature wholly different from the case which you are at this time trying. The law, Gentlemen, is called upon, most imperiously called upon, to put a stop to proceedings like those of the defendant, or the time will come, when a stop will be put to all that remains of the Christian establishment of the Church of England—of every thing entitled to reverence. Whatever may be the opinion of others, I feel that I should not discharge my duty to the public—that I should not do my duty to society, as a member of it, Gentlemen of the Jury, if I had not brought this case of libel before you. I am ready to agree, Gentlemen, that, constitutionally, you are not called upon to find a verdict upon the simple fact of the printing and publishing; but, whatever be the intention of a publication attended with a mischievous tendency, it is no less a libel. This, however, you know, that in a case of libel, as well as in all other cases, it is the duty of a Jury to give in their verdict according to the law, and according to evidence. It was never the meaning of the statute, that the verdict of a Jury should be founded in caprice; it is to be given upon evidence, and that is held to be the law of the land. No man among you can now say that he is mistaken; and it is to prevent such a mistake that I have made any observations of this sort: for he who does not apply his mind to find a verdict upon the evidence, according to the law of the land, is guilty of a misapprehension of duty. It is not necessary for me at the outset to make any further remarks upon this point; I will not therefore proceed. You will hear from my Lord, if I am mistaken in any principle which I have laid down:—if I am wrong, I shall be most happy and most desirous to receive correction in which you will hear stated by the Noble and Learned Judge as to the law; it will be your province to apply your minds to the facts of the case, as to the nature of the paper, and to judge of it according to the law which you will hear laid down. Gentlemen, if such things as this are permitted, no parody, in any terms or in any shape, upon any part of the public worship of the Church of England, or of any part of the Scripture, will be punishable, nor will there be any attack upon Christianity which may not be published with impunity. It is not enough for a man to say, that he did it for another purpose: that cannot be a point for consideration, when the effect of what he has so published is to scoff at the public service of the Church of England. The question is, Did this parody produce this certain effect? If it is answered in the affirmative, by the law of England it is a libel, though at that moment the defendant did not consider what the ultimate effect might be. If a man publish any thing that is obscene and immoral, and say that his object was to ridicule, and that he did not mean to be obscene—that he only meant to ridicule such and such a person; if he did not mean it to be obscene, what does it signify if it is so? He is guilty of producing an effect which is reprehensible. Having stated the case to you, Gentlemen, I shall now proceed to prove it; and if there is any thing like religious principles in your minds—if you are in the practice of looking with veneration upon the service of the Church, you cannot look over this [holding up the publication] without saying that it is a profane and impious parody—that it is calculated to, and actually does bring into contempt, and that it does ridicule, that part of it called the Litany.

The alleged libel was then put in by the ATTORNEY-GENERAL, and read by the Clerk of the Court.

The POLITICAL LITANY; diligently revised; to be said or sung, until the appointed Change come, throughout the Dominion of ENGLAND and WALES, and the Town of BERWICK-UPON-TWEED.—By Special Command.—London: Printed for one of the Candidates for the Office of Printer to the King's Most Excellent Majesty, and sold by WILLIAM HONE, 55, Fleet Street, and 67, Old Bailey, three doors from Ludgate Hill. 1817. Price Two-pence.

THE LITANY.

¶ *Here followeth the Litany, or General Supplication,*
to be said or sung at all times when thereunto especially moved.

O PRINCE, ruler of the people, have mercy upon us, thy miserable subjects.

O Prince, ruler, &c.

O House of Lords, hereditary legislators, have mercy upon us, pension-paying subjects.

O House of Lords, &c.

O House of Commons, proceeding from corrupt borough-mongers, have mercy upon us, your should-be constituents.

O House of Commons, &c.

O gracious, noble, right honourable, and learned rulers of our land, three estates in one state, have mercy upon us, a poverty-stricken people.

O gracious, noble, &c.

Remember not, most gracious, most noble, right honourable, and honourable gentlemen, our past riches, nor the riches of our forefathers; neither continue to tax us according to our long-lost ability—

spare us, good rulers; spare the people who have supported ye with their labour, and spilt their most precious blood in your quarrels; O consume us not utterly.

Spare us, good Prince.

From an unnational debt; from unmerited pensions and sinecure places; from an extravagant civil list; and from utter starvation,

Good Prince, deliver us.

From the blind imbecility of ministers; from the pride and vain-glory of warlike establishments in time of peace,

Good Prince, deliver us.

From all the deadly sins attendant on a corrupt method of election; from all the deceits of the pensioned hirelings of the press,

Good Prince, deliver us.

From taxes levied by distress; from jails crowded with debtors; from poor-houses overflowing with paupers,

Good Prince, deliver us.

From a Parliament chosen only by one-tenth of the tax-payers; from taxes raised to pay wholesale human butchers their subsidies; from the false doctrines, heresy, and schism, which have obscured our once-glorious constitution; from conspiracies against the liberty of the people; and from obstacles thrown in the way of the exertion of our natural and constitutional rights,

Good Prince, deliver us.

By your feelings as men; by your interests as members of civil society; by your duty as Christians,

O Rulers, deliver us.

By the deprivation of millions—by the sighs of the widow—by the tears of the orphan—by the groans of the aged in distress—by the wants of all classes in the community, except your own and your dependents,

O Rulers, deliver us.

In this time of tribulation—in this time of want of labour to thousands, and of unrequited labour to tens of thousands—in this time of sudden death from want of food,

O Rulers, deliver us.

We people do beseech ye to hear us, O Rulers; and that it may please ye to rule and govern us constitutionally in the right way;

We beseech ye to hear us, O Rulers.

That it may please ye to keep yourselves in all sobriety, temperance, and honesty of life—that ye spend not extravagantly the money raised from the production of our labours, nor take for yourselves that which ye need not;

We beseech ye to hear us, O Rulers.

That it may please ye to keep your hearts in fear of oppression, and in love of justice; and that ye may evermore have affiance in our affection, rather than in the bayonets of an hired soldiery;

We beseech ye to hear us, O Rulers.

That it may please ye to be our defenders and keepers, giving us the victory over all our enemies, and redressing the grievances under which we labour;

We beseech ye to hear us, O Rulers.

That it may please ye to lessen the cares of the world unto all Bishops and Church Dignitaries; giving their superabundance to the poor clergy, and no longer taxing us for their support;

We beseech ye to hear us, O Rulers.

That it may please ye to place within the bounds of economy the expenditure of all the Royal Family;

We beseech ye to hear us, O Rulers.

That it may please ye to deprive the Lords of the Council, and all the nobility, of all money paid out of the taxes which they have not earned;

We beseech ye to hear us, O Rulers.

That it may please ye to direct all Magistrates to give up their advanced salaries, which the times no longer render necessary, and to content themselves with their former stipends;

We beseech ye to hear us, O Rulers.

That it may please ye to bless all the people with equal representation, and to keep them safe from borough-mongering factions;

We beseech ye to hear us, O Rulers.

That it may please ye so to govern us, that unity, peace, and concord, may prevail throughout the nation, and the voice of tumult and dissatisfaction be no more heard in our streets;

We beseech ye to hear us, O Rulers.

That it may please ye to give unto all people all their rights as citizens, whatever may be the mode in which their consciences may impel them to worship their Creator, and whatever the creed to which their judgments assent;

We beseech ye to hear us, O Rulers.

That it may please ye to bring into the way of truth those apostates who have erred therefrom, and have deceived us;

We beseech ye to hear us, O Rulers.

That it may please ye to strengthen all such as do stand up for the legal and constitutional rights of the people; to comfort and help the weak-hearted, who want courage in our behalf; to raise up such as do fall; and, finally, to beat down corruption under our feet;

We beseech ye to hear us, O Rulers.

That it may please ye not to tax "until the brow of labour sweats in vain;" but to succour and comfort all that are in necessity and tribulation;

We beseech ye to hear us, O Rulers.

That it may please ye to shew pity to all who are prisoners and captives for the people's sake, or through the oppressive expences of the laws;

We beseech ye to hear us, O Rulers.

That it may please ye to appropriate the 200,000*l.* annually paid to Members of Parliament, contrary to an ancient law, as a provision for fatherless children and widows, and all that are desolate and oppressed;

We beseech ye to hear us, O Rulers.

That it may please ye to have mercy upon us all;

We beseech ye to hear us, O Rulers.

That it may please ye to turn the hearts of our enemies, persecutors, and slanderers, by withdrawing their pensions and emoluments, that they may no longer call us a "rabble," the "swinish multitude," or "ragamuffins," but may once more style us "the real strength of the nation,"—"the body, without which a head is useless;"

We beseech ye to hear us, O Rulers.

That it may please ye to give and preserve to our use the kindly fruits of the earth, untaxed by men in black, whom those who wish for their instruction ought alone to support;

We beseech ye to hear us, O Rulers.

That it may please ye to abolish and destroy all sinecure places, and worthless pensions; to utterly purge and root out all wrong-doers; to thoroughly correct the present mis-representation of the people, by an effectual Reform in Parliament; and otherwise to do, or cause to be done, such further and other acts and deeds, as shall or may conduce to the true interest and benefit of the whole commonwealth;

We beseech ye to hear us, O Rulers.

That it may please ye to lead and strengthen GEORGE Prince of Wales, our present REGENT, in the true fear and knowledge of the principles whereon the people of this commonwealth placed their crown on the head of his ancestors, and continue it towards him; and that it may please ye, as much as in ye lie, to keep and defend him from battle and murder, and sudden death, and from fornication, and all other deadly sin;

We beseech ye to hear us, O Rulers.

That it may please ye to put on short allowance all Bishops, Priests, and Deacons, that their fleshly appetites being reduced, their spiritual-mindedness may be thereby increased, and so that both by their preaching and living they may set it forth, and show it accordingly;

We beseech ye to hear us, O Rulers.

That it may please ye to take to yourselves true repentance, inasmuch as ye have erred from the way of your forefathers; and amend your method of governing according to our free constitution;

We beseech ye to hear us, O Rulers.

Son of George, we beseech thee to hear us.

Son of George, we beseech thee, &c.

O House of Lords, that takest away so many tens of thousands of pounds in pensions,

Have mercy upon us.

O House of Commons, that votest away the money of the whole nation, instead of that of those only who elect you:

Have mercy upon us.

O Prince, hear us.

O Prince, hear us.

George, have mercy upon us.

George, have mercy upon us.

O House of Lords, have mercy upon us.

O House of Lords, have mercy upon us.

O House of Commons, have mercy upon us.

O House of Commons, have mercy upon us.

[Here endeth the Litany.]

¶ THE COLLECT TO BE USED BY HIS MAJESTY'S MINISTERS

Beginneth thus:

LIGHTEN *our darkness, we beseech thee, &c.*

¶ *By whom the following may be used in ordinary.*

THE *Grace of our Lord* GEORGE *the* PRINCE REGENT,
and the Love of LOUIS *the XVIII and the Fellowship of the Pope,
be with us all evermore, Amen.*

Mr. TOPPING rose to call witnesses to prove the fact of the alleged libel being published and sold by the defendant.

Mr. HONE interrupted the learned Counsel, by saying, that it was not his wish to take up the time of the Court by any thing unnecessary; he would admit the fact of the publication.

The ATTORNEY-GENERAL (producing the Common-Prayer Book under seal.)—Do you admit that this is the Common-Prayer Book?

Mr. HONE.—I admit that this is the Common Prayer.

Lord ELLENBOROUGH.—You admit that it is the Common Prayer of the Church of England?

Mr. HONE.—Certainly, my Lord.

Lord ELLENBOROUGH accordingly recorded Mr. Hone's admission, that he was the printer and publisher of the parody in question, at No. 55, Fleet Street, in the parish of St. Dunstan's in the West.

Mr. HONE.—I trust your Lordship will excuse the interruption; but with respect to the disturbance which has occurred in the Court, I beg to observe, that I consider that man to be my enemy, who, in any way—

Lord ELLENBOROUGH.—There is not any thing of that kind before the Court at present; the time for making your observations is not arrived.

Mr. HONE.—I was only desirous, my Lord, to add my feeble assistance in keeping order in the Court.

Lord ELLENBOROUGH.—A very proper disposition.

Here Mr. Sheriff Desanges entered the Court, and Lord ELLENBOROUGH addressed him thus:—"I have sent for you and your colleague, Sir, as there is an absolute necessity for your presence. There was a most unseemly disturbance in the Court yesterday, I understand, and there has been another to-day. You are the persons who are responsible, and shall be responsible; and therefore you will be good enough to use your utmost activity in apprehending any persons who dare to interrupt the course of the proceedings."

Here Mr. Sheriff DESANGES assured the Court, that no endeavour should be wanting on his part to put a stop to conduct so disgraceful and so indecent.

Lord ELLENBOROUGH.—You will understand me; my only motive in admonishing you as to your duty is, that you may attend to it.

The case for the Crown being closed,

Mr. HONE rose.—Before he remarked on the opening speech of Mr. Attorney-General, he would address himself to the persons present; and he must say, he knew of no species of indecency—he knew of no breach of propriety, that more deserved severe reprehension and reprobation, than an act which tended to impede the proceedings of a Court of Justice. Taking his trial there, on a charge which perhaps might consign him to a prison, he felt most solicitous that good order and tranquillity should prevail. Perhaps those indiscreet expressions of feeling might increase his danger—they certainly could not serve any good purpose. The persons who had so loudly expressed themselves ought not, whatever they might think or feel, to have given loose to their feelings in that place. He begged to state, that he was opposed to every such expression in that Court; and he declared that man to be his decided enemy—he cared not where he came from, or who he was—who should attempt to interrupt such solemn proceedings. He did not expect to be so much embarrassed to-day as he was yesterday, but, he confessed, his embarrassment was not abated. This was not surprising, since yesterday was almost the first time that he ever in his life addressed half a dozen sentences to ten persons assembled together. The first time he had ever made such an attempt was when he applied to his Lordship and the other Judges on the subject of the informations filed against him; and when he stood on the floor of the Court, he doubted, so novel was his situation, whether he should be able to utter a single word in objection to the course adopted against him. He was now, from the urgency of the case, thrown into the gap, and he was obliged to fight out as well as he could. The Attorney-General said the *alleged* libel (for he denied that it was one, and if it were, he would not be standing there to defend it) was printed at a cheap rate, in order to be disseminated amongst the common people. The fact was, that the price of the publication was fully commensurate with its size. Where publications were likely to have an extensive circulation, they were sold by the booksellers at four-pence per sheet. The publication for which he was now prosecuted consisted of half a sheet, and it was sold for two-pence, which was the regular price. He would not say that it did not get into the hands of the ignorant and uninformed, for he knew it necessarily must, since a great proportion of the people, even in this enlightened country, were ignorant: but he knew this also, that great numbers of those parodies were sold to persons of a very different description. They were sold to persons of high standing in that Court—to Magistrates of the City of London—to Members of Parliament, and even to his Majesty's Ministers. This publication had a particular object, which every man, who read it with an unprejudiced mind, must at once perceive. That object was a political one; no intention existed to bring religion into contempt. Of course it did not well become him to praise his own publication; but thus much he felt called upon to assert, that the style of it was not the worst he had ever seen, nor did it seem best calculated to make an impression upon the merely vulgar and unlettered. Many men of talent and information were satisfied that the purpose with which it had been published was innocent; and he was persuaded, that every man capable of judging, and who read it without prejudice, would arrive at the same conclusion. The Attorney-General had regretted that certain parodies had been taken from the shelves on which they were placed, and where they might have rotted and been forgotten, had they not been produced in Court on yesterday's trial. He meant nothing dis-respectful to the learned Attorney-General in venturing to differ from him on the present occasion; but he must deny the learned Gentleman's position, that these parodies were brought forward for any improper or irreverent purpose. The production of these books was essentially nec-essary to his defence before a Jury of his country, who were impan-nelled to try this important issue between the crown and himself, the defendant. Without these works it was impossible for the Jury to come to a sound decision upon the allegations of the information,—to which he should afterwards allude more at length than the Attorney-General had thought it necessary to do. Many of the works before him had been placed upon the shelf only within the last ten years; and certainly he should feel it to be his duty to bring those, at least, under the notice of the Jury. Amongst them was a well-known publication, called *The Book of Chronicles of Westminster,* containing Scriptural Parodies, applicable to the Westminster Election.

Lord ELLENBOROUGH.—I think it necessary thus early to apprise you, that if you wish to shew that as a sample of publications of the like tendency which have been written, or for the purpose of proving that the sacred Scriptures have been ridiculed and brought into contempt by other subjects of the realm as well as yourself, I shall not receive it. The commission of crimes, by how many soever persons they may have been committed, does not qualify the guilt of the individual committer. It is my decided purpose not to receive this in evidence; and therefore you may use your discretion, whether you shall dwell further upon a matter of evidence which I declare, judicially, to be inadmissible.

Mr. HONE.—I would ask your Lordship, if you really mean to send me to prison without a fair trial? If your Lordship does not mean to do that, you will let me make my defence to the Jury.

Lord ELLENBOROUGH.—You may state what you know to be of serv-ice to you in your defence upon this particular issue. You may state what you please; but I tell you, that that shall not be given in evidence which falls within the description of evidence I have mentioned.

Mr. HONE (*after a pause.*)—I really do not understand your Lord-ship; I state it seriously, that I am not aware of the exact meaning of your Lordship's intimation.

Lord ELLENBOROUGH.—I think what I have stated is intelligible enough to every other person in Court.

Mr. HONE.—It certainly is not intelligible to my humble apprehension.

Lord ELLENBOROUGH.—I can't help it.

Mr. HONE.—I really don't clearly understand what your Lordship means by the word *evidence*. I am ignorant of the technical rules of evidence, and therefore I apply to your Lordship for a more explicit statement of your meaning. There are certain allegations in this information, which it is necessary for me to explain away, by shewing that they can have no possible reference to the supposed libel. This I propose to do by calling the attention of the Jury to passages in other publications, to shew that this parody has no application whatever to religious matters. I don't know, as a man of plain understanding, what may and what may not be given in evidence. But my intention is to read to the Jury certain other publications that I consider absolutely essential to my defence, and so essential to my defence that I cannot defend myself unless I do read portions of these publications. I state this with all due deference to your Lordship.

Lord ELLENBOROUGH.—You may go on, and exercise your own discretion. I tell you what rule I shall adopt in my direction to the Jury. I don't wish to interrupt you; but I thought it my duty to inform you of the course I meant to adopt. You may exercise your discretion, how far you will conform to that rule or not.

Mr. HONE—If your Lordship had condescended to explain to me your meaning, by saying that these works are not admissible in evidence at all, I should know at once what I am to expect. If your Lordship says, that I am not to read these publications to the Jury—if that is your Lordship's decision against me, then I have no defence to this information, and I am ready to go with your Lordship's tipstaff wherever your Lordship may think proper to send me.

Mr. Hone paused for a few moments as if waiting for an answer, and then continued his address to the jury:—

He insisted, that many of the books from which he had read extracts were modern: it could not surely have escaped the recollection of the Attorney-General, that the first authority to which he had referred yesterday was Blackwood's *Edinburgh Magazine*, published in October last, long subsequent to the date of the alleged libel; yet that contained a parody upon a large portion of the Scriptures, against which no complaint had been ever made. He (the defendant) did not require the Attorney-General to prosecute Mr. Blackwood, a most respectable bookseller; he should be a scoundrel if he did; he only brought it forward as in point, for the writer, bookseller, and printer, must all have been well aware of its nature. Mr. Blackwood's politics were totally different from his (the defendant's); but whatever others might do, he would be the last to suggest a prosecution on account of an honest dissent upon such points. Mr. Hone then read to the jury the extract from the *Edinburgh Magazine* he produced yesterday.

The Attorney-General had said that the Jury were impannelled to try the intention of the party publishing the parody: that was a fair statement of the question; the *intention* constituted the offence, or established the innocence of the accused. If the Jury found that the parody was put forth with a criminal purpose, they would return a verdict of guilty; if, on the other hand, they thought that no such design existed, they would be bound to give him an acquittal. In the year 1771 Mr. Burke clearly explained the principle of a bill which he assisted in bringing into the House of Commons (commonly called Mr. Dowdeswell's Bill), "to explain and declare the office and duties of Jurymen in cases of libel." It had long been held by many eminent Judges, that, in such cases, the Jury had only to find the fact of publication, leaving it to the Court to decide on the question of libel or not libel. As the law then stood, the intervention of a Jury was unnecessary—for the Court might as well procure, by a simple affidavit, the fact of the alleged publication of libel, and then a summary proceeding could be adopted. The old system did, in fact, do away the power of a Jury, by denying their right to decide on the question of libel or not libel. Mr. Burke's great mind was alive to the folly and injustice of this system, and he assisted Mr. Dowdeswell in bringing in his bill; which did not then pass; but in 1790 or 1791 Mr. Fox introduced a bill, nearly similar, "to enlarge and define the power of Juries in cases of libel." The authority formerly vested in the Judge, to declare what was libel, was, as Mr. Justice Blackstone observed, greatly controverted; and Mr. Professor Christian, in one of his notes on Blackstone,[52] stated, that, in consequence of the opposition manifested against the exercise of this authority, the 32d of George III. c. 6, was enacted, by which the Jury were empowered to return a verdict on the whole matter at issue, and not on the fact alone of publishing that which was alleged to be a libel. The Jury were now to decide on all the allegations contained in this information. If they were of opinion that he intended to excite impiety and irreligion in the minds of his Majesty's subjects, they would find him guilty, and his Lordship would, at some future day, pass sentence on him; but if no such intention appeared—and his Lordship would correct him if he were wrong—then they would return a verdict in his favour.

Lord ELLENBOROUGH.—As you call upon me to give my opinion, I say, that if the publication has a tendency to produce that effect upon the minds of persons who read it, it is in law and in fact a libel. I should not have interrupted you, but you called for my direction.

Mr. HONE.—Then all I can say, Gentlemen, is, that that is *his Lordship's* opinion.

Lord ELLENBOROUGH.—It is not merely my opinion; it is the opinion of all lawyers in all ages: publishers must be answerable for the tendency of works they put forth, and they are not to put perverse constructions on their own acts, and thus excuse themselves. If the paper have a tendency to inflame, the law says, the party had an intention to inflame; if to corrupt, that he meant to corrupt. This is no new doctrine; no Judge ever held differently.

Mr. HONE.—Of course, Gentlemen, it is not for me to reply upon his Lordship; but I may observe upon what fell from the Attorney-General: he said, that by Mr. Fox's bill his Lordship, if he think fit, may give his opinion to the Jury upon the question of libel or not libel.

Lord ELLENBOROUGH.—The Judge wanted no such power to be given him by Mr. Fox's bill; it is incidental to his office; it is his sworn duty, and was so before Mr. Fox's bill, or before even Mr. Fox himself existed.

Mr. HONE.—If the Court had that power before, it should seem that it was wholly unnecessary to introduce it into Mr. Fox's bill: it would be absurd in the legislature to pretend to communicate a power which was possessed without it. Recollect, too, that that bill was drawn by a most enlightened and acute man, and it was not adopted until it had been frequently and patiently debated; and let me ask you, if it is likely that a large body of intelligent men, many of them lawyers, would have suffered such unmeaning surplusage to remain on the statute-book, if in truth it had been unnecessary? His Lordship, however, has declared his opinion; but let me say, said Mr. Hone in a triumphant tone of voice, "that, after all, it is but the opinion of *one* man, it is but *his Lordship's* opinion." Of course I speak this in no offensive sense. (*Loud huzzaing.*)

Lord ELLENBOROUGH.—So I understand; but it might be as well if a little decency were preserved at the bottom of the Court. If the officers take any person into custody who makes a disturbance, let him be brought up to me, and I will reward such conduct.

Mr. Sheriff DESANGES.—The first man I see laugh, after such a severe notice, shall be brought up.[53]

* * * * *

Lord ELLENBOROUGH.—This is only wasting time: proceed to the business of your defence. I will hear very anxiously what relates to your defence, but I will not let you be wasting time.

Mr. HONE.—Wasting time, my Lord! I feel the grievance of which I complain; I am to be tried, not you! When I shall have been consigned to a dungeon, your Lordship will sit as coolly on that seat as ever; you will not feel the punishment: I feel the grievance, and I remonstrate against it. I am the injured man. *I* am upon my trial *by those gentlemen,* my jury.

Mr. HONE, after a pause of a few moments, objected to the mode in which the Attorney-General could suspend *ex-officio* informations over the heads of the King's subjects. True it was, the accused could demand a trial; but then it must be at bar, before a special jury[54]—a situation an hundred times worse than that in which he (the defendant) was now placed. Another evil was, that a man was not tried by his peers, and sometimes not by those among whom he lived. He complained of the odium and prejudice under which he had long laboured, because the late Attorney-General had chosen, in a speech, to term these parodies blasphemous publications. He was about to detail some of the facts relating to the putting of his plea, when

Lord ELLENBOROUGH interposed, and observed, that every indulgence had been shewn him on that occasion. Do you remember, said his Lordship, that you were committed until a future day, that you might have time to plead?

Mr. HONE.—Oh, yes, my Lord, I well remember that; you committed me to the King's Bench prison. I well remember the many bitter nights and days I there passed.

Mr. TOPPING (for the Crown) observed, that the defendant had been committed until the next term, that he might have time to plead.

Lord ELLENBOROUGH.—Then, you see, you state false *gravamina.*[55] The Court was extremely studious to give you every indulgence, and means of understanding the information.

Mr. HONE.—I could not plead guilty, when I knew I was not guilty.

Lord ELLENBOROUGH.—Why, you have just admitted the publication.

Mr. HONE.—But have I admitted that it is a libel?

Lord ELLENBOROUGH.—But you yourself had the libel in your possession; you published it, and you might have read it till you were tired of it, as I am.

Mr. HONE further entreated the Jury to dismiss the unfair prejudice which might have been excited against him from the highest authority: for by one of the Secretaries of State—by Lord Sidmouth, night after night, he had been denounced as a blasphemer and a wretch. Many of the newspapers had re-echoed the false and scandalous charge; even after the verdict of acquittal from charge of a profane libel yesterday, some of them had ventured to repeat it. He held in his hand the *Day* newspaper,* published a few hours ago, in which he was designated a blasphemer—

Lord ELLENBOROUGH.—Really, you are getting so far out of the case: what have I to do with the libels published against you? we are not trying that newspaper.

Mr. HONE.—I hope, and firmly believe, that I have an impartial Jury, who will be unprejudiced by every thing they may have heard or seen in or out of court.

Lord ELLENBOROUGH.—Why, nobody can have read that newspaper you speak of; what have I or the Jury to do with—

---

* An obscure Newspaper, called *The Day*, was set up as a trading speculation by some puffing auctioneers, and became a little notorious by a prosecution against it for libel. The editors of this Paper are now

"*Two* single gentlemen roll'd into *one.*"

The unhappy DOCTOR SLOP's[56] imagination is so extravagantly at variance with truth and memory, that he can neither remedy unto himself, nor be controlled by moral management. He runs a-muck at all he meets, with a soft goose-quill, cursing and swearing in the same fashion as Peter in the *Tale of a Tub;* and, unless brought to his senses for a moment by an antagonist who knocks him down, he outstrips pursuit, and bays the moon till he is exhausted. In two respects, however, he is honest to himself—a renegade in politics, he secretly admires the Reformists, whose ranks he left for the Treasury Clerks that crowd his office, and toss him sops;—a high-flier in religion, he really despises the bigotry and fanaticism which he puts forth in his tawdry journal. Hence it is not surprising that the poor man is almost constantly furious or cataleptic; or that, in his lucid intervals, he wears a red night-cap with a *lily* in it, as emblems of his loyalty to the houses of Bourbon and Brunswick, and struts in his *turned coat* as unblushing as a fifty-times-lashed incorrigible *deserter,* when he is drummed to a condemned regiment to the tune of the *Rogue's March.* Mr. HONE, on his third trial, gave the lie direct to Dr. SLOP's aspersions. The crazy charlatan took advantage of Mr. Hone's declaration in court, that he would only rebut the press by the press; and the hypocrite, finding the trials ended, and that Mr. HONE had no means of reply to him, like a bully and a coward, fell to his dirty work again. Let him perish in his own filth!

Mr. HONE.—My Lord! my Lord! it is *I* who am upon my trial, *not your Lordship.* I have to defend myself, not your Lordship.

Long-continued acclamations here interrupted the proceedings of the Court. Lord Ellenborough directed one of the Sheriffs to leave the bench, and to go to the bottom of the Court to quell the disturbance. When order was in some degree restored, his Lordship said,

"It is impossible that the officers can be doing their duty; let them bring any man before me, and I will soon put an end to this."

The SHERIFF, remaining on the bench, asked Mr. Under-Sheriff Smith if he had succeeded in taking any of the offenders, and was answered in the negative.

Lord ELLENBOROUGH.—Open your eyes, and see; and stretch out your hands, and seize.—You must have observed somebody. Mark where the noise comes from, and note the man.

Mr. HONE continued.—The interruption could be occasioned by no friend of his: whoever disturbed the Court was his bitter enemy: his friends could not so conduct themselves; and the noise could only proceed from some designing emissaries, who were anxious that he should be taken from the court to a prison.—He held in his hand two newspapers published this morning—

Lord ELLENBOROUGH.—I must not have the trash of the newspapers produced here, unless you can apply it in some way. If you thought there was any thing in them that would prejudice the Jury on your trial, you ought to have applied at the sitting of the Court upon affidavit, and it might probably have been postponed.

Mr. HONE.—But this attack was much better timed: it was introduced after I had been acquitted by one Jury last night, and before the time of my being tried now—to be acquitted, as I hope, by another.

Lord ELLENBOROUGH.—Still, if you thought that the minds of the Jury had been in any way poisoned, the Court would have given you an opportunity of being tried at a more impartial moment.

HONE.—It did not occur to me that that mode of proceeding was necessary. In fact, both the newspapers who have thus accused me of blasphemy well knew the contrary, for they contain reports of the trial of yesterday, when I was acquitted even of profaneness. One of them begins thus: "It will be seen by our Law Report"—

Lord ELLENBOROUGH.—We cannot enter upon that, after I have said that you might have stated the fact in a way to deserve attention.

Mr. HONE.—I trust that I, being a publisher, shall never apply to a Court of Justice to restrict a publication.

Lord ELLENBOROUGH.—But you will do well to complain if the publication be intended to corrupt the sources of justice. At a proper time I shall be glad to hear you; but do not introduce it as a hash into your speech.

Mr. HONE replied, that he had only heard of it five minutes before he came into court.

The ATTORNEY-General formally objected.

Lord ELLENBOROUGH.—If the defendant has been libelled, he may either bring an action for damages, or put the criminal law in motion; that is the proper mode: but he cannot do it now here.

Mr. HONE.—God forbid that I should force the bitterest enemy I have into the Crown-Office! I have suffered too much there already myself. No, my Lord, I would suffer the foulest imputations before I would take that step even against the man who had most deeply injured me.—The defendant then said, he should now proceed to shew, that for years parodies had existed unquestioned, and even the particular species of parody of which he stood accused. He should also, from this universal practice, and from examples which he should give, establish beyond a doubt, that it was possible to parody without ridiculing the thing parodied.[57]

* * * * *

Mr. HONE said, that having shewn that parodies were not necessarily disrespectful to the work parodied, and that they had been uniformly allowed, he should now shew that his did not deserve to be made an exception to the general rule. In doing this, he said, it became necessary for him to rebut a charge in this information, of seditiously libelling the Prince Regent, the House of Lords, and the House of Commons; and here he felt a *little*, and only a little, embarrassed. His difficulty proceeded from his conceiving the political opinions of the Gentlemen of the Jury might be opposed to his own. But here the difficulty was trifling, because he was sure that prejudices were fast wearing away; that men, as they intermixed more kindly, respected the conscientious opinions of each other; and believing, as he did most sincerely, that opinions wholly opposed to his views were honestly entertained by most respectable and worthy men, he also believed that such men would give him credit for as much honesty in his persuasions, and thus each would tolerate the other. He therefore, from a Jury of enlightened merchants of the City of London, claimed their protection of his right to express his opinions, opposed, as he imagined they might be, to their own; and he was persuaded, that just and liberal feelings would rally in the hearts of his Jurymen, and that they would do unto him as they would that men should do unto them.

Mr. Hone then proceeded to remark upon the several passages of the Litany which was the subject of prosecution, selecting such as appeared to give most offence to the political gentlemen who sought, under the guise of religion, to effect a political object in his ruin. His Parody prayed our delivery, 1st. from "an unnational Debt;" 2d. from "unmerited Pensions;" 3d. from "Sinecure Places;" 4th. from "an extravagant Civil List;" and 5th. from "utter starvation." Now, as to the first, how few were they who doubted that many debts had been contracted by our rulers for purposes by no means national. But good Ministers could have nothing to fear from the promulgation of such things. No government could, indeed, have so much reason to fear any thing as the effects of such a prosecution as he had been subjected to in this instance, in consequence of the frank expression of his mind. Then as to unmerited pensions, that was not to be understood as applying to the reward of public servants; such, for instance, as really performed their duty, upon the bench or elsewhere, but to those who derived fortunes from the public purse, without any public service whatever; and how many such men were to be found in England! Of the "extravagant Civil List," he did not think it necessary to say any thing; nor of "utter starvation" either; for no one acquainted with London, or any of the great towns in the country, for the last twelve months, could require any information upon that point. He had himself, indeed, seen two human beings who had actually expired in the streets from absolute want. But similar scenes must have been witnessed by numbers of those who heard him, as well as by the members of the Jury. In every direction the ravages of distress were visible, and most sensibly felt. Next, our delivery was prayed from the blind imbecility of ministers, as well as from the pride and vain-glory of warlike establishments in time of peace. This prayer might be found fault with by his political prosecutors; but yet, who could doubt the imbecility of Ministers? He, for one, confessed that he could not. There were, he believed, some men of honest purpose among the Ministers, while they evinced the want of wisdom;

but there were others connected with that body, who, while they had reputation for talent, had equal reputation for the want of principle. What then was to be expected from such a combination of integrity without talent, and talent without integrity? Nothing, surely, but imbecility. In asserting that implicitly, however, he did not mean to reflect upon the private life of any man; for, correctly speaking, the private life of a man had no connection with his fitness or capability for the performance of the great duties of a Statesman. A man might be very amiable towards his family and friends, and exemplary in the performance of all the moral duties, while his mind was not large enough to conceive the obligations which attach to the character of a Statesman. The mind of a good private man might indeed be quite incompetent to embrace a Statesman's views, or to understand his duties. A very good man might therefore, from such incapacity, grope as the present Ministers do, like a mole in the dark. Such a man might, notwithstanding the honesty of his intentions, or the purity of his principles, be wholly incapable of devising means to maintain the lustre, the dignity, and the honour of the country. Every little thing would be to them of a distorted importance, as to an animalcule a grain of granite was an universe. He could mean no reflection, therefore, upon the personal character of the Members of the Administration, when he charged them with imbecility. Now, as to the warlike establishments in time of peace, he put it to the Jury, whether such establishments did not at this moment notoriously exist. There was an Act of Parliament, no doubt, to sanction their establishments; but this country had often witnessed Acts of Parliament which were not entitled to public respect—which were, indeed, in direct contradiction to the principles of the British constitution. This he said, because he thought so; and was it not better that he and others should be encouraged to express their mind, than to conceal it, and reserve the expression for secret conspiracies? Every rational man would answer in the affirmative. It was always more desirable to any considerate man to be told when and where he was wrong, than to have the advantage of such information withheld from him. Such must be the case with every man who was not deaf to his own interest. For himself, he could have no hesitation in saying, that he should esteem the friend who frankly told him that he was wrong, because he should thus learn how to correct himself; and the Ministers who did not so feel towards any man who informed them of their errors, must be insensible to their interest, as well as indifferent to their character. A government which would not hear the truth must be a despotism. He did not mean that calumny should be tolerated, but that the expression of truth should be encouraged. No honest men could have any thing to fear even from misrepresentation; for honesty was always sure to defeat that, whether it applied to government or to individuals. Why should government be afraid of truth or falsehood in any case? Nothing but weakness could produce such fear, and that weakness must be pitiable. Another prayer appeared in the Litany, that the country should be delivered from all the deadly sins attendant upon a corrupt method of election—from all the deceits of the pensioned hirelings of the press. But who could deny that the most flagitious corruption prevailed in the prevalent system of election for Members of Parliament. Such corruption was indeed as notorious as the sun at noon-day; and therefore this prayer could not be condemned, unless upon the ground that truth was a libel; and this was a doctrine never recognized by any Jury (who were entitled to judge of the law), although generally asserted by the Judges. But for himself, he could not conceive how truth, with respect to any public act or public officer, could be deemed a libel; and he hoped the Jury whom he had the honour to address would not give up their right of decision upon this material point to the *dictum* of any individual. Another prayer appeared in this Litany, for our deliverance from taxes levied by distress—from gaols crowded with debtors—from poor-houses overflowing with paupers. As to the first, it was universally known that the greater part of the taxes were levied by distress at the time this Litany was published. One tax-gatherer, indeed, employed in the vicinity of Fleet Street, had told him, that he had levied more distress for the payment of taxes within the preceding nine months than he had done within the sixteen preceding years. When, then, such calamity existed—when all things were going wrong, where was the harm of saying so? or was it not rather desirable to make it known? Were an individual told that his affairs were going wrong, his first object would be to cast up his accounts, in order to see the magnitude of his danger, and to provide some remedy, while he would thank the person who roused him to a sense of his danger. And why should not the government be equally grateful for similar information and excitement to inquiry? It would be so, if its members were not imbecile, self-conceited, and supine. Then as to prisons crowded with debtors, was there a quarter of England, or a man in the country, that could not testify to this fact? He himself had seen the condition of the King's Bench prison. The day upon which he was committed to the King's Bench prison in consequence of this prosecution, he was put inside the gate, and found himself, within the walls—at liberty to go where he liked for an abiding place. At length he applied at the door for the tipstaff by whom he was taken into custody, and brought in, requesting to know where he was to get a lodging? In consequence of this application he was conducted to the coffee-room, where alone he could, from the crowded state of the prison, find any sort of decent accommodation. Such was the statement to him at the time, and such he afterwards found to be the fact. At the coffee-room he took up his abode as a boarder; for he was under the necessity of paying three shillings a night for sleeping in a room, in another part of the prison, with three other persons. This inconvenience, which he most sensibly felt, both in person and in pocket, was inevitable, from the extremely crowded state of the prison. Another proof of the crowded state of our prisons he had lately seen at Maidstone, where a prison, to occupy fourteen acres of ground, was nearly completed, avowedly with a view to provide accommodation for the miserable prisoners of the county of Kent, in addition to that afforded by the county-gaol. With respect to the overflow of poor-houses, he did not think it necessary to say any thing upon that point, as every Gentleman of the Jury must, no doubt, be competent, from his own experience and information, fully to decide the truth of that allegation. The next prayer of this publication was as to "a Parliament chosen only by one-tenth of the people—taxes raised to pay wholesale butchers their subsidies—false doctrines, heresy, and schism—conspiracies against the liberty of the people, and obstacles thrown in the way of our natural and constitutional rights." That Parliaments were not chosen by more than one-tenth of the people was, he apprehended, an indisputable fact. He himself had been for the most part of his life a housekeeper, and yet he had never enjoyed the right of voting for a member of the House of Commons. This he must and ever should consider a great grievance. He, and others similarly circumstanced, were no doubt told that they were represented *virtually* as some class. But this was a mere delusion, only aggravating the unjust privation of his right by an insult to his understanding. Then, as to human butchers, in what other light were those to be regarded who let out their subjects to be shot at, or to shoot at others for hire? False doctrines were surely chargeable upon those who sanctioned those notions of "legitimate right," which were inconsistent with the constitution and conduct of this country. But such doctrines were to be expected from those ministers who were inattentive to the wants of the people, who disregarded the example of the noble Sully,[58] the great minister of that truly great sovereign Henry IV. who said, in the spirit of real benevolence and princely duty, that his utmost ambition was that every peasant in his dominions should have each day a pullet in his pot. The existence of conspiracies against the liberties of the people was, he observed, sufficiently obvious from the suspension and re-suspension of the Habeas Corpus Act. The next prayer to the government was, "that ye spend not extravagantly the money raised from the production of our labours, nor take for yourselves that which ye need not." This was surely not to be condemned, especially after government had sanctioned the scandalous Lisbon job, in which Mr. Canning took from the public purse no less than £14,000 for doing nothing, in a situation in which his predecessor, who had something to do, received only £6000.[59] Yet this deduction from the public purse, at a period of dire distress, Ministers made for this most improper purpose, and Mr. Canning accepted the bribe without the excuse of necessity, for his means were ample. Did not such a transaction, amidst a thousand others, justify an allusion to public money spent extravagantly, and given to those who needed it not?

Mr. Hone then adverted to the mode of prosecution by information, which was adopted against him, and said, that the Statesmen who effected the Revolution had expressly stipulated for the abolition of this practice, though the stipulation appeared not to have been subsequently fulfilled. The whole of the recent proceedings of the Administration had his total disapprobation, and therefore he commented upon them through the medium of parodies. Their measures were those of little men of little minds; their measures were the objects of his contempt, and the men themselves, as ministers, were the objects of his pity. It was with pleasure, therefore, that he ever from that quarter heard any thing accidentally advantageous to the country, and thence he was gratified by the declaration of the Attorney-General on the preceding day, that he held in equal estimation all classes of Christians, no matter what were their particular forms of worship.

Mr. Hone said, he was by no means exhausted, but he was afraid of tiring the Jury, whom he most respectfully and sincerely thanked for their patience. If they required it, he would go through every supplication to our Rulers in the parody, to shew that what he said he was justified in saying—that it was true, and not libellous—that if there was ridicule, those who rendered themselves ridiculous, however high their station, had no right to cry out because they were ridiculed. He *intended* to laugh at them. They were his vindictive prosecutors, and his hypocritical persecutors; and laugh at them he would, till they ceased to be the objects of his laughter by ceasing to be Ministers. He expressed a willingness to expound the whole of the parody, in order to remove the imputation of libel, if the Jury thought it necessary; but perhaps the specimen of his remarks on the parts he had read would be sufficient. The Gentlemen of the Jury would take the parody with them, and consider it coolly at their leisure, and draw their own conclusions, whether he proceeded through the whole or not. Mr. Hone was resuming, when he was stayed by

A Juryman.—It is not necessary for you to read any further; we are satisfied.

Mr. Hone said, Gentlemen, I thank ye.—He was glad on many accounts to hear the Jury were satisfied, and would trouble the Jury but a short time longer. He never intended, by these parodies, to excite ridicule against the Christian religion, and none but the weakest men could honestly suppose so, and even they did it without consideration. His intention was merely political. It was done to excite a laugh. Was a laugh treason? Surely not. "The lean-face *Cassius* never laughs."[60] The learned Judge who tried the cause yesterday (Mr. Justice Abbott) had said, that to take the name of the Lord in vain was profanation. Let Mr. Attorney-General look to this; for he found that he had made a free use of this hallowed name at the late trial of Mr. Wooler.[61] When he made this allusion, he begged to assure the learned Gentleman that nothing was further from his mind than any notion that in the extracts from the Attorney-General's speech, which he was about to read, the name of God was introduced in any other way than that which might be done in an earnest and rapid delivery. But the Attorney-General had made, in his speech on Mr. Wooler's trial, the following expressions:—

"There are some persons who suppose, or choose to state they suppose, that persons filling the situation which I fill (*God* knows unworthily) are servants of the Crown."

"The prosecution is not instituted on my own judgment (for *God* knows that is weak), but in concurrence with that of my learned friends."

"If any man can doubt that the defendant meant this as a libel upon Ministers, *God* defend my understanding."

"If he did not mean to violate the law of the country, in *God's* name let him shew it."

"If he can shew, by a preceding or following sentence, that this is not the meaning intended to be expressed, in the name of *Heaven* let him do it."

"*God* knows a great deal of my life has been spent in public."

"*God* forbid that it should be said the highest and lowest man are not equal in the eye of the law."

"Thank *God,* the richest and the poorest man are equally protected."

Mr. Hone begged to remind the Attorney-General of what he had stated yesterday respecting the Ten Commandments, and the reverential awe which ought to be entertained for them. One of these commands was, "Thou shalt not take the name of the Lord thy God in vain;" but it appeared that the learned Gentleman himself had broken this commandment. He was sure that the learned Gentleman had no intention of breaking the commandments, or degrading sacred subjects, and therefore he was morally absolved from the consequences of the impression which such irreverent appeals to the Deity might produce. The defendant absolved him from any intention of taking God's name in vain, and he wished the same construction to be put on the parodies which he had written.

He concluded by imploring the Jury, if they thought him capable of sending forth the publication with the intent attributed to him, to find him guilty; but if, as he anticipated, they disbelieved that he had published with such an intention, then he relied on a verdict of Not Guilty. His politics was his crime; and if he were guilty, the real libellers were those who instituted the prosecution against him, for their punishment should precede his. Why did Mr. Canning escape, if he, Wm. Hone, were guilty? The ministers knew they had among them those who had gone "unwhipped of justice."[62] The Right Hon. George Canning was the man represented in Gilray's graphic parody on the ascent of Elijah, which he had in his hand, as holding forth his arms to catch the mantle falling from Mr. Pitt, who was, like Elijah, mounting in his chariot to the skies. He thanked the Jury for their patience; every thing he valued in life was in their hands—his character, his reputation, his subsistence. He asked from them no mercy, he wanted only justice. If they thought he published the parody with the intent attributed to him, then let him be

"Lash'd for a rascal naked through the world."[63]

If, as his conscience told him, they thought otherwise, then they would send him home to his family instead of the King's Bench prison.

Mr. Hone's address lasted from a quarter to eleven o'clock to a quarter past five o'clock. He was about to call evidence to prove that he stopped the circulation of the parodies when he found they were considered offensive; when

The ATTORNEY-GENERAL rose, and submitted that evidence of stopping the publication could not be received in a case where the mere fact and intent of that publication were to be considered.

Lord ELLENBOROUGH.—You are right as to the rule of evidence. It has nothing to do with the issue on the verdict of Guilty or Not Guilty. At the same time I shall take this evidence as a circumstance to be considered *in mitigation of punishment,* if the defendant should be convicted. This may be a convenient way of taking the evidence for him, as he might be put to the expence of affidavits on a future occasion, if it were now rejected.

Mr. HONE.—I merely adduce it to shew how soon I stopped the publication.

Lord ELLENBOROUGH.—That will not do away the offence, though it may be a very considerable mitigation of the punishment.

The ATTORNEY-GENERAL.—In that light I can have no possible objection to its being received.[64]

*   *   *   *   *

(His Lordship, who appeared much oppressed with indisposition during the latter part of the trial, delivered his charge in so faint a tone, that it was scarcely audible beyond the Bench.)

The Jury then, at a quarter past six, retired; at eight they returned; and their names having been called over, the foreman, in a steady voice, pronounced a verdict of—NOT GUILTY.

The Court was exceedingly crowded; and as soon as the decision was heard, loud and reiterated shouts of applause ensued. His Lordship called upon the Sheriffs to preserve order; but the expression of feeling was so universal, that all interposition was impossible. The crowd then left the Court, and, mixing with the multitude in the hall and in the passages, communicated their feelings with their news, and the loudest acclamations of applause filled the avenues, and were echoed through Guildhall and King-street, which were extremely crowded. Never, indeed, was a greater degree of public interest excited upon any trial. The Court was crowded throughout the day; and for several hours before the Jury retired, Guildhall was as full as upon the assemblage of a Common Hall.[65] The sensation produced by the result of this important trial cannot be described. Before his Lordship left the Court, he asked the Attorney-General what case he would take next. The Attorney-General replied, that he should take next that which stood next in order—"The KING against HONE, for the *Sinecurist's Creed.*"

Mr. HONE endeavoured to leave the Court privately; but he was recognized by some persons in the Court, who, in their exultation, were forgetful of the great fatigue he had undergone during his trials on this and the preceding day. He was pressed upon by innumerable greetings, and hands shaking, and was desired on all sides to get into a coach; but this he positively declined, and, almost overpowered by the eagerness of salutation, escaped into the Baptist-Head Coffee House, Aldermanbury; where he was joined by a few friends. After having taken some slight refreshment, he walked home, unrecognized, to his anxious family. On his arrival he was much indisposed, and apparently too much exhausted to undergo the fatigue of defending himself on the third Trial, which was appointed by the Attorney-General and Lord Ellenborough for the next morning, at half past nine o'clock, on an *ex-officio* information for publishing a third Parody, entitled, *The Sinecurist's Creed.*

THIRD TRIAL

OF

WILLIAM HONE,

ON AN

Ex-Officio Information

AT GUILDHALL, LONDON, ON SATURDAY, DECEMBER 20, 1817

BEFORE

LORD ELLENBOROUGH AND A SPECIAL JURY,

FOR PUBLISHING

A PARODY

ON THE

ATHANASIAN CREED,

ENTITLED

"THE SINECURIST'S CREED."

Fifteenth Edition.

LONDON:

PRINTED BY & FOR WILLIAM HONE, 67, OLD BAILEY;

AND SOLD BY ALL BOOKSELLERS.

1818

PRICE ONE SHILLING.

On the night of Friday, the 19th of December, 1817, immediately after the verdict of Not Guilty on the trial of the second information against Mr. Hone, for the Parody on the *Litany,* it was settled by the Lord Chief Justice and the Attorney-General, that the trial of the third information, for the parody on the *Athanasian Creed,* should commence the next morning; yet it was believed on all hands, that the third information would not be then brought on; and, indeed, it was generally supposed it would be abandoned altogether. The most obvious reasons were, that as two verdicts had been given for Mr. Hone, by two different Juries, the Ministers of the Crown could with no good grace put him upon his trial a third time; and further, that fatigued as he had been, by long previous anxiety, and the exertions of two successive days—on the first of which he spoke near six hours, and on the second near seven hours—it would be indecent to bring him into Court a third time, without the lapse of a single day, and calculate upon the previous exhaustion of his bodily strength for that success which they could not hope for while he retained it.

However, it being understood on the following morning, Saturday, December 20th, that the third information would really be tried, the avenues of the Court were crowded at an earlier hour than on the two former days, and public curiosity was at its height. The Sheriffs, City Marshals, and an increased body of peace-officers, were in attendance. At a quarter past nine the Attorney-General appeared in Court, and about the same time the youth (Mr. Hone's brother)[66] brought in a larger quantity of books than before, which he placed in order on the table of the Court. Mr. Hone himself did not arrive till half an hour afterwards. He appeared exceedingly ill and exhausted.

At a quarter before ten o'clock, Lord Ellenborough being seated on the bench, Mr. Law stated that the prosecution was the King against Hone, on an *ex officio* information; and proceeded to call over the names of the Jury. Though the Court was crowded to excess, the most profound silence prevailed.

Only seven Special Jurymen attending, the Attorney-General prayed a *tales.*

The Attorney-General challenged William Green, one of the talesmen who served on the Jury the day before.

Mr. Hone immediately rose, evidently labouring under great indisposition, and begged that he might be allowed time to recollect himself. A moment after, he said he objected to that peremptory challenge of a common juror, and required the cause of it.

The ATTORNEY-GENERAL observed, that the Crown had a right to challenge, without assigning any cause, until the panel was gone through. If there did not then appear to be a sufficient number to form a Jury, he should, if called upon, state his reasons for challenging any individuals.

Lord ELLENBOROUGH said, the Defendant might in that case call upon the Attorney-General, but not before—that he believed was the rule of law.

Mr. HONE was at this time sitting down, and appeared extremely agitated.

Lord ELLENBOROUGH.—I believe, Mr. Hone, you have not heard the observation of the Attorney-General.

Mr. HONE replied, that he did not distinctly hear it.

His Lordship repeated the words, and assured the Defendant that he should have the benefit of any legal objection that appeared material to his defence.

Mr. HONE—I am thankful to your Lordship.

The ATTORNEY-GENERAL challenged J. MATTHEWS, merchant.

Mr. HONE again rose to object to the challenge.

Lord ELLENBOROUGH repeated the assurance he had made, and the Defendant sat down evidently seriously indisposed—he was much convulsed.

A gentleman at the bar, who sat near the Attorney-General, having made some remark upon the appearance of Mr. Hone,—

The ATTORNEY-GENERAL addressed his Lordship. What he had to state, he said, did not arise from a wish on his part to postpone the proceedings of the Court; it arose from a very different source. Mr. Hone appeared to be very unwell; and it had been just suggested, that a delay of the proceedings might be necessary, in consideration of his probable inadequacy to enter upon his defence with the full command of those energies which he possessed in a very considerable degree. This was a ground of postponement that could by no means be controverted.

Mr. HONE.—I make no request, my Lord—

The ATTORNEY-GENERAL—The Defendant certainly appeared unable to make any great physical exertion; and as it was necessary for him to have a full control upon so serious an occasion, the postponement might be desirable.

Mr. HONE said, he was thankful for the offer of indulgence. He certainly felt much agitation, but it was not agitation of mind. He was merely exhausted from the effort of the day before. In a little time, he hoped to be so far recovered as to be able to enter upon his defence.

Lord ELLENBOROUGH.—Mr. Hone, you will now make a prudent and discreet election; for if the trial begin, I shall not be able to put a stop to it.

Mr. HONE—My Lord, I make my election to proceed now, if your Lordship pleases.

The following most respectable gentlemen were then sworn:—

THE JURY.

George Morewood, Pancras Lane.
GEORGE ELWALL, Love Lane.
ROBERT EDGAR, Fenchurch Street.
DANIEL ECKENSTEIN, College Hill.
JAMES BARRY, Cateaton Street.
JAMES BROCKBANK, Bucklersbury.
WILLIAM CLERK, Philpot Lane.

RICHARD LEWIS.
ALFRED COLES.
JAMES PEARCE.
FREDERICK SANSUM.
ANTHONY KING NEWMAN.

MERCHANTS.

TALESMEN.

Lord ELLENBOROUGH.—The Jury is now formed; and, lest you may suppose that you can object to them hereafter, I must state, that you will not have such an opportunity. If you have any objection, advance it now—there will not be an opportunity at a future time. Should you have any objection to the Attorney-General's challenge, you must rely on it now.

Mr. HONE.—I thought there would be a future time to discuss it.

Lord ELLENBOROUGH.—There will not. I rather think you will find nothing in the challenge to excite suspicion; but don't be advised by me.

Mr. HONE.—The Jury are all strangers to me. I have no doubt that they are respectable and conscientious men, and I wave the objection altogether.

Mr. SHEPHERD then opened the pleadings. This was an information filed by the Attorney-General against the Defendant, for publishing an irreligious and profane libel on that part of the Divine Service of the Church of England, denominated *The Creed of St. Athanasius*, with intent to scandalize and bring into contempt the said Creed.

The ATTORNEY-GENERAL now commenced his address to the Jury,

observing, that the information which he had thought it a part of his official duty to file against this Defendant, charged him with the publication of a profane libel on that part of the service of the Church of England which was called the Creed of St. Athanasius. The tendency, if not the object, of such a libel, appeared to him to be to excite impiety and irreligion in the minds of those who might read it, and to bring into ridicule and contempt the mode of celebrating Divine worship in this country. That Christianity was a part of the law of England, was a proposition which no man could deny; for it had been so held from the earliest periods of our history. At the Reformation, and by several subsequent Acts in the reigns of Edward VI. and of Elizabeth, the form of the national religion was established. But after the restoration of Charles II. the Act of Uniformity, as it was called, was passed, and provided that form of public prayer which was inserted in the Common Prayer Book, and ordained to be kept in all parts of the country, as a record to be produced, if necessary, in Courts of Justice. Whatever relaxation from penalties imposed by this statute might have taken place since that time, the Act, in other respects, remained untouched, the established form of prayer was left sacred, and was to be defended against all who sought to bring it into contempt. Whatever differences of opinion might prevail on the doctrinal points of the Athanasian Creed, amongst different religious sects, it was a part of the church service, as established by law in England. And although the law did not forbid the decent discussion of the theological subjects to which it referred, it ought not to allow it to be scoffed at, or treated with general ridicule. It was for the Jury to decide whether this was not the true character of the publication recited on the record, and whether this did not amount to the offence of libel. There could, he apprehended, be no doubt with regard to the tendency of the work: but it might be urged in the course of the defence, that such was not the object of the author in publishing it. But he must take leave to say, that if a man advisedly did a wrong act, he was answerable for its natural consequences, because it was his duty to reflect upon its tendency and nature before he committed it. Now, writing and publishing were plainly acts of deliberation, in excuse of which, if they were wicked or unjustifiable, it was impossible to allege a momentary impulse or the infirmity of human nature. He was astonished, indeed, that such a pretence should be employed, as that the Defendant was unconscious of the tendency of the writing in question. From the number of books which he saw on the table, it might be attempted to show, that similar works had been circulated by other persons. But whoever they were, or whatever their merits in other respects, he had no hesitation to say, that they had been guilty of the same offence, and that such instances could, therefore, constitute no justification of the Defendant's conduct. The libel in question must be judged upon its intrinsic contents alone, and not by the authority of parodies equally offensive. The Attorney-General then read several passages from the paper he held in his hand, which was entitled "The Sinecurist's Creed," and proceeded to show that those passages were a parody upon many parts of St. Athanasius's Creed, by reading the corresponding paragraphs. The injury likely to arise from the dissemination of this awful system of impiety would be, the Attorney-General observed, particularly great in the case of those who were not enlightened by education, and who were therefore easily initiated into bad principles by publications of that kind. But that was not the only class that would suffer. When children were brought up in the principles of Christianity, the best expectations might be entertained from their mature years; but if they were not protected from these inroads, the great bond that linked man to man would be shaken, and there was no vice that did not afford a speedy promise of becoming greater and more uncontrollable. The man whose acts led to this unfortunate event must be responsible. His fault arose not from oversight or thoughtlessness, but from a cool deliberation. It would be for the Jury to say whether the Defendant's publication was calculated to have the impression he described.

Mr. SWANSON, clerk in the Office of the Solicitor to the Treasury, proved that he purchased the pamphlet on the 17th February, at Mr. Hone's late shop in Fleet-street, &c.

Lord ELLENBOROUGH.—Perhaps it may not be thought necessary by the Defendant, that St. Athanasius's Creed should be read.

Mr. HONE wished it to be read, that he might have the more time to prepare his defence.

Lord ELLENBOROUGH.—I had better give you time expressly than take up the time of the Court unnecessarily. The Creed shall, however, be read, if it is your wish.

Mr. LAW read St. Athanasius's Creed; after which he read the publication charged as a libel.

THE SINECURIST'S CREED, or BELIEF; as used throughout the Kingdom. Quicunque vult.[67] By Authority. From Hone's Weekly

Commentary, No. II. London: Printed for one of the Candidates for the Office of Printer to the King's Most Excellent Majesty, and Sold by WILLIAM HONE, 55, Fleet-Street, and 67, Old Bailey, three Doors from Ludgate-hill. 1817. Price Two-pence.

THE CREED OR BELIEF.

*¶ Upon all suitable occasions may be sung or said
the following CONFESSION
—upstanding and uncovered.
Quicunque vult.*

WHOSOEVER will be a Sinecurist: before all things it is necessary that he hold a place of profit.

Which place except every Sinecurist do receive the salary for, and do no service: without doubt it is no Sinecure.

And a Sinecurist's duty is this: that he divide with the Ministry and be with the Ministry in a Majority.

Neither confounding the Persons: nor dividing with the Opposition.

For there is One Ministry of Old Bags, another of Derry Down Triangle:† and another of the Doctor.[68]

But the Ministry of Old Bags, of Derry Down Triangle, and of the Doctor, is all one: the folly equal, the profusion coeternal.

Such as Old Bags is, such is Derry Down Triangle: and such is the Doctor.

Old Bags a Mountebank, Derry Down Triangle a Mountebank: the Doctor a Mountebank.

Old Bags incomprehensible, Derry Down Triangle incomprehensible: the Doctor incomprehensible.

Old Bags a Humbug, Derry Down Triangle a Humbug: and the Doctor a Humbug.

---

† *Triangle, s. a thing* having three *sides;* the meanest and most tinkling of all musical *instruments;* machinery used in military *torture.*—DICTIONARY.

And yet they are not three Humbugs: but one Humbug.

As also they are not three incomprehensibles, nor three Mountebanks: but one Mountebank, and one incomprehensible.

So likewise Old Bags is All-twattle,‡ Derry Down Triangle All-twattle: and the Doctor All-twattle.

And yet they are not three All-twattles: but one All-twattle.

So Old Bags is a Quack, Derry Down Triangle is a Quack: and the Doctor is a Quack.

And yet they are not three Quacks: but one Quack.

So likewise Old Bags is a Fool, Derry Down Triangle is a Fool: and the Doctor is a Fool.

And yet not three Fools: but one Fool.

For like as we are compelled by real verity: to acknowledge every Minister by himself to be Quack and Fool;

So are we forbidden by state etiquette: to say there be three Quacks, or three Fools.

Derry Down Triangle is made of none: neither born nor begotten.

Old Bags is of himself alone: a Lawyer bred, a Lord created, by his Father begotten.

The Doctor is of Old Bags, and of Derry Down Triangle: neither made, nor created, nor begotten, but proceeding.

So there is one Old Bags, not three Old Bags: one Derry Down Triangle, not three Triangles: one Doctor, not three Doctors.

And in this ministry none is afore or after the other: none is greater or less than another.

But the whole three Ministers are co-Charlatans together, and co-Tricksters.

So that, in all things, as is aforesaid: the Majority with the Ministry, and the Ministry in the Majority, is to be worshipped.

He therefore that will be a Sinecurist, must thus think of the Ministry.

Furthermore it is necessary to his Sinecure's preservation: that he also believe rightly the mystification of Derry Down Triangle.

For the Sinecurist's right faith is, that he believe and confess: that Derry Down Triangle, the *queue* of the Ministry of the great man now no more, is now both Minister and Manager.[70]

---

‡ *All-twattle;* Twattle, *v.n.* to prate, gabble, chatter, talk idly.—ENTICK'S DICTIONARY. [69]

Minister, first selling the substance of his own country to this: Manager scattering the substance of this over all the world;

Perfect Knave and perfect Fool: of unsparing despotic views—on overstrained taxation subsisting;

Equal to Old Bags as touching grave Trickery: and inferior to the Doctor as touching his Mummery.

Who although he be Knave and Fool, yet he is not two, but one Minister;

One; not by a conversion of the Charlatan into the Minister; but by shooting a more showy juggler,[71] who wanted, and still wants, to be a Minister.

One altogether; squandering in profusion our substance: by votes of corrupt Majorities.

For as by power of Dupery, and our Money, he makes whom he will his own: so by Intrigue and Cajolery, he is Minister:—

Who to talk for our Salvation, descended to kiss the Nethermost End of Tally-high-ho;[72] and rose again as a giant refreshed;

He ascended into a higher place, he sitteth at the right hand of the Chair; from whence he shall hear how those who being starved,—'by the Visitation of God,'—became Dead.

At whose nodding all Sinecurists shall rise again, and again; and with their voices cry Aye! Aye! and the Laureate in token of joy, shall mournfully chaunt the most doleful Lay in his Works.

And they that have said Aye! Aye! shall go into place everlasting; and they that have said No! shall go into everlasting Minorities.

And COLERIDGE shall have a Jew's Harp, and a Rabinnical Talmud, and a Roman Missal: and WORDSWORTH shall have a Psalter, and a Primer, and a Reading Easy: and unto SOUTHEY'S Sack-but shall be duly added: and with Harp, Sack-but, and Psaltery, they shall make merry, and discover themselves before Derry Down Triangle, and *Hum* his most gracious Master, whose Kingdom shall have no end.[73]

This is the Sinecurist's duty, from doing more than which, except he abstain faithfully, he cannot be a Sinecurist.

¶ Glory be to old Bags, and to Derry Down Triangle, and to the Doctor.

As it was in the Beginning, is now, and ever shall be, if such *things* be, without end. *Amen.*

[*Here endeth the Creed or Belief.*]

During the Attorney-General's opening, and whilst the Creed and the alleged libel were being read, Mr. Hone was occasionally occupied in making notes, but he seemed weak, and not collected in his mind. He was engaged in writing when Mr. Law concluded the reading of the Sinecurist's Creed.

Mr. HONE rose and stated, that he was not quite prepared; he craved the indulgence of the Court for a short time, whilst he arranged the few thoughts he had been committing to paper; his mind had not been quite cool; he should be ready in five minutes, at farthest; he would certainly not detain the Court longer than that.

Lord ELLENBOROUGH.—The Attorney-General warned you, and admonished you, in the situation you were placed as to health. I offered you the indulgence of postponing the trial, but we really cannot have delay interposed from time to time in the course of the trial. If you shall wish even now to have it postponed, I venture to predict that you will be suffered to request a delay of the trial; but it must be a request, and unless you make it, the trial must go on. Do you make such request?

Mr. HONE (*in a determined tone, and with an expression of countenance which did not indicate much respect for his Lordship personally*)—No! I make no such request! (*His powers seemed renovated by the refusal of the Court to give him time, and pausing a few seconds, he said*) My Lord and Gentlemen of the Jury—(*turning from the Jury to Lord Ellenborough, he exclaimed with earnest vehemence*), my Lord, I am very glad to see your Lordship here to day; (*with increased vehemence*) I say, my Lord, I am very glad to see *your* Lordship here to day, because I feel I sustained an injury from your Lordship yesterday—an injury which I did not expect to sustain. I do not know how very well to measure my words, and yet I know I should do so in any thing I have to remark upon your Lordship's conduct; but if the proceedings of a solemn trial, like that of yesterday, and this to day, are to be interrupted—and I say that, because I think the charge your Lordship gave—

Lord ELLENBOROUGH.—I cannot hear any observations in that way now, on what passed yesterday. You may make common and ordinary observations, but I cannot sit here to be attacked.

Mr. HONE (*pausing, and looking significantly at Lord Ellenborough*) I will not attack your Lordship.

Mr. HONE.—Gentlemen of the Jury, I will not say what his Lordship did on the trial last night; but if his Lordship should think proper, on this trial to day, to deliver his opinion, I hope that opinion will be coolly and dispassionately expressed by his Lordship. I say, if his Lordship should *think proper* to give an opinion, because notwithstanding what has been stated, his Lordship is *not* bound to give an opinion; I repeat, gentlemen (*most vehemently*), by Mr. Fox's Libel Bill,[74] the Judge is *not* bound to give an opinion: the Act does not make it imperative, but leaves it discretionary with the Judge whether he shall give his opinion or not. It is true, there may be Acts of Parliament or difficulties of law, the explanation of which requires the opinion and the intervention of the Judge; but such is not the case upon the occasion to which I allude. I will not relate what passed upon my last trial, but I will suppose the case of a Defendant asking the opinion of the Court for information, and answered in a manner calculated rather to cause confusion in his mind than to clear up the difficulty: and I will ask, whether such ought to be the conduct of a person presiding in a Court of Justice? An Act of Parliament should be so clear, that he who runs may read; and that is, that he who reads it may understand its meaning, without the intervention of a Judge; and I take this Act to be so. But nevertheless, if legal opinion be desired, there is the exposition of the Vinerian Professor of Law[75] upon it, Mr. Christian—no mean authority; for this gentleman is distinguished for his learning and legal knowledge, and is himself a Judge, being Chief Justice of Ely. That learned person, observing on Mr. Fox's Libel Bill, in his notes on Blackstone's Commentaries (B. 4. p. 151, Ed. 1795) says, "That statute provides that the Judge *may* give his opinion to the Jury respecting the matter in issue," not shall—

Lord ELLENBOROUGH.—You are misstating the statute.

Mr. HONE (LOUD)—I beg your Lordship's pardon (*vehemently*), you are interrupting me, my Lord. I was not quoting the statute; I was reading, as the gentlemen of the Jury know, to whom I am addressing myself, the Exposition of Professor Christian upon the words of—

Lord ELLENBOROUGH.—The words in the statute are "shall or may give his opinion."

Mr. HONE.—I shall read the statute presently.

Lord ELLENBOROUGH.—Well, go on.

Mr. HONE (*earnestly and slowly*)—My Lord, I think it necessary to make a stand here. I cannot say what your Lordship may consider to be necessary interruption, but your Lordship interrupted me a great many times yesterday, and then said you would interrupt me no more, and yet your Lordship did interrupt me afterwards ten times as much as you had done before you said you would interrupt me no more. I feel it proper to make this observation upon this interruption. Gentlemen, it is you who are trying me to day. His Lordship is no judge of *me*. You are *my* judges, and *you only* are my judges. His Lordship sits there to receive your verdict. He does not even sit there to regulate the trial—for *the law* has already regulated it. He sits there only as the administrator of that law—to take care that nothing in the regulation of the law prejudice the Prosecutor or the Defendant. I hope that unless I transgress the law I shall not be again interrupted to day—but if I do, I crave interruption, for it will be necessary. I hope for that *necessary* interruption, but then it *must* be necessary interruption. If I transgress the law, I shall do it unwittingly. I trust that I shall not be allowed to do it, and then like a poor fly in the web of a spider, be pounced upon and crushed!

Mr. HONE, resuming his argument, contended that by Mr. Fox's bill the judge was *not* bound to give any opinion on the question, whether the thing under consideration was libel or not, but that it was left discretionary for him to do so or not, as he thought proper. His Lordship seemed to think otherwise, and that it was a part of his duty to give that opinion. His Lordship would, therefore, no doubt, pursue that course to-day—he would not say what his Lordship did yesterday, but he trusted his Lordship to-day would give his opinion *coolly* and *dispassionately*, without using either expression or gesture which could be construed as conveying an entreaty to the Jury to think as he did. He hoped the Jury would not be *beseeched* into a verdict of guilty. He was now brought to answer to a third accusation for a similar alleged offence, by his Majesty's Attorney-General; and he came into Court wholly unprepared, unless from such preparation as he might have collected from the probation of his two former trials. The Attorney-General had behaved towards him most courteously, so far as he was concerned. He had experienced this both on his trial and previous to it. He had no charge to bring against that gentleman. He did not know how far the Attorney-General acted in this business from his own private judgment, or in what degree he was subject to Ministers. He was unacquainted with the relation in which he stood; but had he received any intimation from Ministers to that effect, he believed he would not thus have proceeded to bring him into Court a third time; he should not have been once more dragged from his bed to appear before a Jury. Before coming into Court, he was so ill that he thought he should not have been able to proceed. He had taken no refreshment since yesterday, except one glass of wine, and was so feeble last night, that he could not get into bed without help. He was apprehensive that notwithstanding he had received medical aid, he should not have been able to stand up in Court: but, had he not been able to walk, he should have ordered himself to be brought in his bed, and laid upon the table, for the purpose of making that defence, even in a state of feebleness, which he unexpectedly found himself now able to enter upon with more strength than he had hoped to possess: indeed, his powers were restored in an extraordinary measure. He should, even under the most helpless debility, have defended himself against the charge of circulating a publication which was called a libel, but which he knew, and should prove, to be no such thing. He should regret much, if in the course of his trial any such expression of feeling should be manifested as occurred yesterday. They who were present ought to command themselves, and remember that he was on a trial of life or death. Such was truly the case; for, if found guilty, he knew he should receive sentence for such a term of imprisonment as to deprive him of health, and eventually of life. Those who interrupted yesterday did what was wrong, but it was not the only wrong to be complained of. He had that morning complained to the Sheriff then sitting by his Lordship (DESANGES) that two of his witnesses were refused admission into Court on the trial yesterday, though they produced their subpœnaes at the door. That little indulgence might have been granted to those who lived in his service, and entertained some friendship for him, merely because he had not used them ill. It was attempted to turn the laugh which had been excited yesterday in Court to his disadvantage. It was attributed by the Attorney-General to an irreligious feeling occasioned by the parodies which he had published. This he could not consider very fair; it had a tendency to make the Jury believe that this laugh was one of the irreligious effects arising from the productions he had published; whereas, it was the effect of the ridiculous allusions to his Majesty's ridiculous Ministers, without the least reference or thought for an instant respecting the Athanasian Creed. The parody for which he was at present upon trial, had been reserved, he believed, for no other reason but because it was the weakest of the three. The Attorney-General, no doubt, had selected the parody on the Catechism as the first object of accusation, for no other reason but because he looked upon it as the strongest case; that on the Litany was the next; the last was beyond comparison the weakest. It was an old saying, that experience made fools wise. Experience, however, never made *fools* wise. It made men of understanding wiser, but not fools. If there was any truth in the proverb, he should not then have been a third time in Court, after being twice acquitted upon similar charges. He did not impute folly to the Attorney-General. On his part, the proceedings arose perhaps from an error in judgment; but there were others who, after the experience of the last two days, were so foolish as to allow him to be brought a third time to trial, though the chance of being found guilty was reduced even to less than the proportion of 1 to 999. The Attorney-General, neither upon this, nor upon the former trials, had quoted much by way of authority to enforce his opinion. All the authority was upon his (Mr. Hone's) side. It was contained in the books that lay upon the table. He had selected many passages from them which he should have occasion to read once more. They all proved that parodies upon the Scripture had been in frequent use even among pious and enlightened men. The opinion of Sir Matthew Hale had been mentioned and quoted as the highest authority upon the subject of religion as connected with the State. He was, no doubt, an honest, wise, upright, and pious Judge. He could not say he was in error in the particular opinion alluded to on a former trial, but he was not infallible, and might have been deceived as well as others. That pious and upright Judge actually condemned to death some persons for being witches.[76] He might have been a great man, but this was a proof that he was weak at least in one respect. With respect to the authorities he had quoted upon the subject of parody, there was a great difference of opinion between him and the Attorney-General. He should, however, quote them again, and should tell the Jury that Martin Luther was a parodist as well as William Hone. In the title-page of Wilkes's Catechism, he had stated that it was never before published; he afterwards, however, discovered that it had been printed and published before. This information he had from a gentleman of the bar, Mr. Adolphus, who came into his shop to purchase the Catechism, and seeing it mentioned in the title-page that it had never before been published, informed him that it was printed and published in the 1st volume of the *Morning Chronicle*, remarking at the same time, that the title-page was an imposition. Such was the fact. Was Mr. Adolphus in Court, he believed that gentleman would have no hesitation in admitting it. Truth was always his leading principle, as it should be that of every other man. He defied any person with whom he had the least dealing, to bring a charge of falsehood against him. With respect

to the parody on Wilkes's Catechism, he wrote it himself upon a manuscript which had been put into his hands by a gentleman, who told him,
at the same time, that it was never before published.[77] That gentleman
belonged to the profession of the law. He was a regular attendant upon
church, and his Lordship heard of him every term he sat. Whatever
might be the consequence to himself, no consideration could induce
him to disclose the name of the person who furnished him with the
manuscript of *Wilkes's Catechism*, although that person had not once
called upon him, or in any other way noticed him since this prosecution. He was persuaded though, that if he conceived it to be a blasphemous publication, or to have the evil tendency attached to it upon the
trial, the gentleman to whom he alluded would have been the last man
to put such a production in a train for circulation. The Attorney-
General, in his reply on the former day, seemed to think that the *Litany*
was not published before. The truth, however, was, that three weeks
previous to his publishing it, it had been circulated widely in very populous districts. It was sent to him, not by the author, whom he did not
know at the time, but by another person, whose name had been heard
by every man in England. The author had called on him before the
prosecution, and avowed it to be his; but it would have been courteous
in that person to visit him in prison, or at least to have sent him a line,
were it only with a view of consoling him in his trouble. It was true he
(Mr. Hone) made some alterations in it. He introduced some additional
supplications, the "Glory be to George;" and the Collect for Ministers,
"Enlighten our darkness," &c. This last prayer, however, had no effect
on Ministers; for otherwise, after being acquitted twice before, they
would have been enlightened to the folly of putting him a third time
upon trial. He did not pretend to be well acquainted with the law of libel; but he was far from thinking that all truth was a libel, though there
were many things true that should not be told or written. Were he, for
instance, to give a scandalous history of all he knew, or could learn, of
a certain great personage, from his birth to the present day, however
true it might be, no person could say that the publication of it would not
be equally scandalous. Such a publication differed very much from
what might accidentally or carelessly occur in conversation, or slip
from a person's pen while writing. The doctrine of libel was quite un-
defined; but he had no doubt that the day would come when nothing
would be considered libel until it was declared so by a Jury.

Parodies, it was said by the Court and the Attorney-General, should

Sketch by George Cruikshank. By permission of Berg Collection of English and American
Literature, The New York Public Library, Astor, Lenox and Tilden Foundations

not now be defended by the production of similar publications by other
persons, and at former periods. But why, he would ask, single him out,
after he had been twice before acquitted by two Juries, even after all
the picking and packing of the Crown-office? Why send him now a
third time before another Jury, selected in the same way? With respect
to parody, it was as ancient even as the time of Homer. The finest productions of genius were produced in ancient as well as modern times.
They were parodied because they were generally known, and were in
themselves original and beautiful, obtaining for that reason an extensive popularity. The thing was not done from motives of contempt—
quite the contrary. If parodies on Scripture were criminal, they must
have been so at all times, whoever might have been the author, and
whoever might have then been Attorney-General. The informations
against him were filed by the late Attorney-General. He was brought
into Court on the 5th of May last, and that very day Sir William Garrow
resigned his situation. He would not say the resignation arose from his
being ashamed of his conduct, but it was remarkable that the informa-

tions filed by him upon that occasion were the last acts of his political life as Attorney-General. No information was filed against others who had written parodies. An information had not, and would not, he believed, be filed against Mr. Canning, for his parody on Job. The reason was, perhaps, that it was known that Mr. Canning could make a good defence, while he (Mr. Hone) who was supposed unable to make one, was brought before a Jury three times successively. He never before in his life spoke in the presence of more than ten persons. If Providence ever interfered to protect weak and defenceless men, that interference was most surely manifested in his case. It had interposed to protect a helpless and defenceless man against the rage and malice of his enemies. He could attribute his defence to no other agent, for he was weak and incapable, and was at that moment a wonder unto himself. (*Here a mixed murmur of applause and pity was heard from the crowd assembled.*) As the law of libel stood at present, it was not possible to be understood. It was, in its present state, only calculated to entrap and deceive people into punishment, and reminded him of the conduct of one of those despots, who, in all countries, frequently get into the possession of power, and use it only for the purpose of punishment and oppression. The person to whom he alluded was the tyrant of Syracuse.[78] It was his custom, when laws were promulgated, to have them written in very small letters, and placed so high that they could not be read; but whoever dared to transgress them were punished with all the severity of a despot, though the wretches who suffered the punishment could not possibly have known the law, for the pretended transgression of which they suffered. Such exactly was the law of libel. In fact, there was no such thing as law of libel; or, if there was, the law was written upon a cloud, which suddenly passed away, and was lost in vapour. Nothing was a libel until a Jury pronounced it such. He was pointed at, and showed as one guilty of publishing the most blasphemous productions. When in the King's-Bench, he was shunned as a pestilence, even by those who were, or pretended to be, formerly his friends—by those whom, as David said of Jonathan, his heart loved.[79] His acquaintance, it was true, recommended him to counsel, but some objections were urged against all whom they pointed out to him. Some from motives of etiquette, could not attend upon him in prison. Others, though they might have talent, had not courage to undertake his defence. Without courage it would be useless to attempt it. The question he put, upon such recommendation of counsel being made, was, has he *courage*?

Will he be able to stand up against my Lord Ellenborough? Will he withstand the brow-beating of my Lord Ellenborough? It was necessary that a person undertaking his defence should be a stranger to fear; for if he persisted in saying any thing when once his Lordship had made an objection, the consequence would be to lose what is called the ear of the Court.

The ATTORNEY-GENERAL.—I cannot sit here quietly and hear such language directed to the Court. I submit, my Lord, whether it be right.

Lord ELLENBOROUGH.—Perhaps, Mr. Attorney, you might have interposed your objection sooner; but you have heard the sort of attack which was made upon me. I think the best course will be to let the *thing* blow over us!

Mr. HONE would, he said, entreat pardon, if any thing painful to the gentlemen of the bar had fallen from him. Talent and courage, he perceived, were necessary to his defence. As to talent, he possessed, if any, but a very humble share; but mental fear was a thing to which he was, and ever had been, an utter stranger. He did not know what fear was; and while he conceived himself to have truth and justice on his side, no earthly consideration could deter him from expressing his opinion, and doing what he thought right, which he ever did, and ever should do, without thinking of consequences to himself. There was a circumstance which occurred previous to his coming into Court, that gave him great pain. It proceeded from Dr. *Slop,* the Editor of one of those publications that were always ready to perform any dirty work which they deemed acceptable to men in power. It stated, that a person who had been *tried* and *convicted,* was to receive twelve months' imprisonment for publishing one of those parodies, for which he (Mr. Hone) had been twice acquitted, and would, he hoped, be acquitted again that day. This man applied to a solicitor, by whom he was recommended to let judgment go by default, as the best course which he could adopt.

The ATTORNEY-GENERAL.—I am quite sure nobody on my part, or by my desire, ever had any communication with the person alluded to, or ever advised him to either plead guilty or not guilty.

Mr. HONE observed, that all he meant to say was, that the man was not convicted, was not tried, but suffered judgment to go by default. There were, however, communications between this man and the solicitor who conducted the present prosecution; and yet he received a sentence equal in extent to any thing which might have been expected, even by a man who had been found guilty by a Jury of his country; and, what was very extraordinary, on the very morning this person was brought up to receive his sentence, he (Mr. Hone) received the first notices of his trials. It was equally extraordinary that this person called on him three or four times previous to his going up to Court, to ask him for his advice, although, antecedent to those occasions, he had actually taken advice, and had determined upon the course he should pursue. Williams was what was described as a loyal man; that was to say, a sort of thick and thin man; who, if a person in authority were to say go, he goeth; come, and he cometh.[80] (*Murmurs of approbation.*) He was in a corps of yeomanry, and he told him (Mr. Hone) that he had often printed for Government. His full conviction was, that if he (Hone) had been found guilty, the man would not long have remained in prison. He thought he had a strong right to complain of one or two gross and infamous falsehoods inserted in a paper which was published every morning at six o'clock, and which there had been time, therefore, for every one of the Jury to have seen before he entered the box. At six o'clock every morning did the ghost of Dr. *Slop* (a name acquired by Dr. Stoddart, on account of the profane curses lavished by him upon Buonaparte, before he was dismissed from *The Times* Journal) walk forth in Crane-court, Fleet-street. By this ghost it had been stated (for what purpose, unless to prejudice him on his trial, could not be imagined) that Williams had been found guilty *by the verdict of a Jury* for the same publication. This was as false as was another statement, that he was in the practice of selling obscenity, which he detested and despised as much as any man. Such falsehoods, put forth at such a time, when he was standing up in that Court, in the hour of peril, to vindicate his innocence, could only have proceeded from one who was a *villain to the back-bone.* And such he would proclaim Dr. SLOP to his face, whenever and wherever he should meet him.

Lord ELLENBOROUGH.—Do not use such expressions. You say you have got through life free from private and acrimonious bickering; do not say that now which may hereafter provoke it. I say this merely for your own preservation, and not with a view to interrupt you.

Mr. HONE assured his Lordship that he sincerely acknowledged the propriety of his interference, though it was difficult for him to restrain his feelings. It was nevertheless true that he cherished no hatred against this individual; he was indeed an object of contempt, and not of hatred, and was regarded by him in no other light than as a lost, unfortunate, and abandoned man. He had come into Court with strong feelings of irritation, which he could not well restrain when he found that this man's statements went to impute to him the publication of sedition, blasphemy, and obscenity. He denied that he had ever suffered any obscene work in his shop; and if it could be proved that he had, he called upon the Jury to find him guilty of blasphemy, in order that under that verdict he might receive the punishment due to obscenity; for, next to blasphemy, he considered obscenity the greatest offence which a man could commit. He had, however, no *hatred* for such a man; and although Dr. Slop had attempted to do him this injury in the moment of peril, if the miserable man were in distress to-morrow, and it was in his power to relieve him, he would not hesitate to hold him out a helping hand. This feeling had been cherished in his breast ever since he knew right from wrong. (*Murmurs of Applause.*) He wished he could have had it in his power to say that his trial had not come on that day, merely for the sake of being able to say something in favour of his persecutors. Some of those grave personages went to the Chapel Royal with their Prayerbooks on the Sabbath-day. It was to be lamented that they lost sight of those principles of Christianity which he hoped they were in that place accustomed to hear. He by no means wished that justice should not be done; for to neglect to do justice would be injustice; but he thought, in the present case, they might have borrowed a little of the character, the precept, and the example, of one whose name he could not mention without reverence and humility—he meant Jesus Christ. He would not be so irreverend as to read any passage to illustrate the character of that Divine Being; but he well recollected that when Jesus was on earth, he continually exhorted his followers to the exercise of mercy, charity, love, and good-will. This was exemplified in many instances, but in one more finely than in all the rest. He had heard various sermons on this subject, but none of them produced an impression equal to that which he experienced on reading the relation to which he referred when alone and in his room. That to which he alluded was the story of the woman taken in adultery. The Pharisees went to Christ in the temple, and brought to him a woman whom they had taken in adultery, a crime the greatest that it was possible for a wife to be guilty of. She did not deny her guilt, but Christ, turning to the Pharisees, said, "He that is without sin let him cast the first stone ;" her guilty accusers withdrew in silence, leaving the woman alone with Jesus, who desired her to "Go, and sin no more."[81] If there were nothing but this to excite veneration in the human mind for that Divine Being, it was sufficient; and he had only to lament that such an admirable example had not been followed by those who had brought him there that day. By the Jewish laws, the woman who had committed adultery was liable to be stoned to death, and yet none of her accusers could say they themselves were without sins. Were his Prosecutors without sins, he would ask? Were they not open to impeachment? He would impeach them! These Pharisees were guilty of the same crime for which they were now seeking to punish him! The miserable hypocrites! The wretches! (*Murmurs from the Crowd.*) That was a strong, a very strong phrase; he did not mean to apply it to any person in particular; all he meant to urge was, that his accusers had themselves done what they ought not to have done, and ought therefore to look with the greater lenity towards him. He had now to ask the Jury, for it was too late to ask his accusers, to follow the precept of our Saviour in another part of the Testament, viz.— "to do unto others as you wish others to do unto you."[82] He felt much better to-day than yesterday. He was animated by the consciousness of having done no wrong. For any wrong he might have unwittingly done, he was exceedingly sorry. He was exceedingly sorry if any thing he had written or published had a bad tendency. His Lordship had misconceived the cause of stopping the sale of his publications. He had not stopt it because he thought the publication wrong, but because persons whom he respected had been hurt by them. He esteemed the hearts, though he could not respect the judgment of those persons. He would hurt no man's mind. Sorry, sorry, sorry, was he, that the *prosecution* was not stopt. Although his Prosecutors had thought of bringing him to trial at all, and had actually put him on his trial; although they had done so a second day, after a Jury of honest Englishmen had acquitted him; yet he should have been happy, for their own sake, that his Prosecutors had made some atonement by a twelfth hour repentance. See the odds against me, he exclaimed, in a fervid tone; it is one farthing against a million of gold. My Prosecutors have laid a wager with public opinion; but they will lose it to their irretrievable shame. "Skin for skin (*he exclaimed, vehemently*), all that a man has will he give for his life!"[83] I am here on trial for my life. If you, the Jury, do not protect me, my life must fall a sacrifice to the confinement that shall follow a verdict of guilty. My Prosecutors, my Persecutors, are unrelenting. I feel now as vigorous as when I was in the middle of my defence on Thursday last; and I talk to you as familiarly as if you were sitting with me in my own room; but then, Gentlemen of the Jury, I have not seats for you; I have not twelve chairs in my house; but I have the pride of being independent. None is supposed to be independent without property. I have never had any property. Within the last twelve months my children had not beds. At this moment there is not furniture sufficient for the necessary enjoyment of life. For the last two years and a half I have not had a complete hour of happiness, because my family have been in such misery that it was impossible for a man of my temperament to know any thing of happiness. I have been asked, why I have not employed counsel?—I could not *fee* counsel. I have been asked, when I should publish my trial? I could not pay a reporter; and at this moment I have no reporter in Court. Gentlemen, you do not see me in that dress which my respect for you, and for myself, would make me anxious to appear in. I did resolve to get a suit of clothes for these trials, but the money I had provided for that purpose I was obliged to give for copies of the informations against me. These things I mention to show you what difficulties I had to encounter in order to appear to possess independence of mind, and to let men know how cautious they should be in judging of men. Seven or eight years ago I went into business with a friend in the Strand. I had then a wife and four children, and I was separated from them by evils accumulated from endeavouring to help those who could not help themselves. I attempted, in conjunction with the friend, who originated the plan, to establish something of an institution similar to the saving-banks that are now so general. There was a number associated for this purpose, and I was their secretary. Our object was to get the patronage of Ministers for our scheme. Mr. Fox was then in power. It was the Whig Administration. We hoped to throw a grain into the earth which might become a great tree—in other hands it has succeeded. It was very Quixotic—we were mad; mad because we supposed it possible, if an intention were good, that it would therefore be carried into effect. We were not immediately discouraged, but we met with that trifling and delaying of hope which makes the heart sick.

[Here a person fainted among the crowd, and was carried out. The Court and Jury took the opportunity to take some refreshment. Mr. Hone withdrew, for a few minutes, from the Court, threw off his coat, washed his arms and face with cold water, and rinced his mouth; and when the Court was ready resumed.]

I find I was entering into too much detail. I meant simply to state that I lost every thing, even the furniture of my house. With that friend

I got again into business. We became bankrupts, owing to the terms on which we commenced it. But, on the meeting of our creditors, the first question was, 'Where is your certificate?' All signed it at once, save one, who was unintentionally the cause of my failure, two years and a half ago, when I went into prison for debt, and was discharged by the insolvent act. Having then got some books to sell, being always fond of old books, I took a shop in Fleet-street, at the corner of Lombard-street. It was three feet wide in front. I had no place there for my wife and my seven children. The shop was in consequence broken open three times, and all that was worth any thing in it taken away. I was now in desperation, thrown on a wide ocean without a shore, and without a plank of safety. I then accidentally wrote something which happened to sell. By this success I got a place for my family, which was scarcely a dwelling for human beings. From my anxiety for my family, and the harassed state of my mind, I was attacked with apoplexy, and my family were thrown into the utmost alarm. I was obliged to remove to save my life. I then took a place in the Old Bailey. I could furnish only one room. I would not let lodgings, because I would not expose my state of destitution. Just as I was getting my head a little above water, this storm assailed me, and plunged me deeper than ever. I am as destitute as any man in London. I have not one friend in the world. It has been said that I am *backed*. No! friends are got by social intercourse; and the expense of social intercourse I have never been able to afford. I have as true a relish for the comforts, as well as the elegancies of life, as most men in much higher ranks; but I have ever been independent in mind, and hence I am a destitute man. I have never written or printed what I did not think right and true; and in my most humble station have always acted for the public good, according to my conception, without regard to what other men did, however exalted their rank.

The Defendant now apologized to his Lordship, the Attorney-General, and the Bar, if he had offended them by any thing he had said; and entered upon what was immediately connected with his defence. Informations by the Attorney-General had been defended, he said, as always known in the practice of the law. He denied this. To hold to bail for libel was illegal; and in support of that proposition he quoted a passage from a letter written by Mr. Dunning, afterwards Lord Ashburton,[84] in the following words:—"I never heard, till very lately, that Attorney-Generals, upon the caption of a man, supposed a libeller, could insist upon his giving securities for his good behaviour. *It is a doctrine injurious to the freedom of every subject, derogatory from the old constitution, and a violent attack, if not an absolute breach, on the liberty of the press.* IT IS NOT LAW, AND I WILL NOT SUBMIT TO IT."—(Mr. Dunning's Letter concerning Libels, Warrants, &c. p. 31.) He next referred to the information filed against him, and from which he quoted, and submitted that the only question the Jury had to try was, as to his *intention* when the publication in question issued from his hand. That his intention was such as was imputed to him he utterly denied. Nothing was further from his ideas than to excite irreligion and impiety in the minds of his Majesty's subjects. The *Jury* were his judges. *They* were to decide both upon the law and the fact; and by *their* decision his fate would be decided. He stopt the publication, not, as he was a living man, because he thought it criminal, but he gave way to the wishes of persons not to be argued with.

He would now prove this parody to be no libel. It was possible to parody the most sacred work, without bringing the work itself into ridicule and contempt. The parody might be used as the vehicle of inculcating, by the peculiar language of the thing parodied, an impression of a different tendency. Parody was a ready engine to produce a certain impression on the mind, without at all ridiculing the sentiments contained in the original work. Such was the object of Martin Luther's parody on the first Psalm; and such also was the object of Dr. Letsom's Thermometer of Health, and a number of works applying religious phraseology to give a more solemn impression to the moral or the sentiments inculcated. In illustration of this position, he proceeded to submit to the Jury the same works of which he availed himself on the preceding trials; amongst which were Dr. Boys', the Dean of Canterbury's parody on the Lord's Prayer. There was no doubt that Dr. Boys had written his parody unadvisedly, but certainly without a bad intention. Such was his (the Defendant's) parody on St. Athanasius's Creed. It was not written for a religious, but for a political purpose—to produce a laugh against the Ministers. He avowed that such was his object; nay, to laugh his Majesty's Ministers to scorn; he had laughed at them, and, ha! ha! ha! he laughed at them now, and he *would* laugh at them, as long as they were laughing-stocks! Were there any poor witless men less ridiculous than these Ministers, his persecutors; one of whom was himself a parodist, sitting now in the Cabinet, winking at, instigating, aiding and abetting this prosecution. George Canning was a parodist, with William Hone and Martin Luther (*applause.*) George Canning come into Court! George Canning come into Court! make way for him if you please. No, Gentlemen of the Jury, you will not see Mr. Canning here to-day; but had I him now in the box, I would twist him inside out. Mr. Canning had parodied the Scriptures, but he (Mr. Hone), had only parodied the Common Prayer. He next adverted to the caricature called "The Mantle of Elijah." And who was the *Elijah* personified?—why, Mr. Pitt! And who was the mantle-catcher?—why, this same George Canning, who was now one of his persecutors. Before, he had spoken of this Right Honourable with forbearance; but now he must speak with contempt of the man who could act thus towards the poor miserable, and supposed to be defenceless bookseller of the little shop in Fleet Street. This very caricature was published under the auspices of Mr. Canning; certainly, at least, with his entire knowledge. Mr. Canning ought to have been a willing witness for him on the present occasion; he ought to come into the witness box, to confess his own sins, and plead the Defendant's cause. It was hoped, he had no doubt, by certain very grave members of the Cabinet (my Lord Sidmouth and my Lord Liverpool), that William Hone could not stand the third day— that he would sink under his fatigues and want of physical power. "He can't stand the third trial," said these humane and Christian Ministers; "we shall have him now; he must be crushed." (*Great shouts of applause.*) Oh, no! no! he must *not* be crushed; you *cannot* crush him. I have a spark of liberty in my mind, that will glow and burn brighter, and blaze more fiercely, as my mortal remains are passing to decay. There is nothing can crush me, but my own sense of doing wrong; the moment I feel it, I fall down in self-abasement before my accusers: but when I have done no wrong, when I know I am right, I am as an armed man; and in this spirit I wage battle with the Attorney-General, taking a tilt with him here on the floor of this Court. The consciousness of my innocence gives me life, spirits, and strength, to go through this third ordeal of persecution and oppression. He should order a frame for Elijah's Mantle in his way home to his family, and he should place it over his mantle-piece, for his children to laugh at. He said he should do this to-night, because he had no doubt that the Jury would acquit him without retiring from the box (*great applause*). He next adverted to Lord Somers's tracts, and called in aid the parody of the Genealogy of Christ, and accompanied it with a powerful appeal to the Jury, upon the iniquity of this last effort to overwhelm him—to send him to Gloucester gaol, to rot and perish under the weight of his afflictions. The Harleian Miscellany contained a parody on the Lord's Prayer.

The ATTORNEY-GENERAL objected to its being read, as too indecent for the ears of any persons in these times.

Mr. HONE said, in courtesy to the Attorney-General, he would not persist in reading this work. He then went over the same ground which he had pursued yesterday, bringing under the attention of the Jury a great variety of different parodies, written by churchmen and many other persons, considered in their times as most religious and venerable men. One of which he had not before read, was by the Rev. Mr. Toplady,[85] a very popular preacher, of great talent, amongst the Calvinists, who died greatly lamented, at a very early age. Mr. Toplady's object was to ridicule Lord Chesterfield's Letters,[86] and the morals therein inculcated. It was entitled—

"CHRISTIANITY REVERSED, &C.; *or* Lord CHESTERFIELD'S *New Creed.*

"I believe, that this world is the object of my hopes and morals; and that the little prettinesses of life will answer all the ends of human existence.

"I believe, that we are to succeed in all things, by the graces of civility and attention; that there is no sin, but against good manners; and that all religion and virtue consist in outward appearance.

"I believe, that all women are children, and all men fools; except a few cunning people, who see through the rest, and make their use of them.

"I believe, that hypocrisy, fornication, and adultery, are within the lines of morality; that a woman may be honourable when she has lost her honour, and virtuous when she has lost her virtue.

"This, and whatever else is necessary to obtain my own ends, and bring me into repute, I resolve to follow; and to avoid all moral offences, such as scratching my head before company, spitting upon the floor, and omitting to pick up a lady's fan. And in this persuasion I will persevere, without any regard to the resurrection of the body, or the life everlasting. *Amen.*

"Q. Wilt thou be initiated into these principles?

"A. That is my inclination.

"Q. Wilt thou keep up to the rules of the *Chesterfield* morality?

"A. I will, Lord Chesterfield being my admonisher.

"Then the Officiator shall say,

"Name this child.

"A. A FINE GENTLEMAN.

"Then he shall say,

"I introduce thee to the world, the flesh, and the devil, that thou mayest triumph over all awkwardness, and grow up in all politeness; that thou mayest be acceptable to the ladies, celebrated for refined breeding, able to speak French and read Italian, invested with some public supernumerary character in a foreign Court, get into Parliament (perhaps into the Privy Council), and that, when thou art dead, the letters written to thy bastards may be published, in seven editions, for the instruction of all sober families.

"Ye are to take care that this child, when he is of a proper age, be brought to C——t to be *confirmed.*"

Of the other works to which he particularly alluded, was Mr. Reeves's penny publication entitled the "British Freeholder's Political Catechism."[87] That gentleman had himself been prosecuted; not, however, for his Catechism, but for having depicted the British Constitution as a tree, the branches of which might be lopped off, and yet the trunk remain. For this libel he was prosecuted under the direction of the House of Commons, although it was carried on very unwillingly. Mr. Reeves published his parody on the Catechism no doubt with the best intentions, because he used the parody as a popular mode of inculcating what that gentleman considered wholesome truth. Such was the object of the parody now prosecuted. But what was the difference between his situation and Mr. Reeves's? Mr. Reeves was basking under the sunshine of a Court, and was a placeman. If he (Mr. H.) was convicted, there was no doubt that he also would become a Government placeman: but where?—in Gloucester gaol! To the Jury, however, he looked for his rescue from this bigotted persecution. He was charged with parodying the language and style of sacred works. But what was that style and language?—it happened to be translated nearly three centuries ago, but the language of that time was not, on that account, peculiarly sacred. There was no doubt that if the Bible was re-translated, it must be so altered as hardly to be known, except by its sense. If a parody on the style only was the offence, even Mr. Canning himself, as a literary man, as a man of taste, and a man of words, would acquit him. But whatever might be the motive of this prosecution, there could hardly be any doubt that it was an unchristian feeling on the part of my Lord Sidmouth, to suffer him to stand here for the third time to take his trial for

an offence which two Juries of independent Englishmen had pronounced not to be libels. He would not say that Lord Sidmouth was a
bigot; but he must say, that the spirit of persecution and unchristian
feeling marked this abominable attempt to sacrifice, by all or any
means, a defenceless and innocent man, for party purposes. Lord Sidmouth himself knew, and every man in the country, even the most bigotted, must know, that this parody was not written for irreligious
purposes. The fact was, the hopeful Ministers of the Cabinet wanted to
make him a scape-goat for their political sins; those which were his
own particular sins he should glory in, so long as he lived, because he
knew that his objects were truly constitutional, and aimed at the happiness of his country. The Jury must see that the parodies which he
read were not calculated to injure religion. Most of them had political
or moral objects. Of the former description was the parody in the Oracle newspaper, and the parody on the Te Deum, adapted in five lan-
guages, to the combined royal armies, lately employed against
Buonaparte; and of the latter was the Religious Play-bill, which he had
read on the other trials, which was printed by one of the Society of
Friends. Such also was the parody on the Recruiting Bill, the object of
which was to draw the attention of the idle and dissolute to spiritual
concerns. Of the like description were the hymn tunes played at Rowland Hill's Chapel, although they were the popular and national airs
performed at theatres and other places of amusement. Dr. John Rippon,
an eminent and most respectable teacher of religion amongst the Bap-
tists, had adapted such tunes to the most pious strains of psalmody. For
instance, such tunes as "Drink to me only with thine eyes," "Rule Britannia," "God save the King," &c. The hymns of Dr. Collyer, Lady
Huntingdon,[88] Dr. Watts, and others, were adapted to operatic and military airs, &c. These tunes, no man could doubt, were used as vehicles
for religious worship, and exciting moral feelings. His parody was
adapted exclusively to a similar subject, and was not meant, directly or
indirectly, to affect the sacredness of religious worship. Profaneness
and irreligion must be the same at all times and in all places; and if the
most venerable and sacred pillars of religion had resorted to this mode
of inculcating religious sentiments, the offence must have been as cul-
pable in their times, if it was an offence, as in the present. Bishop Latimer, who had burned at the stake, a martyr for religion, had
spiritualized the pack of cards, as John Bunyan had the fig-tree, for the
most moral purposes. He blamed the Attorney-General for the cruelty of

cutting one crime into piecemeal; for all these three informations might have been included in one. An hundred libels might have been embraced in one information. But no; the object was to embarrass and entrap him. One chance of catching him was not sufficient for the vindictive spirit of his Majesty's Ministers. They were determined to have him at all events; and therefore *three* hooks were baited; but he hoped the Jury would save him from the third. All these snares were laid for his ruin, by a Ministry remarkable alike for bigotry of spirit and hostility to freedom. They were laid by that Ministry, who not long since endeavoured to interfere with those principles of religious toleration which were held sacred by all good and rational men, by introducing a bill into Parliament for restraining the right of preaching among the Dissenters.[89] Yes, that odious bill, which was scouted out of Parliament, through the firm and manly appeals of the Dissenters themselves, originated with Lord Sidmouth, by whom he had been most unjustly held out to the country as a blasphemer, although now persecuted by that Minister only for a profane parody. This Minister endeavoured in Parliament to stigmatize him for an offence which could not be even alleged against him before a Jury. This Minister of the Crown took the advantage of abusing him in a place where he (Mr. Hone) could make him no answer, and this was a practice too common with his unmanly colleagues. But here he would answer that Minister by affirming, that which he would challenge the Attorney-General to contradict, namely, that to impute to him the crime of blasphemy was a foul and unfounded slander. Such slanders, however, were not uncommon. Mr. Canning was quite in the habit of abusing men in the House of Commons, whom he would not venture to meet face to face; while he was in a rage if any the most indirect allusion was made in that House to any member of that confederacy of literary hirelings and political apostates, of which he had been so long the principal leader and active patron. Yes, any man who could write in that style, about which Canning was so peculiarly solicitous, that it seemed, in that gentleman's view, more material than thought, was secure of ministerial patronage, if the writer would only follow Mr. Canning in the desertion of principle and the sacrifice of real independence.

But to return to the subject under the consideration of the Court. He observed that parodies had been so numerous in this country, that no one could suppose them subject to any legal censure. He remembered a parody levelled at Lord Grenville,[90] in the Oracle newspaper, when it was a Ministerial print, as indeed, it had always been for several years before its death; for that paper was dead, notwithstanding the support it received from Ministers; and having mentioned that support, he could not help stating the manner in which it was usually afforded to newspapers. When the venal journalist could write what was deemed a good article in favour of the Ministry, 5 or 600 copies of his journal were bought by the Treasury, and gratuitously circulated among their partisans through the country. Those purchases were made indeed as often as the journalist appeared to his patrons to deserve attention; and they were made, too, with the public money. Thus the money wrung in taxes from the pocket of the people, was distributed among those prostituted writers who were employed in endeavouring to pervert their understanding. How much of this money was given to the Oracle for abusing every principle and advocate of liberty, he could not pretend to say, but its death was a pregnant proof of the integrity, power, and judgment of the people, among whom it could obtain no currency. For after all, if a paper could not obtain circulation among the people, Ministers must feel it of no use to them, and therefore withdraw their patronage from a hireling as soon as the people discard his productions; which they will always do as soon as they clearly understand his character—such had been the fate of many newspapers and other periodical publications in this country. Herriott's paper, the True Briton, met the fate of the Oracle, and for the same reasons.[91] When Herriott was provided with a place, which he now held, Cobbett was offered the True Briton, but he refused it. The True Briton too, under Mr. Herriott, had its share of parodies, which were always of course pointed against the opposition.

He then addressed himself to the particular parody charged as a libel, and adduced a parody on the Athanasian Creed, from the Foundling Hospital for Wit, as follows—

PROPER RULES AND INSTRUCTIONS, WITHOUT WHICH NO PERSON CAN BE AN EXCISEMAN

Quicunque vult.

Whosoever would be an Exciseman, before all things it is necessary that he learns the Art of Arithmetic.

Which Art, unless he wholly understand, he without doubt can be no Exciseman.

Now the Art of Arithmetic is this, we know how to multiply and how to divide. *Desunt pauca.*

The 1 is a figure, the 2 a figure, and the 3 a figure.

The 1 is a number, the 2 a number, and the 3 a number; and yet there are *Desunt plurima.*

For like as we are compelled by the Rules of Arithmetic, to acknowledge every figure by itself to have signification and form:

So we are forbidden, by the rules of right reason, to say, that each of them have three significations or three powers.

The 2 is of the 1's alone, not abstracted, nor depending, but produced.

The 3 is of the 1 and 2, not abstracted, nor depending, nor produced, but derived. So there is one figure of 1. *Desunt nonnulla.*[92]

He therefore that will be an Exciseman, must thus understand his figures.

Furthermore, it is necessary to the preservation of his place, that he also believe rightly the authority of his Supervisor.

For his interest is, that he believes and confesses that his Supervisor, the servant of the Commissioners, is master and man: Master of the Exciseman, having power from the Commissioners to inspect his books: and man to the Commissioners, being obliged to return his accounts.

Perfect master and perfect man, of an unconscionable soul and frail flesh subsisting; equal to the Commissioners, as touching that respect which is shown him by the Excisemen, and inferior to the Commissioners as touching their profit and salary.

Who, although he be master and man, is not two, but one Supervisor.

One, not by confusion of place, but by virtue of his authority; for his seal and sign manual perfect his commission; his gauging the vessels, and inspecting the Excisemen's books, is what makes him Supervisor.

Who travels through thick and thin, and suffers most from heat or cold, to save us from the addition of taxes, or the deficiency in the funds, by corruption or inadvertency.

Who thrice in seven days goes his rounds, and once in six weeks meets the Collectors, who shall come to judge between the Exciseman and Victualler.

At whose coming all Excisemen shall bring in their accounts, and the Victuallers their money.

And they that have done well by prompt payment, shall be well treated.

And those that have done ill, by being tardy in their payment, shall be cast into jail; and the Excisemen whose books are blotted, or accounts unjustifiable, shall be turned out of their places.

These are the rules, which except a man follows, he cannot be an Exciseman.

Honour to the Commissioners, fatigue to the Supervisor, and bribery to the Exciseman.

As it was from the beginning, when taxes were first laid upon Malt, is now, and ever will be till the debts of the nation are paid. *Amen.*

Mr. HONE then read a parody on the Athanasian Creed, from the Wonderful Magazine,[93] entitled—

THE MATRIMONIAL CREED.

Whoever will be married, before all things it is necessary that he hold the conjugal faith, which is this, That there were two rational beings created, both equal, and yet one superior to the other; and the inferior shall bear rule over the superior; which faith, except every one do keep whole and undefiled, without doubt he shall be scolded at everlastingly.

The man is superior to the woman, and the woman is inferior to the man; yet both are equal, and the woman shall govern the man.

The woman is commanded to obey the man, and the man ought to obey the woman.

And yet, they are not two obedients, but one obedient.

For there is one dominion nominal of the husband, and another dominion real of the wife.

And yet, there are not two dominions, but one dominion.

For like as we are compelled by the Christian verity to acknowledge that wives must submit themselves to their husbands, and be subject to them in all things:

So are we forbidden by the conjugal faith to say, that they should be at all influenced by their wills, or pay any regard to their commands.

The man was not created for the woman, but the woman for the man.

Yet the man shall be the slave of the woman, and the woman the tyrant of the man.

So that in all things, as is aforesaid, the subjection of the superior to the inferior is to be believed.

He, therefore, that will be married, must thus think of the woman and the man.

Furthermore, it is necessary to submissive matrimony, that he also believe rightly the infallibility of the wife.

For the right faith is, that we believe and confess, that the wife is fallible and infallible.

Perfectly fallible, and perfectly infallible; of an erring soul and un-erring mind subsisting; fallible as touching her human nature, and infallible as touching her female sex.

Who, although she be fallible and infallible, yet she is not two, but one woman; who submitted to lawful marriage, to acquire unlawful dominion; and promised religiously to obey, that she might rule in injustice and folly.

This is the conjugal faith; which except a man believe faithfully, he cannot enter the comfortable state of matrimony.

There were others, but the next, and only one he should read, was from the New Foundling Hospital for Wit; it was written against the late Lord Chatham,[94] as follows:—

A NEW POLITICAL CREED,

FOR THE YEAR MDCCLXVI.

Quicunque vult.

Whoever will be saved: before all things it is necessary that he should hold the Chatham faith.

Which faith, except every man keep whole and undefiled, without doubt he shall sink into oblivion.

And the Chatham faith is this: that we worship one Minister in Trinity, and the Trinity in Unity:

Neither confounding the persons, nor dividing the substance,

For the Privy Seal is a Minister, the Secretary is a Minister, and the Treasurer is a Minister.[95]

Yet there are not three Ministers, but one Minister; for the Privy Seal, the Secretary, and the Treasurer are all one.

Such as the Privy Seal is, such is the Secretary, and such is the Treasurer.

The Privy Seal is self-create, the Secretary is self-create, and the Treasurer is self-create.

The Privy Seal is incomprehensible, the Secretary is incomprehensible, and the Treasurer is incomprehensible.

The Privy Seal is unresponsible, the Secretary is unresponsible, and the Treasurer is unresponsible.

And yet there are not three incomprehensibles, three self-created, or three unresponsibles: but one incomprehensible, one self-create, and one unresponsible.

For like as we are compelled by the Christian verity, to acknowledge every person by himself to be God and Lord;

So are we forbidden by the articles of the Chatham alliance, to say there are three Ministers:

So that in all things, the Unity in Trinity, and Trinity in Unity, are to be worshipped; and he who would be saved, must thus think of the Ministry.

Furthermore it is necessary to elevation, that he also believe rightly of the qualities of our Minister.

For the right faith is, that we believe and confess, that this son of man is something more than man; as total perfection, though of an unreasonable soul, and gouty flesh consisting.

Who suffered for our salvation, descended into opposition, rose again the third time, and ascended into the House of Peers.

He sitteth on the right hand of the——, from whence he shall come to judge the good and the bad.

And they that have done good, shall go into patent places,[96] and they that have done bad, shall go into everlasting opposition.

This is the Chatham faith; which except a man believe faithfully, he cannot be promoted.

As he was in the beginning, he is now, and ever will be.

Then all the people, standing up, shall say,

O blessed and glorious Trinity, three persons and one Minister, have mercy on us miserable subjects.

These parodies were known to almost every reading man, and yet none of them were ever prosecuted, nor was there an instance upon record of the prosecution of any parody. How then could he suppose the publication of the parody before the Court an illegal, a guilty act? But he had no such feeling—he declared most solemnly that he had no intention to commit any offence in this publication, and the Jury were to judge of intention. But to dissuade the Jury from such a rule of judgment, a course of delusive observation was addressed to them. They were told truly, that they were to judge of a man's intention by his act, and not by his declaration. Granted: but upon what ground should he think his act an offence, or that sort of publication criminal, which had never been so pronounced? There was no analogy between his act and the commission of any crime defined and forbidden by the law, although such analogy had been urged on the other side. If he had committed any act denounced by the law, or deemed a crime by the common sense of mankind, he should not have presumed to speak of the purity of his intentions. No Jury, indeed, could attend to declarations of innocent intention from any man committing an act of acknowledged criminality; but that was not the nature of the publication which he had uttered, and for which he was prosecuted. Therefore he could conscientiously say that he had no guilty intention in sending forth that publication, and he had no doubt that the Jury would believe him, and would send him home to his family, in spite of all the expedients used in this extraordinary prosecution; for extraordinary it truly was, the Attorney-General having split into three indictments matter, which being of the same character, he might have comprehended in one. But were the matter even different, did it consist of two or three different subjects, he was assured by the most eminent barristers, that the Attorney-General could have included them in one information. Why then should so many informations be preferred against him, but for a purpose which he trusted the integrity and judgment of the Jury would defeat? They would not, he was sure, be persuaded to think his publication a fit subject for punishment, after such parodies had been overlooked as he had just read to the Court.

Lord ELLENBOROUGH observed, that every one of the parodies the Defendant had quoted, were as prosecutable as that with which he then stood charged.

Mr. HONE admitted this; but why, he asked, were they not prosecuted? Where were the Attorney-Generals of those days? Why did they abandon their duty? The Attorney-General might any day go into the Crown-office, and file an information against any man who wrote any thing in opposition to the Government. A parody was never seized before. Why was his parody now attacked? Was it because Lord Sidmouth was the only good Secretary of State for the Home Department? He charged that noble Secretary with having put all the people of England against him as a blasphemer. There were persecutions of various kinds for blasphemy, and also for atheism. A man charged with atheism had been punished in Poland, in the beginning of last century, whom he believed to have been certainly as honest a man as the Secretary of State. One of the poor creature's hands was cut off with an axe by the executioner, and afterwards the other was chopped off; his two bleeding stumps were then thrust into boiling pitch, and the miserable man was burned alive, whilst—lifting his eyes and his mutilated arms to heaven—he cried, "Oh God, of Abraham! Oh, God of Judah! have mercy upon me! Oh God, of my fathers! have pity upon me." Who, O who (*cried Mr. Hone, raising his voice to a tone of the utmost vehemence*), who were the blasphemers? Who were the Atheists? Were they not the bloody-minded men who called themselves Christians, rather than the defenceless man whom they put to death in that horrible and cruel manner. (*Great applause instantaneously burst from every part of Guildhall; and Lord Ellenborough declared he would adjourn the Court if greater order were not observed.*) During the whole of Pitt's administration, there was not one prosecution for libel; and yet party feeling never ran higher, and cheap publications were never more numerous. In the volume that contained the parodies on the Westminster election, he could find 100 more of them as strong as his, yet for none of them was ever a prosecution instituted. He on all occasions made frequent use of the language of Scripture. That proceeded from his intimate acquaintance with it. He had ever delighted to read its beautiful narrations. He had long been employed in preparing a publication on the Bible, and he hoped yet to finish it, and to give it to the world, notwithstanding he had been called a blasphemer. In no age of the world was there before a prosecution for parody. He had seen a letter pretended to have been written by Jesus Christ, and found sixty-four years after his death, now in the possession of Lady Cuba, in Mesopotamia. He believed the author was not a blasphemer, but that he ought to be put into a cook-shop, and to be fed on beef-steaks. This letter pretended, that a woman in labour, who had it, should be safely delivered. It gave instructions as to the Sunday and Good Friday. All this was quite absurd; but he would on his knees entreat the Attorney-General not to prosecute the author. Indeed, he had seen such letters from a child; and a gentleman had one of them that was 150 years old. Parodies of all kinds used to be circulated in Westminster, and even to be paid for by the Treasury, before Westminster became independent. Mr. Canning, the Right Honourable parodist, had been a member of Lord Townsend's Committee, though a secret one, for he was then a trimmer;[97] and from them issued many parodies. Why did not the Attorney-General prosecute Mr. Walter Scott, for the "Tales of my Landlord,"[98] a work which abounded with Scriptural phrases, set in the most absurd and ridiculous view? He would ask whether Sir Samuel Shepherd would prosecute this poetical placeman, or would he prosecute him (Mr. Hone,) if he published a dozen pages from the work of Mr. Scott, while the original author was left untouched? Sure he was, that the Attorney-General would not prosecute Mr. Walter Scott, for using Scriptural phrases upon similar subjects, notwithstanding all the solicitude which the learned gentleman professed, to hold the language of the Gospel sacred to religious purposes. But he would ask the Attorney-General which he thought worse, blasphemy or atheism? And did not the learned gentleman know, that there were hundreds of atheistical works at present in circulation? Nay, did he not know that many eminent persons in this country openly professed atheism? And was no solicitude felt for the cause of religion, unless its language were employed to expose the character of Ministers, or to subject them to ridicule?

It had been observed by the Learned Judge, in his charge to the Jury yesterday, that he (Mr. H.) was not entitled to draw any argument in his defence from the parodies which had been heretofore published, because, as his Lordship observed, "the publication of parodies upon the Scripture, or the use of scriptural language for jocular purposes, had never had any legal sanction." Now he held in his hand publications, in which such language appeared, under the direct authority of government.

Lord ELLENBOROUGH said that he did not recollect having used the words imputed to him by the Defendant. He might have used some such words, but he did not remember the precise words that fell from him.

Mr. HONE declared that he quoted the words referred to with accuracy, and that he had no wish whatever to misrepresent his Lordship. He was in the recollection of the short-hand writers in Court. But to the point. He was surely justified in concluding, that his Lordship's impression was rather erroneous; the Lord Chamberlain sanctioned, and a succession of Crown Lawyers and Judges having seen and enjoyed that which he was about to cite. Here Mr. Hone read the following passage from the Hypocrite:[99]

Lady Lamb. O dear; you hurt my hand, sir.

Doctor Cantwell. Impute it to my zeal, and want of words for expression: precious soul! I would not harm you for the world; no, it would be the whole business of my life—

And again, *Lady Lamb* says, you are above the low momentary views of this world.

Dr. Cant. Why, I should be so; and yet, alas! I find this mortal clothing of my soul is made like other men's, of sensual flesh and blood, and has its frailties.

Lady Lamb. We all have those, but yours are well corrected by your divine and virtuous contemplations.

Dr. Cant. Alas! Madam, my heart is not of stone: I may resist, call all my prayers, my fastings, tears, and penance to my aid; but yet I am not an angel; I am still but a man; and virtue may strive, but nature will be uppermost. I love you, then, Madam.

It was well known that the person meant to be represented and ridiculed in the character of Dr. Cantwell, was that celebrated preacher, Mr. Whitfield;[100] and the sentences he was made to utter, as Dr. Cantwell, were varied from his own Journal. This distinguished man had, with John Wesley and others, done great good in promoting morality. If, indeed, those excellent persons had rendered no other service to humanity than that of civilizing the Kingswood colliers,[101] they were entitled to the praise of mankind. Yet Mr. Whitfield and his language were thus caricatured upon the stage, with the authority of one of the first officers of the Crown. But again Mr. Whitfield was still more ridiculed in Foote's Farce of "The Minor,"[102] from which Mr. Hone read the following extracts:

Mrs. Cole. I am worn out, thrown by, and forgotten, like a tattered garment, as Mr. Squintum says. Oh, he is a dear man! But for him I had been a lost sheep; never known the comforts of the new birth! Ay, I have done with these idle vanities; my thoughts are fixed upon a better place. What, I suppose, Mr. Loader, you will be for your old friend the black-ey'd girl from Rosemary-lane. Ha, ha! Well, 'tis a merry little tit. A thousand pities she's such a reprobate!—But she'll mend; her time is not come: all shall have their call, as Mr. Squintum says, sooner or later; regeneration is not the work of a day. No, no, no.—Oh!—

Loader. Crop me, but this Squintum has turned her brains.

Sir Geo. Nay, Mr. Loader, I think the gentleman has wrought most happy reformation.

Mrs. Cole. Oh, it was a wonderful work. There had I been tossing in a sea of sin, without rudder or compass. And had not the good gentleman piloted me into the harbour of grace, I must have struck against the rocks of reprobation, and have been quite swallowed up in the whirlpool of despair. He was the precious instrument of my spiritual sprinkling.

Dr. Squintum was the character in which Mr. Whitfield was again ridiculed, and Mother Cole was meant to represent an infamous woman of that day, whose name was Douglas.[103] In the preface to this farce, the writer says, that "it must be useful, while there was a bawd in the street, an auctioneer in the rostrum, or a Methodist in the pulpit." All this was tolerated, and no one was heard to complain of any disposition in these dramatic writers to make use irreverently of scriptural language, although applied to the most ludicrous purpose. But it was not directed against Ministers, nor against the Established Church, and it seemed that in such cases alone was the use of scriptural language calculated to bring religion into contempt. To those, however, who dissented from the Church, or the Ministers, scriptural language could, it would seem, be applied with impunity. So it appeared from the parodies which he had quoted, as well as from the following passages in "The Weathercock,"[104] which was a farce not long since written:

Variella. Yea, verily, I saw a damsel, friend, clad in gaudy apparel.

Tristram Fickle. You say true; very gaudy and fantastical, unlike the modest attire which thy fair form gives grace to.

Var. [aside] So! so!

Tris. Zounds! what a most delectable creature she is! I was always fond of the Quakers. There is something so neat about them, such a charming modesty.—You did see that person then?

Var. Yea, the sight of her flaunting attire did offend my eyes.

Tris. 'Tis a pity such a pair of eyes should be offended. Poor conceited little ape! Why you look a thousand times better in that simple dress, than she did in all her frippery.

Var. I seek not to look well.

Tris. And therefore thou art a thousand times more lovely. For thy sake, fair maid, I will become a stiff Quaker. Wilt thou introduce me to thy con-ven-*ticle*?

Var. Yea; and it does rejoice me exceedingly, that the spirit doth move thee towards us—Hum!

Tris. Hum!

Var. And wilt thou listen to the good things which are said unto thee? Wilt thou learn therefrom? And wilt thou not sigh for the damsel in the colours of vanity?

Old Fickle. What is here? May I believe my eyes?

Trist. If they tell thee that thou seest before thee one of the faithful, verily thou mayst believe what they say, for they speak unto thee that which is true.

O. F . And you are turned Quaker?

Tris. Yea, a damsel hath wrought my conversion—yea, a fair damsel. Wilt thou give thy consent that I espouse her, and make her a thing of my own? Verily I do expect the damsel to join with me in the request, that we two may be made one.

Here there was the use of scriptural language tolerated on the stage, for the very purpose of ridiculing a most amiable and respectable class of Dissenters, the *Quakers;* yet this Farce had the sanction of the Lord Chamberlain. But, with facts before them, how could the Jury, whom he had the honour to address, or any body of respectable men, conclude, that he, in publishing the parody under prosecution, could suppose he was committing a criminal or an illegal act? The parodies, however, which he had quoted, and in reading which he feared he had trespassed upon the attention of the Jury, formed but a small part of those which he had it in his power to bring forward. He could, indeed, have covered the table with such compositions. How many could he have taken from Chalmers' Poets:[105] and was it meant, if he should be convicted, to have an *index expurgatoris* applied to this, and the numerous other works in our language which contained parodies upon the Scriptures? He referred to the History of the Westminster Election, in which Lord J. Townshend was a candidate, for a number of parodies from both sides.[106] Some of those parodies were probably from the pen of Mr. Canning, who had a notorious taste for such composition, and that Gentleman was, in the contest alluded to, a Member of the Committee for conducting Lord John Townshend's election. But he was a secret member; for this Gentleman was then ready to serve the Foxites, with whom he professed to concur, while he wished to conceal his operations from the Minister, whose patronage he was intriguing to obtain. Thus Mr. Canning played the same double game many years ago which he had lately performed towards his militant friend Lord Castlereagh. But how would the Jury feel, as honourable men, towards a prosecution instituted against him by the authority of this very Minister? Was he to be punished for imitating the example of Mr. Canning, in writing parodies, while that Gentleman enjoyed impunity and power? Was it becoming on the part of Mr. Canning, or of Lord Sidmouth, who was also, he understood, a party in the Westminster contest to which he had alluded, to institute this prosecution against him? But, independently of the parodies he could have quoted from the history of this contest, he could adduce many others from the first periodical publications. Who that had, for instance, been in the habit of reading *The Morning Chronicle,* could forget the many interesting parodies which appeared, especially in the early numbers of that excellent paper—yes, most excellent paper, he must call it; he meant for the character of its politics.

Mr. HONE here presented several prints which he had adduced on his previous trials. He exhibited M. Fuseli's celebrated print of "The Night Mare;" and then showed a parody upon it representing the Lord Mayor (Wood) as the night mayor (mare), upon the breast of a girl.[107] What, he would ask, did this parody ridicule? Was it Fuseli's print, or was it Alderman Wood? The Attorney-General had not prosecuted—for ridicule upon Alderman Wood was not unacceptable to Ministers. Did the Alderman bring an action? That excellent man, and able magistrate, had too much sense to do so. The print ridiculed his well-meant, though perhaps injudicious, efforts to clear the streets from prostitutes. By neglecting it he made it harmless. He was afraid that his Lordship would think the introduction of all the prints he had before him unmeaning.

Lord ELLENBOROUGH (*smiling*). I am afraid I may say so.

Mr. HONE. The object was to show that the design and effect in all those parodies were to impress something on the mind quite unconnected with the thing parodied, and that the thing parodied had suffered nothing from such an use of it.

Lord ELLENBOROUGH. The picture is ground for indictment.

Mr. HONE granted it; but what was gained by indicting? Where was a man more ridiculed than Sir William Curtis?[108] Yet he only bought as many as he saw of them, to laugh at them. Prosecution created a demand for the thing prosecuted; and, in consequence either of prosecution or suppression, curiosity was always excited to a publication supposed to be unattainable or scarce. When Mr. Horne Tooke's *Diversions of Purley* (a work which every man who knew the English language read and admired) was first published, it was in octavo.[109] A second edition in quarto was preparing, but, in the mean time, a well-known book-seller, still living, pirated the octavo edition, and sold it for one guinea the copy. It was thus that a great demand was created, by giving publicity to a work. He then read the subject of libel, and commented with great spirit and force upon the different parts of it. He would ask any man coolly to lay his hand on his breast, and to say that the Sinecurist's Creed was written with the design and intention to ridicule St. Athanasius's Creed. His Lordship was once a member of the Cabinet, and had differed on a great question of state from the other members. His Lordship was of one opinion, and the rest were of another opinion; yet there were not two Cabinets, but one Cabinet. Was this parodical phrase impiety? He had taken that mode of expressing truths which he could not otherwise have declared; for if he had attended the Prince Regent's levee, and in his presence called any of his Ministers incomprehensible, a fool, a humbug, or a mystificator, his Royal Highness might, perhaps, be of a different opinion. At least, his telling his thoughts in that way would be rather useless and unpleasant. He then exhibited several prints by Gillray, the Prodigal Son, representing two high personages; the Devil addressing the Sun, representing Buonaparte and the Prince Regent; the Hand-writing on the Wall, representing Buonaparte in the midst of his council; the ascent of Mr. Pitt, as Elijah; and General Hoche's apotheosis.[110] He now recapitulated the principal points of his defence. Luther had parodied the Bible, and yet no information had been filed against him. The Attorney-General and his Lordship had excused Luther as he had done it, in a moment of irritation, against persons who had been troublesome to him. Could not the same persons find any excuse for William Hone? He had been attacked as showing a bad example to his family. He had, indeed, written this parody in twenty minutes, while he held his infant on his knee. But let them recollect that Martin Luther had a family. He had not always continued a Monk. Yet he parodied the first Psalm. He was as pure as Luther, and claimed the same excuse. But no excuse was necessary, for there was no wrong done. Gillray was a parodist; he employed his transcendent talents in parodying Scripture for political purposes. In the ascent of Mr. Pitt, as Elijah, George Canning was represented as catching the dropping mantle. Fox, the most humane, the best man that ever sat in an English Cabinet, was represented on a dunghill, with a Jacobin red cap on his head. He wished Mr. Fox's spirit predominated now in our counsels, and the nation would be in a far different state. The power of government would not be made execrable by the persecution of an innocent and defenceless man. O the persecutors, the persecutors, the persecutors, that obliged him now to stand the third day on his trial! Why did they not, to save Mr. Canning's character, abstain from this prosecution? Mr. Canning would have thanked them, and said, "Hone is a poor fellow; I am a parodist too: this prosecution is a nasty thing; I don't like it." There was Lord Sidmouth, a grave, a good, a religious, and surely a charitable man; there was Lord Ellenborough, a very grave man (*his Lordship could not resist a smile here*); why did they not step forward to help a poor oppressed man? O no! he could not stand three days; their united force would surely crush the insect! No, he defied their powers. They could only immortalize him. He would at least go down to posterity with George Canning. If this Right Honourable parodist ascended after Mr. Pitt, he would lay hold of his left leg, and ascend along with him. They would perhaps have spared him this third trial, if he had implored their mercy. But no; he disclaimed, he anathematized their mercy. They were below the contempt of William Hone, the humble bookseller of No. 67, in the Old Bailey. Walter Scott had edited the parody of Lord Somers.[111] Why was he not prosecuted? O no! this Mr. Scott, a man of great talents, was ministerial, and had held a little ogling for the laureateship with Robert Southey, who was plain Robert Southey, when he wrote Wat Tyler, and such publications as displeased Ministers. He was now a pensioner and Robert Southey, *Esq.*[112] He (Mr. Hone) had occasion, when he edited the Critical Review, which he did for six months, to see the Stuart Papers.[113] They were published by the librarian to the Prince Regent. There was no prosecution against that gentleman publishing a partial and insidious apology for those tyrants. No; a great deal of the spirit of 'the bonny king and mickle wise mon' was still to be perceived. The Stuarts must be excused and spoken gently of; they must not be talked of as the tyrants, the hypocrites, the bloody-minded persecutors they really were. Such language was unacceptable to courtly taste. Mr. Reeves had parodied the Catechism, but afterwards obtained a pension.[114] But his politics were different. Royalty had singled *him* (Mr. Hone) out for *persecution,* on account of his politics. He could not pretend to have become known to Royalty, but Ministers would make him known. This was entirely a political prosecution. Lord Sidmouth had before tried his hand at persecution, when he brought in his bill against the Dissenters. The same noble Lord left him to stand three days in that Court. When such a man was Secretary of State, there was very little chance of the liberty of England being protected. The Morning Herald, of the 4th of May, 1812, parodied Scripture to ridicule Lord Grenville,[115] but it was for and on behalf of Ministers, and there was no prosecution. The language of Ministers was, "Every thing must be done to keep down those confounded fellows, the Whigs, curse them." The people were taxed to pay these expenses. He, poor as he was, contributed to pay the secret service money. Every morsel of bread that went into his children's mouths was taxed for the paltry purposes of his pitiful Prosecutors. He now made a solemn appeal to his conscience as to the innocence of his intentions. He would submit to be posted up as a liar, and to bend his head whenever he walked in public, if he once uttered there, or any where else, what he did not believe to be true. Upon his conscience, then, he assured them, that he had no more intention to ridicule St. Athanasius's Creed, than he had now of murdering his wife and children when he went home; for he was sure the Jury would send him home to his family. He knew none of them: but he hoped, and he believed that they were honest-minded and independent men. The Sinecurist's Creed had an extraordinary sale, but not so extraordinary as the Litany. However, he stopped it, from the motives he had mentioned. He confidently put himself under their protection. As to St. Athanasius's Creed, Gibbon stated that it was not written by Athanasius.[116] Some said that it was in fact a parody upon his creed, and written by Vigilius,[117] four centuries after Athanasius had died. Warburton expressly states that it was not his. Waterland mentions that it was doubted. Archbishop Tillotson on one occasion exclaimed, "I wish we were well rid of it;" and in recent days, upwards of 200 Clergymen met, and solicited the late Dr. Porteus, Bishop of London, to take some steps to put an end to the obligation at present imposed on them to read it. Even his Lordship's father, the Bishop of Carlisle,[118] he believed took a similar view of the creed. ——

Lord ELLENBOROUGH.—I do not know what his opinion was on this point; you, perhaps, have had better opportunity of knowing his belief.

Whatever that opinion was, he has gone many years ago, where he has had to account for his belief and his opinions.

Mr. HONE was about to make some particular references to the Bishop of Carlisle's opinions, when

Lord ELLENBOROUGH interrupted him, and said, "For common delicacy forbear"——

Mr. HONE—(*In a subdued and respectful tone*),—O, my Lord, I shall most certainly! Sure he was, that this creed was not generally believed even by churchmen.

Lord ELLENBOROUGH.—It is not alleged to be Athanasius's Creed here. It is said only to be commonly called the Creed of St. Athanasius.

Mr. HONE.—Then it would seem to be the Attorney-General's opinion, from the form of the information to which your Lordship has just referred, that the Athanasian Creed is *apocryphal,* and cannot be viewed as genuine by my Prosecutors.

Lord ELLENBOROUGH.—Yes; but the Act of Uniformity[119] made it that which it is now described to be.

Mr. HONE.—The Act of Uniformity! God forbid that the Act of Uniformity could have had the effect of making this what it is deemed to be, from its import, by some persons. God forbid that this Act could make all men think alike on such a subject as this.

Lord ELLENBOROUGH.—It is not intended to have that effect. It merely operates to create uniformity amongst those who conform to certain religious opinions. It is not intended to compel those of a different persuasion to believe it.

Be it so (resumed Mr. Hone); whether this creed were written by St. Athanasius or not, he was not himself prepared to state. He had intended to read a speech made by the Bishop of Clogher[120] on this creed, but it was long, and not essentially material to the case; for the question here was, whether the publication before the Court was meant to bring that creed into contempt, and to that he could give the most conscientious negative. But the Jury would, he had no doubt, consider, not the tendency, but the intention. They were not bound to follow his Lordship's opinion. If his Lordship's opinion were adopted, he should at once have to walk to the King's Bench. To the Jury he looked, and to them alone, for protection; for from them alone could he expect aid or advice; and he took leave to observe that it would answer the ends of justice to pay more attention to what he said, than to what might be urged by the Judge or the Attorney-General. He had declared that he had no intention to publish a libel, and this declaration was entitled to credit upon this ground, which he would undertake to affirm was the law of the land, namely, that the production before the Court was not a libel, until the Jury had so pronounced it. With them alone the power of making that decision rested; and he appealed to them as men, as Christians, as men and brethren, to consider what he had said. For whether they differed from him in political or religious opinions, he trusted they would, in the spirit of justice and Christian charity, examine his case, and consider the terrible sentence that awaited him if they should find a verdict against him. He might happen to differ in political opinions from many of the Gentlemen of the Jury, but he hoped that they would feel that tolerant spirit towards him which he himself had always practised and recommended to others. For he never could conceive any man entitled to that infallibility, which, by some people, was attributed to the Pope; and without such arrogance no man would attempt to prescribe or censure those who conscientiously differed from his opinions. Were such a practice indeed indulged, perpetual disputes must arise, harmony be destroyed, and men be reduced to the savage state. But the liberality that was especially of late years so widely spreading, promised to guard the world from such a state of discord and misery. Differences on politics and religion were not now found to interfere with the charities of social life, or the performance of moral duties, and therefore he could not apprehend that prejudice could be found to operate in the breast of any Englishman acting under the solemn obligation of an oath. He felt the most unqualified confidence in the principles and judgment of the Jury, whose attention, he feared, he had too long occupied. But he felt that he was struggling for life, for should he have the misfortune to be pronounced guilty by the Jury, the punishment which awaited him would be equal to the loss of it. In such a struggle he fancied himself gifted with supernatural powers, but he feared he had trespassed too much upon the time of the Court. He had, however, no disposition to give offence, and this he begged to be understood. He might have been in some instances too eager or peremptory in replying to the Judge and the Attorney-General, but he most sincerely assured his Lordship and the Learned Gentleman, that he had no intention whatever to offend. Feeling that his all was at stake, he hoped he should be excused for the many materials he had brought forward, perhaps unnecessarily. He could still go to the King's Bench, and lay his head down there with the greatest composure, but for his family. If the Jury

felt doubts, they would be reasonable doubts, and they knew that he
was entitled to the benefit of them. He committed himself to them. The
liberty of the press was attacked through him. The prosecution had
nothing but a political ground-work. Two Juries of cool honest men had
already acquitted him. He had no doubt but they, too, would send him
home to dine on Sunday with his family.

After a speech of precisely eight hours and five minutes, he concluded, amid the applause of the immense multitude that crowded the
Court and all the passages to it.

Mr. HONE declined to adduce the witnesses who proved on the former trials that he had stopped the publication of the parodies as soon
as he understood that they were deemed libellous by Government, upon
Lord Ellenborough's undertaking to read his notes of that evidence to
the Jury. The notes were read by his Lordship, and Mr. HONE called

THOMAS CLEARY, Esq. who deposed, that on the 21st of February (a
day he had reason to remember), he met Mr. Hone near Charing-cross,
who stated to Witness his intention of stopping the publication of the
parodies, as they had been called, in the Report of the House of Lords,
profane and seditious, or something to that effect. That Witness remarked, their being so characterized in the Report, did not make them
profane or seditious, and strongly recommended Mr. Hone not to take
what Witness considered so ill-advised a step; as it would by implica-
tion be an admission that he (Mr. Hone) considered the parodies profane and seditious, while nobody but the Borough-mongers so
considered them. That notwithstanding this advice, Hone stopped the
publication the following day; for which Witness told him he was a fool.

The ATTORNEY-GENERAL rose to reply.—He observed upon the remark of Mr. Hone, as to the division of the charges against him into
three informations, stating, that such proceeding was agreeable to practice, especially where the publications charged as libellous were quite
distinct and separate, as was the case in this instance.—Therefore the
Defendant had no right to complain, and still less could he warrant the
complaint which he had made, of having the present trial brought forward to-day, after two days of previous trials. For it must be in the recollection of the Court, that before the Jury were sworn, he proposed to
postpone this trial, in consequence of an understanding that Mr. Hone
was indisposed, from the fatigue of the two preceding days, and that
that gentleman declined to avail himself of the proposition.—Were Mr.
Hone unequal to make his defence, or did he feel unable to proceed, he

could have had time for repose and recovery; and therefore he could not attribute to the Counsel for the prosecution, the slightest disposition to subject him to any unnecessary inconvenience. But the propriety of persisting in this prosecution, notwithstanding the previous acquittals of Mr. Hone upon similar charges, would, he hoped, be felt by every reflecting mind, from the very principle upon which Mr. Hone had rested his defence this day; for Mr. Hone had distinctly asserted his right to publish the paper which was under prosecution, and, having stood upon that ground, he (the Attorney-General) should have felt himself guilty of gross dereliction of duty, if he had not persevered in this prosecution. On the former days, the Defendant, with a view to induce a belief that he had no intention to publish a libel, rested particularly upon his stoppage of the publication of the parodies, but to-day he had openly contended for his right to publish them. But if this plea of right were admitted, what was to prevent the Defendant from publishing those parodies again on Monday? He would not say, that the Defendant expressed or entertained any such intention, but if his claim of right were admitted, what was to prevent him or any other person from republishing this parody? and to abandon the present prosecution would be tantamount to an admission of that claim. What a serious responsibility, then, should he incur, if he exposed the cause of religion, and of the country, to the evils too likely to result from such an admission. What a door would be opened for the incursion of profaneness. In his notions of the duty of a Judge upon the trial of libel, he undertook to say that Mr. Hone was quite mistaken. For the Judge derived no authority from the statute, commonly called Mr. Fox's, which he did not possess before. His Lordship had unquestionably the right of stating his opinion upon the law to the Jury, upon this as well as upon every other question; and if he did not enjoy that right, what would become of the function and office of a Judge? But the Judge was invested with the power of stating the law upon the subject of libel, with a view to guard against inconsistent decisions, or the establishment of capricious conceptions, as to the principles of the law. Besides, by the statute alluded to, provision was made peculiarly favourable to the accused, if any special verdict were found, or any appeal made to the Judges upon the finding of a verdict against him contrary to law. But the Defendant seemed entirely to misunderstand the character and object of the statute. Now as to the question before the Court, the Defendant had adduced a number of parodies, some of which were even worse than that which he had himself published, and none of which were such as he (the Attorney-General) was disposed to defend. Being of opinion that the more becoming course was to reserve scriptural language for appropriate purposes, he could not approve of its application to different objects. Then as to the prints, it might be that the caricature of Mr. Fuseli's Night-mare was meant merely to ridicule the late Lord Mayor, but even so it was an indictable publication. So would any print, reflecting upon an individual. But if any painter were to make a ludicrous application of the sufferings of our Saviour, who could doubt that such application would outrage the feelings of every Christian, and amount to a profane libel? So if any one who should parody the paintings of Rubens, or Mr. West,[121] upon sacred subjects, he would be indictable for a profane libel; for no man would be justified in exciting mirth, or ridicule, or prejudice, through the medium of sacred subjects. So of certain obscene airs, which were too familar to the vulgar, and which he was sorry to have ever heard were applied to the Psalms of David, such an application would be profane. As to the parodies quoted from Luther and others, he heard them with regret; but they were the effusions of excessive zeal, and he apprehended that zeal in excess was generally vice. Of the parodies adduced by Mr. Hone, he thought it proper to take some notice. First, as to that from Mr. John Reeves, it was clear that it was not the object of that parody to bring religion into contempt, although Scriptural phrases were made use of, from which it would have been better to abstain. The same might be said of the parody from Mr. Toplady. But there were other parodies adduced by Mr. Hone, which all Christians must condemn—must review indeed with disgust and abhorrence. With respect to the "Tales of my Landlord," Mr. Walter Scott had no doubt made use of a great deal of scriptural language, which, however, was put into the mouths of zealots, at a time that such language was much more familiar than in modern times. But yet the object of this language was by no means to bring religion into contempt. On the contrary, the evident end of the author was to ridicule fanaticism, and to expose the artifice of hypocrites, who sought to palliate vice and knavery by the use of scriptural language. Mr. Hone was therefore mistaken in supposing the "Tales of my Landlord" any precedent for his system of parody, or any excuse for his conduct. He was also mistaken in his conception of the several acts of the legislature with respect to toleration; for no act, either ancient or modern, tolerated that which was forbidden by the common law, namely, railing or scoffing at the Trinity, or the Ritual of the Church. To illustrate this, the Learned Gentleman referred to the Acts of James I. Charles I. and Charles II. upon the subject of religious toleration. As to the paper before the Court, the Learned Gentleman read several passages of it, from which he argued that its object was to ridicule the Creed of St. Athanasius, which was a part of the Church Ritual. The whole, he thought, evidently a scoffing at the Trinity, in the terms of "Old Bags, Derry Down Triangle, and the Doctor." But Mr. Hone had said that he did not intend to ridicule the Trinity or the Creed of St. Athanasius; but a man's intention was to be judged by his acts or their effects, and not by what he declares to be his intention. For, if the declaration of an intention on the part of the accused were to be taken as evidence, no one accused would ever be found guilty. But so far indeed from that being the conception of the law, there was a case in the books where a man who had thrown a piece of wood from the top of a house into the street, was found guilty of murder, because that wood killed a passenger upon whom it had fallen. Therefore, the law would not excuse any one who committed a crime, whatever might be said as to his intention. The man who flung down the wood had most probably no intention to kill the passenger, but then he was bound not to do that from which mischief was likely to accrue. So Mr. Hone was answerable for the evil but too likely to result from that publication which he deliberately published; for it could avail nothing to any man to make protestations of innocent intention, while he scattered about his firebrands and arrows of death. The Jury would recollect, that the object of prosecution was to repress offences. Blackstone had very properly observed, that the end of punishment was not to afflict individuals, but to prevent offences. Such, and such alone, he declared to be the object and end of the present prosecution. For he had no personal animosity whatever towards Mr. Hone; but he felt it his duty to the public to institute this prosecution, with a view to prevent the issue of such publications in future as were calculated to undermine the religion of the country, and so to destroy the basis of morality, comfort, happiness, and prosperity.

Lord ELLENBOROUGH then charged the Jury. He pronounced the complaint of the Defendant as to his peculiar grievances, in consequence of the conduct of the present prosecution, to be entirely groundless. It was the duty of the Attorney-General to institute this prosecution; and although the defendant was right in his opinion, that the Attorney-General might include different charges in the same indictment, yet it was indisputably at his discretion to do so; and the course the Learned Gentleman had taken was agreeable to practice. The Defendant appeared to think that libels upon the Scriptures formed a sort of composition exempted by law from prosecution or punishment; but the cases of Woolston and Paine[122] should have informed him that his impression was unfounded; so was his assertion that there was no law of libel; for from the earliest records that law had existed, and been well understood by the Judges. The act of Mr. Fox, as it was called, had indeed made no change in that law. That was no doubt a proper legislative provision. Chief Justice Eyre[123] had stated, that if the Jury had only the power of deciding upon the fact of publication, the printer of the libel itself might be liable to conviction for libel. He thought the case put by that Learned Judge quite too strong, because the interposition of the Judge must in such a case serve to prevent a verdict; but still he approved of the statute. In this statute, however, there was nothing to prevent a libel from being tried like all other offences, in which the Judge was called upon to state his opinion upon the law to the Jury. For, according to his construction of the Statute, the Judge was bound to state his opinion upon such prosecutions, and that was also the construction of his learned predecessor; otherwise, indeed, the functions of a Judge would cease in such a case. Mr. Hone had, no doubt, told the Jury, not to attend to the opinion of the Judge, and he might think himself justified in so saying. Unquestionably the Jury were not bound to adopt the opinion, or follow the advice of the Judge; but without wishing to invade their province, he felt himself imperatively called upon to perform his duty, by stating his opinion upon the paper under prosecution. After that opinion was stated, it would be for the Jury, from a calm and candid review, as well as of that opinion, as of the paper charged as a libel, to declare their judgment. The main defence was parodies written by other men at different times. The Exciseman's Creed was very offensive. In Bishop Latimer's time much greater familarity was used in public discourses than at the present period. The parodies quoted by the Defendant appeared to his mind to offer nothing in defence of the paper before the Court, which was in fact worse than any of those parodies, even bad as they were. But if the mode of defence pursued by the Defendant were valid, what criminal could be convicted? For there was not one offender perhaps, who could not quote 100 instances in which persons committing the offence with which he stood charged had escaped with impunity. Mr. Hone had, he apprehended, very truly conceived, that if he had employed any Barrister, the course of defence upon which he had determined would not be followed up by such Barrister; for from his (Lord E's) experience of the profession, he did not think that there was a gentleman at the bar, who would outrage decency and propriety so far as to exhibit such disgusting parodies and prints, or at least persist in such exhibitions, especially after the Judge had expressed his decided disapprobation of them. God knows that he (Lord E.) had no wish to do the Defendant or any other man an injury, but he felt it due to the ends of public justice and the preservation of individual character, to interpose occasionally his advice to Mr. Hone. Finding that advice, however, unavailing, he had declined to interfere, and let the Defendant pursue his own course. But yet he called upon the Jury not to allow the numerous libels which Mr. Hone had thought proper to read, or the gross calumnies which he had uttered against individuals, to operate upon their mind in considering the question, whether the paper before them was or was not a profane libel. The Defendant had repeatedly declared that he had no intention to publish a libel in sending forth this paper, but upon that point the observations of the Attorney-General were perfectly just, for the law always concludes as to the intent of any man from his act; and here the question being, whether the Defendant intended to bring into ridicule the Athanasian Creed, the Jury were to decide that question from a review of the paper before them, and not from the declarations of the Defendant. Here the learned Lord read the Parody itself, and expressing his belief that the terms of "Old Bags, Derry Down Triangle, and the Doctor," were meant to be applied to some public men, commented on each article as he proceeded. The only question for them was, whether this was a libel. Did it force ludicrous and absurd images into the mind when the Creed was read? The Father was Old Bags, the Son was Derry Down Triangle, the Holy Ghost was the Doctor. The Defendant asked whom the laugh excited by this was against? But although the laugh might be against the persons represented under those terms, did not the Father, the Son, and the Holy Ghost, form a part of the association in this laugh? If they found that there was a mixed profanity of this kind in the subject of the libel, they must find a verdict of guilty; if both the subject and the object of the parody were made ridiculous in the conjunction, they must come to this conclusion. He had not a doubt that the parody before them was a profane and impious libel. This paper was not charged as a political libel, and therefore it must be found as a profane libel, which it was described in the record. His Lordship entreated the Jury to consider the importance of the case which they were called upon to decide—that the temporal comforts and spiritual interests of their countrymen might defend their verdict. He begged them to recollect, that if such publications as that before them were not prohibited and punished, the country was too liable to be deluged by irreligion and impiety, which had so lately produced such melancholy results in another nation. The Learned Lord, after some comment upon the Defendant's stoppage of this publication, which fact would no doubt have due weight upon those who, in the event of a verdict of conviction, would be called upon to pronounce sentence, observed that it should have no weight whatever with the Jury.

The Jury retired at half-past eight to consider their verdict.

In twenty minutes the Jury returned into Court, and the foreman, after the usual forms had been observed, pronounced Mr. Hone NOT GUILTY.

The moment the verdict was announced, a spontaneous burst of applause issued from the crowd in the Court.

This soon extended to the crowd without; and for some minutes the Hall and adjoining avenues rung with the loudest acclamations. The crowd waited for some time for Mr. Hone, in order to greet him as he passed. By an intended manœuvre, however, two groups passed out, in one of which it was expected he was, and it was cheered accordingly. He afterwards passed out through the immense multitude, alone and unnoticed.

During the absence of the Jury, a gentleman was brought into Court in the custody of the Chief and Deputy Marshals of the City, charged with riotous conduct on the steps leading from Guildhall to the Court. It appeared, that towards the close of the evening a prodigious crowd of persons, amounting to the number of not less than 20,000, had assembled in the Hall, and in the avenues leading thereto. Many of these persons were desirous of forcing their way into the Court, but their efforts were resisted. Among others, the gentleman now brought forward. He attempted to push up the steps, when Mr. Wontner, the Chief Marshal, told him he could not pass. He replied that it was an open Court, and he had a right to admission. This observation attracted the attention of the crowd, which moved towards the spot. Mr. Wontner then said, if he questioned his authority to prevent his entrance, he must take him before Lord Ellenborough. With this view, he laid his hand on his arm, when a scuffle ensued, and some disturbance, which ended by two of the officers being struck, and one of them knocked down, principally, as it was stated, through the conduct of the prisoner. These facts were proved by several Witnesses. The gentleman on being called on for his defence, stated his name to be Mr. Thomas Wetherell; that he had been five years at King's College, Cambridge, and had but recently returned from the West Indies. He had certainly attempted to come up the steps, and did not conceive he was acting improperly by attempting to enter an open Court. The City Marshal had laid hold of his arm, and in attempting to extricate himself from his grasp, all the subsequent confusion happened.—A gentleman named Marsh corroborated this statement.

Lord Ellenborough fined Mr. Wetherell twenty pounds, and directed that he should be detained in custody till the fine was paid.

On Thursday, the first day's Trial, before Mr. Justice Abbott, Mr. Hone spoke near six hours. On Friday, the second day's Trial, he spoke near seven hours. On Saturday, the third day, he spoke in his defence upwards of eight hours.

PART TWO

—

SATIRES

—

Between 1819 and 1821 the prolific collaboration of William Hone and George Cruikshank produced "no fewer than sixteen pamphlets, some of which sold in excess of a hundred thousand copies" (Robert L. Patten, *George Cruikshank's Life, Times, and Art* [New Brunswick, N.J.: Rutgers University Press, 1992], 144). These pamphlets drew on a wide variety of popular forms, were astonishingly successful, and became, at this time, "the most widely circulated of all illustrated political literature" (Patricia Anderson, *The Printed Image and the Transformation of Popular Culture 1790–1860* [Oxford: Clarendon Press, 1990], 36). Recited in coffee- and alehouses, on the street, and at reformist meetings (Kyle Grimes, "Spreading the Radical Word: The Circulation of William Hone's 1817 Liturgical Parodies," in *Radicalism and Revolution in Britain, 1775–1848*, ed. Michael T. Davis [London: Macmillan, 2000], 146–50), they vigorously and hilariously attacked the government while affirming central reform objectives such as freedom of the press.

Of the four illustrated satires printed below, *The Political House that Jack Built* was the most popular and influential, going through forty editions in 1819 and thirteen more over the following two years (Bowden, "Hone's Political Journalism," 1:244). The immediate occasion for the publication was Hone's outrage at the Peterloo Massacre in Manchester on 19 August 1819. Like its successors and its imitations, *The Political House* married a relatively short text (in this instance based on a nursery rhyme that had been frequently adapted) with a striking illustration in a simple but boldly impudent manner. For someone like Southey, *The Political House* was a sign that the "tendency of the age is plainly toward revolution," and he asserted that such a publication ought to be "prosecuted immediately on its appearance" (*Selections from the Letters of Robert Southey*, ed. John Wood Walter [1856; reprint, New York: AMS Press, 1977], 3:176, 177). The Prince Regent, a central target of the satire, did indeed want to have Hone prosecuted again, but he was persuaded that this would not be a prudent course of action (Patten, 165).

The Queen's Matrimonial Ladder (August) and *Non Mi Ricordo* (September) were both pamphlets connected with the 1820 trial of

Princess Caroline and her efforts to become Queen when her husband was crowned George IV. The first of these, its success (forty-four editions in 1820: Bowden, 2:319) second only to *The Political House,* uses a children's toy to trace the treatment of Caroline. The second cross-examines the Regent about his personal behaviour and attributes the phrase "Non mi ricordo" ("I don't remember") to him; the response had been repeated some eighty times by an Italian witness, Teodoro Majocchi, who was believed to have been paid for his services by the prosecution. This pamphlet reached thirty-one editions before year's end (Bowden, 2:326). Two pages of bogus, pun-filled advertisements in this pamphlet have been omitted.

The Political Showman—At Home! was published in April 1821 and went through twenty-seven editions (Bowden, 2:390). The showman is actually a printing press which is personified and brought to life. Freedom of the press is strongly asserted in the face of harsh, repressive legislation from a ruthless government. There are more illustrations in *The Political Showman* than in any of the earlier pamphlets, and they picture a menagerie of often grotesque creatures. The more than one hundred quotations (most often from Cowper and Shakespeare but also from works on natural history) that form the texts and allusive framework for the piece were another ingenious strategy to avoid prosecution.

THE POLITICAL

HOUSE

THAT

JACK BUILT.

"A straw—thrown up to show which way the wind blows."[1]

WITH THIRTEEN CUTS.

The Pen and the Sword.

𝕱𝖎𝖋𝖙𝖞-𝖙𝖍𝖎𝖗𝖉 𝕰𝖉𝖎𝖙𝖎𝖔𝖓.

LONDON:
PRINTED BY AND FOR WILLIAM HONE,
LUDGATE HILL.
1821.

ONE SHILLING.

——"Many, whose sequester'd lot
Forbids their interference, looking on,
Anticipate perforce some dire event;
And, seeing the old castle of the state,
That promis'd once more firmness, so assail'd,
That all its tempest-beaten turrets shake,
Stand motionless expectants of its fall."

COWPER.[2]

NOTE.

Each Motto that follows, is from Cowper's "Task."

"A distant age asks where the fabric stood."[4]

THIS IS THE HOUSE THAT JACK BUILT.

—"Not to understand a treasure's worth,
Till time has stolen away the slighted good,
Is cause of half the poverty we feel,
And makes the world the wilderness it is."[5]

THIS IS

THE WEALTH

that lay

In the House that Jack built.

————"A race obscene,
Spawn'd in the muddy beds of Nile, came forth,
Polluting Egypt: gardens, fields, and plains,
Were cover'd with the pest;
The croaking nuisance lurk'd in every nook;
Nor palaces, nor even chambers, scap'd;
And the land stank—so num'rous was the fry."[6]

THESE ARE

THE VERMIN

That plunder the Wealth,

That lay in the House,

That Jack built.

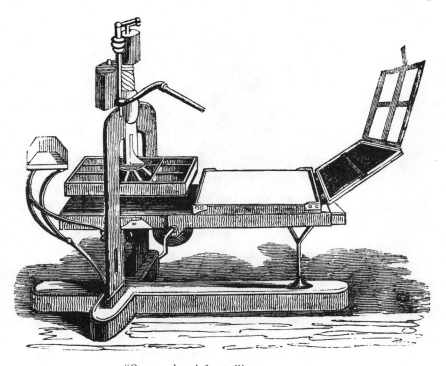

"Once enslaved, farewell!

* * * * * *

Do I forbode impossible events,
And tremble at vain dreams? Heav'n grant I may!"[7]

THIS IS

THE THING,

that in spite of new Acts
And attempts to restrain it,
by Soldiers or Tax,
Will *poison* the Vermin,
That plunder the Wealth,
That lay in the House,
That Jack built.

"The seals of office glitter in his eyes
He climbs, he pants, he grasps them—
To be a pest where he was useful once:"[8]

THIS IS

THE PUBLIC INFORMER,

who

Would put down the *Thing*,

that, in spite of new Acts,

And attempts to restrain it,

by Soldiers or tax,

Will *poison* the Vermin, that plunder the Wealth,

That lay in the House, that Jack built.

"Ruffians are abroad—

*   *   *   *

Leviathan is not *so* tamed."[9]

THESE ARE

THE *REASONS* OF LAWLESS POWER,
That back the Public Informer,
who
Would put down the *Thing*,
that, in spite of new Acts,
And attempts to restrain it,
by Soldiers or Tax,
Will *poison* the Vermin,
That plunder the Wealth,
That lay in the House,
That Jack built.

——"Great offices will have
Great talents."[10]

**This is THE MAN—all shaven and shorn,
All cover'd with Orders—and all forlorn;**

THE DANDY OF SIXTY,
who bows with a grace
And has *taste* in wigs, collars,
cuirasses, and lace;
Who, to tricksters and fools,
leaves the State and its treasure,
And, when Britain's in tears,
sails about at his pleasure,
Who spurn'd from his presence
the Friends of his youth,[11]
And now has not one
who will tell him the truth;
Who took to his counsels,
in evil hour,
The Friends to the Reasons
of lawless Power;
That back the Public Informer
who
Would put down the *Thing*,
that, in spite of new Acts,
And attempts to restrain it,
by Soldiers or Tax,
Will *poison* the Vermin,
That plunder the Wealth,
That lay in the House,
That Jack built.

"Portentous, unexampled, unexplain'd!
————————What man seeing this,
And having human feelings, does not blush,
And hang his head, to think himself a man?
————————I cannot rest
A silent witness of the headlong rage,
Or heedless folly, by which thousands die—
Bleed gold for Ministers to sport away."[12]

THESE ARE

THE PEOPLE

        all tatter'd and torn,

Who curse the day

        wherein they were born,

On account of Taxation

        too great to be borne,

And pray for relief,

        from night to morn:

Who, in vain, Petition

        in every form,

Who, peaceably Meeting
>> to ask for Reform,
Were sabred by Yeomanry Cavalry,[13]
>> who
Were thank'd by THE MAN,
>> all shaven and shorn,
All cover'd with Orders—
>> and all forlorn;
THE DANDY OF SIXTY,
>> who bows with a grace,
And has *taste* in wigs, collars,
>> cuirasses, and lace:
Who, to tricksters and fools,
>> leaves the state and its treasure,
And, when Britain's in tears,
>> sails about at his pleasure:
Who spurn'd from his presence
>> the Friends of his youth,
And now has not one
>> who will tell him the truth;
Who took to his counsels, in evil hour,
The Friends to the Reasons of lawless Power,
That back the Public Informer, who
Would put down the *Thing*, that, in spite of new Acts,
And attempts to restrain it, by Soldiers or Tax,
Will *poison* the Vermin, that plunder the Wealth,
That lay in the House, that Jack built.

THE DOCTOR.
"At his last gasp—as if with opium drugg'd."
DERRY-DOWN TRIANGLE.
"He that sold his country."
THE SPOUTER OF FROTH.
"With merry descants on a nation's woes—
There is a public mischief in his mirth."

———————

THE GUILTY TRIO.
"Great skill have they in *palmistry*, and more
To conjure clean away the gold they touch,
Conveying worthless dross into its place;
Loud when they beg, dumb only when they steal.
    *   *   *   *
————————————Dream after dream ensues!
And still they dream, that they shall still succeed,
And still are disappointed."[14]

———————

This is THE DOCTOR
of *Circular* fame,
A Driv'ller, a Bigot, a Knave
without shame:

And *that's* DERRY DOWN TRIANGLE
        by name,
From the Land of mis-rule,
        and half-hanging, and flame:
And *that* is THE SPOUTER OF FROTH
        BY THE HOUR,
The worthless colleague
        of their infamous power:
Who dubb'd *him* 'the Doctor'
        whom now he calls 'brother,'
And, to get at his Place,
        took a shot at the other;[15]
Who haunts their *Bad House*,
        a base living to earn,
By playing Jack-pudding,[16] and Ruffian,
        in turn;
Who bullies, for those
        whom he bullied before;
Their *Flash*-man, their Bravo,[17]
        a son of a————;
The hate of the People,
        all tatter'd and torn,
Who curse the day
        wherein they were born,
On account of Taxation
        too great to be borne,
And pray for relief
        from night to morn;

Who, in vain, petition
       in every form:
Who peaceably Meeting
       to ask for Reform,
Were sabred by Yeomanry Cavalry,
       who
Were thank'd by THE MAN,
       all shaven and shorn,
All cover'd with Orders—
       and all forlorn;
THE DANDY OF SIXTY,
       who bows with a grace,
And has *taste* in wigs, collars,
       cuirasses and lace:
Who to tricksters and fools,
       leaves the State and its treasure,
And, when Britain's in tears,
       sails about at his pleasure:
Who spurn'd from his presence
       the Friends of his youth,
And now has not one
       who will tell him the truth;
Who took to his counsels, in evil hour,
The Friends to the Reasons of lawless Power;
That back the Public Informer, who
Would put down the *Thing*, that, in spite of new
       Acts,
And attempts to restrain it, by Soldiers or Tax,
Will *poison* the Vermin, that plunder the Wealth
That lay in the House, that Jack built.

————"Burghers, men immaculate perhaps
In all their private functions, once combin'd,
Become a loathsome body, only fit
For dissolution.
————————Power usurp'd
Is weakness when oppos'd; conscious of wrong,
'Tis pusillanimous and prone to flight.
————————I could endure
Chains nowhere patiently; and chains at home,
Where I am free by birthright, not at all."[18]

This **WORD** is the Watchword—
the talisman word,
That the **WATERLOO-MAN**'s to crush
with his sword;[19]

But, if shielded by NORFOLK
> and BEDFORD's alliance,
It will set both his sword,
> and him at defiance;
If FITZWILLIAM, and GROSVENOR, and
> ALBERMARLE aid it,
And assist its best Champions,
> who then dare invade it?[20]
'Tis the terrible WORD OF FEAR,
> night and morn,
To the *Guilty Trio*,
> all cover'd with scorn;
First, to the Doctor,
> of *Circular* fame.
A Driv'ller, a Bigot, a Knave
> without shame:
And next, Derry Down Triangle
> by name,
From the Land of Mis-rule,
> and Half-hanging, and Flame:
And then, to the Spouter of Froth
> by the hour,
The worthless colleague
> of their infamous power;
Who dubb'd *him* 'the Doctor,'
> whom now he calls 'brother',
And to get at his Place,
> took a shot at the other;

Who haunts their *Bad House*,
   a base living to earn,
By playing Jack-Pudding, and Ruffian,
   in turn;
Who bullies for those,
   whom he bullied before;
Their *Flash*-man, their Bravo,
   a son of a——;
The hate of the People,
   all tatter'd and torn,
Who curse the day
   wherein they were born
On account of Taxation
   too great to be borne,
And pray for relief,
   from night to morn;
Who, in vain, Petition
   in every form,
Who peaceably Meeting,
   to ask for Reform,
Were sabred by Yeomanry Cavalry,
   who
Were thank'd by THE MAN,
   all shaven and shorn,
All cover'd with Orders—
   and all forlorn;
THE DANDY OF SIXTY,
   who bows with a grace,

And has *taste* in wigs, collars,
              cuirasses and lace;
Who, to tricksters and fools,
              leaves the State and its treasure,
And, when Britain's in tears,
              sails about at his pleasure;
Who spurn'd from his presence
              the Friends of his youth,
and now has not one
              who will tell him the Truth;
Who took to his counsels,
              in evil hour,
The friends to the Reasons
              of lawless Power;
That back the Public Informer,
              who
Would put down the Thing
              that, in spite of new Acts,
And attempts to restrain it
              by Soldiers or Tax,
Will *poison* the Vermin
That plunder the Wealth,
That lay in the House,
That Jack built.

END OF THE HOUSE THAT JACK BUILT.

THE CLERICAL MAGISTRATE.[21]

The Bishop. Will you be diligent in Prayers—laying aside the study of the
  world and the flesh?—*Priest.* I will.
The Bishop. Will you maintain and set forwards, as much as lieth in you,
  quietness, peace, and love, among all Christian people?—*Priest.* I will.
¶ The Bishop laying his hand upon the head of him that receiveth the order
  of Priesthood, shall say, "RECEIVE THE HOLY GHOST."
                                        The Form of Ordination for a Priest.

--------"The pulpit (in the sober use
Of its legitimate peculiar pow'rs)
Must stand acknowledg'd, while the world shall stand,
The most important and effectual guard,
Support, and ornament of virtue's cause.
 *   *   *   *
Behold the picture! Is it like?"[22]

THIS IS A PRIEST,

made 'according to Law,'

Who, on being ordain'd, vow'd, by rote, like a daw,

That he felt himself call'd, by the Holy Spirit,

To teach men the Kingdom of Heaven to merit;

That, to think of the World and the flesh he'd cease,

And keep men in quietness, love, and peace;

And, making thus his profession and boast,

Receiv'd, from the Bishop, the Holy Ghost:

Then—not having the fear of God before him—

Is sworn in a Justice, and one of the *Quorum*;[23]

'Gainst his spiritual Oath, puts his Oath of the Bench,

And, instead of his Bible, examines a wench;

Gets Chairman of Sessions—leaves his flock, sick
                    or dying,

To license Ale-houses—and assist in the trying

Of prostitutes, poachers, pickpockets, and thieves;—

Having *charged* the Grand Jury, dines with them,
                    and gives

"CHURCH AND KING without day-light;" gets *fresh*,
                    and puts in—

To the stocks vulgar people, who fuddle with gin:

Stage-coachmen, and toll-men, convicts as he pleases;

And beggars and paupers incessantly teazes:

Commits starving vagrants, and orders Distress

On the Poor, for their Rates[24]—signs warrants to press,

And beats up for names to a Loyal Address:

Would indict, for Rebellion, those who Petition:

And, all who look peaceable, try for Sedition;

If the People were legally Meeting, in quiet,
Would pronounce it decidedly—*sec. Stat.*[25]—a Riot,
And order the Soldiers 'to aid and assist,'
That is—kill the helpless, who cannot resist.

He, though vowing 'from all worldly studies to
cease,'
Breaks the Peace of the Church, to be Justice of Peace;
Breaks his vows made to Heaven: a pander for power;
A Perjurer—a guide to the People no more;
On God turns his back,
when he turns the State's Agent;
And damns his own Soul,
to be friends with the————.

THE END.

"'Tis Liberty alone, that gives the flow'r
Of fleeting life its lustre and perfume
And we are weeds without it."[26]

The Queen's Matrimonial Ladder

EMIGRATION
EXCULPATION
IMPUTATION
ALTERATION
ACCEPTATION
DECLARATION
QUALIFICATION

THE QUEEN'S
MATRIMONIAL LADDER.

REMIGRATION
CONSTERNATION
ACCUSATION
PUBLICATION
INDIGNATION
CORONATION
DEGRADATION

PRINTED BY WILLIAM HONE,
LUDGATE HILL, LONDON.
Price (with the Pamphlet) One Shilling.

A cardboard miniature step ladder was presented as a free "toy" with the pamphlet *The Queen's Matrimonial Ladder*. The two sides of the ladder are shown above.

THE QUEEN'S
MATRIMONIAL LADDER,
𝔄 National Toy,
WITH FOURTEEN STEP SCENES;
AND
ILLUSTRATIONS IN VERSE,
WITH EIGHTEEN OTHER CUTS.

BY THE AUTHOR OF "THE POLITICAL HOUSE THAT JACK BUILT."

"The question is not merely whether the Queen shall have her rights, but whether the rights of any individual in the kingdom shall be free from violation."

Her Majesty's Answer to the Norwich Address.[1]

"Here is a Gentleman, and a friend of mine!"
Measure for Measure.[2]

𝔉orty–third 𝔈dition.

LONDON:
PRINTED BY AND FOR WILLIAM HONE, LUDGATE HILL

1820.

"It is a wonderful thing to consider the strength of Princes' wills when they are bent to have their Pleasure fulfilled, wherein no reasonable persuasions will serve their turn: how little do they regard the dangerous sequels, that may ensue as well to themselves as to their Subjects. And amongst all things there is nothing that makes them more wilful than Carnal Love, and various affecting of voluptuous desires."

Cavendish's Memoirs of Card. Wolsey.[3]

NOTE.

All the Drawings for this Publication are
By Mr. George Cruikshank.

Give not thy strength unto women, nor thy ways to that which destroyeth kings.

Solomon.[4]

QUALIFICATION.

In love, and in drink, and o'ertoppled by debt;
With women, with wine, and with duns on the fret.

Penury incurr'd
By endless riot, vanity; the lust
Of pleasure and variety!————.
——————Ministerial grace
Deals him out money from the public chest.

Cowper.[5]

DECLARATION.

The Prodigal Son, by his perils surrounded,
Vex'd, harass'd, bewilder'd, asham'd, and con-
    founded,
Fled for help to his Father,
      confessed his ill doing,
And begged for salvation
      from stark staring ruin;
The sire urged—"The People
      your debts have twice paid,
"And, to ask a third time,
      even Pitt is afraid;
"But he shall if you'll marry, and lead a new life,—
"You've a cousin in Germany—make her your
      wife!"[6]

Lured from her own, her native home,
  The home of early life,
And doom'd in stranger realms to roam;
  A widow! yet a wife!

Phillips's Lament.[7]

ACCEPTATION.

From the high halls of Brunswick, all youthful and
  gay,
From the hearth of her fathers, he lured her away:
How joy'd she in coming—
    how smiling the bower;
How sparkling their nuptials—
    how welcome her dower.
Ah! short were her pleasures—full soon came her
  cares—
Her husbandless bride-bed was wash'd with her
  tears.

The most desolate woman in the world!

Thy daughter, *then,* could hear thee weep;
But now she sleeps the dreamless sleep.
Phillips's Lament[8]

ALTERATION.

Near a million of debts gone,
          all gone were her charms—
What! an Epicure have *his own* wife
          in his arms?
She was not to his *taste*—
          what car'd *he* for the 'form,'
'To love and to cherish'
          could not mean reform:
'To love' meant, of course, nothing else
          but neglect;—
'To cherish' to leave her,
          and shew disrespect.

————faded appetite resign'd
The victim up to shame.

Phillips's Lament.[9]

IMPUTATION.

Was it manly, when widow'd,
       to spy at her actions;
To listen to eaves-droppers,
       whisp'ring detractions;
And, like an old WATCHMAN,
       with faults to conceal,
Get up a *false Charge*,
       as a proof of his zeal?
If desertion was base, Oh base be his name,
Who, having deserted, would bring her to shame.

God, and your Majesty, protect mine innocence!
King Henry VIII.[10]

EXCULPATION.

Undaunted in spirit, her courage arose,
With encrease of charges, and encrease of foes.
Despising the husband,
   who thus had abused her,
She proved to his father,
   his son had ill used her:—
Her conduct examin'd, and sifted, shone bright,
Her enemies fled, as the shadows of night.

—A wanderer, far away,
Neglected and reviled—
Phillips's Lament.[11]

EMIGRATION.

Her father and king, while with reason yet blest,
Protected her weakness, and shielded her rest;
Infirmity seizes him, false friends draw near,
Then spies gather round, and malignants appear;
And cajole, wait, watch, insult,
      alarm, and betray,
Till from home, and her daughter,
      they force her away.

'A hundred thousand welcomes!'
Coriolanus.[12]

REMIGRATION.

Still pursued, when a 'wanderer,'
   her child sleeps in death,
And her best friend, in England, her king,
   yields his breath;
This gives her new rights—
   they neglect and proscribe her;
She threatens returning—they then try to bribe her!
The bullies turn slaves, and, in meanness, fawn on her:
They feel her contempt, and they vow her dishonour;
But she 'steers her own course,' comes indignantly
  over,
And the shouts of the nation salute her at Dover!

He smelt — O Lord! how he did smell!
Southey's Minor Poems, vol. iii. p. 108.[13]

CONSTERNATION.

Ah, what was that groan!—
      'twas the Head of the Church,
When he found she was come—
      for he dreaded a search
Into what *he*'d been doing:
      and sorely afraid, for
What *she* might find out,
      cried *'I'll not have her pray'd for'*;
And the B——ps, obeying their *pious* Head,
      care took
That the name of his wife
      should be out of the prayer book!

"———A BURNING SHAME!"

———I will kill thee, if thou dost deny
Thou hast made me a cuckold.

————What false Italian
(As poisonous tongued as handed) hath prevailed
On thy too ready hearing?

Cymbeline.[14]

ACCUSATION.

On searching for precedents, much to their dread,
They found that they couldn't well cut off her head;

And the 'House of Incurables' raised a 'Report'
She was not a fit person to live in *his* Court.
How like an OLD CHARLEY
       they then made him stand,
In his lanthorn a *leech*,
       the 'Report' in his hand.
'Good folks be so good as not go near that door
'For, though my own wife, she *is*—I could say more
'But it's all in this *Bag*, and there'll be a fine pother,
'I shall get rid of her, and I'll then get another!'

Yet he thought, to himself,—
       'twas a thought most distressing,—
'If *she* should discover
       I've been M—ch—ss—g,
'There's an end of the whole!
       D——rs C——ns, of course,[15]
'If *my own* hands are dirty,
       won't grant a D—ce!'

  He tried to look wise, but he only look'd wild;
The women laugh'd out, and the grave even smiled;
The old frown'd upon him—the children made sport,
And his wife held her *ridicule* at his 'Report'!

MORAL.
Be warn'd by his fate
    Married, single, and all;
Ye elderly Gentlemen,
    Pity his fall!

Give me but the Liberty of the Press, and I will give to the minister a venal House of Peers.

Sheridan.[16]

PUBLICATION.

As yon bright orb, that vivifies our ball,

Sees through our system, and illumines all;

So, sees and shines, our MORAL SUN, THE PRESS,
Alike to vivify the mind, and bless;
Sees the rat *Leech* turn towards Milan's walls,
'Till the black slime betrays him as he crawls;'
Sees, from that recreant, vile, and eunuch-land,
Where felon-perjurers hold their market-stand,
Cooke,[17] with his 'cheek of parchment, eye of stone,'
Get up the evidence, to go well down;
Sees who, with eager hands, the Green Bag cram,
And warns the nation of the frightful flam;
Sees Him, for whom they work the treacherous
    task,
With face, scarce half conceal'd, behind their mask,
Fat, fifty-eight, and frisky, still a beau,
Grasping a half-made match, by *Leech*-light go;
Led by a passion, prurient, blind, and batter'd,
Lame, bloated, pointless, flameless, age'd and
        shatter'd;
Creeping, like Guy Fawkes, to blow up his wife,
Whom, spurn'd in youth, he dogs through after-life.

    Scorn'd, exiled, baffled, goaded in distress,
She owes her safety to a fearless Press:
With all the freedom that it makes its own,
It guards, alike, the people and their throne;
While fools with darkling eye-balls shun its gaze,
And soaring villains scorch beneath its blaze.

I am wrapp'd in dismal thinkings!—
THE KING, in *All's well that ends well.*[18]

INDIGNATION.

The day will soon come, when 'the Judge and the
    Ponderer,'
Will judge between thee, and the charge-daring
    'Wanderer;'
Will say—'Thou who cast the first stone at thy wife,
Art thou without sin, and is spotless *thy* life?'[19]
Ah! what if *thy* faults should 'outrival the sloe,'
And thy wife's, beside thine, should look 'whiter
    than snow'![20]
   Bethink thee! the old British Lion awoke,
Turns indignant, and treads out thy bag-full of smoke.
Spurn thy minions—the traitors, who counsel thee,
    banish;
And the soldiers will quickly forget all their *Spanish!*[21]

"Le Roy le veut!" G. R.

See Blackstone's Com. b.1. c.2.[22]

CORONATION.

Shakespeare says, in King John, it's a curse most
    abhorrent,
That '*Slaves* take the humours of Kings for a warrant.'[23]
A more *useful* truth never fell from his pen,
If Kings would apply it like sober-bred men.
The Slaves of *your* will,
        will make your reign, in History,
A misrule of force, folly, taxing, and mystery:
Indulging your wish for
        what, with law, 's incompatible,
For the present, they've render'd your crown
        not come-at-able;
And the tongues of old women and infancy wag,
With, 'He call'd for his crown—and
        they gave him the *Bag!*'[24]

So let him stand • • • • •
• • • • •   *Byron.*[25]

DEGRADATION.

To this have they brought thee, at last!

Exposed thee, for all men to see!
Ah, surely, their pandering
    shall quickly be past:—
'How wretched their portion
    shall be!
'Derision shall strike them
    forlorn,
 'A mockery that never shall die:
'The curses of hate and the hisses
    of scorn,
 'Shall follow wherever they fly;
'And proud o'er their ruin
    for ever be hurl'd,
'The laughter of triumph,
    the jeers of the world!'

THE END

"Cats' Meat!"

English Cry.

I say, HUM, how fares it with Royalty now?
Is it *up?*— Is it *prime?*— Is it *spooney?*— or how?
The Fudge Family.

THE JOSS AND HIS FOLLY,

An Extract of an overland Dispatch.

I stare at it from out my casement,
And ask for what is such a place meant.

Byron.[26]

July 29, 1820.

——The queerest of all the queer sights
I've set sight on;——
Is, the *what d'ye-call-t thing,* here,
THE FOLLY at Brighton:

The outside—huge teapots,
>all drill'd round with holes,
Relieved by extinguishers,
>sticking on poles:
The inside—all tea-things,
>and dragons, and bells,
The show rooms—*all* show,
>the sleeping rooms—cells.
>But the *grand* Curiosity
>>'s not to be seen—
The owner himself—
>an old fat MANDARIN;
A patron of painters
>who copy designs,
That grocers and tea-dealers
>hang up for signs:
Hence teaboard-taste artists
>gain rewards and distinction,
Hence his title of 'TEAPOT'
>shall last to extinction.
I saw his great chair
>into which he falls—*soss*—
And sits, in his CHINA SHOP,
>like a large JOSS;
His mannikins round him,
>in tea-tray array,
His pea-hens beside him,
>to make him seem gay.
>It is said when he sleeps
>>on his state Eider-down,

And thinks on his Wife,

         and about *half* a Crown;

That he wakes from these horrible dreams

         in a stew;

And that, stretching his arms out,

         he screams, Mrs. Q.!

He's cool'd on the M—ch——ss,

         but I'm your debtor

For further particulars—

         in a C letter.

You must know that he hates *his own* wife,

         to a failing;—

And it's thought, it's to shun her,

         he's now gone out

           SAILING.[27]

A living teapot stands, one arm held out,
One bent; the handle this, and that the spout.
         Rape of the Lock.[28]

FINIS.

"NON MI RICORDO!"

&c. &c. &c.

"This will witness outwardly, as strongly as the conscience does within"

Cymbeline.[1]

"Who are you?"

𝕿𝖍𝖎𝖗𝖙𝖎𝖊𝖙𝖍 𝕰𝖉𝖎𝖙𝖎𝖔𝖓.

LONDON:
PRINTED BY AND FOR WILLIAM HONE, LUDGATE HILL.

1820.
SIXPENCE.

"NON MI RICORDO!"

CROSS EXAMINED BY MR. BESOM.[2]

WHO are you?   Non mi ricordo.

What countryman are you?—a foreigner or an Englishman?

Non mi ricordo.

Do you *understand* ENGLISH?   No not at all.

Will the Oath you have taken *bind* you to speak the truth, or do you know of any other Oath *more* binding?

The TURNSTILE GENERAL objected to the question; upon which a discussion arose as to the nature of the Oath likely to bind the Witness, who appeared to be playing with a thread. The Witness was accordingly asked, by way of illustration, to what degree he thought the thread was *binding*, and whether he knew of any thing else *more* binding?

The Lord PRECEDENT FURTHERMORE said, if the Witness believed the thread he held was *binding*, that was sufficient.

The LORD PRECEDENT'S opinion gave rise to a long discussion as to whether *more* binding was *binding*, and binding was *more* binding; which ended in a reference to the ERMINIANS, who delivered the following solemn opinion:—If the Witness shall answer that he thinks the bit of thread is *binding*, there is no doubt it *is* binding; but he cannot be asked if a cord is *more* binding, because he in fact says that the thread itself is *binding*. If the Witness twists the thread round his little finger he is so far bound by it, and it is *binding*; and having done that, it is unnecessary to inquire whether a cord, round another part of his body, would be *more binding*.[3]

Question over-ruled.

CROSS EXAMINATION RESUMED.

You are a master tailor, I think?   I was cut out for a tailor.

You have been a tailor, then?   I only follow tailoring as a mere amusement.

Fond of *Goose* I suppose—but pray Mr. Mereamusement what is your business?   I was brought up a *Cabinet* maker.

What can you get at it?—are you a good hand?   I can't say I am; I'm badly off; my *tools* are worn out.[4]

What is your place of residence?

(Order Order).

The TURNSTILE GENERAL protested against the consequences of this mode of Examination.

Lord JURYMAN[5]—Why does not the Interpreter give the Witness's Answer?

The Lord PRECEDENT FURTHERMORE—Because the Bench objects to the question.

Lord MUDDLEPOOL[6]—Does the Turnstile General object to the question?

The TURNSTILE GENERAL—I do object to it, my Lord. This is perhaps the most important question that ever occurred. By this dealing out, the party is placed in such a situation as he never was placed in before.

Mr. BESOM—I ask him where he now lives, and the Turnstile General objects to this, because I do not put all the questions I might put, in a single breath.

The Lord PRECEDENT FURTHERMORE—I feel great difficulty—I doubt.

Lord WHEELBARROW thought there was a *great* deal in what the noble Lord had said; and *he* doubted.

CROSS EXAMINATION RESUMED.

How much money has been expended on you since you were born? Non mi ricordo.

What have you done for it in return?   More less than more.

How do you get your living?   I was waiter for some years at the Hotel *de Grand Bretagne*, and succeeded my father as head waiter at the *Crown* Inn.

What wages have you?   Non mi ricordo.

Have you any perquisites?   *Veils.*

Are you *head waiter*, or by what other name than head waiter you may be called, at the Crown Inn?[7]

I am after building a new place called the *Wellington Arms*, and try-ing to be *Barrack-master*;[8] if I don't gain the *Trial* I shall be glad to re-main at the old *Crown*.

This answer appeared to excite considerable sensation.

The TWISTER GENERAL thought the meaning was, 'if I don't gain what I attempt to gain.'

[The Short-hand writer was desired to read the answer, and the word *Trial* was retained as the correct translation.]

I do not ask what you are to be hereafter, but whether you are *still* head waiter at the Crown?

The head waiter is dismissed occasionally.

Are you married?   More yes than no.

Do you live with your own wife?   No.

Is she in this country?   Yes.

Why did you marry?   To pay my debts.[9]

Then why did you part?   Because my debts were paid.

Were you not up to the eyes in debt?   Si Signor.

Are you not bound to manifest some gratitude towards those who have paid your debts?

The Interpreter said the witness was a mere *fanfaron*, [10] and that he found it difficult, if not impossible, to explain to the witness's under-standing what was meant by *gratitude*.

CROSS EXAMINATION RESUMED.

Did you not write to your wife a licentious letter, called a letter of license?[11]—*(Order, order.)*

I ask you again the cause of your separation? She left me.

On what account? I did not like her, and I told her I'd have nothing to do with *her* any more.

After that what did you do? Oh, I rambled about.

Where did you go? To Jersey and elsewhere.

Well, Sir, go on. Non mi ricordo.

Do you mean to say that you never went to Manchester Square?[12] More yes than no.

Were you in the house on the footing of a private friend? No, not as a friend.

You mentioned your father just now:—you did not go in your father's *cart*, I presume; in what sort of carriage did you go? In the old yellow chariot.[13]

How long did it take you to travel from Manchester Square to Richmond? Non mi ricordo.

How many other places did you go to? Non mi ricordo.

Is the Marquis of C. a married man?[14]

(Order Order).

After you parted from your wife, on what terms did you live?

I've been *trying* to get rid of her.

Do you know what Matthew says (c.v.v. 32)?[15]

Matthew? Matthew? *(trying to recollect)*—what Matthew?—he's no friend of mine.

In what light do you consider your oath at the marriage ceremony? A ceremony.

If your marriage oath has not bound you, can you expect people to believe you if ever you should take a solemn public oath? More yes than no.

By The Roman law, a divorce was granted for Drunkenness, Adultery, and *False Keys:* [16] what is your opinion of that law?

The TWISTER GENERAL said, that it was contrary to common sense to ask the witness's opinion about any *Law.*

How many Wives does *your* Church allow you? Non mi ricordo.

How many have you had since you separated from your own? Non mi ricordo.

Are you a Member of the Society for the Suppression of Vice?[17] Yes *(with great energy).*

The Cross-examining Counsel said that the Interpreter had materially altered the sense of the last question; he had in fact asked, if the Witness was Member of the Society for the suppression of *Wives, (a loud laugh)* which Witness had eagerly answered in the affirmative.

The Witness's answer was expunged, and on the question being repeated correctly, he answered that he was told it was his duty to encourage the *Vice* Society, because it professed to diminish the influence of bad example.

Have they ever prosecuted you?   Me!—*(with astonishment)*—they like *me* too well!

What do you mean then by *Suppression*—is your Society to prevent little vice from being committed, or great vice from being found out?

More Yes than No.

It was here moved by Lord LE CUISINIER[18], that 4 o'Clock, the hour of dinner, was arrived.

Another, in a maiden Speech, said, that during his long silence in that Court he had had leisure to observe, that 4 o'Clock in the *morning* was a more usual hour of adjournment.

Another considered that Lord LE CUISINIER'S suggestion ought not to be entertained for a moment. We only exist in our formalities. If we suffer ourselves to be put a stop to by the motion, we may find that we are travelling round again into the obsolete usages of our early ancestors; which will be to describe a circle that must be generally considered as nothing less than a revolution! I therefore deprecate the least innovation, and move, as an amendment, that 4 o'Clock is *not* arrived.

The MASTER GENERAL of the *Black* Barracks at Exeter, rose without his wig, and declaring upon the memory of his whiskers, that he had just heard it strike 4, he enquired whether the Clock was in *Order.* *(Loud and continued* cries of *hear hear.)*

The HOME DOCTOR felt his pulse alarmingly quicken one and a fraction in the minute, and nervously said, that the clock was clearly guilty of a barefaced libel, and ought to be instantly held to bail for breach of the peace. The simultaneous action of all the Clocks throughout the nation and their open communication by circulars, was an index to the existence of an organized correspondence and a systematic affiliation. He trembled at the 'positive intelligence' he had received, that millions at that moment held their hands in an attitude ready to strike; but it was the proudest day of his life that he had so far succeeded by a *circular* movement of his own, as to enable his workmen to hold them to the peace for an hour together.[19]

Lord BATHOS[20] assured the Black-Barrack Master-General that the Clock *was* out of Order, and he congratulated the Home Doctor on his efficiency; but he thought they had not sunk low enough into the subject; for he had strong doubts whether the striking might not be construed into an overt act of High Treason, and if he saw any probability of being supported he should conclude with a substantive motion. Did not the Lord Precedent remember a Clock Case, in which, immediately after the chain had been locked up, a principal link suddenly disappeared? and whether, after the most minute inquiry, there was not every reason to believe from the best information that could be obtained at that time, that that link had been *prigged?*[21] *(Hear hear.)* Take even the very last Clock Case, where the chain was kept together with the greatest pains, and the utmost care. If the smallest link in that chain had been *prigged,* it would have been fatal to the works, and yet in that very case, two days after the chain was locked up, a link was obtained, which, if sooner discovered, would have lengthened the chain to the necessary extent, and brought home in the most conclusive manner the guilt of the Clock. He therefore moved that the Clock be examined, and the chain kept in their own custody, with liberty to add to the number of links.

Lord RATSTAIL with his usual animation seconded the Motion.

Marquiz BOUDOIR moved as an Amendment, that the Clock being in contempt, the *Black stick* be ordered to *walk him* in to-morrow.[22] Seconded.

Upon this Amendment the following Amendment was moved and seconded, that the word 'to-morrow' be expunged, and the word 'yesterday' be inserted in its place.   *Ordered.*

CROSS EXAMINATION RESUMED.

Does the Witness recollect whether he was at B——?[23]   Non mi ricordo.

Who usually closed the Pavilion?   I did.

Was it so close as to exclude any person outside from seeing what passed within, or was it partially open?   It was quite closed— When I could not close it with C*********[24] entirely, I did it with other pieces.

What do you mean by saying with other pieces?   I mean with other pieces of the same quality.

Symptoms of impatience were now expressed, with loud cries of *Withdraw, withdraw.*

Do you remember any thing particular occurring one night? No.

Do you not recollect whether a new wing was added during the time you and your mistress were absent?   Non mi ricordo.

Do you know a certain Colonel Q.?[25]   Yes, he has *too* little mustachios.

Are you a sober man?   More no than yes.

How many bottles a day do you drink?   Non mi ricordo.

Do you drink six bottles?   Non mi ricordo.

Five bottles?   Non mi ricordo.

How many nights in the week do you go to bed sober?   Non mi ricordo.

Are you sober now?   More no than yes.

Where do you spend your mornings?   At Curaçao.[26]

Where do you spend your evenings?   At the *Cat and Fiddle.*[27]

What is your favorite dish?   Trifle.

What is your favorite game?   *Bag-at-L—*

What is your favorite amusement?   The C.[28]

After Dressing, Drinking, and Dreaming, what time remains for thinking?   Non mi ricordo.

I hold in my hand a list of immense sums of money that have been advanced to you, how much have you left?   None.

Well, but you have something to show for it?   No.

How do you live?   I have a *doll*-shop, and a large stable in the country, and some *cow*-houses in different parts.

Are not your favourite friends *horn*-boys and flashmen?[29]—*(Order, order.)*

Can you produce a certificate of good character from those who *know* you?   Yes, from the *minister*.

Pho! pho! don't trifle: can you from any *respectable* person? More no than yes.

I understand you have the *scarlet* fever, do you not know that it ends here in a *putrid* fever?[30]   Non mi ricordo.

You have many companions and advisers, but have you to your knowledge one *real* friend in the world; and if not, why not?   Non mi ricordo.

By what acts of your life do you expect you will be remembered hereafter?   I shall not answer you any more questions; you put questions to me I never dreamt of.

Suppose every man in society were to do as you do, what would become of society; and what right have you to do so, more than any other man?—*(Witness greatly agitated.)*

The Witness from the *Grillery* asked whether the *Cross* Examination was nearly concluded? *(Cries of* KEEP ON!)—Supposing that the business would close to day at 4 o'clock, he had made a private *assignation*, although he was quite ready to *stop* if necessary.

The Lord PRECEDENT FURTHERMORE was in favour of adhering to a square rule; he had not entered the Court till five seconds past ten by his *stop*-watch, in consequence of consulting with his Wife upon a motion-of-course which they had contemplated; and their further deliberation had been postponed until after the adjournment to-day. It was impossible to know what questions might turn out to be doubtful or doubtless; yet adjourning at Five o'Clock would gain a delay of six hours in the Week, and the *gaining of any thing* he considered very material in the present case.

An Adjournment then took place, the Witness remaining on

THE GRILLERY.

"The *Fat* in the Fire!"

STRAYED AND MISSING.

AN INFIRM ELDERLY GENTLEMAN in a Public Office, lately left his home, just after dreadfully ill-using his wife about half a Crown, and trying to beat her. He had long complained a great deal of his forehead, and lately had a leech put upon him. He was last seen walking swiftly towards the Horns without a Crown to his hat, accompanied by some evil disposed persons, who tied a great green bag to his tail full of crackers,[31] which he mistook for sweetmeats, and burnt himself dreadfully. Every person he met in this deplorable condition tried to persuade him to go back, but in vain. He is very deaf and very obstinate, and cannot bear to be looked at or spoken to. It is supposed that he has been seduced and carried off by some artful female. He may be easily known by his manners. He fancies himself the politest man in Europe, because he knows how to bow, and to offer a pinch of snuff; and thinks himself the greatest man in Europe, because people have humoured him and let him have his own way. He is so fond of tailoring, that he lately began a suit that will take him his life to complete. He delights in playing at soldiers, supposes himself a cavalry officer, and makes speeches, that others write for him, in a field marshal's uniform.[32] Sometimes he fancies himself 'Glorious Apollo,' plays 'Hailstones of Brunswick' on the base fiddle, and qualifies his friends to perform 'Cuckolds all on a row.' His concerns are very much deranged. Not long ago he imported a vast quantity of Italian images at enormous prices, upon credit, and hoarded them up in a waterside cotton warehouse.[33] Since then, things have gone all against him, and he has been in a very desponding state. It is of the utmost consequence to himself that he should be at his post, or he may lose his place; one of his predecessors some time ago having been cashiered for his misconduct. If this should meet his eye, it is earnestly requested that he will return to his duty, and he will be kindly received and no questions asked.

N.B. He has not a friend in the world except the advertiser and a few others, who never had an opportunity of speaking to him and letting him know the real state of his affairs.

PUBLIC OFFICE, LUDGATE HILL

1st **September, 1820.**

WHEREAS that well known old established Public House, (formerly a *free* house) called the POLITICAL HOUSE THAT JACK BUILT, has been feloniously entered into and damaged, and the property therein carried off to a large amount, by a numerous gang of desperate Villains, who, by various vile arts and contrivances, have not only kept possession thereof, but also of the Head Waiter, who was intrusted by MR. BULL, the owner, with the management of the concern, and was a very promising young man when Mr. Bull first knew him, and might have done very well if he had followed the advice of his old friends, and not suffered these desperadoes to get him into their clutches; since when he seems to have forgotten himself, and by neglecting his duty sadly, and behaving ill to the customers who support the House, has almost ruined the Business, and has also dreadfully injured the Sign, which Mr. Bull had had fresh painted after he dismissed a former waiter for his bad manners. Whoever will assist Mr. Bull in bringing the offenders to Justice, will be doing a great service to the young man, and he will still be retained in his situation, unless he has actually destroyed or made away with the Sign, which Mr. Bull very much admires, it being a *heir-loom*. If offered to be pawned or sold it is requested the parties may be stopped, and notice given as above. As the young man has not been seen for some time, there is no doubt the ruffians have either done him a serious mischief, or secreted him somewhere to prevent Mr. Bull, who is really his friend, from speaking to him.[34]

"What are you *at*? what are you *after*?"

THE END.

Printed by W. Hone, 45, Ludgate Hill.

THE

POLITICAL SHOWMAN—AT HOME!

EXHIBITING HIS CABINET OF CURIOSITIES AND

Creatures—All Alive!

BY THE AUTHOR OF THE
POLITICAL HOUSE THAT JACK BUILT.

"I lighted on a certain place where was a *Den*."   *Bunyan.*[1]

WITH TWENTY-FOUR CUTS.

"The putrid and mouldering carcase of exploded Legitimacy."

Mr. Lambton[2]

Twenty-Sixth Edition.

LONDON:
PRINTED BY AND FOR WILLIAM HONE, 45, LUDGATE HILL.

1821.

ONE SHILLING.

   THE PRESS, invented much about the same time with the *Reformation*, hath done more mischief to the discipline of our Church, than all the doctrine can make amends for. 'Twas an happy time, when all learning was in manuscript, and some little officer did keep the keys of the library! Now, since PRINTING came into the world, such is the mischief, that *a man cannot write a book but presently he is answered!* There have been ways found out to *fine* not the people, but even the *grounds and fields where they assembled:* but no art yet could prevent these SEDITIOUS MEETINGS OF LETTERS! Two or three brawny fellows in a corner, with meer ink and elbow-grease, do more harm than an *hundred systematic divines.* Their ugly printing *letters*, that look but like so many rotten teeth, how oft have they been pulled out by the public tooth-drawers! And yet these rascally operators of the press have got a trick to fasten them again in a few minutes, that they grow as firm a set, and as biting and talkative as ever! O PRINTING! how hast thou *"disturbed the peace!"* Lead, when moulded into bullets, is not so mortal as when founded into *letters!* There was a mistake sure in the story of Cadmus; and the *serpent's teeth* which he sowed, were nothing else but the *letters* which he invented.

Marvell's Rehearsal transprosed, 4to, 1672.

Being marked only with *four and twenty letters,—variously transposed* by the help of a PRINTING PRESS,—PAPER works miracles. The Devil dares no more come near a *Stationer's* heap, or a *Printer's Office,* than *Rats* dare put their noses into a Cheesemonger's Shop.

A Whip for the Devil, 1669, p. 92.[3]

THE SHOWMAN.

LADIES AND GENTLEMEN ,

Walk *up!* walk *up!* and see the CURIOSITIES and CREATURES—all alive! alive O! Walk *up!*—now's your time!—*only* a shilling. Please to walk *up!* Here is the strangest and most wonderful *artificial CABINET* in Europe!—made of NOTHING—but *lacker'd brass, turnery,*[4] and *papier mâché*—all FRET *work* and *varnish,* held together by *steel points!*—very CRAZY, but very CURIOUS!

Please to walk in, Ladies and Gentlemen—it's well worth *seeing!* Here are the most wonderful of all wonderful LIVING ANIMALS. Take care! Don't go within their *reach*—they mind nobody but *me!* A short time ago they got loose, and, with some other *vermin* that came from their *holes and corners,* desperately attacked a LADY OF QUALITY; but, as luck would have it, *I,* and *my 'four and twenty men,* happened to come in at the very moment;—we *'pull'd* 'em away, and prevented 'em from doing her a *serious mischief.* Though they *look tame,* their vicious dispositions are unchanged. If any thing was to happen to *me,* they'd soon break out *again,* and shew their natural ferocity. *I'm in continual danger from 'em myself*—for if I didn't watch 'em closely they'd *destroy* ME. As the clown says, 'there never *was* such times,'—so there's no telling what *tricks* they may play *yet.*

Ladies and Gentlemen,—these animals have been exhibited *at Court,* before the KING, and all the Royal Family! Indeed His Majesty is so *fond* of 'em that he often sees 'em *in private,* and *feeds* 'em; and he is so *diverted* by 'em that he has been pleased to express his gracious approbation of all their *motions.* But they're as cunning as the *old one* himself! Bless you, *he* does not know a thousandth part of their *tricks.* You, Ladies and Gentlemen, may see 'em just as they are—the BEASTS and REPTILES—all *alive! alive* O! and the BIG BOOBY—all *a-light! a-light* O!

Walk in, Ladies and Gentlemen! walk in! just a-going to begin.— Stir 'em up! Stir 'em *up* there with *the long pole!*

Before I describe the ANIMALS, please to look at the SHOW-CLOTH opposite——— ☞

The CURIOSITIES have *labels* under them, which the company can *read.*

THE TRANSPARENCY, of which this is a copy, was exhibited by WILLIAM HONE during the ILLUMINATION commencing on the 11th, and ending on the 15th of November, 1820, in celebration of the VICTORY *obtained by* THE PRESS *for the* LIBERTIES OF THE PEOPLE, which had been assailed in the Person of *The Queen*: the words "TRIUMPH OF THE PRESS," being displayed in variegated lamps as a motto above it. On the 29th, when *The Queen* went to St. Paul's, it was again exhibited with Lord Bacon's immortal words, "KNOWLEDGE IS POWER," displayed in like manner.—The Transparency was painted by Mr. GEORGE CRUIKSHANK.[5]

―――― COURT VERMIN that buzz round
And fly-blow the King's ear; make him suspect
His wisest, faithfullest, best counsellors—
Who, for themselves and their dependants, seize
All places, and all profits; and who wrest,
To their own ends, the statutes of the land,
Or safely break them.

Southey's Joan of Arc. b. x.[6]

¶ **These creaturis sere not to teche us to corecte owr maners and amende our lyuynge.**

Dialoges of Creatures Moralysed. Prologe.[7]

To exalt virtue, expose vice, promote truth, and help men to serious reflection, is my first moving cause and last directed end.

De Foe's Review, 4to., 1705, Preface.[8]

――――――Oh that I dared
To basket up the family of plagues
That waste our vitals; peculation, sale
Of honour, perjury, corruption, frauds
By forgery, by subterfuge of law,
By tricks and lies――――――
Then cast them, closely bundled, every brat
At the right door!

Cowper.[9]

NOTE.

All the Drawings are by Mr. GEORGE CRUIKSHANK.

"JUGLATOR REGIS."   *Strutt's Sports*, 188.[10]

————————a most officious Drudge,
His face and gown drawn out with the same budge,
His pendant Pouch, which is both large and wide,
Looks like a Letters-patent:
He is as *awful*, as he had been sent——————
From Moses with the eleventh commandement.

                 Bp. Corbet's Poems, 1672, p. 3.[11]

He begins his DECISION by saying, *Having had* DOUBTS *upon this for twenty years*.
               Maddock's Chancery Practice, Pref. ix.[12]

    He is like a tight-rope dancer, who, whenever he leans on *one side*, counteracts his position by a corresponding declination on *the other*, and, by this means, keeps himself in a most *self-satisfied equipoise*.   *Retrospective Review*, No. V. p. 115.[13]

    Trust not the cunning waters of his eyes:—
His eyes drop millstones.   *Shakspeare*.[14]

BAGS.—(*a Scruple Balance.*)

————————'tis the veriest madness, to live poor,
And die with *Bags*——   *Gifford's Juvenal*, Sat. xiv.[15]

DUBIUS is such a *scrupulous* good man—
Yes—you may catch him tripping, if you can!
He would not, with a PEREMPTORY tone,
Assert the nose upon his face HIS OWN.
With HESITATION, admirably slow,
He humbly hopes—presumes—it MAY be so.
Through constant dread of giving truth offence,
He ties up all his hearers in SUSPENSE!
His sole opinion, whatsoe'er befall,
Cent'ring, AT LAST, in having—NONE AT ALL.

                  Cowper.[16]

    Well! he is a *nimble* gentleman; set him upon BANKES, his horse, in a saddle rampant, and it is a great question, which part of the Centaur shews better tricks.

               Cleveland's Poems, 1665, p. 183.[17]

By some the Crocodile is classed among fishes. A person born under this Zodiacal Sign, (*Pisces*), shall 'be a mocker and shall be *covetous*, he will *say* one thing and *doe* another, he shall *find money*, he will trust in his *sapience*, and shall have *good fortune*, he shall be *a defender of Orphelins and widdowes* and shall live lxxiii year and v months after nature.'

Shepheard's Kalender, 1497, c. liii.[18]

> Pitty not him, but fear thyself,
> Though thou see the crafty elfe
> Tell down his silver-drops unto thee,
> They're counterfit, and will undoe thee.

Crashaw's Poems, 1670, p. 112.[19]

A CROCODILE.

LADIES AND GENTLEMEN,

I begin the Exhibition with the Crocodile, which is of the Lizard tribe; yet, from his *facility of creeping through narrow and intricate ways,* he has been classed among SERPENTS.* He has a monstrous appetite, his *swallow* is immense, and his legs are placed *side*-ways. It is a vulgar error to suppose that he cannot *turn;* for, although he is in appearance very heavy, and his back very strong, and proof against the hardest blows, yet he is so *pliable,* that he can *wheel* round with the utmost facility. When in his HAUNT, and apparently torpid, he sometimes utters a piteous *whine* of distress—almost human; *sheds tears,* and, attracting the unwary, suddenly darts upon a man and gorges him with all he has. His *claws* are very long and tenacious. If a victim eludes his grasp, he infallibly secures him by his FLEET power. He is sometimes used for purposes of *state and show,* and his BAGS are much coveted for their *peculiar* qualities.+

* By Linnaeus.+ Goldsmith's Animated Nature, v. 283.[20]

Above the steeple shines a plate,
That *turns, and turns,* to indicate
From what point blows the weather;
Look up.—

Cowper.[21]

    Having by much dress, and secrecy, and dissimulation, as it were *periwigged** his sin, and covered his shame, he looks after no other innocence but *concealment.*

Bp. South's Sermons.[22]

A MASK.—*(an Incrustation—a Relique.)*[23]

A shallow brain behind a serious *mask,*
An oracle within an empty cask,
A solemn fop.———
———A sooty *Film.*   Cowper.[24]

——————————————————The THING on Earth

Least qualified in honour, learning, worth,
To occupy a sacred, awful post,
In which the best and worthiest tremble most.
The ROYAL LETTERS are a thing of course,
A King, that would, might recommend his horse;
And deans, no doubt, and chapters, with one voice,
As bound in duty, would confirm the choice.
       *   *   *   *   *   *   *   *

A piece of mere CHURCH-FURNITURE at best.

Cowper.[25]

---

*There is a similarity, amounting almost to absolute identity, in the two Greek words that signify an *Impostor* and a *Periwig:*—

         φεναξ-ακος———*Impostor.*
         φενακη———*Periwig.*

Hederict Lexicon.

There are a number of us creep
Into this world, to eat and sleep;
And know no reason why they're born,
But merely to consume the corn.

Watts on Hor. L. i. Ep. ii. 27.[26]

Very grievous were they; before them there were no such locusts as they, neither after them shall be such: for they covered the face of the whole earth, so that the land was
darkened.

Exodus, x. 14, 15.

THE LOCUST.

LADIES AND GENTLEMEN,

The Locust is a destructive insect, of the GRILL US tribe. They are
so numerous, and so rapacious, that they may be compared to an ARMY,
pursuing its march to devour the fruits of the earth, as an instrument of
divine displeasure towards a devoted country. They have LEADERS, who
direct their motions in preying on the labours of man *in fertile regions.*
No insect is more formidable in places where they breed: for they
wither whatever they *touch.* It is impossible to recount the *terrible dev-
astations* which historians and travellers relate that they have committed at different times, in various parts of the world. Many are so
venomous, that persons *handling* them are immediately stung, and
seized with shivering and trembling; but it has been discovered that, in
most cases, their hateful qualities are completely assuaged by *palm*
oil.*

* Goldsmith, vi. 21.

It preys upon and destroys itself with its own poison. It is of so malignant and ruinous a nature, that it ruins itself with the rest; and with rage mangles and tears itself to pieces.

Montaigne, v. 3. c. xi.[27]

A SCORPION.

Ladies and Gentlemen,

The Scorpion is a REPTILE that resembles the *common lobster,* but is much more hideous. They are very terrible to mankind, on account of their size and malignity, and their large *crooked stings*. They often assault and kill people in their houses. In ITALY, and some other parts of Europe, they are the greatest pests of mankind; but their venom is most dreadful in the *East*. An inferior species sally forth at certain seasons, in battalions;—scale houses that stand in the way of their march;—wind along the course of rivers;—and on their retreat entrench themselves. Scorpions are so irascible, that they will attempt to sting a *constable's staff*; yet even a harmless little MOUSE* destroyed three of them, *one after the other,* by acting on the *defensive,* survived their venomous wounds, and seemed pleased with its victory. When in a confined space, they exert all their rage against each other, and there is nothing to be seen but universal carnage. If this mutual destruction did not prevail, they would multiply so fast as to render some countries uninhabitable.+

* Confined for the sake of experiment in a vessel, by Maupertuis.[28]   + Goldmsith, v. 428.

THE LOBSTER.

———————————they preferre
Broiles before Rest, and place their Peace in Warre.
Du Bartas, 4to. 131.[29]

LADIES AND GENTLEMEN,

The Lobster is very similar to the scorpion. It is *armed* with *two* great *claws,* by the help of which it moves itself *forwards*. They *entrench* themselves in places that can be easily defended where they acquire defensive and offensive *armour*. They issue forth from their *fortresses* in hope of *plunder,* and to surprise such inadvertent and weak animals as come within their reach. They have little to apprehend except from each other, the more powerful being formidable enemies to the weaker. They sometimes continue in the same habitations for a long time together; in general they get *new coats once a year*. When in *hot water* they make a great noise, attack any one that puts a hand towards them, and knowing their danger, use violent efforts to escape. In a sufficient heat they *change their colours*.*

*Goldsmith, v. 163.

————With huge fat places stored,
A *prop* that helps to shoulder up the state.
                              Tom of Bedlam, folio. 1701, p. 4.[30]
————a *Crutch* that helps the *weak* along,
Supports the *feeble*—but *retards the strong*.   *Smith*.[31]
He knows not what it is to feel within
A comprehensive faculty, that grasps
Great purposes with ease, that turns and wields,
Almost without an effort, plans too vast
For his conception, which he cannot move.   *Cowper*.[32]
One of that class of individuals of but moderate talents, who by habitual exercise of their
faculties are enabled to figure in the world by mere *imitation*; to become learned moral-
ists, jurists, and theologians; to go through the ceremonies of professional life with an im-
posing gravity and regularity, and to run round the mill-horse circle of routine with a
scrupulous precision.   *Sir C. Morgan's Phil. of Life*, 370.[33]

A *PRIME* CRUTCH.—
(From the Westminster Infirmary—Upper Ward). [34]

He fondly 'IMITATES' that wondrous LAD,
    That durst assay the sun's bright flaming team;
Spite of whose feeble hands, the horses mad
    Fling down on burning earth the scorching beam;—
        So MADE *the flame in which* HIMSELF *was fired;*
        THE WORLD THE BONFIRE WAS—*when* HE *expired*!*
        Like HIM of Ephesus, HE HAD WHAT HE DESIRED.

Fletcher's Purple Island.[35]

*The 'LAD' died in the midst of war, ejaculating heaven to save the country from the mis-
eries of his system of misrule.

I don't think myself obliged to play tricks with my own neck, by putting it *under his feet*, to inform myself whether he wears sparrow-bills in his shoes or no.

Asgill's Defence, 1712, p. 15.[36]

THE OPOSSUM.

LADIES AND GENTLEMEN,

This is a *quick climbing* animal; but is, in other respects, *heavy* and helpless. When it is pursued on *level ground* and overtaken, it feigns itself dead, to deceive the hunters. A faculty in its *seat*, enables it to suspend itself from a high branch, by that part, for a long time together; and, in this position, watching for whatever is weak that comes within its reach, it falls upon it and usually destroys it. By this elevating power in its *nether end*, it not only seizes its prey more securely, but preserves itself from pursuers; looking down on them, in a sort of *upright* position, heels upwards. It is very domesticated, but proves a disagreeable inmate, from its *scent*; which, however fragrant in *small* quantities, is uniformly ungrateful when *copiously* supplied. *It is a* BOROUGHING *creature.**

* Goldsmith, iii, 322. Stedman's Surinam. Shaw's Zoology.[37]

Full of business, bustle, and chicanery;   *Dibdin's Bibl. Decam.* iii. 301.[38]
An odious and vile kind of creatures that fly about the *House;*   *B. Jonson's Discov.*[39]

> They seem———*descending*, at some direful blow,
> To *nibble brimstone* in the realms below!   *Salmagundi*, 139.[40]

Suppose one to be "boring" on *one side* for two hours, and his opponent to be "bothering" for a like period on the *other side*, what must be the consequence?
                    Sir Jos. Yorke, in H. of Com. March 30, 1821.[41]

> Of torrent tongue, and never blushing face;
> ———Knaves, who, in truth's despite,
> Can white to black transform, and black to white!
>   *Gifford's Juvenal*, Sat. iii.[42]

When they were fewer, men might have had a Lordship safely conveyed to them in a piece of parchment no bigger than your hand, though several sheets will not do it safely in this wiser age.   *Walton's Angler* (4to. Bagster) 93.[43]

They'll argue as confidently as if they spoke gospel instead of law; they'll cite you six hundred several Precedents, though not one of them come near to the case in hand; they'll muster up the authority of Judgments, Deeds, Glosses, and Reports, and tumble over so many dusty Records, that they make their employ, though in itself easy, the greatest slavery imaginable; always accounting that the best plea which they have took most pains for.   *Erasmus of Folly*, 96.[44]

In other countries, they make laws upon laws and add precepts upon precepts, till the endless number of them makes the fundamental part to be forgotten; leaving nothing but a confused heap of explanations, which may cause ignorant people to doubt whether there is really any thing meant by the laws or not.   *Bp.Berkeley's Gaudentio di Lucca*, 166.[45]

In the country of the *Furr'd Law-cats*, they gripe all, devour all, conskite all, burn all, draw all, hang all, quarter all, behead all, murder all, imprison all, waste all, and ruin all, without the least notice of right or wrong: for among *them* vice is called virtue; wicked-ness, piety; treason, loyalty; robbery, justice: *Plunder* is their motto; *and all this they do, because they dare*—*Gripe-men-all*, the *Chief* of the *Furr'd Law-cats*, said to Pantagruel '*Our* Laws are like cobwebs; your silly *little* flies are stopt, caught, and destroy'd therein, but your *stronger* ones break them, and force and carry them which way they please. Don't think we are so mad as to set up our nets to snap up your *great* Robbers and tyrants: no, *they* are somewhat too hard for us, there's no meddling with them; for they will make no more of *us*, than we make of the little ones.'—   *Rabelais*, b. v. c. xi. xii.[46]

BLACK RATS.—*(Stuffed.)*

LADIES AND GENTLEMEN,

These are most pernicious animals. They BOROUGH, and prey on our food, drink, clothing, furniture, live-stock, and every convenience of life; furnishing their residences with the plunder of our property. They have particular HAUNTS, to which they entice each other in large numbers, for the sake of *prey;* where they often do incredible damage to our *mounds,* and undermine the strongest *embankments.* Sometimes they hoard their plunder in *nests,* that they make at a distance from their usual *places of congregating.** They are very bold and fierce. Instead of waiting for an attack, they usually become the aggressors, and, *seizing their adversaries by the lips,* inflict dangerous, and even deadly wounds. While they subsist on our industry, and increase our terrors, they make no grateful returns, and, therefore, mankind have studied various ways for diminishing their numbers; but their *cunning* discovers the most distant danger, and if any are disturbed or attacked, in an unusual manner, the rest take the alarm, and, becoming exceedingly shy, and wary, elude the most ingenious devices of their pursuers. When, unhappily, you come in contact with one of these *vermin,* the best way of dispatching it is by a single squeeze; but novices who hesitate, are sure to prove sufferers. They have been found on a BENCH, so *interwoven* by their tails, that *by reason of their entanglement, they could not part.*† A DEAD RAT, *by altering the look of his* HEAD *and the appearance of his* SKIN, may be transformed into the appearance of a much more *powerful* animal; and THIS, Ladies and Gentlemen, *has been considered a* MASTER PIECE *in cheating.*‡

* White's Selborne, 4to. 75.† Letters from Bodleian Library, i. 12.[47]
‡ Ibid, ii. 160, *note.* See also Goldsmith, iii, 169.

A *bait,* such wretches to beguile.

Spenser.[48]

Cadger. *n. s.* A *Low* Character.   *Pierce Egan.*[49]

One of
"The blessings of this *most indebted* land."
* * *
Useless in him alike both brain and speech,
Fate having plac'd all truth above his reach.   *Cowper.*[50]

A most damnable swearer and inventor of new oaths. A tongue-libelling lad of the sea—
he matters not the truth of any thing he speaks; but is prone to fasten his stings in the
reputation of those that would scorn to be like him. I wonder to see this unquiet disposition in a brute creature—a Swill-tub.

Pell's Improvement of the Sea, 1695, p. 101, *et seq.*[51]

————

A *CADGE* ANCHOR.—*(a Remora— a sucking Fish.)*[52]

WHAT have we here? a man or a fish? A FISH: he *smells* like a fish; a
very *ancient* and fish-like smell; a kind of, not of the newest, Poor John.
Were I in England now (as once I was) and had but this fish painted, not
a holiday fool there but would give a piece of silver: *there* would this
monster make a man; any *strange beast* there makes a man. His gab-
bling voice is to utter FOUL SPEECHES, and to DETRACT. He is as dispro-
portioned in his manners, as in his shape. As with age his body grows
uglier, his mind cankers.

CALIBAN.[53]

Reptil, with spawn abundant—   *Milton, Par. L.* b. 7.[54]

A WATER SCORPION.

LADIES AND GENTLEMEN,

This offensive INSECT lives in *stagnant* waters, continually watching for prey. Its feelers resemble the claws *of* a scorpion; the EYES are *hard and prominent,* the SHOULDERS *broad and flat.* It wastes twenty times as much as its appetite requires; one can destroy thirty or forty of the LIBELLULA kind,[55] each as large as itself. It is nevertheless greatly overrun with a small kind of lice, which probably repay the injuries it inflicts elsewhere. At certain seasons it flies to *distant waters* in search of food; but it remains where it was produced until fully grown, when *it sallies forth in search of a companion of the other sex, and soon begets an useless generation.*[*56]

* Martyn's Dict. Nat. Hist. 2 vols. Folio, 1785.   Goldsmith, vi. 35.

He that maketh the wound *bleed inwards*— *Bacon*[57]

Gives Liberty the last, the mortal shock;
Slips the slave's collar on, and *snaps* the lock. *Cowper.*[58]

What is his *Character*?—A man of amiable *Manners*—mild and civil.
Character of the Murderer of the Marrs.[59]
I never judge from *Manners*, for I once had my pocket picked by the *civilest* gentleman
I ever met with; and one of the *mildest* persons I ever saw was Ali Pacha. *Lord Byron.*[60]

DIRKPATRICK.
(a Petrified Putrefaction.—a Bloodstone.)

The Bloodstone is *green*, spotted with a bright *blood* red. *Woodward on Fossils.*[61]

Moral.

I recommend it to all that read this *History,* that when they find their lives come up,
in any degree, to a similitude of cases, they will inquire and ask themselves, is not this
the time to repent? *De Foe's Col. Jack,* 1723, p. 399.[62]

——————— *Raised* in blood. *Shakespeare.*[63]

THE BLOODHOUND.

LADIES AND GENTLEMEN,

This is the most terrible animal in the Collection. Its character is that of decided *enmity to man;* it hunts down those who endeavor to regain their *Liberty,* and is called the *Ban* Dog.[64] When it scents a human victim it follows his track with cruel perseverance, flies upon him with dreadful ferocity, and, unless dragged off, tears and rends the form until every noble feature of humanity is destroyed. It has an exquisite smell for blood. The species vary little throughout the world: there is scarcely any difference between the trans-atlantic *Spanish* bloodhound and the *Irish* wolf-dog, whose ferocity has been much diminished by the animal being frequently *crossed.* It is still kept on some of the old *royal grounds.**

* Edwards's West Indies. Goldsmith. Rainsford's St. Domingo. Scott's Sportsman's Repository.[65]

I do remember an APOTHECARY—
A THREE-INCH FOOL;——*unmannerly breech'd:*—— *Shakespeare.*[66]
Inflated and astrut with self-conceit:—— *Cowper*[67]
To *bleed* adventured he not, *except the Poor.* *Swift's Mem. of P. P.*[68]
He had heard of *Politics*, and long'd to get
A *Place;*————————and now,
With *all his Fam'ly* crowding at his heels,
His brothers, cousins, followers, and his son,
He shows himself *Prime Doctor*— *Rt. Hon. G. Canning.*[69]
He is that CANTING SLAVE foretold,
By one Dan Barnaby of old,
That would hang up his cat on Monday,
For killing of a mouse on Sunday;
Who, that *his* beer mayn't work the latter day,
Forbids the brewer's call on Saturday. *Anon.*[70]

A *go-cart* of superstition and prejudice, never stirring hand or foot but as he is pulled by the wires and strings of the state conjurers.
Hazlitt's Table Talk, 366.[71]

His A. B. C. is a great deal better employment for him, than the grave and weighty matters of state, and the study of politics.
Dr. Bastwick against Col. J. Lilburne, 42.[72]

Shall I lose my *Doctor?* No; he gives me the potions, and the *motions.*
What ho! APOTHECARY!— *Shakespeare.*[73]

THE DOCTOR.—*(a Dejection.)*[74]

In these days the grand "primum mobile" of England is CANT—*Cant political, Cant religious, Cant moral,* but *always* CANT—a thing of words, without the smallest influence upon actions; the English being no wiser, no better, and much poorer, and more divided among themselves, as well as far less moral, than they were before the prevalence of this *Verbal Decorum.* *Lord Byron on Mr. Bowles*, 16.[75]

DIARY.—April 1st. I grew *melancholy.*—My father lying sick, told me, in syllables, the *Philosopher's stone.*—It pleased God to put me in mind that I was now placed in the condition I always desired.—I hung three spiders about my neck (*for a charm*).—I kissed the king's hand.—*Caetera desunt.*[76]
Elias Ashmole's Diary.[77]

—————————the most notorious geck and *Gull*
That e'er Invention play'd on.   *Shakespeare.*[78]

THE BOOBY.[79]

LADIES AND GENTLEMEN,

The *Creature* you now see is a sort of *Noddy*[80] of the GULL kind. Observe his uncouth form and his ludicrously wise looks! He is the most stupid of the *feathered* tribe; yet he has a *voracious* appetite, and an enormous swallow. You perceive that he feigns the appearance of being *upright,* of seeming to comprehend objects he sees, of listening to what he hears, and that he shakes his head with *gravity,* as though he had a certain degree of understanding. His greatest pleasure is in *standing still.* He has not sense enough to *get out of People's way;* speaking to him or making *motions* never disturb him. There is no compelling him to the fatigue of *changing* his position till he feels a *blow;* for he keeps his PLACE till he is approached quite close, and *knocked down.* He is a living *full stop.* When he is *forced to walk,* which is very seldom, he goes from *side to side.* Like others of similar tribes, he BOROUGHS. In this respect the union and affection of these *Creatures* towards each other is wonderful; for, when undisturbed by the encroachments of *men,* they construct their *nests* as convenient as if they expected them to be *permanent;* arranging their different PLACES with such an amazing degree of uniformity, as to resemble a *regular plantation.* Sometimes they draw up side by side, in rank and file, and sit brooding together as if in deep counsel, on affairs of moment—their *silliness* and *solemnity* exciting involuntary *laughter!* This *burlesque* takes place, in particular, about the month of *November.* The habits of these tribes are known through those who visit the haunts they have forsaken for more obscure *retreats,* where they can *build aloft,* and settle in their *nests* at ease: a practice which confirms the remark of a great naturalist, that the presence of *men* not only destroys the society of the *meaner* animals, but even extinguishes their *grovelling* instincts. Hitherto the BOOBY has been considered of no service whatever; yet a similar species,* by drawing a wick through the body and lighting it, is made into a *candle.†* If this BOOBY could be thus used, the *illumination of* BOTH HOUSES *and the* PUBLIC OFFICES might be speedily effected, and the tribe he belongs to be rendered available to human purposes. At any rate a skilful tallow-chandler might try his hand at converting the *Creature* into

A TWOPENNY FLAT[81]

FOR A COBBLER'S STALL;

—————————————which, with short cotton wicks,
Touch'd by *th' industr'ous Cobb's* Promethean art,
Starts into light—and makes the lighter start!   *Rejected Addresses.*[82]

* Mother Carey's Chickens—the *Peterel.*[83]   † Martyn. Bewick.[84]

The Creature's at his *dirty* work again.   *Pope.*[85]

THE SLOP PAIL.

LADIES AND GENTLEMEN,

THE "SLOP PAIL" being occupied by "SLOP" keeping his *tri-colored* cockade in it, with the hope of bleaching it *white*, has become more and more offensive daily, and will be *kicked down.**[86]

---

*So 'the Jacobite Relics of Scotland' *fall low,*
When MENDACITY HOGG dares *his betters* to brow,
And turns up *HIS* SNOUT, with derision and scorn,
At those, who *less cringing*, to labor are born:—
The *parasite* pride of his *mendicant* mind
Pimps himself "to bewilder, and dazzles to blind;"
Yet I still wish him well—for I wish that he may
Learn, that wrong can't be right, and—be *honest* as they.

See Dedication of *Hogg's Jacobite Relics*
to the Highland Society of London.[87]

THE GREAT BOOTS having been *out of order*, were *welted*, and afterwards new *vamped*, and *polished*.[88] Dr. SOUTHEY, *the Varnisher*, has them in hand at present, and is '*doing them up*' as fast as possible.[89]

LADIES AND GENTLEMEN,

I thank you for your company. Opposite to you is a description of THE MONSTER, that my people are now *hunting* on the Continent. When *destroyed*, its skin will be stuffed and preserved among the other Antiquities and Curiosities in the *European Museum*.

LADIES AND GENTLEMEN, I wish you *a good day*.—*Keep to* THE RIGHT. Walk *steadily* FORWARD. The *Animals* may make an *uproar*, but don't be alarmed; I'll see you safe OUT. Remember they are *under my control*, and cannot take a step beyond the reach of

MY EYE

I'll watch them *tame*.   *Shakespeare*.[90]

THE
BOA DESOLATOR,
OR
LEGITIMATE VAMPIRE.

It overlays the continent like an ugly Incubus, sucking the blood and stopping up the breath of man's life. It claims Mankind as its property, and allows human nature to exist only upon sufferance; it haunts the understanding like a frightful spectre, and oppresses the very air with a weight that is not to be borne.   *Hazlit's Political Essays and Characters, p. 91.*[91]

THIS hideous BEAST, not having at any time put forth all his *members,* cannot be accurately described. Every *dark* Century has added to his frightful bulk. More disgusting than the filthiest reptile, his strength exceeds all other *brute force.*

His enormous, bloated, toad-like body is *ferruginous:*[*][92] the under surface appears of *polished steel.*[†] His cavern-like mouth is always open to devour; 'his teeth are as *swords,* and his jaw-teeth as knives'— as millions of *bristling bayonets* intermingled with *black fangs* containing mortal venom. His roar is a voice from the sepulchre. He is marked *'in form of a cross,'*[‡] with a series of *chains,* intersected by the TRIANGLE,[§] and glittering colours, variegated with *red.*

His aspect is cruel and terrible. He loves the *dark,* but never sleeps. Wherever he makes his lair, nature sickens, and man is brutified. His presence is 'plague, pestilence, and famine, battle, and murder, and sudden death.'[93] His bite rapidly *undermines the strongest* CONSTITUTION, and dissolves the whole into an entire mass of CORRUPTION. He has no *brain,* but the *walls* of the skull emit a *tinkling* sound, that attracts his victims, and lulls them into *passive obedience.* In this state he clutches them in his coils, and *screws* and *squeezes* them to destruction—*slavering* them over, and sucking in their *substance* at leisure. It is difficult to witness the half-stifled cries of his harmless prey, or to behold its anxiety and trepidation, while the monster writhes hideously around it, without imagining *what our own case would be in the same dreadful situation.*[||]

---

* Shaw's Zoology. Art. Boa, iii, 344.   † Ibid. 366.
‡ Linnæus's Nat. Hist. by Gmelin, 8vo. (Jones) 1816. Art. Boa Constrictor, xii. 437.[94]
§ Shaw's Zoology, iii. 339. || Macleod's Wreck of the Alceste, 291, 295.[95]

His rapacity is increased by *indulgence.* He grinds, cranches,[96] and devours whole multitudes, without being satisfied. His blood is cold. His ravening maw does not digest: it is an ever-yawning grave that *engulphs*—a 'bottomless pit' continually crying *'give, give!'* Sometimes he 'rests from his labours,' to admire his loathsome *limbs,* and *slime* them over. He has no affections: yet he appears charmed by the *hum* of the INSECTS that follow him, and pleased by the *tickling crawl* of the MEANEST REPTILES—permitting them to hang upon his lips, and partake of his leavings. But his real pleasure is in listening to the cries of his captives, the wail of the broken hearted, and the groans of the dying.

He lives in defiance and scorn of Providence, and in hatred to the happiness of man. When distended with human carnage, and wet with the gore of the innocent and the helpless, he lifts an impious *form* to heaven in solemn mockery. He was predicted of by the Seer of old, as the BEAST with many heads and crowns, bearing the name of BLASPHEMY.[97]

The garish *colours* that denote his malignity, excite only horror and detestation in the lover of nature, and of his species. They are most *lively* when he is engaged in the work of death, and cause him to be admired by the vulgar multitude, learned and unlearned, who hold him *sacred,* pay him *divine honors,* call him *holy,* and fall down before him as an object of worship, while priests glorify him, and minister to him, and pray for his murderous successes in the temples. Hence the good and the wise, in all ages, have devised and practised various methods for the destruction of a FIEND that creates nothing but *terror* and *imposture,* and between whom and rational man there is a natural antipathy.

He is filled with the deadliest rage by the encreasing growth of the *pop'lar* TREE:—

THAT TREE, beneath whose shade the Sons of Men
Shall pitch their tents in peace.
————BRISSOT murder'd, and the blameless wife
Of ROLAND! Martyr'd patriots, spirits pure,
Wept by the good, ye fell! Yet still survives,
Sown by your toil, and by your blood manured,
That imperishable TREE; and still its roots
Spread, and strike deep.————
                    Southey's Joan of Arc, b. iii.[98]

His existence is drawing to a close. It has been ascertained that the way of putting him *quietly* out of the world is by a 𝕭𝖑𝖆𝖈𝖐 𝕯𝖔𝖘𝖊, consisting of the *four and twenty letters* * of the alphabet, properly *composed*, made up in certain *forms*, covered with sheets of white *paper*, and well *worked* in a *Columbian* PRESS. These PAPERS are to be *forced down his throat* DAILY, morning and evening, and on every *seventh* day a *double* dose should be administered. The operation is accelerated by the powerful *exhibition* of the WOOD DRAUGHTS. In a short time his *teeth* will fall out—he will be seized with catalepsy—in the last stage of MORTIFICATION, he will STING HIMSELF *to death*;—and all mankind, relieved from the deadened atmosphere under which they had been *gasping*, will make the first use of their *recovered breath*, to raise an universal shout of joy at the extinction of

THE LEGITIMATE VAMPIRE.

Those Lords of pray'r and prey—that *band* of Kings,
That Royal, rav'ning BEAST, whose vampire wings
O'er sleeping Europe treacherously brood,
And fan her into dreams of *promis'd* good,
Of Hope, of Freedom—but to drain her blood!   Moore[99]

THE END.

---

* Philostratus[100] relates that the Indians destroy the most monstrous serpent by spreading *golden* LETTERS, *on a field of* RED, before his hole. They dazzle and confound him, and he is taken without difficulty.

PART THREE

—

PROSE

The Every-Day Book (1825–26), together with its successors The Table Book (1827) and The Year Book (1832), gave Hone's antiquarian interests and research abilities full expression. He had grown eager to withdraw from controversy and felt that the most practical activity would be to publish information useful to the public at large. He was fascinated with popular historical customs, and he successfully encouraged readers to contribute their own examples. Many became regular correspondents as a result. Hackwood suggests that Hone was indebted to Brand's Popular Antiquities (William Hone, 258) and to Defoe's Time's Telescope for the idea behind The Every-Day Book (William Hone, 320), and John Wardroper provides a brief list of some of the other sources Hone used in his compilations (The World of William Hone, ed. John Wardroper [London: Shelfmark Books, 1997], 314). Nevertheless, all three of these projects are Hone's distinctive products. All three were serial publications and combined elements of almanac, antiquarian miscellany, literary anthology, newspaper, and encyclopedia (Marsh, Word Crimes, 51). Hone's poetic enthusiasms were a conspicuous feature. In addition to his own occasional verses, extracts from the major English poets appeared frequently, and he also included notices of contemporary poets such as Keats, Clare, and Wordsworth. Charles Lamb became a regular contributor, and the two men became close friends.

Priced at threepence, The Every-Day Book appeared each Saturday, "a sheet of thirty-two columns with engravings" (Hackwood, 246) by artists Hone commissioned or based on old prints and drawings. Although Cruikshank did make some contributions, Hone's chief illustrator in the three works was Samuel Williams. The first volume having achieved a popular success, a second was published and the two volumes comprising 1,700 pages went on sale at the close of 1826. Although Hone was arrested for debt in April 1826 and had to reside within King's Bench Prison for the next two years (he was released, a bankrupt, in September 1828), he continued to edit, compile, and solicit contributions while in debtors' prison. A successor to The Every-Day Book, The Table Book, a literary miscellany, was undertaken at the beginning of 1827 and it, too, attracted broad support. Thomas Tegg enlisted Hone to compile yet another companion volume, The Year Book, in 1831–32. This was a sixty-four-page monthly magazine. Hone was paid four hundred pounds for editing a year's issues, but he involved Tegg in such heavy expenditures, notably for high-quality engravings, that the enterprise ended in severe financial acrimony. Desperate for money, Hone was forced to sell for a pittance all his printing materials and original stereotypes connected with these prose volumes. Tegg purchased them and made a small fortune exploiting them for many years.

All three books were reprinted singly and together many times during the nineteenth century, and even as late as 1927. *The Year Book*, for example, was reprinted in at least the following years: 1838, 1839, 1841, 1845, 1848, 1850, 1864, 1866, 1878, and 1892. The Gale Research Company of Detroit published a reprint in 1967, edited by Leslie Shepard. As mentioned above, more recently Shelfmark Books of London has published *The World of William Hone*, edited by John Wardroper, an annotated selection from the series.

While the prose volumes compiled by Hone range over all parts of England in highlighting local customs and traditions, London had always been his home and central point of reference. As a result, his concern over rapid urbanization in London also receives attention in his prose, especially in articles that describe excursions on foot. A draft article in manuscript, "Walks and Talks," states his perspective: "London is familiar to me; I know every street & turning in the city, have walked over half the metropolis when the land covered with houses and churches was green fields" (Add MS 40117, f.68). Our brief selections especially aim to give examples of Hone's own contributions to his prose volumes.

FROM THE EVERY-DAY BOOK, VOL. 1

PREFACE.

THIS volume is a specimen of a work undertaken for the purpose of forming a collection of the manners and customs of ancient and modern times, with descriptive accounts of the several seasons of popular pastime.

Each of the three hundred and sixty-five days in the year is distinguished by occurrences or other particulars relating to the day, and by the methods of celebrating every holiday; the work is therefore what its title purports, THE EVERY-DAY BOOK.

It is an EVERLASTING CALENDAR—because its collection of facts concerning the origin and usages of every remarkable day, including movable feasts and fasts, constitute a calendar for *every* year.

It is a HISTORY OF THE YEAR—because it traces the commencement and progress of the year from the first day to the last.

It is a HISTORY OF THE MONTHS—because it describes the appearances that distinguish each month from the other months.

It is a HISTORY OF THE SEASONS—because it describes the influences and character of the four quarters into which the year is divided, and the most remarkable objects in natural history peculiar to each season.

It is a PERPETUAL KEY TO THE ALMANACK—because it explains the signification of every name and term in the almanack.

Its antiquarian and historical notices are calculated to engage the attention of almost every class of readers, and to gratify several who would scarcely expect such particulars in such a miscellany. The perplexities attending the discovery of certain facts, and the labour of reducing all into order, will be appreciated by the few who have engaged in similar pursuits. Some curious matters are now, for the first time, submitted to the public; and others are so rare as to seem altogether new.

As regards the engravings, to such as are from old masters, notices of their prints are always annexed. The designs for the allegorical and other illustrations have originated with myself; and the drawings been accommodated, and the engravings executed, according to my own sense of subject and style. In numerous instances they have been as satisfactory to me as to my readers; many of whom, however, are less difficult to please than I am, and have favourably received some things which I have been obliged to tolerate, because the exigency of publication left me no time to supply their place. I know what art can accomplish, and am therefore dissatisfied when artists fail to accomplish.

I may now avow that I have other aims than I deemed it expedient to mention in the prospectus:—to communicate in an agreeable manner, the greatest possible variety of important and diverting facts, without a single sentence to excite an uneasy sensation, or an embarrassing inquiry; and, by not seeming to teach, to cultivate a high moral feeling, and the best affections of the heart: —to open a storehouse, from whence manhood may derive daily instruction and amusement, and youth and innocence be informed, and retain their innocency.

To these intentions I have accommodated my materials under such difficulties as I hope may never be experienced by any one engaged in such a labour. To what extent less embarrassed and more enlarged faculties could have better executed the task I cannot determine; but I have always kept my main object in view, the promotion of social and benevolent feelings, and I am persuaded this prevailing disposition is obvious throughout. The poetical illustrations, whether "solemn thinkings," or light dispersions, are particularly directed to that end.

I may now be permitted to refer to the copious indexes for the multifarious contents of the volume, and to urge the friends to the undertaking for assistance towards its completion. There is scarcely any one who has not said—"Ah! this is *something* that will do for the *Every-Day Book:*" I crave to be favoured with that "something." Others have observed—"I expected *something* about so and so in the *Every-Day Book.*" It is not possible, however, that I should know *every* thing; but if each will communicate "something," the work will gratify every one, and my own most sanguine wishes.

And here I beg leave to offer my respectful thanks to several correspondents who have already furnished me with accounts of customs, &c. which appear under different signatures. Were I permitted to disclose their real names, it would be seen that several of these communications are from distinguished characters. As a precaution against imposition, articles of that nature have not been, nor can they be, inserted, without the name and address of the writer being confided to myself. Accounts, so subscribed, will be printed with any initials or mark the writers may please to suggest.

From the publication of the present volume, a correct judgment may be formed of the nature and tendency of the work, which incidentally embraces almost every topic of inquiry or remark connected with the ancient and present state of manners and literature. Scarcely an individual is without a scrap-book, or a portfolio, or a collection of some sort; and whatever a kind-hearted reader may deem curious or interesting, and can conveniently spare, I earnestly hope and solicit to be favoured with, addressed to me at Messrs. Hunt and Clarke's, Tavistock-street, who receive communications for the work, and publish it in weekly sheets, and monthly parts, as usual.

May, 1826.

May 8

CANONBURY TOWER.

People methinks are better, but the scenes
Wherein my youth delighted are no more.
I wander out in search of them, and find
A sad deformity in all I see.

Strong recollections of my former pleasures,
And knowledge that they never can return,
Are causes of my sombre mindedness:
I pray you then bear with my discontent.[1]

A walk out of London is, to me, an event; I have an *every-day* desire to bring it about, but weeks elapse before the time arrives whereon I can sally forth. In my boyhood, I had only to obtain parental permission, and stroll in fields now no more,—to scenes now deformed, or that I have been wholly robbed of, by "the spirit of improvement." Five and thirty years have altered every thing—myself with the rest. I am obliged to "ask leave to go out," of time and circumstance; or to wait till the only enemy I cannot openly face has ceased from before me— the north-east wind—or to brave that foe and get the worst of it. I did so yesterday. "This is the time," I said, to an artist, "when we Londoners begin to get our walks; we will go to a place or two that I knew many years ago, and see how they look now; and first to Canonbury-house."

Having crossed the back Islington-road, we found ourselves in the rear of the *Pied Bull*. Ah! I know this spot well: this stagnant pool was a "famous" carp pond among boys. How dreary the place seems! the yard and pens were formerly filled with sheep and cattle for Smithfield market; graziers and drovers were busied about them; a high barred gate was constantly closed; now all is thrown open and neglected, and not a living thing to be seen. We went round to the front, the house was shut up, and nobody answered to the knocking. It had been the residence of the gallant Sir Walter Raleigh,[2] who threw down his court mantle for Queen Elizabeth to walk on, that she might not damp her feet; he, whose achievements in Virginia secured immense revenue to his country; whose individual enterprise in South America carried terror to the recreant heart of Spain; who lost years of his life within the walls of the Tower, where he wrote the "History of the World," and better than all, its inimitable preface; and who finally lost his life on a scaffold for his courage and services. By a door in the rear we got into "the best parlour;" this was on the ground-floor; it had been Raleigh's dining-room. Here the arms of Sir John Miller are painted on glass in the end window; and we found Mr. John Cleghorn sketching them. This gentleman, who lives in the neighbourhood, and whose talents as a draftsman and engraver are well known, was obligingly communicative; and we condoled on the decaying memorials of past greatness. On the ceiling of this room are stuccoed the five senses; Feeling in an oval centre, and the other four in the scroll-work around. The chimney-piece of carved oak, painted white, represents Charity, supported by Faith on her right, and Hope on her left. Taking leave of Mr. Cleghorn, we hastily passed through the other apartments, and gave a last farewell look at Sir Walter's house; yet we bade not adieu to it till my accompanying friend expressed a wish, that as Sir Walter, according to tradition, had there smoked the first pipe of tobacco drawn in Islington, so *he* might have been able to smoke the last whiff within the walls that would in a few weeks be levelled to the ground.

We got to Canonbury. Geoffrey Crayon's "Poor Devil Author" sojourned here:[3]—

"Chance threw me," he says, "in the way of Canonbury Castle. It is an ancient brick tower, hard by 'merry Islington;' the remains of a hunting-seat of Queen Elizabeth, where she took the pleasure of the country when the neighbourhood was all woodland. What gave it particular interest in my eyes was the circumstance that it had been the residence of a poet. It was here Goldsmith resided when he wrote his 'Deserted Village.'[4] I was shown the very apartment. It was a relic of the original style of the castle, with pannelled wainscots and Gothic windows. I was pleased with its air of antiquity and with its having been the residence of poor Goldy. 'Goldsmith was a pretty poet,' said I to myself, 'a very pretty poet, though rather of the old school. He did not think and feel so strongly as is the fashion now-a-days; but had he lived in these times of hot hearts and hot heads, he would no doubt have written quite differently.' In a few days I was quietly established in my new quarters; my books all arranged; my writing-desk placed by a window looking out into the fields, and I felt as snug as Robinson Crusoe when he had finished his bower. For several days I enjoyed all the novelty of change and the charms which grace new lodgings before one has found out their defects. I rambled about the fields where I fancied Goldsmith had rambled. I explored merry Islington; ate my solitary dinner at the Black Bull, which, according to tradition, was a country seat of Sir Walter Raleigh, and would sit and sip my wine, and muse on old times, in a quaint old room where many a council had been held. All this did very well for a few days; I was stimulated by novelty; inspired by the associations awakened in my mind by these curious haunts; and began to think I felt the spirit of composition stirring with me. But Sunday came, and with it the whole city world, swarming about Canonbury Castle. I could not open my window but I was stunned with shouts and noises from the cricket ground; the late quiet road beneath my window was alive with the tread of feet and clack of tongues; and, to complete my misery, I found that my quiet retreat was absolutely a 'show house,' the tower and its contents being shown to strangers at sixpence a head. There was a perpetual tramping up stairs of citizens and their families to look about the country from the top of the tower, and to take a peep at the city through the telescope, to try if they could discern their own chimneys. And then, in the midst of a vein of thought, or a moment of inspiration, I was interrupted, and all my ideas put to flight, by my intolerable landlady's tapping at the door, and asking me if I would 'just please to let a lady and gentleman come in, to take a look at Mr. Goldsmith's room.' If you know any thing what an author's study is, and what an author is himself, you must know that there was no standing this. I put a positive interdict on my room's being exhibited; but then it was shown when I was absent, and my papers put in confusion; and on returning home one day I absolutely found a cursed tradesman and his daughters gaping over my manuscripts, and my landlady in a panic at my appearance. I tried to make out a little longer, by taking the key in my pocket; but it would not do. I overheard mine hostess one day telling some of her customers on the stairs that the room was occupied by an author, who was always in a tantrum if interrupted; and I immediately perceived, by a slight noise at the door, that they were peeping at me through the key-hole. By the head of Apollo, but this was quite too much! With all my eagerness for fame, and my ambition of the stare of the million, I had no idea of being exhibited by retail, at sixpence a head, and that through a key-hole. So I bade adieu to Canonbury Castle, merry Islington, and the haunts of poor Goldsmith, without having advanced a single line in my labours."

Now for this and some other descriptions, I have a quarrel with the aforesaid Geoffrey Crayon, gent. What right has a transatlantic settler to feelings in England? He located in America, but it seems he did not locate his feelings there; if not, why not? What right has *he* of New York to sit "solitary" in Raleigh's house at Islington, and "muse" on *our* "old times;" himself clearly a *pied* animal, mistaking the *pied* bull for a "black" bull. There is "black" blood between us. By what authority has *he* a claim to a domicile at Canonbury? Under what international law laid down by Vattel or Martens,[5] or other jurist, ancient or modern, can *his* pretension to feel and muse at Sir Walter's or Queen Elizabeth's tower, be admitted? He comes here and describes as if he were a *real* Englishman; and claims copyright in our course for his feelings and descriptions, while he himself is a copyist; a downright copyist of *my* feelings, who *am* an Englishman, and a forestaller of *my* descriptions— baiting the "black" bull. He has left me nothing to do.

My friend, the artist, obligingly passed the door of Canonbury tower to take a sketch of its north-east side; not that the tower has not been taken before, but it has not been given exactly in that position. We love every look of an old friend, and this look we get after crossing the bridge of the New River, coming from the "Thatched house" to "Canonbury tavern." A year or so ago, the short walk from the lower Islington-road to this bridge was the prettiest "bit" on the river nearest to London. Here the curve of the stream formed the "horse-shoe." In bygone days only three or four hundred, from the back of Church-street southerly, and from the back of the upper street westerly, to Canonbury, were open green pastures with uninterrupted views easterly, bounded only by the horizon. Then the gardens to the houses in Canonbury-place, terminated by the edge of the river, were covetable retirements; and ladies, lovely as the marble bust of Mrs. Thomas Gent, by Behnes,[6] in the Royal Academy Exhibition, walked in these gardens, "not unseen," yet not obtruded on. Now, how changed!

My ringing at the tower-gate was answered by Mr. Symes, who for thirty-nine years past has been resident in the mansion, and is bailiff of the manor of Islington, under Lord Northampton.[7] Once more, to "many a time and oft" aforetime, I ranged the old rooms, and took perhaps a last look from its roof. The eye shrunk from the wide havoc below. Where new buildings had not covered the sward, it was embowelling for bricks, and kilns emitted flickering fire and sulphurous stench. Surely the dominion of the brick-and-mortar king will have no end; and cages for commercial spirits will be instead of every green herb. In this high tower some of our literary men frequently shut themselves up, "far from the busy haunts of men."[8] Mr. Symes says that his mother-in-law, Mrs. Evans, who had lived there three and thirty years, and was wife to the former bailiff, often told him that her aunt, Mrs. Tapps, a seventy years' inhabitant of the tower, was accustomed to talk much about Goldsmith and his apartment. It was the old oak room on the first floor. Mrs. Tapps affirmed that he there wrote his "Deserted Village," and slept in a large press bedstead, placed in the eastern corner. From this room two small ones for sleeping in have since been separated, by the removal of the pannelled oak wainscotting from the north-east wall, and the cutting of two doors through it, with a partition between them; and since Goldsmith was here, the window on the south side has been broken through. Hither have I come almost every year, and frequently in many years, and seen the changing occupancy of these apartments. Goldsmith's room I almost suspect to have been tenanted by Geoffrey Crayon; about seven years ago I saw books on one of the tables with writing materials, and denotements of more than a "Poor Devil Author." This apartment, and other apartments in the tower, are often to be let comfortably furnished, "with other conveniences." It is worth while to take a room or two, were it only to hear Mr. Symes's pleasant conversation about residences and residentiaries, manorial rights and boundaries, and "things as they used to be" in his father's time, who was bailiff before him, and "in Mrs. Evans's time," or "Mrs. Tapps's time." The grand tenantry of the tower has been in and through him and them during a hundred and forty-two years.

Canonbury tower is sixty feet high, and seventy feet square. It is part of an old mansion which appears to have been erected, or, if erected before, much altered about the reign of Elizabeth. The more ancient edifice was erected by the priors of the canons of St. Bartholomew, Smithfield, and hence was called Canonbury, to whom it appertained until it was surrendered with the priory to Henry VIII.; and when the religious houses were dissolved, Henry gave the manor to Thomas Lord Cromwell; it afterwards passed through other hands till it was possessed by Sir John Spencer, an alderman and lord mayor of London, known by the name of "rich Spencer."[9] While he resided at Canonbury, a Dunkirk pirate came over in a shallop to Barking creek, and hid himself with some armed men in Islington fields, near to the path Sir John usually took from his house in Crosby-place to this mansion, with the hope of making him prisoner; but as he remained in town that night, they were glad to make off, for fear of detection, and returned to France disappointed of their prey, and of the large ransom they calculated on for the release of his person. His sole daughter and heiress, Elizabeth, was carried off in a baker's basket from Canonbury-house by William, the second lord Compton, lord president of Wales. He inherited Canonbury, with the rest of Sir John Spencer's wealth at his death, and was afterwards created Earl of Northampton; in this family the manor still remains. The present earl's rent-roll will be enormously increased, by the extinction of comfort to the inhabitants of Islington and its vicinity, through the covering up of the open fields and verdant spots on his estates.

As a custom it is noticeable, that many metropolitans visit this antique edifice in summer, for the sake of the panoramic view from the roof. To those who inquire concerning the origin or peculiarities of its erection or history, Mr. Symes obligingly tenders the loan of "Nelson's History of Islington," wherein is ample information on these points.[10] In my visit, yesterday, I gathered one or two particulars from this gentleman not befitting me to conceal, inasmuch as I hold and maintain that the world would not be the worse for being acquainted with what every one knows; and that it is every one's duty to contribute as much as he can to the amusement and instruction of others. Be it known then, that Mr. Symes says he possesses the ancient key of the gate belonging to the prior's park. "It formerly hung there," said he, pointing with his finger as we stood in the kitchen, "withinside that clock-case, but by some accident it has fallen to the bottom, and I cannot get at it." The clock-case is let into the solid wall flush with the surface, and the door to the weights opening only a small way down from the dial plate, they descend full two-thirds the length of their lines within a "fixed abode." Adown this space Mr. Symes has looked, and let down inches of candle without being able to see, and raked with long sticks without being able to feel, the key; and yet he thinks it there, in spite of the negative proof, and of a suggestion I uncharitably urged, that some antiquary, with confused notions as to the "rights of things," might have removed the key from the nail in the twinkling of Mr. Symes's eye, and finally deposited it among his own "collections." A very large old arm chair, with handsome carved claws, and modern verdant baize on the seat and back, which also stands in the kitchen, attracted my attention. "It was here," said Mr. Symes, "before Mrs. Tapps's time; the old tapestry bottom was quite worn out, and the tapestry back so ragged, that I cut them away, and had them replaced as you see; but I have kept the back, because it represents Queen Elizabeth hunting in the woods that were hereabout in her time—I'll fetch it." On my hanging this tapestry against the clock-case, it was easy to make out a lady gallantly seated on horseback, with a sort of turbaned headdress, and about to throw a spear from her right hand; a huntsman on foot, with a pole in one hand, and leading a brace of dogs with the other, runs at the side of the horse's head; and another man on foot, with a gun on his shoulder, follows the horse; the costume, however, is not so early as the time of Elizabeth; certainly not before the reign of Charles I.

This edifice is well worth seeing, and Mr. Symes's plain civility is good entertainment. Readers have only to ring at the bell above the brass plate with the word "Tower" on it, and ask, "Is Mr. Tower at home?" as I do, and they will be immediately introduced; at the conclusion of the visit the tender of sixpence each, by way of "quit-rent," will be accepted. Those who have been before and not lately, will view "improvement" rapidly devastating the forms of nature around this once delightful spot; others who have not visited it at all may be amazed at the extensive prospects; and none who see the "goings on" and "ponder well," will be able to foretell whether Mr. Symes or the tower will enjoy benefit of survivorship.

To Canonbury Tower.

As some old, stout, and lonely holyhock,
Within a desolate neglected garden,
Doth long survive beneath the gradual choke
Of weeds, that come and work the general spoil;
So, Canonbury, thou dost stand awhile:
Yet fall at last thou must; for thy rich warden
Is fast "improving;" all thy pleasant fields
Have fled, and brick-kilns, bricks, and houses rise
At his command; the air no longer yields
A fragrance—scarcely health; the very skies
Grow dim and townlike; a cold, creeping gloom
Steals into thee, and saddens every room:
And so realities come unto me,
Clouding the chambers of my mind, and making me—like thee.

May 18, 1825.

May 23

WHITSUNTIDE AT GREENWICH.

I have had another holiday—a Whitsuntide holiday at Greenwich: it is true that I did not take a run down the hill, but I saw many do it who appeared to me happier and healthier for the exercise, and the fragrant breezes from the fine May trees of the park.

I began Whit-Monday by breakfasting on Blackheath hill.[11] It was my good fortune to gain a sight of the beautiful grounds belonging to the noblest mansion on the heath, the residence of the princess Sophia of Gloucester.[12] It is not a "show house," nor is her royal highness a woman of show. "She is a noble lady," said a worthy inhabitant of the neighbourhood, "she is always doing as much good as she can, and more, perhaps, than she ought: her heart is larger than her purse." I found myself in this retreat I scarcely know how, and imagined that a place like this might make good dispositions better, and intelligent minds wiser. Some of its scenes seemed, to my imagination, lovely as were the spots in "the blissful seats of Eden." Delightful green swards with majestic trees lead on to private walks; and gladdening shrubberies terminate in broad borders of fine flowers, or in sloping paths, whereon fairies might dance in silence by the sleeping moonlight, or to the chant of nightingales that come hither, to an amphitheatre of copses surrounding a "rose mount," as to their proper choir, and pour their melody, unheard by earthly beings,

> ————————————save by the ear
> Of her alone who wanders here, or sits
> Intrelissed and enchanted as the Fair
> Fabled by him of yore in Comus' song,
> Or rather like a saint in a fair shrine
> Carved by Cellini's hand.[13]

It may not be good taste, in declaring the truth, to state "the whole truth," but it is a fact, that I descended from the heights of royalty to "Sot's hole." There, for "corporal refection," and from desire to see a place which derives its name from the great Lord Chesterfield,[14] I took a biscuit and a glass of ginger-beer. His lordship resided in the mansion I had just left, and his servants were accustomed to "use" this alehouse too frequently. On one occasion he said to his butler, "Fetch the fellows from that sot's hole:" from that time, though the house has another name and sign, it is better known by the name or sign of "Sot's hole." Ascending the rise to the nearest parkgate, I soon got to the observatory in the park. It was barely noon. The holiday folks had not yet arrived; the old pensioners, who ply there to ferry the eye up and down and across the river with their telescopes, were ready with their craft. Yielding to the importunity of one, to be freed from the invitations of the rest, I took my stand, and in less than ten minutes was conveyed to Barking church, Epping Forest, the men in chains, the London Docks,

St. Paul's Cathedral, and Westminster Abbey. From the seat around the tree I watched the early comers; as each party arrived the pensioners hailed them with good success. In every instance, save one, the sight first demanded was the "men in chains:" these are the bodies of pirates, suspended on gibbets by the river side, to warn sailors against crimes on the high seas. An able-bodied sailor, with a new hat on his Saracen-looking head, carrying a handkerchief full of apples in his left hand, with a bottle neck sticking out of the neck of his jacket for a nosegay, dragged his female companion up the hill with all the might of his right arm and shoulder; and the moment he was at the top, assented to the proposal of a telescope-keeper for his "good lady" to have a view of the "men in chains." She wanted to "see something else first." "Don't be a fool," said Jack, "see *them* first; it's the best sight." No; not she: all Jack's arguments were unavailing. "Well! what is it you'd like better, you fool you?" "Why I wants to see our house in the court, with the flower-pots, and if I don't see that, I wont see nothing—what's the men in chains to *that?* Give us an apple." She took one out of the bundle, and beginning to eat it, gave instructions for the direction of the instrument towards Limehouse church,[15] while Jack drew forth the bottle and refreshed himself. Long she looked, and squabbled, and almost gave up the hope of finding "our house;" but on a sudden she screamed out, "Here Jack! here it is, pots and all! and there's our bed-post; I left the window up o' purpose as I might see it!" Jack himself took an observation. "D'ye see it, Jack?" "Yes." "D'ye see the pots?" "Yes." "And the bed-post?" "Ay; and here Sal, here, here's the cat looking out o' the window." "Come away, let's look again;" and then she looked, and squalled "Lord! what a sweet place it is!" and then she assented to seeing the "men in chains," giving Jack the first look, and they looked "all down the river," and saw "Tom's ship," and wished Tom was with them. The breakings forth of nature and kind-heartedness, and especially the love of "home, sweet home," in Jack's "good lady," drew forth Jack's delight, and he kissed her till the apples rolled out of the bundle, and then he pulled her down the hill. From the moment they came up they looked at nobody, nor saw any thing but themselves, and what they paid for looking at through the telescope. They were themselves a sight: and though the woman was far from

whatever fair
High fancy forms or lavish hearts could wish,

yet she was all that to Jack; and all that she seemed to love or care for, were "our house," and the "flower-pots," and the "bed-post," and "Jack."

At the entrances in all the streets of Greenwich, notices from the magistrates were posted, that they were determined to put down the fair; and accordingly not a show was to be seen in the place wherein the fair had of late been held. Booths were fitting up for dancing and re-freshment at night, but neither Richardson's, nor any other itinerant company of performers, was there. There were gingerbread stalls, but no learned pig, no dwarf, no giant, no fire-eater, no exhibition of any kind. There was a large round-about of wooden horses for boys, and a few swings, none of them half filled. The landlord of "the Struggler" could not struggle his stand into notice. In vain he chalked up "Hagger's entire, two-pence a bottle:" this was ginger-beer; if it was not brisker than the demand for it, it was made "poor indeed;" he had little aid, but unsold "Lemmun aid, one penny a glass." Yet the public-houses in Greenwich were filling fast, and the fiddles squeaked from several first-floor windows. It was now nearly two o'clock, and the stage-coaches from London, thoroughly filled inside and out, drove rapidly in: these, and the flocking down of foot passengers, gave sign of great visitation. One object I cannot pass by, for it forcibly contrasted in me mind with the joyous disposition of the day. It was a poor blackbird in a cage, from the first-floor window of a house in Melville-place. The cage was high and square; its bars were of a dark brown bamboo; the top and bottom were of the same dolorous colour; between the bars were strong iron wires; the bird himself sat dull and mute; I passed the house several times; not a single note did he give forth. A few hours before I had heard his fellows in the thickets whistling in full throat; and here was he, in endless thrall, without a bit of green to cheer him, or even the decent jailery of a light wicker cage. I looked at him, and thought of the Lollards at Lambeth, of Thomas Delaune in Newgate, of Prynne in the Gate-house, and Laud in the Tower:[16]—all these were offenders; yet wherein had this poor bird offended that he should be like them, and be forced to keep Whitsuntide in prison? I wished him a holiday, and would have given him one to the end of his life, had I known how.

After dining and taking tea at the "Yorkshire Grey," I returned to the park, through the Greenwich gate, near the hospital. The scene here was very lively. Great numbers were seated on the grass, some re-freshing themselves, others were lookers at the large company of walkers. Surrounded by a goodly number was a man who stood to exhibit the wonders of a single-folded sheet of writing paper to the sight of all except himself; he was blind. By a motion of his hand he changed it into various forms. "Here" said he, "is a garden-chair for your seat—this is a flight of stairs to your chamber—here is a flower-stand for your mantle-piece;" and so he went on; presenting, in rapid succession, the well-shaped representation of more than thirty forms of different utensils or conveniences: at the conclusion, he was well rewarded for his ingenuity. Further on was a larger group; from the centre whereof came forth sounds unlike those heard by him who wrote—

> "Orpheus play'd so well, he moved old Nick,
> But thou mov'st nothing but thy fiddle-stick."

This player so "imitated Orpheus," that he moved the very bowels, uneasiness seemed to seize on all who heard his discords. He was seated on the grass, in the garb of a sailor. At his right hand lay a square board, whereon was painted "a tale of woe," in letters that disdained the printer's art; at the top, a little box, with a glass cover, discovered that it was "plus" of what himself was "minus;" its inscription described its contents—"These bones was taken out of my leg." I could not withstand his claim to support. He was effecting the destruction of "Sweet Poll of Plymouth," for which I gave him a trifle more than his "fair" audience usually bestowed, perhaps. He instantly begged I would name my "favourite;" I desired to be acquainted with his; he said he could not "deny nothing to so noble a benefactor," and he immediately began to murder "Blackeyed Susan." If the man at the wall of the Fishmongers' almshouses were dead, he would be the worst player in England.

There were several parties playing at "Kiss in the ring," an innocent merriment in the country; here it was certainly not merriment. On the hill the runners were abundant, and the far greater number were, in appearance and manners, devoid of that vulgarity and grossness from whence it might be inferred that the sport was any way improper; nor did I observe, during a stay of several hours, the least indication of its being otherwise than a cheerful amusement. One of the prettiest sights was a game at "Thread my needle," played by about a dozen lasses, with a grace and glee that reminded me of Angelica's nymphs.[17] I indulged a hope that the hilarity of rural pastimes might yet be preserved. There was no drinking in the park. It lost its visitants fast while the sun was going down. Many were arrested in their progress to the gate by the sight of the boys belonging to the college, who were at their evening play within their own grounds, and who, before they retired for the night, sung "God save the King," and "Rule Britannia," in full chorus, with fine effect.

The fair, or at least such part of it as was suffered to be continued, was held in the open space on the right hand of the street leading from Greenwich to the Creek bridge. "The Crown and Anchor" booth was the great attraction, as indeed well it might. It was a tent, three hundred and twenty-three feet long, and sixty feet wide. Seventy feet of this, at the entrance, was occupied by seats for persons who chose to take refreshment, and by a large space from whence the viands were delivered. The remaining two hundred and fifty feet formed the "Assembly room," wherein were boarded floors for four rows of dancers throughout this extensive length; on each side were seats and tables. The price of admission to the assembly was one shilling. The check ticket was a card, whereon was printed,

VAUXHALL.
CROWN AND ANCHOR,
WHIT MONDAY.

This room was thoroughly lighted up by depending branches from the roofs handsomely formed; and by stars and festoons, and the letters G. R.[18] and other devices, bearing illumination lamps. It was more completely filled with dancers and spectators, than were convenient to either. Neither the company nor the scene can be well described. The orchestra, elevated across the middle of the tent, consisting of two harps, three violins, a bass viol, two clarionets, and a flute, played airs from "Der Freischütz,"[19] and other popular tunes. Save the crowd, there was no confusion; save in the quality of the dancers and dancing, there was no observable difference between this and other large assemblies; except, indeed, that there was no master of the ceremonies, nor any difficulty in obtaining or declining partners. It was neither a dancing school, nor a school of morals; but the moralist might draw conclusions which would here, and at this time, be out of place. There were at least 2,000 persons in this booth at one time. In the fair were about twenty other dancing booths; yet none of them comparable in extent to the "Crown and Anchor." In one only was a price demanded for admission;

the tickets to the "Albion Assembly" were sixpence. Most of these booths had names; for instance, "The Royal Standard," "The Lads of the Village," "The Black Boy and Cat Tavern," "The Moon-rakers," &c. At eleven o'clock, stages from Greenwich to London were in full request. One of them obtained 4*s.* each for inside, and 2*s.* 6*d.* for outside passengers; the average price was 3*s.* inside, and 2*s.* outside; and though the footpaths were crowded with passengers, yet all the inns in Greenwich and on the road were thoroughly filled. Certainly, the greater part of the visitors were mere spectators of the scene.

* * * * *

THE SLUICE GATE.

From Canonbury tower onward by the New River, is a pleasant summer afternoon's walk. Highbury barn, or, as it is now called, Highbury tavern, is the first place of note beyond Canonbury. It was anciently a barn belonging to the ecclesiastics of Clerkenwell; though it is at present only known to the inhabitants of that suburb, by its capacity for filling them with good things in return for the money they spend there. The "barn" itself is the assembly-room, whereon the old roof still remains. This house has stood in the way of all passengers to the Sluice-house, and turned many from their firm-set purpose of fishing in the waters near it. Every man who carries a rod and line is not an Isaac

Walton,[20] whom neither blandishment nor obstacle could swerve from his mighty end when he went forth to kill fish.

> He was the great progenitor of all
> That war upon the tenants of the stream,
> He neither stumbled, stopt, nor had a fall
> When he essay'd to war on dace, bleak, bream,
> Stone-loach or pike, or other fish, I deem.

The Sluice-house is a small wooden building, distant about half a mile beyond Highbury, just before the river angles off towards Newington. With London anglers it has always been a house of celebrity, because it is the nearest spot wherein they have hope of tolerable sport. Within it is now placed a machine for forcing water into the pipes that supply the inhabitants of Holloway, and other parts adjacent.

JUNE 26

THE EVERY-DAY BOOK.—JUNE 26.

COTTAGE FORMERLY IN HAGBUSH-LANE.

" Why this cottage, sir, not three miles from London, is as secluded as if it were in the weald of Kent."

COTTAGE FORMERLY IN HAGBUSH-LANE.

"Why this cottage, sir, not three miles from London, is as secluded as if it were in the weald of Kent."

This cottage stands no longer: its history is in the "simple annals
of the poor."[21] About seven years ago, an aged and almost decayed
labouring man, a native of Cheshunt, in Hertfordshire, with his wife
and child, lay out every night upon the road side of Hagbush-lane, under what of bough and branch they could creep for shelter, till "winter's cold" came on, and then he erected this "mud edifice." He had
worked for some great land-holders and owners in Islington, and still
jobbed about. Like them, he was, to this extent of building, a specula-
tor; and to eke out his insufficient means, he profited, in his humble
abode, by the sale of small beer to stragglers and rustic wayfarers. His
cottage stood between the lands of two rich men; not upon the land of
either, but partly on the disused road, and partly on the waste of the
manor. Deeming him by no means a respectable neighbour for their
cattle, they "warned him off;" he, not choosing to be houseless, nor
conceiving that their domains could be injured by his little enclosure
between the banks of the road, refused to accept this notice, and he
remained. For this offence, one of them caused his labourers to level
the miserable dwelling to the earth, and the "houseless child of want,"
was compelled by this wanton act to apply for his family and himself to
be taken into the workhouse. His application was refused, but he received advice to build again, with information that his disturber was
not justified in disturbing him. In vain he pleaded incompetent power
to resist; the workhouse was shut against him, and he began to build
another hut. He had proceeded so far as to keep off the weather in one
direction, when wealth again made war upon poverty, and while away
from his wife and child, his scarcely half raised hut was pulled down
during a heavy rain, and his wife and child left in the lane shelterless.
A second application for a home in the workhouse was rejected, with
still stronger assurances that he had been illegally disturbed, and with
renewed advice to build again. The old man has built for the third
time; and on the site of the cottage represented in the engraving,
erected another, wherein he dwells, and sells his small beer to people
who choose to sit and drink it on the turf seat against the wall of his
cottage; it is chiefly in request, however, among the brickmakers in the

neighbourhood, and the labourers on the new road, cutting across Hag-bush-lane from Holloway to the Kentish-town road, which will ulti-mately connect the Regent's-park and the western suburb, with the eastern extremity of this immensely growing metropolis. Though im-mediately contiguous to Mr. Bath, the landlord of "Copenhagen-house," he has no way assisted in obstructing his poor creature's endeavour to get a morsel of bread. For the present he remains unmo-lested in his almost sequestered nook, and the place and himself are worth seeing, for they are perhaps the nearest specimens to London, of the old country labourer and his dwelling.

From the many intelligent persons a stroller may meet among the thirty thousand inhabitants of Islington, on his way along Hagbush-lane, he will perhaps not find one to answer a question that will occur to him during his walk. "Why is this place called Hagbush-lane?" Before giving satisfaction here to the inquirer, he is informed that, if a Lon-doner, Hagbush-lane is, or ought to be, to him, the most interesting way that he can find to walk in; and presuming him to be influenced by the feelings and motives that actuate his fellow-citizens to the im-provement and adornment of their city, by the making of a *new* north road, he is informed that Hagbush-lane, though now wholly disused, and in many parts destroyed, was the *old*, or rather the *oldest* north road, or ancient bridle-way to and from London, and the northern parts of the kingdom.

Now for its name—Hagbush-lane. *Hag* is the old Saxon word *hæg*, which became corrupted into *hawgh*, and afterwards into *haw*, and is the name for the berry of the hawthorn; also the Saxon word *haga* sig-nified a hedge or any enclosure. *Hag* afterwards signified a bramble, and hence, for instance, the blackberry-bush, or any other bramble, would be properly denominated a *hag*. Hagbush-lane, therefore, may be taken to signify either Hawthornbush-lane, Bramble-lane, or Hedgebush-lane; more probably the latter. Within recent recollection, Whitcomb-street, near Charing-cross, was called *Hedge*-lane.

Supposing the reader to proceed from the old man's mud-cottage in a northerly direction, he will find that the widest part of Hagbush-lane reaches, from that spot, to the road now cutting from Holloway. Cross-ing immediately over the road, he comes again into the lane, which he will there find so narrow as only to admit convenient passage to a man on horseback. This was the general width of the road throughout, and the usual width of all the English roads made in ancient times. They did not travel in carriages, or carry their goods in carts, as we do, but rode on horseback, and conveyed their wares or merchandise in pack-saddles or packages on horses' backs. They likewise conveyed their money in the same way. In an objection raised in the reign of Elizabeth to a clause in the Hue and Cry bill,[22] then passing through parliament, it was urged, regarding some travellers who had been robbed in open day within the hundred of Beyntesh, in the county of Berks, that "they were clothiers, and yet travailed not withe the great trope of clothiers; they also carried their money openlye in wallets upon their saddles."* The customary width of their roads was either four feet or eight feet. Some parts of Hagbush-lane are much lower than the meadows on each side; and this defect is common to parts of every ancient way, as might be exemplified, were it necessary, with reasons founded on their ignorance of every essential connected with the formation, and perhaps the use, of a road.

It is not intended to point out the tortuous directions of Hagbush-lane; for the chief object of this notice is to excite the reader to one of the plesantest walks he can imagine, and to tax his ingenuity to the discovery of the route the road takes. This, the *ancient* north road, comes into the *present* north road, in Upper Holloway, at the foot of Highgate-hill, and went in that direction to Hornsey. From the mud-cottage towards London, it proceeded between Paradise-house, the residence of Mr. Greig, the engraver, and the Adam and Eve public-house, in the Holloway back-road, and by circuitous windings approached London, at the distance of a few feet on the eastern side of the City Arms public-house, in the City-road, and continued towards Old-street, St. Luke's. It no where communicated with the back-road, leading from Battle-bridge to the top of Highgate-hill, called Maiden-lane.

Hagbush-lane is well known to every botanizing perambulator on the west side of London. The wild onion, clowns-wound-wort, wake-robin, and abundance of other simples, lovely in their form, and of high medicinal repute in our old herbals and receipt-books, take root, and seed and flower here in great variety. How long beneath the tall elms and pollard oaks, and the luxuriant beauties on the banks, the infirm

* Hoby MSS

may be suffered to seek health, and the healthy to recreate, who shall say? Spoilers are abroad.

Through Hagbush-lane every man has a right to ride and walk; *in* Hagbush-lane no one man has even a shadow of right to an inch as private property. It is a public road, and public property. The trees, as well as the road, are public property; and the very form of the road is public property. Yet bargains and sales have been made, and are said to be now making, under which the trees are cut down and sold, and the public road thrown, bit by bit, into private fields as pasture. Under no conveyance or admission to land by any proprietor, whether freeholder or lord of a manor, can any person legally dispossess the public of a single foot of Hagbush-lane, or obstruct the passage of any individual through it. All the people of London, and indeed all the people of England, have a right in this road as a common highway. Hitherto, among the inhabitants of Islington, many of whom are opulent, and all of whom are the local guardians of the public rights in this road, not one has been found with sufficient public virtue, or rather with enough of common manly spirit, to compel the restoration of public plunder, and in his own defence, and on the behalf of the public, arrest the *highway* robber.

Building, or what may more properly be termed the tumbling up of tumble-down houses, to the north of London, is so rapidly increasing, that in a year or two there will scarcely be a green spot for the resort of the inhabitants. Against covering of private ground in this way, there is no resistance; but against its evil consequences to health, some remedy should be provided by the setting apart of open spaces for the exercise of walking in the fresh air. The preservation of Hagbush-lane therefore is, in this point of view, an object of public importance. Where it has not been thrown into private fields, from whence, however, it is recoverable, it is one of the loveliest of our green lanes; and though persons from the country smile at Londoners when they talk of being "rural" at the distance of a few miles from town, a countryman would find it difficult to name any lane in his own county, more sequestered or of greater beauty.

LINES
WRITTEN IN HAGBUSH-LANE.

A scene like this,
Would woo the care-worn wise
    To moralize,
And courting lovers court to tell their bliss.

Had I a cottage here
I'd be content; for where
    I have my books
        I have old friends,
    Whose cheering looks
        Make me amends
For coldnesses in men: and so,
With them departed long ago,
    And with wild-flowers and trees
    And with the living breeze,
    And with the "still small voice"[23]
    Within, I would rejoice,
    And converse hold, while breath

Held me, and then—come Death!

JULY 9
QUATRAINS

TO THE EDITOR OF THE EVERY-DAY BOOK

[From the London Magazine.]

I like you, and your book, ingenuous Hone,
    In whose capacious all-embracing leaves
The very marrow of tradition's shown;
    And all that history—much that fiction—weaves.

By every sort of taste your work is graced.
    Vast stores of modern anecdote we find,

With good old story quaintly interlaced—
    The theme as various as the reader's mind.

Rome's lie-fraught legends you so truly paint—
    Yet kindly—that the half-turn'd Catholic
Scarcely forbears to smile at his own saint,
    And cannot curse the candid Heretic.

Rags, relics, witches, ghosts, fiends, crowd your page;
    Our father's mummeries we well-pleased behold;
And, proudly conscious of a purer age,
    Forgive some fopperies in the times of old.

Verse-honouring Phoebus, Father of bright *Days*,
    Must needs bestow on you both good and many,
Who, building trophies to his children's praise,
    Run their rich Zodiac through, not missing any.

Dan Phoebus loves your book—trust me, friend Hone—
    The title only errs, he bids me say:
For while such art—wit—reading—there are shown,
    He swears, 'tis not a work of *every day*.

C. Lamb[24]

QUATORZIANS[25]

TO THE AUTHOR OF "QUATRAINS."

In feeling, like a stricken deer,[26] I've been
    Self-put out from the herd, friend Lamb; for I
Imagined all the sympathies between
    Mankind and me had ceased, till your full cry
Of kindness reach'd and roused me, as I lay
    "Musing—on divers things foreknown:" it bid
Me know, in you, a friend; with a fine gay
    Sincerity, before all men it chid,

Or rather, by not chiding, seem'd to chide
   Me, for long absence from you; re-invited
Me, with a herald's trump, and so defied
   Me to remain immured; and it requited
Me, for others' harsh misdeeming—which I trust is
Now, or will be, known by them, to be injustice.

I *am* "ingenuous:" it is all I can
   Pretend to; it is all I wish to be;
Yet, through obliquity of sight in man,
   From constant gaze on tortuosity,
Few people understand me: still, I am
   Warmly affection'd to each human being;
Loving the right, for right's sake; and, friend Lamb,
   Trying to see things as they are; hence, seeing
Some "good in ev'ry thing"[27] however bad,
   Evil in many things that look most fair,
And pondering on all: this may be mad-
   ness, but it is my method; and I dare
Deductions from a strange diversity
Of things, not taught within a University.

No schools of science open'd to my youth;
   No learned halls, no academic bowers;
No one had I to point my way to truth,
   Instruct my ign'rance, or direct my powers
Yet I, though all unlearned, p'rhaps may aid
   The march of knowledge in our "purer age,"
And, without seeming, may perchance persuade
   The young to think,—to virtue some engage:
So have I hoped, and with this end in view,
   My little *Every-Day Book* I design'd;
Praise of the work, and of its author too,
   From you, friend Lamb, is more than good and kind:
To such high meed I did not dare aspire
As public honour, from the hand of Allworthy Elia.

As to the message from your friend above:—
   Do me the favour to present my best

Respects to old "Dan Phoebus," for the "love"
    He bears the *Every-Day Book:* for the rest,
That is, the handsome mode he has selected
    Of making me fine compliments by you, 'tis
So flatt'ring to me, and so much respected
    By me, that, if you please, and it should suit his
Highness, I must rely upon you, for
    Obtaining his command, to introduce me
To him yourself, when quite convenient; or
    I trust, at any rate, you'll not refuse me
A line, to signify, that I'm the person known
    To him, through you, friend Lamb, as

Your Friend
WILLIAM HONE

DECEMBER 31

It must have been obvious to every reader of the *Every-Day Book*, as it has been to me, of which there have been several indications for some time past, that the plan of the work could not be executed within the year; and I am glad to find from numerous quarters that its continuance is approved and even required. So far as it has proceeded I have done my utmost to render it useful. My endeavours to render it agreeable may occasion "close" readers to object, that it was more discursive than they expected. I am afraid I can only answer that I cannot unmake my making-up; and plead guilty to the fact, that, knowing the wants of many, through my own deficiencies, I have tried to aid them in the way that appeared most likely to effect the object, with the greater number of those for whom the work was designed. Nor do I hesitate also to acknowledge, that in gathering for others, I have in no small degree been teaching myself. For it is of the nature of such an undertaking to constrain him who executes it, to tasks of thought, and exercises of judgment, unseen by those who are satisfied when they enjoy what is before them, and care not by what ventures it was obtained. My chief anxiety has been to provide a wholesome sufficiency for all, and not to offer any thing that should be hurtful or objectionable. I hope I have succeeded.

I respectfully desire to express my grateful sense of the extensive favour wherein the conduct of the publication is held. And I part from my readers on New Year's-eve, with kind regards till we meet in the new volume of the *Every-Day Book* on New Year's day—to-morrow.

FROM THE EVERY-DAY BOOK, VOL. 2

PREFACE.

2. Respecting this second volume of the *Every-Day Book*, it is scarcely necessary to say more than that it has been conducted with the same desire and design as the preceding volume; and that it contains a much greater variety of original information concerning manners and customs. I had so devoted myself to this main object, as to find no lack of materials for carrying it further; nor were my correspondents, who had largely increased, less communicative; but there were some readers who thought the work ought to have been finished in one volume, and others, who were not inclined to follow beyond a second; and their apprehensions that it could not, or their wishes that it should not, be carried further, constrained me to close it. As an "Everlasting Calendar" of amusements, sports, and pastimes, incident to the year, the *Every-Day Book* is complete; and I venture, without fear of disproof, to affirm, that there is not such a copious collection of pleasant facts and illustrations, "for daily use and diversion," in the language; nor are any other volumes so abundantly stored with original designs, or with curious and interesting subjects so meritoriously engraven.

3. Every thing that I wished to bring into the *Every-Day Book*, but was compelled to omit from its pages, in order to conclude it within what the public would deem a reasonable size, I purpose to introduce in my *Table Book*. In that publication, I have the satisfaction to find myself aided by many of my "*Every-Day*" correspondents, to whom I tender respectful acknowledgments and hearty thanks. This is the more due to them here, because I frankly confess that to most I owe letters; I trust that those who have not been noticed as they expected, will impute the neglect to any thing rather than insensibility of my obligations to them for their valuable favours.

Although I confess myself to have been highly satisfied by the general reception of the *Every-Day Book,* and am proud of the honour it has derived from individuals of high literary reputation, yet there is one class whose approbation I value most especially. The "mothers of England" have been pleased to entertain it as an everyday assistant in their families; and instructors of youth, of both sexes, have placed it in school-libraries. This ample testimonial, that, while engaged in exemplifying "manners," I have religiously adhered to "morals," is the most gratifying reward I could hope to receive.

February, 1827.

FEBRUARY 23
CHRONOLOGY.

1821. John Keats, the poet, died. Virulent and unmerited attacks upon his literary ability, by an unprincipled and malignant reviewer, injured his rising reputation, overwhelmed his spirits, and he sunk into consumption. In that state he fled for refuge to the climate of Italy, caught cold on the voyage, and perished in Rome, at the early age of 25. Specimens of his talents are in the former volume of this work. One of his last poems was in prospect of departure from his native shores. It is an *Ode to a Nightingale* [the Ode follows].

APRIL 23
SPRING IN THE CITY,
and
JEMMY WHITTLE.

At Laurie and Whittle's print-shop "nearly opposite St. Dunstan's church, Fleet-street,"[28] or rather at Jemmy Whittle's, for he was the manager of the concern—I cannot help calling him "Jemmy," for I knew him afterwards, in a passing way, when *every* body called him Jemmy; and after his recollection failed, and he dared no longer to flash his merriment at the "Cock," at Temple-bar, and the "Black Jack," in Portugal-street, but stood, like a sign of himself, at his own door, unable to remember the names of his old friends, they called him "*poor* Jemmy!"—I say, I remember at Jemmy Whittle's there was always a change of prints in spring-time. Jemmy liked, as he said, to "give the public something alive, fresh and clever, classical and correct!" One print, however, was never changed; this was "St. Dunstan and the

Devil." To any who inquired why he always had "that *old* thing" in the window, and thought it would be better out, Jemmy answered, "No, no, my boy! that's *my* sign—no change—church and state, you know!—no politics, you know!—I hate politics! there's the church, you know, [pointing to St. Dunstan's,] and here am I, my boy!—it's *my* sign, you know!—no change, my boy!" Alas, how changed! I desired to give a copy of the print on St. Dunstan's day in the first volume of the *Every-Day Book*, and it could not be found at "the old shop," nor at any printsellers I resorted to. Another print of Jemmy Whittle's was a favourite with me, as well as himself; for, through every mutation of "dressing out" his window it maintained its place with St. Dunstan. It was a mezzotinto, called The Laughing Boy.

* * * * *

I am now speaking of five and thirty years ago, when the shop windows, especially printsellers', were set out according to the season. I remember that in spring-time "Jemmy Whittle," and "Carrington Bowles, in St. Paul's Church-yard," used to decorate their panes with twelve prints of flowers of "the months," engraved after Baptiste,[29] and "coloured after nature,"—a show almost, at that time, as gorgeous as "Solomon's Temple, in all its glory, all over nothing but gold and jewels,"[30] which a man exhibited to my wondering eyes for a halfpenny.

Spring arrives in London—and even east of Temple-bar—as early as in the country. For—though there are neither hawthorns to blossom, nor daisies to blow—there is scarcely a house "in the city," without a few flower pots inside or outside; and when "the seeds come up," the Londoner knows that the spring is "come to town." The almanac, also, tells him, that the sun rises earlier every day, and he makes his apprentices rise earlier; and the shop begins to be watered and swept before breakfast; and perchance, as the good man stands at his door to look up, and "wonder what sort of a day it will be," he sees a basket with primroses or cowslips, and from thence he hazards to assert, at "the house he uses" in the evening, that the spring is very forward; which is confirmed, to his credit, by some neighbour, who usually sleeps at Bow or Brompton, or Pentonville or Kennington, or some other adjacent part of "the country."

To the east of Temple-bar, the flower-girl is "the herald of spring." She cries "cowslips! sweet cowslips!" till she screams "bow-pots! sweet, and pretty bow-pots!" which is the sure and certain token of full spring in

London. When *I* was a child, I got "a bow-pot" of as many wall-flowers and harebells as I could then hold in my hand, with a sprig of sweet briar at the back of the bunch, for a halfpenny—*such* a handful; but, now, "they can't make a ha'penny bow-pot—there's nothing under a penny;" and the penny bow-pot is not half so big as the ha'penny one, and somehow or other the flowers don't smell, to *me*, as they used to do.—

It will not do however to run on thus, for something remains to be said concerning the patron of the day;[31] and, to be plain with the reader, the recollections of former times are not always the most cheering to the writer.

SEPTEMBER 2
ROMAN REMAINS AT PENTONVILLE,
and
THE WHITE CONDUIT

I am not learned in the history or the science of phrenology, but, unless I am mistaken, surely in the days of "craniology," the organ of "inhabitiveness" was called the organ of "travelling." Within the last minute I have felt my head in search of the development. I imagine it must be very palpable to the scientific, for I not only incline to wander but to locate. However that may be, I cannot find it myself—for want, I suppose, of a topographical view of the cranium, and I have not a copy of Mr. Cruikshank's "Illustrations of Phrenology" to refer to.[32]

At home, I always sit in the same place if I can make my way to it without disturbing the children; all of whom, by the by, (I speak of the younger ones,) are great sticklers for rights of sitting, and urge their claims on each other with a persistence which takes all my authority to abate. I have a habit, too, at a friend's house of always preferring the seat I dropped into on my first visit; and the same elsewhere. The first time I went to the Chapter Coffee-house, some five-and-twenty years ago, I accidentally found myself alone with old Dr. Buchan, in the same box; it was by the fireplace on the left from Paternoster-row door: poor Robert Heron presently afterwards entered, and then a troop of the doctor's familiars dropped in, one by one; and I sat in the corner, a stranger to all of them, and therefore a silent auditor of their pleasant disputations. At my next appearance I forbore from occupying the same seat, because it would have been an obtrusion on the literary community; but I got into the adjoining box, and that always, for the period of my then frequenting the house, was my coveted box. After an absence of twenty years, I returned to the "Chapter," and involuntarily stepped to the old spot; it was pre-occupied; and in the doctor's box were other faces, and talkers of other things. I strode away to a distant part of the room to an inviting vacancy, which, from that accident, and my propensity, became my desirable sitting place at every future visit. My strolls abroad are of the same character. I prefer walking where I walked when novelty was charming; where I can have the pleasure of recollecting that I formerly felt pleasure—of rising to the enjoyment of a spirit hovering over the remains it had animated.

One of my oldest, and therefore one of my still-admired walks is by the way of Islington. I am partial to it, because, when I was eleven years old, I went every evening from my father's, near Red Lion-square, to a lodging in that village "for a consumption," and returned the following morning. I thus became acquainted with Canonbury, and the Pied Bull, and Barnesbury-park, and White Conduit-house; and the intimacy has been kept up until presumptuous takings in, and enclosures, and new buildings, have nearly destroyed it. The old site seems like an old friend who has formed fashionable acquaintanceships, and lost his old heart-warming smiles in the constraint of a new face.

In my last Islington walk, I took a survey of the only remains of the Roman encampment, near Barnesbury-park. This is a quadrangle of about one hundred and thirty feet, surrounded by a fosse or ditch, about five-and-twenty feet wide, and twelve feet deep. It is close to the west side of the present end of the New Road, in a line with Penton-street; immediately opposite to it, on the east side of the road, is built a row of houses, at present uninhabited, called Minerva-place. This quadrangle is supposed to have been the praetorium or head quarters of Suetonius, when he engaged the British queen, Boadicea, about the year 60.[33] The conflict was in the eastward valley below, at the back of Pentonville. Here Boadicea, with her two daughters before her in the same war-chariot, traversed the plain, haranguing her troops; telling them, as Tacitus records, "that it was usual to the Britons to war under the conduct of women," and inciting them to "vengeance for the oppression of public liberty, for the stripes inflicted on her person, for the defilement of her virgin daughters;" declaring "that in that battle they must remain utterly victorious or utterly perish; such was the firm purpose of her who was a woman; the men, if they pleased, might still enjoy life and bondage." The slaughter was terrible, eighty thousand of the Britons were left dead on the field; it terminated victoriously for the Romans, near Gray's-inn-lane, at the place called "Battle Bridge," in commemoration of it.

PRETORIUM OF THE ROMAN CAMP NEAR PENTONVILLE.

The pencil of the artist has been employed to give a correct and picturesque representation as it now appears, in September, 1826, of the last vestige of the Roman power in this suburb. The view is taken from the north-east angle of the prætorium. Until within a few years the ground about it was unbroken; and, even now, the quadrangle itself is surprisingly complete, considering that nearly eighteen centuries have elapsed since it was formed by the Roman soldiery. In a short time the spirit of improvement will entirely efface it, and houses and gardens occupy its site. In the fosse of this station, which is overrun with sedge and brake, there is so pretty a "bit," to use an artist's word, that I have caused it to be sketched.

THE OLD WELL IN THE FOSSE.

This may be more pleasantly regarded when the ancient works themselves have vanished. Within a few yards of the western side of the fosse, and parallel with it, there is raised a mound or rampart of earth. It is in its original state and covered with verdure. In fine mornings a stray valetudinarian or two may be seen pacing its summit. Its western slope has long been the Sunday resort of Irishmen for the game of foot-ball.

Getting back into the New Road, its street which stands on fields I rambled in when a boy, leads to "White Conduit-house," which derives its name from a building still preserved, I was going to say, but I prefer to say, still standing.

The old well in the fosse

THE WHITE CONDUIT.

* * * * *

About 1810, the late celebrated Wm. Huntington, S.S.,[34] of Providence chapel, who lived in a handsome house within sight, was at the expense of clearing the spring for the use of the inhabitants; but, because his pulpit opinions were obnoxious, some of the neighbouring vulgar threw loads of soil upon it in the night, which rendered the water impure, and obstructed its channel, and finally ceasing to flow, the public was deprived of the kindness he proposed. The building itself was in a very perfect state at that time, and ought to have been boarded up after the field it stood in was thrown open. As the New buildings proceeded it was injured and defaced by idle labourers and boys, from mere wantonness and reduced to a mere ruin. There was a kind of upper floor or hayloft in it, which was frequently a shelter to the houseless wanderer. A few years ago some poor creatures made it a comfortable hostel for the night, with a little hay. Early in the morning a passing workman perceived smoke issuing from the crevices, and as he approached heard loud cries from within. Some mischievous miscreants had set fire to the fodder beneath the sleepers, and afterwards fastened the door on the outside: the inmates were scorched by the fire, and probably they would all have been suffocated in a few minutes, if the place had not been broken open.

The "White Conduit" at this time merely stands to shame those who had the power, and neglected to preserve it. To the buildings grown up around, it might have been rendered a neat ornament, by planting a few trees and enclosing the whole with an iron railing, and have stood as a monument of departed worth. This vicinity was anciently full of springs and stone conduits; the erections have long since gone to decay, and from their many waters, only one has been preserved, which is notoriously deficient as a supply to the populous neighbourhood. During the heats of summer the inhabitants want this common element in the midst of plenty. The spring in a neighbouring street is frequently exhausted by three or four o'clock in the afternoon, the handle of the pump is then padlocked till the next morning, and the grateful and necessary refreshment of spring-water is not to be obtained without going miles in search of another pump. It would seem as if the parochial powers in this quarter were leagued with publicans and sinners, to compel the thirsty to buy deleterious beer and bowel-disturbing "pop,"[35] or to swallow the New River water fresh with impurities from the thousands of people who daily cleanse their foul bodies in the stream, as it lags along for the use of our kitchens and tea-tables.

"White Conduit-house," has ceased to be a recreation in the good sense of the word. Its present denomination is the "Minor Vauxhall," and its chief attraction during the passing summer has been Mrs. Bland. She has still powers, and if their exercise here has been a stay and support to this sweet melodist, so far the establishment may be deemed respectable. It is a ground for balloon-flying and skittle-playing,[36] and just maintains itself above the very lowest, so as to be one of the most doubtful places of public resort. Recollections of it some years ago are more in its favour. Its tea-gardens then in summer afternoons, were well accustomed by tradesmen and their families; they are now comparatively deserted, and instead, there is, at night, a starveling show of odd company and coloured lamps, a mock orchestra with mock singing, dancing in a room which decent persons would prefer to withdraw their young folks from if they entered, and fire-works "as usual," which, to say the truth, are usually very good.

Such is the present state of a vicinage which "in my time," was the pleasantest near spot to the north of London. The meadow of the "White Conduit" commanded an extensive prospect of the Hampstead and Highgate hills, over beautiful pastures and hedge-rows which are now built on, or converted into brick clamps,[37] for the *material* of irruption on the remaining glades. The pleasant views are wholly obstructed. In a few short years, London will distend its enormous bulk to the heights that overlook its proud city; and, like the locusts of old, devour every green field, and nothing will be left to me to admire, of all that I admired.

DECEMBER 31

On taking leave, as Editor of this work, I desire to express my thanks for its favourable acceptation. It seems to have been regarded as I wished—a miscellany to be taken up by any body at any time. I have the pleasure to *know* that it is possessed by thousands of families of all ranks: is presented by fathers to their sons at school; finds favour with mothers, as suited to the perusal of their daughters; and is so deemed of, as to be placed in public and private libraries enriched with standard literature. Ascribing these general marks of distinction to its general tendency, that tendency will be maintained in my next publication,

THE TABLE BOOK.

This publication will appear, with cuts *every Saturday*, and in monthly parts, at the same price as the *Every-Day Book*, and will contain several original articles from valued correspondents, for which room could not be here made.

The first number and the present year will be "out" together. I gratefully remember the attachment of my friends to the present sheets, and I indulge a hope that they will as kindly remember me, and my new work

THE TABLE BOOK.

Cuttings with Cuts, facts, fancies, recollections,
Heads, autographs, views, prose and verse selections,
Notes of my musings in a lonely walk,
My friends' communications, table-talk,
Notions of books and things I read or see,
Events that are, or were, or are to be,
Fall in my TABLE BOOK—and thence arise
To please the young, and help divert the wise.

December 23, 1826.

FROM THE TABLE BOOK

My
TABLE BOOK.

THE TITLE is to be received in a larger sense than the obsolete signification: the old table books were for private use—mine is for the public; and the more the public desire it, the more I shall be gratified. I have not the folly to suppose it will pass from *my* table to *every* table, but I think that not a single sheet can appear on the table of *any* family without communicating some information, or affording some diversion.

On the title-page there are a few lines which briefly, yet adequately, describe the collections in my *Table Book:* and, as regards my own "sayings and doings," the prevailing disposition of my mind is perhaps sufficiently made known through the *Every-Day Book.* In the latter publication, I was inconveniently limited as to room; and the labour I had there prescribed to myself, of commemorating *every* day, frequently prevented me from topics that would have been more agreeable to my readers than the "two grains of wheat in a bushel of chaff,"[1] which I often consumed my time and spirits in endeavouring to discover— and did not always find.

In my *Table Book,* which I hope will never be out of "season," I take the liberty to "annihilate both time and space,"[2] to the extent of a few lines or days, and lease, and talk, when and where I can, according to my humour. Sometimes I present an offering of "all sorts," simpled from out-of-the-way and in-the-way books; and, at other times, gossip to the public, as to an old friend, diffusely or briefly, as I chance to be more or less in the giving "vein,"[3] about a passing event, a work just read, a print in my hand, the thing I last thought of, or saw, or heard, or, to be plain, about "whatever comes uppermost." In short, my collections and recollections come forth just as I happen to suppose they may be most agreeable or serviceable to those whom I esteem, or care for, and by whom I desire to be respected.

My Table Book is enriched and diversified by the contributions of my friends; the teemings of time, and the press, give it novelty; and what I know of works of art, with something of imagination, and the assistance of artists, enable me to add pictorial embellishment. My object is to blend information with amusement, and utility with diversion.

My Table Book, therefore, is a series of continually shifting scenes—a kind of literary kaleidoscope, combining popular forms with singular appearances—by which youth and age of all ranks may be amused; and to which, I respectfully trust, many will gladly add something, to improve its views.

* * * * *

Note.

Communications for the *Table Book* addressed to *me*, in a parcel, or under cover, to the care of the publishers, will be gladly received.

Notices to Correspondents will appear on the wrappers of the monthly parts *only*.

The Table Book, therefore, after the present sheet, will be printed continuously, without matter of this kind, or the intervention of temporary titles, unpleasant to the eye, when the work comes to be bound in volumes.

Lastly, because this is the last opportunity of the kind in my power, I beg to add that some valuable papers which could not be included in the *Every-Day Book,* will appear in the *Table Book.*

Moreover Lastly, I earnestly solicit the immediate activity of my friends, to oblige and serve me, by sending *any* thing, and *every* thing they can collect or recollect, which they may suppose at all likely to render my *Table Book* instructive, or diverting.

THE NEWSMAN.

"I, that do *bring* the news."

Shakespeare.[4]

Our calling, however the vulgar may deem,
Was of old, both on high and below, in esteem;
E'en the gods were to much curiosity given,
For Hermes was only the Newsman of heaven.

Hence with wings to his cap, and his staff, and his heels,
He depictured appears, which our myst'ry reveals,
That *news* flies like wind, to raise sorrow or laughter,
While leaning on Time, *Truth* comes heavily after.

Newsmen's Verses, 1747.

The newsman is a "lone person." His business, and he, are distinct from all other occupations, and people.

All the year round, and every day in the year, the newsman must rise soon after four o'clock, and be at the newspaper offices to procure a few of the first morning papers allotted to him, at extra charges, for particular orders, and despatch them by the "early coaches." Afterwards, he has to wait for his share of the "regular" publication of each paper, and he allots these as well as he can among some of the most urgent of his town orders. The *next* publication at a later hour is devoted to his remaining customers; and he sends off his boys with different portions according to the supply he successively receives. Notices frequently and necessarily printed in different papers, of the hour of final publication the preceding day, guard the interests of the newspaper proprietors from the sluggishness of the indolent, and quicken the diligent newsman. Yet, however skilful his arrangements may be, they are subject to unlooked for accidents. The late arrival of foreign journals, a parliamentary debate unexpectedly protracted, or an article of importance in one paper exclusively, retard the printing and defer the newsman. His patience, well-worn before he gets his *"last* papers," must be continued during the whole period he is occupied in delivering them. The sheet is sometimes half snatched before he can draw it from his wrapper; he is often chid for delay when he should have been praised for speed; his excuse, *"All* the papers were *late* this morning," is better heard than admitted, for neither giver nor receiver has time to parley; and before he gets home to dinner, he hears at one house that "Master has waited for the paper these two hours;" at another, "Master's gone out, and says if you can't bring the paper earlier, he won't have it at all;" and some ill-conditioned "master," perchance, leaves positive orders, "Don't take it in, but tell the man to bring the bill; and I'll pay it and have done with him."

Besides buyers, every newsman has readers at so much each paper per hour. One class stipulates for a journal always at breakfast; another, that it is to be delivered exactly at such a time; a third, at any time, so that it is left the full hour; and among all of these there are malcontents, who permit nothing of "time or circumstance" to interfere with their personal convenience. Though the newsman delivers, and allows the use of his paper, and fetches it, for a stipend not half equal to the lowest paid porter's price for letter-carrying in London, yet he finds some, with whom he covenanted, objecting, when it is called for,—"I've not had my breakfast,"—"The paper did not come at the proper time,"—

"I've not had leisure to look at it yet,"—"It has not been left an hour,"—or any other pretence equally futile or untrue, which, were he to allow, would prevent him from serving his readers in rotation, or at all. If he can get all his morning papers from these customers by four o'clock, he is a happy man.

Soon after three in the afternoon, the newsman and some of his boys must be at the offices of the evening papers; but before he can obtain his requisite numbers, he must wait till the newsmen of the Royal Exchange have received theirs, for the use of the merchants on 'Change. Some of the first he gets are hurried off to coffee-house and tavern keepers. When he has procured his full quantity, he supplies the remainder of his town customers. These disposed of, then comes the hasty folding and directing of his reserves for the country, and the forwarding of them to the post-office in Lombard-street, or in parcels for the mails, and to other coach-offices. The Gazette nights, every Tuesday and Friday, add to his labours,—the publication of second and third editions of the evening papers in a super-addition. On what he calls a "regular day," he is fortunate if he find himself settled within his own door by seven o'clock, after fifteen hours of running to and fro. It is now only that he can review the business of the day, enter his fresh orders, ascertain how many of each paper he will require on the morrow, arrange his accounts, provide for the money he may have occasion for, eat the only quiet meal he could reckon upon since that of the evening before, and "steal a few hours from the night" for needful rest, before he rises the next morning to a day of the like incessant occupation: and thus from Monday to Saturday he labours every day.

The newsman desires no work but his own to prove "Sunday no Sabbath;" for on him and his brethren devolves the circulation of upwards of fifty thousand Sunday papers in the course of the forenoon. His Sunday dinner is the only meal he can ensure with his family, and the short remainder of the day the only time he can enjoy in their society with certainty, or extract something from, for more serious duties or social converse.

The newsman's is an out-of-door business at all seasons, and his life is measured out to unceasing toil. In all weathers, hail, rain, wind, and snow, he is daily constrained to the way and the fare of a wayfaringman. He walks, or rather runs, to distribute information concerning all sorts of circumstances and persons, except his own. He is unable to allow himself, or others, time for intimacy, and therefore, unless he had

formed friendships before he took to his servitude, he has not the
chance of cultivating them, save with persons of the same calling. He
may be said to have been divorced, and to live "separate and apart"
from society in general; for, though he mixes with every body, it is only
for a few hurried moments, and as strangers do in a crowd.

Cowper's familiar description of a newspaper, with its multiform intelligence, and the pleasure of reading it in the country, never tires, and
in this place is to the purpose.

> This folio of four pages, happy work!
> Which not ev'n critics criticise; that holds
> Inquisitive Attention, while I read,
> Fast bound in chains of silence, which the fair,
> Though eloquent themselves, yet fear to break,
> What is it, but a map of busy life,
> Its fluctuations, and its vast concerns?
> Houses in ashes, and the fall of stocks,
> Births, deaths, and marriages————————
> ————————————————The grand debate,
> The popular harangue, the tart reply,
> The logic, and the wisdom, and the wit,
> And the loud laugh————————————
> Cat'racts of declamation thunder here;
> There forests of no meaning spread the page,
> In which all comprehension wanders lost;
> While fields of pleasantry amuse us there,
> With merry descants on a nation's woes.
> The rest appears a wilderness of strange
> But gay confusion; roses for the cheeks,
> And lilies for the brows of faded age,
> Teeth for the toothless, ringlets for the bald,
> Heav'n, earth, and ocean, plunder'd of their sweets,
> Nectareous essences, Olympian dews,
> Sermons, and city feasts, and fav'rite airs,
> Æthereal journies, submarine exploits,
> And Katerfelto, with his hair on end
> At his own wonders, wand'ring for his bread.
> Tis pleasant, through the loopholes of retreat,
> To peep at such a world; to see the stir
> Of the great Babel, and not feel the crowd;

To hear the roar she sends through all her gates,
At a safe distance, where the dying sound
Falls a soft murmur on th' uninjured ear.
Thus sitting, and surveying thus, at ease,
The globe and its concerns, I seem advanced
To some secure and more than mortal height,
That lib'rates and exempts us from them all.

This is an agreeable and true picture, and, with like felicity, the poet paints the bearer of the newspaper.

Hark! tis the twanging horn o'er yonder bridge,
That with its wearisome but needful length
Bestrides the wintry flood, in which the moon
Sees her unwrinkled face reflected bright;—
He comes, the herald of a noisy world,
With spatter'd boots, strapp'd waist, and frozen locks;
News from all nations lumb'ring at his back
True to his charge, the close pack'd load behind
Yet careless what he brings, his one concern
Is to conduct it to the destin'd inn;
And, having dropp'd th' expected bag, pass on.
He whistles as he goes, light-hearted wretch,
Cold and yet cheerful: messenger of grief
Perhaps to thousands, and of joy to some;
To him indiff'rent whether grief or joy.

Methinks, as I have always thought, that Cowper here missed the expression of a kind feeling, and rather tends to raise an ungenerous sentiment towards this poor fellow. As the bearer of intelligence, of which he is ignorant, why should it be

"To him indifferent whether grief or joy?"

If "cold, and yet cheerful," he has attained to the "practical philosophy" of bearing ills with patience. He is a frozen creature that "whistles," and therefore called "light-hearted wretch." The poet refrains to "look with a gentle eye upon this *wretch*," but, having obtained the newspaper, determines to enjoy himself, and cries

Now stir the fire, and close the shutters fast,
Let fall the curtains, wheel the sofa round,
And, while the bubbling and loud-hissing urn
Throws up a steamy column, and the cups,
That cheer, but not inebriate, wait on each,
So let us welcome peaceful ev'ning in.[5]

This done, and the bard surrounded with means of enjoyment, he directs his sole attention to the newspaper, nor spares a thought in behalf of the wayworn messenger, nor bids him "God speed!" on his further forlorn journey through the wintry blast.

In London scarcely any one knows the newsman but a newsman. His customers know him least of all. Some of them seem almost ignorant that he has like "senses, affections, passions," with themselves, or is "subject to the same diseases, healed by the same means, warmed and cooled by the same winter and summer."[6] They are indifferent to him in exact ratio to their attachment to what he "serves" them with. Their regard is for the newspaper, and not the newsman. Should he succeed in his occupation, they do not hear of it: if he fail, they do not care for it. If he dies, the servant receives the paper from his successor, and says, when she carries it up stairs, "If you please, the newsman's dead:" they scarcely ask where he lived, or his fall occasions a pun—"We always said he *was,* and now we have proof that he *is,* the *late* newsman." They are almost as unconcerned as if he had been the postman.

Once a year, a printed "copy of verses" reminds every newspaper reader that the hand that bore it is open to a small boon. "The Newsman's Address to his Customers, 1826," deploringly adverts to the general distress, patriotically predicts better times, and seasonably intimates, that in the height of annual festivities he, too, has a heart capable of joy.

———————"although the muse complains
And sings of woes in melancholy strains,
Yet Hope, at last, strikes up her trembling wires,
And bids Despair forsake your glowing fires.
While, as in olden time, Heaven's gifts you share,
And Englishmen enjoy their Christmas fare,
While at the social board friend joins with friend,

And smiles and jokes and salutations blend,
Your Newsman wishes to be social too,
And would enjoy the opening year with you:
Grant him your annual gift, he will not fail
To drink your health once more with Christmas ale:
Long may you live to share your Christmas cheer,
And he still wish you many a happy year!"

The losses and crosses to which newsmen are subject, and the minutæ of their laborious life, would form an instructive volume. As a class of able men of business, their importance is established by excellent regulations, adapted to their interests and well-being; and their numerous society includes many individuals of high intelligence, integrity, and opulence.

WEST WICKHAM CHURCH, KENT.

—From Beckenham church we walked about two miles along a nearly straight road, fenced off from the adjoining lands, till we reached West Wickham. It was from a painted window in this church that I made the tracing of St. Catherine engraved in the *Every-Day*

Book, where some mention is made of the retired situation of this village.

"Wickham Court," the ancient manor-house adjacent to the church, was formerly the residence of Gilbert West, the translator of Pindar, and author of the "Observations on the Resurrection of Christ," for which the university of Oxford conferred on him the degree of doctor of laws.[7] "He was very often visited by Lyttelton and Pitt,[8] who, when they were weary of faction and debates, used, at Wickham, to find books and quiet, a decent table, and literary conversation."[*] It was in West's society at Wickham, that lord Lyttelton was convinced of the truth of Christianity. Under that conviction he wrote his celebrated "Dissertation on the Conversion and Apostleship of St. Paul," which, until the appearance of Paley's "Horae Paulina," was an unrivalled treatise.[9] Mr. Pitt, (the great earl of Chatham,) during his intimacy with West, formed a walk at Wickham Court. In a summer-house of the grounds, Mr. West inscribed the following lines, in imitation of Ausonius,[10] a Latin poet of the fourth century, "Ad Villam:"—

Not wrapt in smoky London's sulphurous clouds,
    And not far distant stands my rural cot:
Neither obnoxious to intruding crowds,
    Nor for the good and friendly too remote.

And when too much repose brings on the spleen,
    Or the gay city's idle pleasures cloy:
Swift as my changing wish I change the scene,
    And now the country, now the town enjoy.

The ancient manor of West Wickham was vested in Sir Samuel Lennard, bart., from whom it passed to his daughter Mary, the present dowager Lady Farnaby, who resides in the manor-house, and with whose permission we were permitted a look at the hall of the mansion, which contains in the windows some painted remains of armorial bearings on glass, removed from the windows of the church. A view in Hasted's "History of Kent"[11] represents the towers of this mansion to

---

[*] Dr. Johnson

have been surmounted by sextagon cones, terminated at the top with the fleur de lis, a bearing in the family arms; these pinnacles have been taken down, the roofs of the towers flattened, and the walls castellated. By a charter of free warren, in the eleventh year of Edward II, a weekly market was granted to West Wickham, but it is no longer held, and Wickham, as a town, has lost its importance.

The manor-house and church are distant from the village about half a mile, with an intervening valley beautifully pleasant, in which is a road from Hayes Common to Addington and Croydon. The church is on a hill, with an old lich-gate,[12] like that at Beckenham, though not so large. At this spot W. sat down, and made the sketch here represented by his graver. Although I had been in the edifice before, I could not avoid another visit to it. At the north-east corner, near the communion table, are many ancient figured tiles sadly neglected, loose in the pavement; some displaced and lying one upon the other. Worst of all,—and I mean offence to no one, but surely there is blame somewhere,—the ancient stone font, which is in all respects perfect, has been removed from its original situation, and is thrown into a corner. In its place, at the west end, from a nick (not a niche) between the seats, a little trivet-like[13] iron bracket swings in and out, and upon it is a wooden hand-bowl, such as scullions use in a kitchen sink; and in this hand-bowl, of about twelve inches diameter, called a font, I found a common blue-and-white Staffordshire-ware halfpint basin. It might be there still; but, while inveighing to my friend W. against the depravation of the fine old font, and the substitution of such a paltry modicum, in my vehemence I fractured the crockery. I felt that I was angry, and perhaps, I sinned; but I made restitution beyond the extent that would replace the baptismal slop-basin.

The fragments of old painted glass in the windows of this church are really fine. The best are, St. Anne teaching the virgin to read; whole lengths of St. Christopher wading, with the infant Saviour bearing the globe in his hand; an elderly female saint, very good; and a skeleton with armour before him. Some years ago, collectors of curiosities paid their attentions to these windows, and carried off specimens: since then wires have been put up on the outside. On the walls are hung pennons, with an iron helmet, sword, spurs, gloves, and other remains of a funereal pageant. A small organ stands on the floor: the partitions of some of the pewings are very ancient.

𝔑ote.

Under severe affliction I cannot make up this sheet as I wish. This day week my second son was brought home with his scull fractured. To-day intelligence has arrived to me of the death of my eldest son.[14]

The necessity I have been under of submitting recently to a surgical operation on myself, with a long summer of sickness to every member of my family, and accumulated troubles of earlier origin, and of another nature, have prevented me too often from satisfying the wishes of readers, and the claims of Correspondents. I crave that they will be pleased to receive this, as a general apology, in lieu of particular notices, and in the stead of promises to effect what I can no longer hope to accomplish, and forbear to attempt.

December 12, 1827.

FROM *THE YEAR BOOK*

PREFACE.

ALFRED THE GREAT was twelve years old before he could read. He had admired a beautifully illuminated book of Saxon poetry in his mother's hands, and she allured him to learn by promising him the splendid volume as a reward. From that hour he diligently improved himself; and, in the end, built up his mind so strongly, and so high, and applied its powers so beneficially to his kingdom, that no monarch of the thousand years since his rule attained to be reputed, and called, like Alfred, the *great*. He always carried a book in his bosom, and amidst the great business and hurries of government, snatched moments of leisure to read. In the early part of his reign, he was

> Cast from the pedestal of pride by shocks,
> Which Nature gently gave, in woods and fields.[1]

Invaded, overwhelmed, and vanquished by foreign enemies, he was compelled to fly for personal safety, and to retreat alone, into remote wastes and forests:—"learning policy from adversity, and gathering courage from misery."[2]

* * * * *

Alfred became our greatest legislator, and pre-eminently our patriot king for when he had secured the independence of the nation, he rigidly enforced an impartial administration of justice; renovated the energies of his subjects by popular institutions for the preservation of life, property and order, secured public liberty upon the basis of law; lived to see the prosperity of the people, and to experience their affection for the commonwealth of the kingdom; and died so convinced of their loyalty, that he wrote in his last will, "The English have an undoubted right to remain free as their own thoughts."[3] It was one of his laws that freemen should train their sons "to know God, to be men of understanding, and to live happily."[4] The whole policy of his government was founded upon "the beginning of Wisdom."[5] The age was simple, and the nation poor; but the people were happy. Little was known of the arts, and of science less. A monarch's state-carriage was like a farmer's waggon, and his majesty sat in it holding in his hand a long stick, having a bit of pointed iron at the top, with which he goaded a team of oxen yoked to the vehicle.

Ours is an age of civilization and refinement, in which art has arrived to excellence, and science has erected England into a great workhouse for the whole world. The nation is richer than all the other nations of Europe, and distinguished from them by Mammon-worship, and abject subserviency to Mammon-worshippers, the enormous heaps of wealth accumulated by unblest means; the enlarging radius of indigence around every Upas-heap;[6] the sudden and fierce outbreakings of the hungry and ignorant; and, more than all, a simultaneous growth of selfishness with knowledge; are awful signs of an amalgamation of depravity with the national character. Luxury prevails in all classes: private gentlemen live "like lords," tradesmen and farmers like gentlemen, and there is a universal desire to "keep up appearances," which situations in life do not require, and means cannot afford. The getters and keepers of money want more and get more; want more of more, and want and get, and get and want, and live and die—wanting happiness. Thoughtless alike of their uses as human beings, and their final destiny, many of them exhibit a cultivated intellect of a high order, eagerly and heartlessly engaged in a misery-making craft. Are these "the English" contemplated by Alfred?[7]

*   *   *   *   *

Most of us may find, that we have much to *unlearn:* yet evil indeed must we be, if we do not desire that our children may not be worse for what they learn from us, and what they gather from their miscellaneous reading. In selecting materials for the *Every-Day Book,* and *Table Book,* I aimed to avoid what might injure the youthful mind; and in the *Year Book* there is something more, than in those works, of what seemed suitable to ingenuous thought. For the rest, I have endeavoured to supply omissions upon subjects which the *Every-Day Book* and the *Table Book* were designed to include; and, in that, I have been greatly assisted by very kind correspondents.

13, *Gracechurch-street,*
January 1832.

FEBRUARY 21

A CHILD READING.

I sometimes avail myself of a friend's invitation to set off at night and sleep a few miles from town in wholesome air, and glad my eyes in the morning with the fresh green of the grass. On a visit of this sort, last winter, I casually took up a stray volume and carried it to my bedchamber, and began to read—where it is not my usual practice to begin—at the beginning. I became deeply interested, and read till between three and four in the morning. Before day-break I awoke, impatiently awaited the light, resumed my reading, and regretted the call to the breakfast-table. There was another volume of the work: I borrowed and pocketed both; and instead of walking briskly to town for health, as had been my purpose, I cornered myself in the earliest stage, and read till it stopped near my own home. I had business to transact, and bustled in doors; but the book was a spell upon me: I could think of nothing else, and could do nothing that awaited my doing. To escape observation and interruption I rushed out of the house, stepped into a stage, going I knew not whither, and read till the coachman, having set down all my fellow passengers, inquired where I wished to stop:—"At the house where the coach stops."—"Will you be set down at the Plough, Sir?"—"Yes"— and, in a cold dreary winter's day, I found myself in the passage of the Plough at Blackwall, a house of summer entertainment. A wondering waiter showed me into an upper room having a long reaching view of the noble river, with "many a rood" of ice floating past large moored ships and floating craft. I flung myself, book in hand, into a chair; a fire was lighted, and I read, unconscious of time, and only annoyed by the men coming in now and then to stir the fire, till I had finished the fascinating volumes. That done, I took a hasty dinner, and a place to town in the stage. The work which clutched me was Sir Walter Scott's "Heart of Mid Lothian."[8] While it was in my hands I was an infant. It is certain that "I have not yet arrived at the period of life which may put me on a

level with childhood;" but I am not wiser than when I was a child:—I
only know more.

Oh! Spirit of the days gone by—
Sweet childhood's fearful ecstasy!
The witching spell of winter night
Where are they fled with their delight:
When list'ning on the corner seat,
The winter evening's length to cheat,
I heard my mother's memory tell
Tales Superstition loves so well:—
Things said or sung a thousand times,
In simple prose or simpler rhymes!
Ah! where is page of poesy
So sweet as this was wont to be?
The magic wonders that deceived,
When fictions were as truths believed;
The fairy feats that once prevail'd,
Told to delight, and never fail'd:
Where are they now, their fears and sighs,
And tears from founts of happy eyes?
I read in books, but find them not,
For Poesy hath its youth forgot:
I hear them told to children still,
But fear numbs not my spirits chill.
I still see faces pale with dread,
While mine could laugh at what is said;
See tears imagined woes supply,
While mine with real cares are dry.
Where are they gone?—the joys and fears,
The links, the life of other years?
I thought they twined around my heart
So close, that we could never part;
But Reason, like a winter's day,
Nipp'd childhood's visions all away,
Nor left behind one withering flower
To cherish in a lonely hour.

Clare.[9]

I love to hear little ones talk of the books they admire; and should like to know, above all things, which were the favourite authors of "Hugh Littlejohn, Esq.," before he was pictured "at his grand-father's gate," with his friend the noble lurcher, keeping watch and ward. When I see a child with a book, I am restless for a peep at the title page. On looking at the artist's sketch of the little girl, printed on the other side, I said, "What is she reading?" and I imagined it must be "Mrs. Leicester's School—the history of several young ladies related by themselves"—containing a story of a little girl who had never been out of London all her life, nor seen a bit of green grass, except in the Drapers' garden, near her father's house; with the touching tale of "The Changeling;" and the narrative of "Susan Yates," who lived with their parents in the Lincolnshire fens, in a lone house, seven miles distant from the nearest village, and had never been to church, nor could she imagine what a church was like. When the wind set in from a particular point, and brought over the moor the sound of the bells from St. Mary's, little Susan conceived it was "a quiet tune,"[10] occasioned by birds up on the air, so that it was made by the angels. She then tells of the Sunday morning of her first going to church, from her remote home; of the anxiety and awe she felt, and her child-like wonder at the place, and at what she heard—and ever afterwards, when she listened to the sweet noise of bells, of her thinking of the angels' singing, and remembering the thoughts she had in her uninstructed solitude.—These are things which I would wish gentle readers to conceive, with me, may engage the attention of the little girl in the engraving.

THE SABBATH BELLS.

THE cheerful sabbath bells, wherever heard,
Strike pleasant on the sense, most like the voice
Of one, who from the far-off hills proclaims
Tidings of good to Zion: chiefly when
Their piercing tones fall *sudden* on the ear
Of the contemplant, solitary man,
Whom thoughts abstruse or high have chanced to lure
Forth from the walks of men, revolving oft,

And oft again, hard matter, which eludes
And baffles his pursuit—thought-sick and tired
Of controversy, where no end appears,
No clue to his research, the lonely man
Half wishes for society again.
Him, thus engaged, the sabbath bells salute
Sudden! his heart awakes, his ears drink in
The cheering music; his relenting soul
Yearns after all the joys of social life,
And softens with the love of human kind.

Charles Lamb[11]

THE ROYAL CLARENCE VASE.

This engraving held at arms length for a moment, and no more, may convey a slight notion of the superb glass Vase designed and executed at Birmingham, by Mr. John Gunby, and exhibited at the Queen's Bazaar, Oxford Street, London.

An immense bason of copper, and its iron shaft, or foot, clothed with two thousand four hundred pieces of glass, construct a vase fourteen feet high, and twelve feet wide across the brim, weighing upwards of eight tons, and capable of holding eight pipes of wine. Each piece of glass is richly cut with mathematical precision, and is beautifully colored; the colors are gold, ruby, and emerald, and they are enamelled upon one side of the glass. These colored sides being cemented upon the metal body, and rendered perfectly air-tight in that junction, the exterior is a gem-like surface of inconceivable splendor.

On entering the room in which it is exhibited, I was not so much struck by the first sight of the vase, as I expected to be from the account I had received respecting it. The room being small, a few steps from the entrance door had brought me too near to the object, and the eye sought relief from a mass of brilliancy. On continuing to look at it, the strong light of a sunny summer afternoon, commixing with the full blaze from several gas-burners, made out the details too clearly. Ascending a small gallery at the back of the apartment, I saw down into the concavity of the immense vessel. After admiring, for a few minutes, the Thyrsis-like[12] ornaments of the interior, and then proceeding to descend the stairs, my eye was caught by the shadow which dimmed a portion of the exterior, and rendered more lustrous the gleams shining from other parts. It seemed to me that this was a good place for a view; and lingering on the stair-case, the beauty of the vase, as a whole, appeared to gradually unfold. But, upon reaching the floor of the room, the sudden drawing of a curtain obscured the day-light; and the vase, by the illumination of gas alone, glittered like diamonds upon melting gold. From a remote corner I observed the magic splendor at leisure, and watched the varying effects of different degrees of the light, as it was heightened or lowered by a valve regulating to the burners of the surrounding lamps. Waiting till the visitors had retired, who were better pleased with its full lustre, the doors were closed, and I was then allowed half an hour's contemplation in a partial and subdued light. By causing some of the gas-burners to be extinguished, and the flame in the others to be reduced to a finger's breadth, one side of the room was darkened, parts of the vase were in deep shadow, and the rest seemed a glowing golden fire, silently consuming precious gems; while the transparent edge of the encircling rim above became a sparkling nimbus of starlight. I coveted to be shut up with the stillness, and banquet my eyes through the night upon the gorgeous vision. By elevating and adjusting my hands to exclude the illuminating burners from my sight, the colossal gem appeared through the gloom mysteriously self-lighted, and I gazed and mused till I might have imagined it to be the depository of the talismans of Eblis,[13] which disclosed forbidden secrets and exhaustless treasures to the impious caliph who preferred knowledge to wisdom, and who discovered too late that the condition of man is—to be humble and ignorant.

This gorgeous wonder produced solely by native art, at the opening of a new and auspicious aera in our history, should be destined to the palace of a King who holds the hearts of the people to his own, and rules by the law of kindness. Let them respectfully tender it to His Majesty, as the splendid first fruits of British ingenuity in the first year of his beneficent reign, and in testimony of their unanimous sense of his paternal purposes. To a subscription properly originated and conducted, the poorest man that could spare a mite would doubtless contribute; and the "Royal Clarence Vase" may be an acceptable present from the Nation to William the Fourth.

July, 1831.

PART FOUR

—

LETTERS

Reading (and particularly transcribing) Hone's correspondence provides a peculiar sensation of intimacy with his lively and likeable personality at its most unguarded. The letters he wrote to friends such as Francis Place or John Childs were evidently spontaneous compositions, often full of jokes and word play, though at other times his correspondence is marked by candid advice or sympathy, if the circumstances of friends demanded it. The less numerous letters he wrote to individuals who had power over him or from whom he sought assistance are noticeably more strained and self-conscious.

At their best, the letters seem clearly to reproduce the rhythms, intonations, and sudden plunges of Hone's conversation. In those that follow may be traced his changing attitudes toward radicalism as well as his increasing religious preoccupations. Hone was carefully courteous to all his correspondents, with the sole exception of his letter to Cruikshank's mother (8 July 1822), in which his anger and hostility are nevertheless delivered with measured control. Also noteworthy is the evidence of the network of mutual support and reciprocal consultations on strategy among radical reformers under the pressure of legal dangers. A frequent note of urgency ("by four o'clock this afternoon") reflects this drama of deadlines in law as well as in publishing. A similar air of anxiety often informs his many allusions to the straits to which his family was endlessly reduced. As the years pass, while Hone still remarks on public matters and the state of the country, he attends less to particular issues, generalizes more, and becomes increasingly disengaged, even somewhat pessimistic ("I take little interest in the immediate strife"). Yet, to the end, cheerfulness keeps breaking in, and always the endearing touch of self-mockery.

A very helpful source in identifying the repositories of Hone's letters in the United Kingdom is *Location Register of English Literary Manuscripts and Letters: Eighteenth* and *Nineteenth Centuries,* vol. 1, ed. David C. Sutton (London: British Library, 1995).

LETTERS

King's Bench Prison
8 May 1817

[To John Hunt]
Sir[1]

Your kind conversation with my wife on Monday sensibly affects me—I am often backward in expressing acknowledgements of services but I am never insensible of them. On the present occasion, however, many untoward accidents have combined to prevent me from dropping you a line until now—I was ill when I came here, seriously ill. My application to the Court for leave to sit until the Second information was read proceeded from real Indisposition. I was ready to fall & I believe had the Court declined it in civil terms I should have fallen.—But Lord Ellenborough's *No!*—(you might have heard it to the Entrance door of Westminster Hall from Palace Yard)—was as good as Thieves' Vinegar;[2] it startled me & recovered me till I was taken out of Court. I have met with very little accommodation too at this place—so that, though I am in general pretty adaptable to circumstances, no great comfort has been my portion. The prison is very full and a decent room not to be had but at an enormous price. I think I shall have one tomorrow which though dark & not very airy will be better than wandering in the area or idling in the Coffee room without the power of writing in it. Like the Seer of old I shall get a table & a chair & a stool (& a few books withal) and make myself as happy as I can. If my conduct have the approbation of such men as you I desire nothing further. I have no wish to goad Government to extremity but were all their force in array against me and if I stood single handed, *in a just quarrel,* I should defy their efforts and say as the man did to Jove "Ah Jupiter! You are in a passion—you are wrong and you fly to your thunder."

I have received so many kindnesses from you and I owe you so much of service on the Fenning account that nothing I can say on paper or verbally will put you in possession of my feelings.[3] There is an abundance of the heart which the mouth cannot utter; when all that a man hopes for is the power which the mouse had of shewing hers, as we read in the spelling book, to the fine old Lion who was caught in a net after he had been kind to her.

All this, by the by, is to apologize to you for not writing as soon as I heard you had called in the Old Bailey—Will you do more?—drop me a few lines directed there unless you reckon upon coming this way before "the first day of next Term" & do me the honour of a call. *I want your opinion on the stand I take to obtain Copies of the Informations before pleading*—this you see is refused on the ground of custom-precedent—which I say would be more honoured in the breach than in the observance. When the powers that be encroach so much & so daily by new precedents against us it is worth trying, surely, to make them go back a little & create a precedent *for* us—.

> I am Sir, with great respect,
> Your faithful servant
> W. Hone

Place[4]

No circumstance has befallen me of more real concern since I came into this place than the delay of your Shorthand writer with Mr. Wooler's trial[5]—Mr. Wooler has been *wholly precluded* from obtaining & publishing a Report as he had originally purposed and certainly if there was a strong interest any where to prevent the gratification of laudable curiosity & feeling in the public when at their height the disappointment could not have been more effectual.—If the object was to serve Mr. Wooler by this Report—it has robbed him of £200 or £300: if the object was to serve his enemies—it has been completed. Again I say I feel the deepest regret for this affair—you *must* in justice to him & above all to the cause he has so eminently, so nobly served make him reparation & atone to the public to the fullest extent in your power.— Wooler is a brave fellow & I am sick & savage at his usage.

> W. Hone
> King's Bench Prison
> 26 June 1817

67 Old Bailey
(Sunday) 23 Nov. 1817

[To Sir Samuel Shepherd]
Sir[6]

Last night I was served with Rules for nominating Juries & Notices of Trial for the Sittings after Term on the Three Informations filed against me for the Parodies—

I confess I was much surprised at this because after the waiver of the Juries & my liberation on my own Recognizance I did not expect further Proceedings. It has occurred to me that these measures in the multiplicity of Business may have escaped your notice for I can scarcely imagine that I should continue to attract the attention of a public Officer on account of publications of which I have not sold a single Copy within the last nine Months.

As it would be extreme hardihood in me, with a very large Family and wholly inadequate means to court a contest with the purse and power of the Crown so I should feel no less pleasure in being indebted to your liberality for putting an end to the Prosecutions—in that case I pledge myself not to reissue the publications and indeed the entire quantity in my possession may be disposed of as you direct.

I might enhance on my having suspended their Sale nearly three Months before the Informations were filed—on my never having resumed it—on my two Months Confinement in the King's Bench Prison—on consequent estrangement of connexion and domestic suffering during that period—

I forbear to say more than that the Appointment of the Master of the Crown Office to nominate the Juries is for the day after Tomorrow (Tuesday). I am already indebted to you for the politeness of something more than a mere Acknowledgment to a former Communication & I persuade myself that I may be obliged by a line in the course of Tomorrow (Monday) which, in my unexpected, unadvized & wholly unprepared situation I take the liberty of soliciting & anxiously await.

I have the honour to be Sir
Your most obedient Servant
W. Hone

Sir Samuel Shepherd Knt.
His M's Attorney General Lon.

45 Ludgate hill
22 July 1818

[To William Upcott]
Dear Sir[7]

My Trials have not yet been published in a form that many of my friends desire to see them in—they are certainly so forward that I can promise them before the Anniversary—I purpose printing the names of my Juries in Letters of Gold to precede each Trial—the name of Lord Ellenborough to require no illumination—

I am Dear Sir
Yours faithfully
W. Hone

45 Ludgate hill
8 Jan. 1819

[To John Childs]
My dear Sir[8]

On the 21st of last Month, or so soon after as conveniently could be conveyed, I received from you what in London we call an Alderman in chains[9]—this was reserved for our Christmas day dinner when we, that is, my Wife and our seven young ones, played our many parts and drank your health, and carolled away till our eighth little one in my wife's lap crowed herself so hoarse that we were obliged to adjourn our mirth. It was not forgotten that the day of the date of your note was the Anniversary of the day after the Trials which Ministers and their myrmidons designed should send me to keep Christmas in the custody of the Marshal of the Marshalsea of our Sovereign Lord the King—it was not forgotten either that this attempt brought me acquainted with some of the best of my Countrymen who with stout english hearts in their bodies are unsubduable by all the powers of Despotism—nor was it forgotten that to a contempt for Tyranny and a proud hate of it, Britain is indebted for all her Liberties and I for my Christmas dinner.

My dear Sir my wife and I thank you heartily for your kindness—it was my *duty* to have done so before but—(now for a civil lie)—procrastination is the thief of time & I put off, & put off, even unto this day, when finding my conscience troublesome, that is, the burden of the reproach greater than I could bear, I mustered courage to say "thank ye" with my pen, my heart & mind having done so as often as I thought of you.

I have been, and am, ill—dying—but not dead. Blood at the head—apopleptic affection—cupping—bleeding—blistering—lowering—a fortnight at Bath &c—vexation at home & habitual melancholy, which encreases upon me, all these are indications of that sure & certain event which happeneth unto all and which may happen to me in an instant—I am in fact in a very bad way—the Trials have given me a physical shake which has compelled me to abandon what I entered upon with alacrity & spirit, the sales by Auction of Libraries &c for which I had made expensive & extensive arrangements & had neglected my other business to further.—I have therefore now to begin the world afresh nearly.

From my bad health the Prospectus of the Trials has been delayed—of course the Trials themselves not much forwarded. When the prospectus is ready I will send you some down knowing they will be where they will be used. Wishing you and yours health and happiness,

I am My dear Sir Yours faithfully

W. Hone
Mr. Childs. Bungay.

[To Matthew D. Hill, 1820]

My dear Sir[10]

I am no publisher—I am too quick for an enemy and too tardy and uncertain in my operations for a friend—Blow me up, cut me up, make mincemeat of me or scatter me among the Stars—which you please.

Here is your reforming again! All alike!—E'en so My Lord.

But what is the occasion of all this? why could not you send me a Copy of the Argument before?

Ans.—I was indisposed by too large a dose of the powder of *projection.*[11]

Reply—Sir I've done with you—I'll never bring you anything more! Thank ye!

You are such a d—d careless fellow—you know I've been waiting for *a single copy* of this God knows how long and now here you come and——.

I told you I was no bookseller, did I not?

Go to the Devil!

Hastily
W. Hone

———◦———

London 11 Dec: 1820

Dear Childs

I have great satisfaction from your letter this morning, announcing that enough has been obtained for Mr. Scraggs, and a little mortification on learning that part of the sums subscribed are to be directed to some public charity. Assuredly *some* of those who have subscribed here, will be dissatisfied if the surplus be thus appropriated, and I, for one, can conceive no reason for it unless Scraggs be unworthy of further assistance, which you have given me no reason to imagine. Pray do not suffer any clamour of the Bungay loyalists to misdirect a single shilling from its intended object—*Give it him all*. I have however returned a Guinea to George Cruikshank from whom I extracted it, over "a pint stoup,"[12] on Saturday night, or, (orthodoxy forgive me) rather on Sunday Morning—and I have likewise returned another guinea to another good fellow who could better afford a sentiment than a sixpence—To revert however to the surplus—Scraggs is a fool, & does not know what is good for him, and therefore you & his other friends ought to, and *must*, secure the amount whatever it be, *for his exclusive benefit*. Do this.

Property is encumbering in some forms. In the shape of *money* it is confoundedly annoying. If you have it, you naturally divide it with some destitute and distressed fellow creatures, and then divide the remainder, till the quotient is indivisible. And if you have it in the shape of a *house* you as naturally let in some unhappy shelterless devil as a tenant, upon whom you haven't the heart to levy a distress for the rent—. That is, I mean that cash & tenements are to *me* teazing alike— and if I had not surrendered myself to certain Trusties, who kindly convert to their own use and behoof, all and all manner of Income and Proceeds, arising out of and from divers, to wit, sundry, Houses, and Ladders, and other things, or from the sale thereof, I say were it not for said Trusties viz. 1 Sarah 2 Matilda, 3 Fanny, 4 William 5 Alfred, 6 John 7 Emma 8 Rose, &, 9, Samuel Parr Hone, on the body of my wife Sarah (another Trustie for *us 10*) lawfully begotten, I say I do believe were it not for said kind case & consumption, as aforesaid, I should have been not worth a groat[13] or a family. Money is the Devil to me— and, if I had it, Land would be Hell, which being interpreted signifieth Torment.

Thank you & your good brother for Hares—*such* Hares!—I am absolutely under an indigestion from devouring part of one because I could not abstain from the temptation to eat as much as I could of it—and then *a brace* today. "Visions of glory spare my aching sight!"[14] I sent the stoutest to the wife of our friend the tall Stationer—the other will be jugged[15] for our dinner on Wednesday, when we shall laugh at recollections of the donor and drink his & his wife's, & his family's health. I am not fond of giving advice but pray tell your brother to get married without delay—it sharpens a man's capabilities, & enlarges his powers of usefulness, and concentrates his mind to one object. Tell him that Marriage is Nature's art of stereotyping—besides a man should begin while he can fuse—years roll over him & he vitrifies.[16]

> I am Dear Childs Yours faithfully
> W. Hone

[on the cover] I forgot poor Bill. Thank you for him——I *must* [? obscured by seal] you the beginning of this [?] *will*. More anon.

> Ludgate hill
> 20 Dec: 1820

Friend Place

I want to get as many *facts* in proof of the flagrant corruption of the House of Commons as I can possibly procure by 4 o'clock this afternoon and I have full assurance of your readiness to aid me when I tell you it is for my friend John Hunt's Defence of the alleged libel in the Examiner[17]—Pamphlets expository of the various branches of State corruption will likewise be very serviceable—I only received Notice last night and I must send off the parcel to him at Taunton this afternoon—He will not be the less pleased for knowing that *you* are a contributor to his fund of knowledge—

Now it strikes me that every *fact* or recollection of fact or reference to fact within Newspaper reference is *most* desireable but I leave this to your judgment with only one word more—that as to myself I am the most unprovided at this time of any politician with books or tracts on Parliamentary reform—all my heavy ones were sold to raise the wind

for my Defences in 1817 and since then my means have been entirely
directed to Parodial collection

> I am Friend Place
> Yours faithfully
> W. Hone

———◦———

> Ludgate hill
> 16 March 1821

Dear Childs

Here is the "Right Divine of Kings to Govern Wrong" and here is
"The Spirit of Despotism"[18]—the first I will not degrade by my
praise—and the other, for obvious reasons, I modestly leave to be
praised by others—

Friend Filby was here a day or two ago—full of wool and good
spirits—I am very *very* anxious about my boy William, and asked Mr.
Filby what business he thought he might be put to—He could give me
very little idea for he had form'd none—Now my good fellow if your observation of him has enabled you to judge of likings and capabilities
what *sort* of a trade do you suppose him inclined to, or fitted for? seden-
tary or active? brain work or handwork? either is hard work—but as to
authorship or bookselling, I would rather he were a sweep, for I don't
want him a stultus or a knave.[19]

Mr. Filby will tell you what I said about him—he drags at my heart
poor fellow very greatly. If I did not know you for a prompt *"man of
business"* (now I shall have a letter!) I might expect to wait your arrival
in town before I learn your thoughts—however as my correspondence
has been very active of late (this is the *second* letter you have had since
we last met remember) perhaps you will drop a line about him.

Remember me to Edwards (I like a dog that carries his heart in his
mouth) & to your brother —& tell Mrs. Childs that my wife (who has
been no better than she should be of late) and I (who am much as
usual—up and down) thank her very greatly for her kindness to
William—As to you, you will take silence from me as gratitude.

> God bless you John Childs &
> Yours
> W. Hone

I suppose I shall see Donkin when you come to town. I never see him but at those times—he's *"a man of business."*

[On Cover] "With 6 Spirits & 13 Rights."

"We twa hae paidl't"— BURNS.

From Hone's *Facetiae and Miscellanies* (1827) by George Cruikshank.

Ludgate hill
8 July 1822

[Mrs. Mary Cruikshank]
Madam[20]

On Saturday when a letter arrived from you by the twopenny post dated the 2[d] instant I was not in town. I lose no time in acknowledging, that the unjust spirit towards me that it is written in, does not excite my curiosity to be acquainted with the occasion of an address, evidently designed for the purpose of rude offence.

Whatever of kindness I entertain, and I entertain *much*, for your son George, has been from *admiration of his talents* and respect for his honorable disposition. For everything that could diminish either of those qualities, I have expressed to him not only deep regret, but re-monstrated with him more severely than any one but a *sincere friend* feeling deeply for his *best interests* and *real welfare* would venture to do. If he has, as you say, left your house for three years past, you must be better acquainted with the reasons for his seeking a home elsewhere than I am, or desire to be—because, after the wanton unprovoked expressions of malignity in your letter, towards my family and me, I decline all communication with you upon that or any other subject. But, though I do not choose to expose myself to a repetition of the insult, yet I wish you well—and I trust, that, by forbearing from uncharitable surmises and hasty judgments, you may attain to a knowledge that you desire somewhat of that Christian Character you assume—the chief ornament of which, I find myself constrained to remind you, is a meek and quiet spirit.

I am Madam
Your most obedient Servant
W. Hone

Mrs Cruikshank
[Cover] For Mrs Cruikshank
   Middleton Terrace
    Pentonville

Ludgate hill
4 January 1823

[To Mr. Rhodes]
My dear Sir
If you can excuse a timeless cold-toed wight for not taking the trouble to leave watergruel,[21] and knocking at the portal of Lyons Inn to ascend the south west turret to your enchanted chamber—do: not forgetting that he has a favor to ask which if you can confirm—do also. Boldly then *can* you oblige me with the loan of that pageant wherein the devil holds converse with St. Dunstan.[22] If not I desire no reason—such a collection as yours ought not to be assailable by every Tarquin,[23] and if I thought myself one because you had permitted me a flirtation I ought to set about the abduction in another way. However so many things fall out between the cup and the lip that I am offended with no one for circumspection.—Yet if you dare trust me with the

fiend and the Saint till Monday you shall see us three in company that afternoon

I am
My dear Sir
Very respectfully Yours
W. Hone

Pre-Script—(there being no room for a Post-Script)—If you take this letter ill, we shall both be mistaken.

Wm. Hone
London
22 January 1823

Dear Wilson[24]

I am half angry with you, not for scolding or half scolding me but because you are doing, what you ought not to attempt, without adequate means. Now I am not conscious of having affected to be *"a busy man"*— but I have had the business of others thrust upon me, to the occupation of time that ought to have been devoted to my own, and "in my sear and yellow leaf"[25] I am seeking fresh sap to put forth a few branches for the protection of my family. Yet *you* I acquit wholly of having been one of these depredators on the "stuff that life is made of"[26]—but I am compelled to say NO, for the first time almost I ever did to an old friend, and that simply because I cannot say Yes without injury to myself of which you can scarcely form a notion. Still I cannot forbear to exemplify by telling you that my work on "the Mysteries"[27] did not come out at Christmas as announced, nor can it on the last of this month as *positively* announced, because I literally cannot make the time necessary for its completion, and I have only about a sheet of it to do.

Concerning the "many things which I *have*" towards assisting you in the Life of De Foe your friend Williams misinforms you. When I last saw you in town you entreated me to get together what I could in that way, and appointed a certain morning to call upon me and see what I had done. Though heavy to move on a slight application, yet the name of De Foe was a "word of power,"[28] and, in rummaging, I employed myself diligently, and till the hour of three on that morning, when I expected you between 9 & 10, very anxiously—waited at home the whole forenoon fidgetting—your presence would have been as grateful to me as "the breath of Maia to the lovesick Shepherdess"[29]—but lo! on sending to Ely Place I found you had gone off for Somersetshire, which seemed to me as though you were too uxorious for a De Foeite, and I will frankly confess that the disappointment very much mortified me. By degrees what I had got together were once more dispersed by my own occasions for reference, and the thing is to me as though it were not. "*You* do not mean to see London again till *you* have finished the book"—the more to your shame. "It is impossible" you say—very well. You cannot make a *bad* book I know, but will not make so *good* an one as you may, and I acknowledge to you that I take little interest in that which does not interest *you* sufficiently to forsake the "fat contented easy ignorance"[30] of a country town, in search of knowledge that is to be got by seeking for it in London. Were I as you are, and with the same object in view, neither hedge-row elms, nor Christmas festivities, nor aught in "bed or board" I love, would detain me from the laborious inquiries essential to its final and successful accomplishment. The Life of De Foe is to be dug for in the writings of his contemporaries, and where they are in large masses there should you excavate—at the British Museum, Sion College, Dr. Williams's[31]—in short, into all public and private collections you should burrow—and access is easy to all. Without this the life of De Foe will be no more. I thought I knew you better, and nothing but your own acknowledgment on paper would convince me that you were about to commit *murder*. "Conjure *me*, by *my* love of De Foe!" fie! fie! I *do* love him and so much *better than you do* that I would rather he reposed in his grave with no other record than Mr. Chalmers's Memoir,[32] and his own works as his imperishable monument, than see his *ghost* raised by you who can do so much better, and all that I, and all, could wish, if you *will*. You have no right to call upon Mr. Dyer, or myself, or any one, for assistance, till you can show that you have spent, not 3, but 6 months in London *alone*, seeing no one, and thinking of nothing, but about De Foe—You must have collected materials, of course, and the fat of the "Review"[33] is a fine block to chip from, but you have not got *all*, I mean all that you *can*. This is what I quarrel with you for, to excite you to. Do this, and be like the Walter Wilson that I knew a dozen years ago—*he* was a fine fellow at a scent, and when the hunt was up would follow in a steeple chace. Your *power* is greater now than it was then—let your *resolves* be equal and we may have a Life of De Foe yet—but not without 6 months of *your* 'Life in London'—Yours truly, W. Hone.

P.S. The first 3 pages may be   45 Ludgate hill
passed—the *beginning*   6 Oct. 1824 *night*
is at the *end.*

Dear Place

Yes! Dear *"Sir,"* is not the *thing* between *us*—plain *"Place"* is too much like *"plain* Place" *himself,* to be the language of William Hone, who is not less plain but a little more modish, and *so* it is to be as it stands at the top—thus I jump over the awkwardness I feel and always have felt, in answering any one of your notes—*I must do things in my own way,* and *one* of my ways is to be in *some* things like other people, and *this* is one of *them.* I dare to say that *I* am, on a few points, as prominently *out* of the way as *you* are in the commencement of a letter—and *between us* (you know it's a *secret* to every body else) we are two *queer* fellows. However, *this* I *do* know as regards *myself,* and jok-ing aside, that *if I cannot do a thing in my own way I never can do it at all.* I do not *aim* to do things differently from other people, and yet they *are* different, and I sometimes think that *I* differ *myself* from others' selfs—that *I am,* as Sir F. Burdett said of the Speaker's warrant, *"a thing sui generis."* I never metaphysicized about myself, to inquire *how* all this is, or *why* it is—the "causation" I have never tried to trace, and I think it quite likely that I shall die without having informed myself upon a point which others may be quite acquainted with—*you,* for in-stance, & *in particular.*

All *this* comes of not being able to get over plain "Place"—and I think I hear *him* saying "Why *what* is the fool about? did you ever *hear* such a fool? He's *drunk!" "No,* I am *not* drunk!" "Why then you are as great a *fool* as you *were!" "Very* likely" "Why, I *say,* what the L's the matter with you?" "Oh I'm only a little merry or so." "*So*! Go and *sew* below along with Frank's men—you're *drunk!"* I tell you *what* Mr. Place I've had nothing but broth, and gruel, and slops, since last Sun-day fortnight, when I became "possessed" by the *Cholera-morbus*[34] and notwithstanding all the exorcisms of the ministering apothecary he remained in me for fourteen days—as soon as I found myself incapable of moving, I *"set to"* upon "Another article for the Quarterly,"[35] and I got that *out* as soon as I did my tormentor, whereupon I *"disport me"* before going to bed tonight; and I don't know why a man may not as well laugh upon paper, as in another man's face. I have been all that time shut up in my bedroom, without seeing one *strange* face (not even *my own* in a looking glass) except that worthy fellow John Evans's (of Tooks Court) and tomorrow I crawl down to meal with my family, in prospect of which I give you my last word—Good Night!

"Well, well" says Place "but you're not off without telling me what you've got to *say*." "Oh, aye! *true!*"

I have sent Mr. Mill a copy of the "Aspersions Answered,"[36] which I think I did not send him before, and "Another Article."—You will see from the bulk & price of the latter tract, that, though it was "made to *sell*," it was not published to get *money* by—in fact *I shall lose by it*. I cannot afford to advertize it, as I used to advertize pamphlets by the sale of which I profited, and I need *the aid of the press* mightily. I imagine it is the *greatest blow,* in the shape of a *separate* publication, that the *Quarterly* has had. I do not know that I have made it *clear* to *others*, and therefore I assure *you* of the *fact,* that I have not in the *slightest* degree misrepresented the reviewer—there is not a trick or feint in any one instance—it is all heavy, hard, fair, stand-up fighting on my part (Turn to the last Quarterly & you'll see I've not missed one of his points.)—It will therefore be *no discredit* to the *Morning Chronicle*[37] to lend its aid. The pamphlet furnishes materials for a *thorough exposure* of the *rascally* methods by which the *Quarterly* catches and macerates victims who have not courage to defend themselves by re-reviewing the Arch Enemy's articles—*Do oblige me & further the interests of* <u>*Truth and Justice*</u> *by getting our friend Black to do his best at it*. I am too ill to get out. I sent him one on Monday afternoon. I thank you sincerely for your intimation of *"satisfaction"*—Yours truly

W. Hone

—— ⊸⊙⊶ ——

45 Ludgate hill London
12th April 1825

[To James Montgomery]
Sir[38]

If you have seen the weekly sheet entitled the "Every-Day Book" you may have perceived somewhat of a feeling in it, akin to what I conceive to be your own, as regards the condition of the helpless—if that feeling were strongly put forth it might defeat the object I have in view—the gradual persuasion of unthinking persons in behalf of those who may be served by right dispositions, and consequently the engendering of gentle feelings in common readers. It is this alone that I urge as excuse for acquainting you, that "MayDay" being a "holiday" with the poor Sweeps in the metropolis, I designed a few words in their favor; and, to show that they had not wholly been neglected aforetime, I purposed some account of a custom (I heard talk of when a child) with the late Mrs. Montague to give them a feast on that day at her house at Soho. I turned to your volume, "The Chimney Sweepers Friend," hoping I might find some particulars of that lady's festival, and though I do not find them I take the liberty of writing to you with a query as to whether you can direct me to any channel wherein they may be found. I have looked to several Journals and met with nothing. I need not say that I shall be the more obliged if you have any old newspapers or publications that you can lend me to supply my want—it is an *immediate* one, because what I do must be at press on Tuesday next. Expense of carriage &c is no object, and whatever you may be pleased to favour me with I will carefully return. Possibly too, if you conceive the matter in the light I mean it, you would be good enough to inform me if any and what custom exists at Sheffield on the first of May connected with "Chimney Sweepers"—as relates to others I do not presume to trouble you.

You must be aware that in a work professedly relating to "Amusements" and "Customs" it is an affair of some difficulty to depart from the usual course of "merriment"—but I have not hesitated to aberrate occasionally, and if I can feel my way among my readers may do so more frequently as regards their higher relations—this however must be a work of time, and not to intrude further on yours, with the hope also that you will not conceive offence when my desire is furthest from that of giving it. I beg to assure you that the sense I have of your writings, and of their purpose, is more accordant with your own than I can have any ground to suppose you may imagine in him to whom self vindication is irksome ever against more than common misconception and misrepresentation.

I am, Sir, very respectfully,
Your obedient Servant
W. Hone

45 Ludgate hill
5 Oct. 1825

[To Robert Childs]
My dear Sir[39]

I received the Old Lady[40] and shall treat her if I find her of good repute as tenderly as I would a young one—distinguishing her & *you* at
the same time.

So!—you send me an "Account sent to the Newspapers"—! *you*!
This won't do—I must have more. Answer me these.

Did she survive her husband?

What was she? by occupation or profession?

Where did he live? Did he leave her a competence?

Was she remarkable for nothing but living beyond her time?

Acquaint me with—her temper? & her usual diet?

Did she rise early? & if early how early? how long did she sleep?
How was her appetite? her eyesight? her memory? Was she of any religious persuasion? and what? bigoted or tolerant? Had she any
mind? & how much? distinguishing the qualities thereof? (Had she
any bumps? I beg pardon—"organic developments" on the cranium?
had she the organ of destructiveness? or of self destructiveness? & by
what organ was it counteracted?—All this is in a parenthesis—she
had amativeness I presume—with PhiloproJenny & Jackeytiveness[41]
of course—still in the parenthesis.) Seriously though I will thank you
to give me as many particulars as you can collect or re-collect respecting this want—and you shall have an article if you will give me
the materials—

Was she temperate in drinking? & how temperate? drinking no, or little, spirits or wine or beer? or water only? &c. &c.—talkative or taciturn?

But a few *anecdotes* respecting her would be very acceptable—
these are the *materiel* of article-writing.

Now tell "Uncle Filby" that his best wishes have my hearty thanks
and that I don't forget him or "Brother John" whom that I did not see
when he was in town I lament me in vain—I c^d not—I was mal-a-tete
as the French say, & rambling head or heels or both together in or about
"Hagbush Lane,"[42] the old North Road where he might have found me
if he c^d. have found anybody near or on the spot that knew the aforesaid
way by either of those denominations—or even as a way—*I* keep to the
"good *old* ways."

Remember me yourself and remember me to "brother John" and

ask him if the division of Poland was justifiable?[43] and therewith he will associate the division of Turkey, or see that I do and that I recollect "Christmas is a-coming."

In woful haste I have made wanton waste of paper—as you & "brother John" do—all I have said might have been said thus

My dear Sir

If you forward me some particulars of Mrs. Want by Tuesday next you shall see her portrait with an Account of her in the E.D.B.–

I am My dear Sir
Yours most sincerely
W. Hone

24 April 1826

Dear Childs

My family is thrust out from Ludgate hill and I am in the Rules of the King's Bench Prison.[44] From the moment I found my affairs irretrievable which was within two hours after I was arrested—(it being made plain to me by my solicitor and I had not dreamed of it before)— I worked like a horse to put the "Every Day Book" beyond the reach of destruction by transferring it to Messrs. Hunt & Clarke, in trust for my Creditors, & every sheet, of every thing, out of my own power, or the power of any one man to touch in preference to another. All was removed into their warehouse in a few hours, & my papers secured, with the books necessary to the conduct of the work, and I was transferred hither, after writing a No. in the Lock up house, since when I got out last week's, arranged the Index to make the first volume an immediately productive asset, & have just got the proofs from the printers which when read will go to press. But my family are in great distress. My wife & six of the children, as I am informed, sleep in one room of my father's house whither they ran for shelter when executions came in. I went to prison, with 3/6 in my pocket, a week before my daughter Fanny was to have been married—this state of affairs rendered it necessary to defer *that*, but it can be deferred no longer without more than the risk, I may add with the *certainty*, of the match being off and my poor girl being deserted and heart-broken—that step therefore is indispensable immediately for the sake of her future happiness—it can't even have taken place at the time first appointed if I had possessed the means of raising Ten pounds to clothe her—my sudden destitution & the necessity, under the exigency of my resigning all power to reach a single shilling, deprived me of the least ability, and now, that, for the reasons I have stated, the day is fixed for *next Saturday*—she must go to her future home, without under-linen, or other than the gown she has on her back, exposed to the derision of her husband's family, who by their jeers at my downfal, & remonstrances against the marriage have nearly swayed him from it; & also subject to the chance of his contempt under such circumstances of harassing from his own friends. He is an honest & worthy young man, but the poor fellow has been nearly worried out of his life, & though he will be able to maintain her, yet, from having expended his little all in providing a humble home for her, it cannot be expected that a demand on her part for money for clothing would contribute towards an outfit of happiness if it were even in his power to comply with it—it is *not*, & therefore the anticipation we all have is, that her marriage will be embittered in the outset. In this state of things, & not knowing to whom to fly, I represent the facts to *you*, with the hope that you may find it in your means & disposition to aid me with the means of obviating the condition wherein she will appear on her wedding day & afterwards. They are absolute necessaries that she is in want of—for I should be ashamed of myself if in my present circumstances she were to appear otherwise than accommodated to them. It is not possible, I think, that my creditors will refuse the proposition that will be submitted to them generally, & to which those who have been already seen have assented, for the continuation of the "Every Day Book," and employing me, under Trustees, at such a rate as shall barely maintain the family on the smallest weekly allowance until I have satisfied them *in full*—it is my wish, & will be my endeavor to do it, & nothing short of being allowed to make that endeavor, & pay them 20 shillings in the £ will satisfy *me*. To remove all suspicion that I might desire the benefit, as it is called, of the Insolvent Court, I have forborne entering the prison walls, which is a requisite enjoined by the law before a debtor can petition for relief. Bankruptcy seems altogether out of the question. It would be the best thing for *me*, & the worst for my creditors, & as I am willing to work for them, at the price of a bare existence, they will scarcely reject the offer. Either way I should be unable to repay the money. If this arrangement I seek takes place I would liquidate it by a pound a month—if Bankruptcy ensues, it is not possible to confine my pen & I should be enabled to repay it, probably even earlier. You will enter into my feelings, I think, as a father, & if I could here state all the particulars that render it desirable, you would see that they are more strong than you will imagine from what I have written. I know not whether Mr. John Childs be at home, but I direct so as for this to be opened by either him or Mr. Robert Childs—and to both, or either, I say I shall highly value the obligation, if both, or either, can confer it. My direction (and on account of similar numbers in the street it is necessary to be precise) is "Mr. Hone at Mr. Poole's Tobacconist No. 2 Great Suffolk Street, opposite the Old Windsor Castle, Borough, London." Though I have even lacked necessaries, I mean meals, since I have been here, I have not made known that I had not wherewithal to obtain them, for I am not a beggar—had I been dishonest to my creditors I should not have been in want, &, as it is, I am as above the meanness of a begging letter, as I am of appropriating a farthing of the money I now speak of to other than my child's use. I am Dear Childs

Yours sincerely W. Hone

13 Gracechurch Street, London
23 April 1830

[To Robert Southey]
Sir[45]

Late last night I got a copy of the new edition of the Pilgrim's Progress at Mr. Major's, and this morning my first employment is to obtrude upon you my most sincere and respectful thanks for your unexpected mention of my name and latter writings in the conclusion of your Life of Bunyan.[46] Such a notice, from *you,* is especially grateful to *me,* and is the more gratifying now, when the humble doings you are pleased to publicly favor can benefit me no otherwise than by occasioning reflection on the honesty of purpose which stimulated my labours, and which consoles me after I have lost every thing on earth except my integrity, and ten children, and these, I trust, I shall be enabled to keep to my life's end. To further literary exertion I am beyond the reach of "encouragement." At this moment the last remains of my ruined fortunes, a few of the books that assisted me in working out my Every Day Book and Table Book—which, by the bye, are mine no longer—are passing under the hammer of an auctioneer, to realise a small instalment towards insufficient means for commencing a business wholly foreign to all my former pursuits and addictions.[47] I have thrown down my pen forever, and am struggling to enter on a strange drudgery for the future support of my wife and family.

In the autumn of last year, while sojourning in a quiet hamlet, I packed up a book or two respecting the Pilgrim's Progress with the intention of sending them to you. I had misgivings, however, as to whether *you* would receive, from *me*, as a token of good-will, what I unfeignedly desired to communicate in that spirit, and the parcel was put aside, sealed up, as it still remains. In that state I shall forward it for conveyance to you through Mr. Major—simply to evidence my feelings towards you several months ago. You may be convinced by it that your liberality has a kin in my own mind. After all, perhaps, the best testimony I can give to the fact, that I am duly sensible of your unlooked-for kindness, is the promptitude with which I acknowledge the obligation.

         I am,

             Sir,

                 Your very respectful,
                    and most obedient Servant
                         W. Hone

---

                    13 Gracechurch St. London
                             5 May 1830

Dear Wilson

I imagine that Will. Hazlitt's article in the Edinburgh Review has long since compensated you for imaginary loss of anything I might have done in the Westminster, which I assigned reasons to Mr. Thomas Hurst for not being able to do, though I so desired and purposed.[48] I wrote him from Lancashire, whither I had gone to raise means for getting into premises which by the advice of friends I had taken, & now date from. I succeeded to an extent which enabled me to obtain the Lease & Fixtures, & pay for altering & fitting up the place, for a respectable Coffee House on economical principles to be conducted by my eldest daughter. It was suggested to me by my best well-wishers, and, as the house is situated where the stages resort, & is surrounded by great commercial & banking establishments, besides a constant thoroughfare, there is every reasonable prospect of complete success. But, unhappily, from having paid away our money & the bills for carpentry, bricklaying, plastering, plumbing, glazing & paper hanging & painting, having exceeded the calculations, we are short by £200 for lamps, gas fitting, steam apparatus, boilers, earthenware, glass, and a large variety of smaller sundries, which are indispensable to the opening of the place. This happens at a time when, in all other respects, it is ready for business, & persons are coming to town, who, if they could be accommodated otherwise, would occupy our beds which will be a daily profit. In short, we have paid for what we have in the place to the extent of £700, which, by wear & tear of body & mind, I ravaged together from every one in town & country whom I could think of as likely to assist me & my family in making the last struggle I ever can make with them for a standing place in this life. I now sit down heart-sore, & sick in mind, to write to a few persons, most of whom are strangers to me, and I venture to communicate to you my situation—that of Tantalus with the cup at his lips.[49] Among those who contributed to our undertaking, by gift, are Joseph Birch Esq. M.P.—Charles Blundell Esq. of Ince, a possessor of rich stores of books & ancient sculpture, at his seat near Liverpool, where I visited him—Arthur Heywood Esq., Banker, of Liverpool— William Rathbone Esq. of the same place—Rev. W. Shephard of Gateacre—the Earl of Sefton—Mr. Behnes the eminent sculptor— T. M. Alsager Esq. of *The Times*—& Joseph Parkes Esq. of Birmingham, author of the History of the Court of Chancery, the evidence of whose friendship to me was the sum of £50.[50] I am prohibited by an exemplary member of the Society of Friends from mentioning *his* name as a donor of a Two Hundred Pound Bank Note. After a rigidly economical disposition of the sums received in this way, which, as they were received, were paid by me into the hands of Alfred A. Fry Esq. of 53, Great Ormond Street, and by him paid to the Tradesmen employed, himself being a donor, and, as a man of business, making the disbursements for the work to do, I say, after this you will scarcely be surprised that I should be in no small degree affected on finding myself aground, and turn with anxious eyes to whomsoever I can think of for aid. If the amount can be obtained, *without loss of time,* it will be of indescribable benefit, inasmuch as it will enable the family to commence business, & put an end to the grievous disadvantages & expenses inescapable from delay. Let me supplicate you in this exigence to assist us to a convenient extent by way of gift, or loan (to be repaid at a stipulated time, not too early.) For anything that you can do for us I & my wife & family shall be very grateful.

> I remain,
>> Dear Wilson,
>>> Yours sincerely
>>>> W. Hone

———◆———

[To Francis Place]   13 Gracechurch Street   23 September 1830

You do not "tease" me I assure you. I had purposed answering your first letter respecting Spence[51] as soon as I had finished correcting the "Annals," from the sheets of the 4th edition in a more decent state than those of the three former.[52] I thank you for wishing the publication a "large sale"—if it have not, I shall have labored to a small purpose, for I divide profits with the publisher. I have just ridded off the last sheets, and now have at you.

Beginning with your first letter, respecting my "Short Publications in 1817," I believe it is not profitable to procure any of them—if I had any they should be yours.

"*Thomas Spence.*" The only things I have of his I deem the rarest, & most curious of his works—they are 1. The Real Reading-made-Easy 2. A Supplement to the History of Robinson Crusoe—Both are printed at Newcastle in 1702.

The latter has a version in the "Kruzonian M'an'ir"—this is clearly what he afterwards called the "*Spensonian*" manner. The tract is pregnant with his "Plan." I will lend you, with pleasure, the little volume (24mo), & would send it by post, but I fear miscarriage. I have nobody to send with it, but will leave it at the bar of the "Grasshopper" for anyone who may ask for it in your name. I do not know anybody that has tracts by Spence which you have not.

It will be a fortnight before I can get to see you, & hear you read your sketch, for I must immediately turn to commencing "The Year Book," which I am under articles for, in the manner of the Every Day Book. Among the papers that I have to turn over, I expect to find a printed sheet of a work containing a more minute account of Spence than I ever saw. It was done by I forget whom, & sent to me about three years ago by the author from Newcastle.[53] He knew Spence. More I cannot tell you respecting this sheet, for I recollect no more. I shall come to it within a fortnight, & you shall have it as soon as I find it.

I only know of Spence's Son that he had one. The last time I saw or heard of him was when Spence lived in Turnstile. He was then publishing a Dictionary of the "Spensonian" Language in numbers [?]—it was, in form, like the square Entick, but, I imagine, never finished.[54]

You speak in your last letter, just received, as though you had some paper before you, written by me, respecting Spence. I have no remembrance of such a paper. To say the truth my memory is not so good as it was. I have a faint notion only of [Fugion?] in connection with Spence. I *saw* Spence with his "vehicle," & bought his Trial from it in Parliament Street, near the Duke of Richmond's. My personal intercourse with him was very little, for I disliked his manner—but I was a frequent observer of him, on account of his fearless thinking & printing. About 1808 or 9 he came to the Strand for one of Sir F. Burnett's speeches, and talked away about his "Plan" & the Landlords, against whom he was inveterate. On leaving he gave me a card (long since lost) admitting the bearer to a meeting at the *Something* & Lamb in or near Windmill Street, where he said he met his friends to talk over & cooperate towards his "Plan." I should not have objected to being there as a mere spectator, but I knew that could not be, & therefore did not go. Really, at present, I cannot remember more of him. His "vehicle" mentioned before, was very like a Baker's close barrow—the pamphlets were exhibited outside, & when he sold one he took it from within, & handed & recommended others with strong expressions of hate to the powers that were, & prophecies of what would happen to the whole race of "Land Lords."

I *know* that Spence was arrested where he kept the long stall in Chancery Lane at the Middle Row Corner, for I was passing at the time, & heard him in dispute with the officer. He had just got his shutters down in the morning when he was pounced upon. It was early therefore & no one but myself was present at first. I remained only a minute or so, for I had to hasten to a situation I then had to attend at 9 o'clock. Dates I cannot fix as I might have done 6 or 7 years ago. Since then my head has cullendered.[55]

It gave me great pleasure to hear on coming home the other day, that honest Thomas Hardy had been to the Grasshopper, & broke the rules, by breaking into the bar, & kissing my daughter Matilda before all the visitors.[56]

I remain Friend Place
Yours sincerely
W. Hone

13 Gracechurch Street
25 November 1830

[To Robert Southey]
Dear Sir,

It did not occur to me yesterday to enclose the printed paper I now send you. I read it cursorily a few weeks ago, & was much impressed by many of its remarks—it is especially worth your perusal & thinking over, when you are considering the Machinery question.—Machinery is the Jaggernaut[57] of our country. The progress of the idol carriage is imposing and devastating—it will level all ranks & conditions to a common mass—property, title, all will be crushed—nothing will be saved or spared by this Giant Radical. It concentrates the power of money-getting, & the money-getter is a land-getter. Hence a new & heartless aristocracy is rapidly growing up on the ruins of the old. This is the age of science—we have "sought out many inventions,"[58] & discovered one which displaces human labour, & will displace every being of society. Jews & Jobbers are mortgagers of the land-owners—there will, of necessity, be foreclosures, for the mortgagers cannot return with a sterling currency & maintain their profession which they mistake for dignity. This dignity they will not abate, it will evaporate, & the monied-man will become the landed-man.

I will not however weary you with crude dogmatising. You set my head at work a little yesterday & I scribbled much seeming nonsense to you—yet I could work out my sayings, but I assure you I have not put to paper a line on politics for the last seven years, & now I desire nothing but quiet & books—liberty to rest.

Let me now direct your eye most particularly to a careful reading of the three columns in the *Times* of this morning on the "State of the Country." The article "Berkshire" is important—but far more applicable to your inquiry is the "Lewes" article, which contains an account of an extraordinary parley between the discontented laborers at *Ringmer* and Lord Gage.[59] Did I not tell you yesterday of the ignorance of the rich respecting the poor—and to-day we find a nobleman ignorant of his own affairs—the proceedings of his own steward! I pray God that the land-owners may yet see their interest. But what think you of Fox-hunting landlords in farming districts? I entreat you, my dear Sir, to cry aloud & spare not—awaken, if it be possible, the gentry to a sense of their true condition. They will be criminal to the laborers, to themselves, & to the country, if they suffer the people to rise instead of themselves. The faces of the half-famished have appealed to them—their voices have been disregarded—they now speak to them with tongues of fire.

Do I justify these outrages? God forbid! M. Chateaubriand says he warned the French court against headlong proceedings, because he was "a believer in Revolutions, & in facts."[60] Our government requires no warnings of that kind, but our aristocracy need a trumpet-tongued alarum—not to arms, but to do justice as between man & man. There is a social difference, & it may be settled socially—but if it be not now *finally* settled in the disturbed counties, & voluntary concessions made in other parts before the claims are urged, we shall have extended insurgency. At present the question seems to be between the laborers and the farming tenantry—but in reality it is between the tenantry & the landowners. And the landowners cannot see this!

I remain,
    Dear Sir,
        Yours most respectfully, & sincerely
            W. Hone

---

13 Gracechurch Street
4 June 1831

[To Robert Childs]
In the name of sacred Phrenology, & yourself, Mr. Robert Childs, and every thing else that is sacred, and laughable, & wonderful, to a poor half daft body like me, what can you assign to me as a reason—the reason is another thing—but I ask what will you give as a reason, you thief of the world and me, for taking off, and causing me to leave behind, & yourself detaining, witholding, & keeping, my head and ears, face and features, & the appurtenances thereof & thereto belonging or appertaining? Answer me that, and get out of it as you can, if it is in your power, without forfeiting your honor, & standing naked before me, as you would do if you got up in the morning in my presence, without your breeches, like a snake that has crawled through a bush & left his skin behind him, & works his way tenderly over the young green grass, reptile as he is, while it's growing for the food of the innocent beasts

that perish, after the manner of yourself working among the harmless printing types, as they would be, if it was not for your changing them about into skimble-skamble stuff, & perplexing the heads of the people with knowledge and sorrow—knowledge today, & sorrow tomorrow— botheration! Botheration! I say, where's my head?—Am I to go about everlastingly, as I have done for the last two months, with people asking me where's *my* head; & they know *you've* got it, & I know you've got it, & I have not got it myself, & the craters[61] laughing at me for a fool, as I am, & you made me so, and I want to know why? What have you done with it? What did you want it for? What do you want it for? What are you going to do with it? What right have you to it? Is not it my head, & not yours? And is not your own enough for you? Have you no respect for the *head-hitter*[62] of the "Year Book"? Don't you know you are only just outside of his *rapper*,[63] and, if he gets you within, the better for him, & the worse for yourself, & your brother perhaps. It is not Christmas yet, & what care I for turkey, or Turks like you? And, for aught I know, my head may be stuck up at your door, for the pigs to look at, like the heads at the gate of the great Turk's palace upon poles. And their's the poor creatures in Poland, half of them, perhaps, by this time, without *their* heads—all taken off by barbarians, like you, with bumps of destructiveness—or blown away at the cannon's mouth, as I may be, some day, in a hard winter, from the top of a—stage-coach, going somewhere to increase my means of living, & so meeting with my death.

Now I have it!—I have it! May you not feel another bump, if you are not keeping my head till I'm dead! But I'll be up with you—I'll be down upon you—Down at Bungay will I be, as sure as my head's my own, & I live to reach the place—or—I'll bring an action in trover—or file a bill of discovery & get you into Chancery, & recover my head—or get an order to have it referred to the master to take an account of the bumps, & report the proceeds—or an interlocutory judgment for the profits to be paid to the Accountant General, with interest, and I'll ruin you with costs—I'll proceed *Informer pauper us*[64]—make your brother a co-defendant, & work at that same Treasury check he would not let me see in his breeches pocket, buttoned up, which he got out of our present finance-ministers, & could not have got from the others, for flabbergasting at the *Come at he*[65] for parliamentary printing—*that* was your brother—why don't you get *his* head?

———◦———

Mr. Robert Childs
Sir

Please to take notice, that I hereby demand & require of you to forthwith surrender, & give, or yield up, the entire & quiet possession of a certain cast or mould of, from, or off, my head, to wit, the sides top back & face of the said head, in such & so many piece or pieces, or in one whole piece, as the same, to wit, the whole of the said mould, may be—or a full and perfect cast thereof, or, in default, I shall daily and every day, from a certain day, put a letter into the post office directed to you, without any further notice or contents than my signature in manner and form following, as the same followeth, or is hereunto subjoined. As Witness my hand, as aforesaid, this present late blessed old King's Birthday that was, in the year 1831.[66]

I am Sir
Your humbug Servant

H

P.S. Please to ask, & tell him I bid you ask "how he gets on"—I mean your brother—& be sure to let me know his answer.

13 Gracechurch Street
13 June 1831

Dear Robert

Without a joke out of, from, belonging, appertaining unto, respecting, or concerning, or on, or about, my head—but, seriously, intending and devising how to obtain or procure it—I say, seriously, "I wish I may get it."

Your letter, courting the infliction of penalties I proposed, would be a baffler, were I to let you *have* your wicked wish, epistolarily, (*see* Johnson) or visitorially. I can neither write nor see you—"Come and hear the grasshoppers." In truth I hear enough of "the Grasshopper in Gracechurch Street," and I almost premise, from these premises, I shall never be able to go in search of another. You tell me of "shores" & "skies" & "mouldering ruins" in Norfolk (or, 'save you, Suffolk)—I beg to tell *you* that, from the room in which I write at this instant, the *old walls* of the X keys inn are before me, & confine my view to the *sky* only and I nose the "common *shore*" at every change of the weather. Think of that, Master Robert, in "*this* blessed month of June," and wonder, when I tell you, that I am content. I have little of encumbrances, but many duties upon me, and have suffered too much from waywardness, to give way to fidgetty wants & wishes. It would pleasure me, and do me much good, to have the run of a friend's house in the country this summer, but I must walk cautiously about my own, & there only, or the "Grasshopper" will cease to hop as it ought.

I caught up a pamphlet at John Atkinson's which you advised him to read, & brought it away to read myself—"Mr. Beverley's Pamphlet"[67]—it is a most *tremendous* blow, & if he follows it up, will be "the beginning of the end." Clearly he is a young man, & throws away much of his power, by his fierceness. If he does not cool, or fanaticise, into weakness, he has the bull by the horns, & notwithstanding some monstrous exaggerations, he, *alone*, may bring down the *whole* enormous mass of clerical encumbrance. Still, to *my* eye, *he* is not the man who will achieve this—much he can & will do—he knows the great points, & therefore cannot fail of doing *much*—but to effect *all*, a man who attempts it must be a lover of the truth for the truth's sake, forget himself wholly, be unmoved by scorn & threats, and, above all, be insensible to the greater calamity—which besets well-doers, & obstructs their well-doing—*praise*. Singleness of purpose is the essential requisite to an honest & able reformer—Mr. Beverley has the ability, is he *honest?* If he is, why does he *judge* so unsparingly? I confess I do not admire certain wholesale denunciations of *estimated* numbers. The cause of which he volunteers to be the champion is too good, or it might be vitally injured by some of his misrepresentations—nor does it require the aid of such auxiliaries as his clap-trap, about restoring the churches to their former owners, seems to entice: scrupulous readers may incline to imagine something *esoteric* in the meaning of those passages.

However, the cause, as I said, is good—but it cannot be worked out to its fulness of result by unholy hands—neither will the accomplishment of the work be delayed unduly, by its remaining for a time unattempted. One of the very good portions of Mr. Beverley's pamphlet, which must tell with every one, is the irrefutable exposition of the fact, that the Church with all its corruptions has reformed nothing since it was established. It has not—it can not—and for this reason, it *dare* not

move—and it being of the nature of corruption to extend, the putres-
cence has enlarged with increasing years—the longer it remains the
worse it will become—"it *must* become worse." Shall I tell you a *true*
story. A young medical friend of mine from the North, had an infant patient, which he was called to after it was beyond his skill to help. The
child died, and in a few days the father brought the body to him with a
request to preserve it & inject the veins & arteries—they differed about
the charge & negotiated day after day, the child remaining all the while
in the surgeon's cellar, till the parents' ardour for preservation cooled,
& the body became a nuisance—the more it smelt, the more my friend
pestered the father with messages to take it away, & the more inclined
was the fond parent not to meddle with it—at length the smell wholly
ceased & the body was almost forgotten when Tim the surgeon observed, in place of it, a shapeless mass of blue mould—so it remained
till, the last time I asked him about it, and then he told me it had wasted
& withered, melted & dried, that it almost defied discrimination to de-
tect what it had been—at first it was too noisome to tolerate, and now
"it's past," as Tim says, "egad sir, it's *past* throwing away."

> Yours finally & sincerely
> W. Hone.

P.S. <u>*Mind*</u>—*no more letters from me.* I find reading & writing bad
things. Reading is a lazy-making employment, & writing a worthless
one, & above all things I hate letter writing—I cannot write letters of
business, U no Y & my other letters, having no others to write, always
run into length. I took up this sheet merely to say that I wrote you before,
when I was hypp'd from keeping indoors, & that all I desired & desire
amounts to this—that, as soon as you can, I shall really be glad if *you*
will let me have the *cast* of my head, for my wife & girls desire to see it.
To this I add that, as a particular favor, I request you will put on paper a
plain (not a jocose) statement of the developments, & absence of development, as they appear from the cast. If you are a cunning man you will
hesitate—if you are honest you will do it at once, &, if there be truth in
Phrenology, you will find enough upon my skull to assure you that you
may safely communicate the truth & the *whole* truth to me, for whose eye
alone it is intended. I make this request in sober earnestness—

> My dear Childs,
> W. H.

Memory. "Philosophers place it in the rear of the head, and it seems the mine of memory lies there, because there men naturally dig for it, scratching it when they are at a loss." *Fuller.*[68]

---

13 Gracechurch Street, London
27 September 1831

[To Charles Sturgeon]
Dear Sir

I received a letter from you with great pleasure, and if you knew how bad a correspondent I am, this would be evidence of the fact—for I write you almost immediately. How could you conceive I forgot you— certainly, when we were together, "Our time, oh ye Muses, was happily spent." What! could I forget him who led me to the Camp-field, and there in drenching weather, explored inches below its surface—did we not toe up, and toe down, for Roman pottery in the mirey clay till we were half drenched, and having lost our feet might have lost our shoes and legs—can I forget friend Taplis's kindly cup of tea after that cold adventure, and his specimens from the site we had troddden in vain— or that you and I took counsel together over our cups in a Manchester Alehouse, whither you carried me for "good ale?"—I suspect it was the "Trafford Arms."

I have a distinct recollection of Mr. Taplis, poor man. He seemed a broken-spirited man, and though he let us see his leaves from Caxton, and other odd matters, his heart appeared to be from this world, and himself dead to it. To my eye, at that time, he was preparing for his jour- ney home—and since then I have often thought of him, as awaiting his hour.

Your proffer of "other articles," in addition to the memoranda, I am obliged to you for, leads me to expect them. But why have you delayed till now—you will recollect that the Year Book concludes with the year—hasten then "local customs" to me without delay, or any thing else you may desire to see in print, or I cannot ensure insertion. What has come shall go in except the "Last shift." I studiously avoid vulgar- ities, or what *refined* people might so deem of. If the Year Book were for Antiquarians only I should give many curious things which from the general nature of the work I am constrained to omit. The Wakefield Monks I know not what to say to. Mr. Atkinson of your town had my most perfect matrice[69]—I shall be happy in receiving what you write, as I am in your affording me an opportunity of saying that I do not & shall not forget you.

    I remain Dear Sir   Yours sincerely,

                                                  W. Hone

---

                                      56 New Hall Street
                                            Birmingham
                                  14 October 1831

Friend Mott[70]

Your letter dated Tuesday arrived with my letters & trowsers yesterday afternoon. I am, I assure you, deeply concerned to hear of your indisposition, which, I think, with you, may be mainly occasioned by the close weather. Today it blows fresh here & is cooler, and I hope before now you have experienced an advantageous change.

    Thanks for your opinion concerning public matters. Lord Brougham's exhortation to peaceable demeanor, coupled with his assurance that a bill equally efficient with the former will be brought in, is tranquillising to the best spirits here—but the wilder sort are displeased by Lord Wharncliffe's concurrence, and acknowledgment of the necessity for Reform[71]—they apprehend a "cross," and will not relax of their hold, yet know not what to do—A requisition is signing for a *Town's* Meeting at the Royal Hotel, at which I imagine the Political Unionists will attend, and more amendments which they will be sure to carry. This will be connived at by the intelligent of the "reputable" inhabitants, as opening a safety valve for the escape of much heat, which if carried to another New Hall Hill Meeting might explode mischievously. I seriously think that another Meeting there would jeopardize the town, and the Union leaders will not resort to it, until they fail of expectation from the ministers. The votes of the Bishops have reduced their term of voting in the Lords to a few years—and then, out they go. I am satisfied they have irrecoverably lost themselves—I have not met with a churchman that will put forth a finger to keep them on the crossbench.

    The burning of Nottingham Castle occasioned much dismay, but now, when it is known that the military acted thus, and at Derby, a salutary quiet prevails.[72] My own opinion is, that a measure of Reform considerably short of the late Bill will pass under a compromise, but that pacification will not be final till the whole measure be conceded—yet, *if* the monetary question be disposed of so as to raise prices, and give the agricultural laborer sufficiency of maintenance, things may jog on steadily for a while. At the next outbreak the privileged orders will be shaken to the centre. The Lords are blind—they see only through their feelings, as Miss McEvory saw with the ends of her fingers. They will be made to feel by the rage of the people, and then they will *see*—

In my own affair I am anxious, and uncertain. Mr. Parkes[73] flies off to Coventry, and elsewhere, without notice, and I expect may be in London before me. We saw Mr. Redfern together on Wednesday, but not satisfactorily. Mr. P. appointed me to meet him afterwards in an hour, but I had only the mortification of seeing him dragged away by anxious clients without his being able to say a word to me. I could not catch him again till last night, and then sat with him till he finished letters for the London post, before which two gentlemen broke in, and all ended by his saying that this morning he must be off to Warwick by the first coach & return by the last to-day—My time is slaughtered and my heart sickened. I have determined, if I cannot *fix* him tomorrow, to write him an earnest letter, and urge him to a conclusion at once.

Meantime I shall be glad if Matilda will send me *by the first Coach,* a thin quarto Volume "Guest's History of Spinning," and an octavo volume by the same author, both in boards, they are both, I think, on the small shelves (at the top) between the closet & the fireplace, *also, Clare's Poems.*[74] I shall attend forthwith to the *gratis* & lamps, & send up a parcel for Haddon by the Coach tomorrow—Love to all—I address this to Matilda, lest you should be in Sussex—Yours ever

W. Hone

Grasshopper Hotel
Gracechurch Street, London
7 February 1832

My dear [John] Childs

I duly received a very kind letter from you dated 22 Dec. 1831 introductory to the annual Turkey, which as duly arrived and which you will have pleasure in knowing was eaten in more comfort, with more of heart's-ease for sauce, than some of its predecessors. This perennial recollection of me and mine, the recurrence of it at a stated season, without one interruption, is an instance of continued desire to maintain an intimacy of feeling, to which the unfrequency of our meeting has not seemed very favorable. I must add too, that there has been very little on my part, which, if you were an ordinary-minded man, would tend to perpetuate the remembrance of a promise you have so well kept—and I have not unfrequently endeavored to account for your constancy. I have looked at you as "a man of the world," or, in other words, "a man of business," and in this light you would not object to be considered—but how, or why, a *mere* man of the world, a *mere* man of business, should, or could, think it his interest to bestow a thought or an acceptable token of regard upon one who is notoriously not much of either, has occasioned me some perplexity—for, in the way of business, you could have no expectation of deriving anything from me, and I have made no return of the obligation, have not always, perhaps, acknowledged it, and, mostly, when I have, it has been sent in an over-due period of time. Then, again, when we have met, our conversation, as regards ourselves personally, has been usually in the tone of banter. I have sometimes endeavored with some earnestness to get you, upon such occasions, into a serious and holding mood, but always to my discomfiture. Well then, coupling these matters & considerations, with our seldom seeing each other, I tell you that I begin to scrutinize more closely how it is that you and I are still "friends," beyond the vulgar erroneous meaning of the term; and, in downright earnest, in plain truth and sincerity, I shall be glad if you will, as you can, assist me in answering the question. Now this letter, at so long a lapse from the coming of the "beast," cannot be any evidence to you, as a man of the world, or of business, that I have assimilated to you in either character, and yet I almost persuade myself that, apart from joking, you will in sober earnestness, acquaint me with so much as will set me right upon the point. I know you for a *close* man. I wish you would *open* to me on the matter in question—if you do I know you will not deceive me, for I know you are not a deceiver. We are in many respects opposite, I want to know our points of junction. You are not a *mere* man of business, not a *mere* man of the world, what are you else though? Answer me *that*, John Childs, and so far, I shall be satisfied.

In re Turkey. You intimated that on Xmas day at four o'clock you should "fill a bumper" to our house & home. We did not dine till within a quarter of an hour of that four o'clock, and then, allowing for difference of clocks, at that number of strokes upon the bell, I and mine stood up with half empty mouths, and brimmers, and drank, to the founder of the feast and all around his table, health and happiness, and all that heart can desire that is good for it.

To your inquiry in matters of Politics I answer, what you know to be the fact, the potsherds are striving with the potsherds—in fact, though I cannot be indifferent to the result, I take little interest in the immediate strife. Whatever power rectitude may have in the political affairs of the world, will be after the battle has been fought between the conflicting parties—for *this* is not a mere adjustment of differences between men who think differently on points of policy, but it is a death-grapple between fiends, wherein the greater will destroy the lesser, and they who may be of less infernal minds will assuredly perish if they enlist into the ranks. I care not for the *seeming* virtue of the "cause"—I know that the *real* virtue will not be actively employed during the on-slaught without being trodden down into the filth & bloody mire of the furious combatants. The present is a mere affair of pickets—the driving in of the outposts—the engagement is to come, and it will be between the Apollyons of Toryism and the Belials of Reform[75]—thus, and after they have destroyed each other, and Pride & servile baseness lie with death-wounds on the field of the unholy fight, then, and not till then, can the humble & the honest come forth with any chance of contributing to the freedom & happiness of human beings. I speak of no events that are likely to happen soon—but in my mind's eye I see "a dark hour coming."[76] I am My dear Childs

Sincerely
W. Hone

———

Woodland Cottages, Grove Lane,
Camberwell, London
29 March 1833

[To Matthew D. Hill]
My dear Sir

I hasten to thank you for your letter, and above all for your most prompt application in my behalf to the Chancellor. But what can I say in apology for having thus interested you, when I regret that I addressed you on the subject. The sole gratification it affords me is, that I am assured of your steady substantial friendship—for, as respects my being a candidate for the Museum Print Room it is out of the question. Mr. William Young Ottley applies for it.[77] Were I sure of success I should not persevere, because I should prevent a better man than myself. Mr. Ottley is the most erudite man in Chalcography,[78] Printing, and Painting, of any Antiquary in Europe—he ought to have the place—the Trustees will do themselves and the Museum *an honour* by appointing him without delay. No claim ought to stand for an hour against Mr. Ottley's—I would be the rival of any man but this gentleman, with whom I have no intimacy; yet whom, I dare not conscientiously oppose, and who will remain perfectly ignorant that my humble testimony in his favor may be added, perhaps, to the strong recommendations his merits enable him to command.

Alas! my dear Sir, I "did *not* recollect" you were on circuit—one of the qualities of paralysis is to suspend mental as well as bodily faculties—this, unhappily, I know—My memory has been as water spilt on the earth—my right side powerless—and, now, though I am rapidly recovering a dividend of my former self, it is by small weekly instalments, and I shall never "be myself" again. I had contemplated, and prepared, to struggle for, and carry the office of Bridgemaster[79] upon the next vacancy, but this I must not think of for a moment—my great chance of success would be from hustings speaking, and now a speech of five minutes would kill me. I cannot, and shall not be able to bear physical exertion, but I find my mind fast recruiting, and there are certainly little things dropping, here and there, which I might tend to advantage. At present I am not able to walk more than a mile out and in, though I feel, on this sunny day with a S.W. zephyr, that a fortnight of real Summer may enable me to a real stroll, and to risk converse with strangers. May God keep you, my friend, from this awful disturbance of the frame and spirit. I now live as with a sense of having been buried, and being out of my grave upon furlough—and with this consciousness I am not the less qualified for some employment which may require diligence and attention, if such a thing can be got, without mixing in turmoil. My children, and my poor wife, lie heavy at my heart—You know my hatred to Attornies, and my love for the law—is there nothing suitable to me about the Courts?!

I'll tell you what would just suit me—A fellowship at Oxford, Magdalen Coll. gardens, and the Bodleian Library!

I am My dear Sir
Most gratefully and Sincerely Yours
W. Hone

Peckham Rye Common, near London
22 April 1834

[To Joseph Hone]
My dear Brother[80]

I find among a heap of papers which I may never have health or spirits to sort, a letter I wrote to you near twelve months ago to acquaint you with our Mother's death. It was then a great effort with me to write, for my faculties were stunned by a paralytic stroke in January preceding, which deprived me in an instant of the use of my right side, and for many weeks an hour of further life was not with me a probability. The blow impaired my memory, and even now I have not recovered the recollection of many occurrences, and I continue to forget things I did an hour ago. In a far worse state I received intelligence on the 20th of April last that my mother had died that morning, and unfit as I was to go to Perceval Street, I yet went thither and with all the ability I could muster, arranged for her funeral. I returned home to suffer consequences from such exertions which I had not anticipated, and my wife went to the funeral. Before this event I found myself in a furnished lodging at Camberwell, to which I had been removed in a helpless state from Gracechurch Street, and while in that state the property of the family had been taken possession of by creditors of the business, and finally I was stripped of every atom I possessed in the world, dispossessed of a home to return to, my family dispersed, and I without a friend I could look to, but Almighty God, who had been my merciful support throughout my affliction. In my deep sorrows He and He alone has been my helper. This language from me will be new to you, but you will understand it better than I did at one time. For more than two years before God in his Providence laid his hand upon me, I had been led to seek Him if haply I might find Him, and I was drawn to earnest and anxious prayer, to be enabled to pray aright, at the same time reading intently in the scriptures, yet comprehending little of what I read, for I sought the conviction of my natural understanding, and missed ground at every step for want of faith, and through ignorance of the way. The Almighty however was dealing with me, and, ever and anon, I had gleams of light upon his blessed word, which showed me the darkness in which I groped, and caused me to pray for further illumination. I picked up a little book "Scougal's Life of God in the Soul of Man," which was very useful to me, but, above all, "Cecil's Remains," which had been presented to me by a quaker gentleman from the country in 1825 upon the express condition that I would read it, and which I had read.[81] I read again with other eyes, so that it scarcely seemed the same work. I had not been accustomed to attend a place of worship, but, shortly after my residence commenced in Gracechurch Street, I went regularly to the Parish Church of Allhallows Lombard Street, and in most of the supplications in the Church Liturgy my heart unfeignedly concurred during the service. The pulpit was not ill filled, but, to me, it was not well filled. I wanted more than the simple plain discourse of a well intentioned clergyman. I wanted food, and came away comparatively hungry. At length on New Year's Day 1832, the first time I had deviated from Allhallows, I sent the children into the church and passed on, not knowing or determining into what place I should go, but thinking of going to Surrey Chapel I went down Fish Street hill until coming to Eastcheap it struck me that as Mr. Clayton had left the Weigh-house, somebody worth hearing must have succeeded him. I had been there only once, about thirty-five years before, and making my way upstairs got in just before the text was taken. Through the Minister, Mr. Binney,[82] a startling summons was delivered to me in the course of the sermon and I came away with my mind disturbed but deeply solemnized. I must be brief. In a very short time it pleased God to break down my self-will, and enable me to surrender my heart to him. I read his word with prayer for his light upon it, and I seemed to know though I could not comprehend, to feel though I could not understand, its truth. To my wonder everything appeared changed, the world and its pleasures, literature and its choicest works, had lost their charms—in short, I found that I myself was changed, and the mystery of salvation, through the blood of Christ, God manifest in the flesh, is to me, through the eye of Faith, and by the power of Grace, a precious truth by which my rebellious will has been subjugated, and my heart reconciled to God. My rationalizing of scripture, to carve out from it a rational religion which could afford to God a little of my heart, and allow the rest of it to the world, is, long since, at an end—it has vanished with all my unworthy derogatory views of Christ as a prophet, the greatest of prophets, anything and everything short of what he was, Christ himself, the saviour of sinners, who took away the sins of the world, through faith in whom as our great sacrifice we have pardon, in whom dwelt the fulness of the Godhead bodily, and who lives, as the great Intercessor and Mediator, until time shall be no more, when we shall know him as the Judge of all flesh, the Creator of all things & in whom all things consist. Dark, cold, unfeeling, unscriptural Unitarianism was my stumbling-block for years. I humbly thank our heavenly Father that of his great mercy I have been raised from that charnel house of Christianity by the vivifying power of his gracious Spirit, to the enjoyment of marvellous light. I pray for grace to be emptied of self, to be kept low, and to be kept crying for power to pray, until prayer shall be turned into praise before the throne.

My dear Brother, I know if you are what you were, which I earnestly and fervently hope you will be preserved to be, you will rejoice in what I have communicated. I do not know that I have a friend in existence but Him who is the friend of all who are ready to perish—certainly in England I have no relative that I know of except my poor wife and children—and to you, my Brother, my heart yearns with increased affection. The last letter that has arrived in England from you was one in which you required me to tell my mother she should hear from you very soon—she was then no more.

1839

Botheration John!

Is there to be no end to the botheration? "Shrink not from the *word*" (I quote from memory). "Rejoice rather that there is such a word signifying such a thing," but shrink from the *thing*—for observe:—

BOTHER, is a word compounded of *be* and *other*; to bother, is, to *be other:* hence *being*

other is, by transposition, *bothering:* hence also comes, by corruption, *botheration*. Again:—

BOTHER, or *Bothering*, *being other*, though continually in practice, is *being* with the mind

out of oneself, a state of *being* not definable in words, but altogether metaphysical, vulgarly called being out of one's mind, or *being* beside oneself, which is, rare, two beings, one *being* beside the other, this not being that, but both being this, which is inexplicable, *bothering*.

For example, a little—i.e. a little for example—"You shall have Cruden for Missus—and Adams for Peter"[83]—So you say, and so you have said, for months, and we are but where we were,—nothing done but bother, nothing doing but bothering, not being yourself, being beside yourself. I have the promise of *that*, a nonentity, a *thing*, to use metaphysical language, not *in esse*. And then your I.O.U., when I look at it, among the bills in my Cash-box, gives me as much anxiety as they do. But come, come here I mean to tea, and prove by action to "Missus" & me, that the promise of the books is not to be an "everlasting no," and the I.O.U. I'll make a present of to Mrs. —'s next boy.

Observe, lastly, as the old postillers[84] said, I am in Winter quarters for the whole season, and possibly for life. This secession discloses to me the difference between Free Will and Free Agency, and affords to me leisure for thinking, in drear hours, when too worn to write, or speak. Adams I hear of to such a purport, that, if I could buy any book, I should buy that.

Observe moreover, that I *cannot* get out and therefore if we meet it must be *here*. From 3 to 5 I endeavour for sleep. At 5 we drink tea. I don't rise till near ten, & get to bed early. Rest and warmth are *essential* to me—that I experience. So *come*, with your opium story. You cannot go to Bungay during Guy Fawkes time—it's against the New Metropolitan Police Act to let off *crackers!*[85]

Observe moreover, lastly, we have an inmate about Sam's age—a fine youth, son of Rev. Mr. Kent of Barnstaple, formerly of Bungay. The young man was appointed to a printer at Exeter, & since he came to me, has engaged himself to Messrs. Roake & Varty of the Strand. He has been well trained every way, and we deem him a valuable addition to our family—morally valuable, and pecuniarily.

I am,
My dear Childs,
Yours faithfully
W. Hone

5 Bolt Court
2 November 1839
[On cover.] I am told I made a mistake as to duration of time—but it seems to me as long as I supposed it to be. So take this explanation outside, by way of Postscript within.

W. H.

4 Nov. 1839
Church Road, Tottenham
30 Novr. 1840

My dear Alice[86]

I write to you a line to tell you that though my hand writing appears to have been fast, it was really very slowly executed. I have begun wrong, I mean this letter is begun wrong—it ought to have *ended* with what I have said. I should have written, at first, my dear child, I very much love you, and then my letter might have closed. For, I have thought so for such a length of time, that I am filled with the feeling of simple affection, and the pure sentiment comes out all at once; and in reality little more than my love can be found to talk of upon paper. It is love for you which causes me to add I have read all your letters to Mother & Ellen, and have said, after getting to the end, of each "Poor child!" For each was dolorous & expressive of anxiety for time to elapse, that you might see us again. And how fast it has rolled on! If God permit, in less than three weeks, we shall meet again; and you will let us know *how* you come, at what time *punctually*, & to what spot in London. Your mother or Ellen will meet you, if you are very particular in your statement, and conduct you hither.

Our dwelling is a little *tot* of a house. The room I write is where my books are, and is our living room—it is about 7 feet wide by 10 feet long with one window in it, and looks down *our garden* which is about 14 feet wide, and fifty feet long, with some kale & brocoli plants in it, & room for more. There are no trees in it for birds, except a young sycamore, which is only a tree-*ling*, at one side. On the other side is *our wash-house* up which, & over the low roof, runs a vine which branches over our living-parlour window. At the side of our house a hedge, parts us from a bit of land, set with mangel-wurzel, & beyond that at the side, are the gardens of Bruce Castle (a School) with timber trees, now "barren as lances," but which in summer become a harbour for birds. This is our view in the rear, which is to the *South*—over our living room is Ellen's Bedroom with the same view. Your mother's is in front, to the North, with our front Parlour below it. Above all, is one room filled with lumber, boxes &c. The North View is over a market gardener's ground.

Such is our house. Our provision for living affords us a *short bite*, but we, thank God, have enough, & are contented.

And now, my dear Child, you [have a?] letter from me. Probably it is the last I may address [to you?] but, as you may address us, I send you some stamps to prevent your letters costing 2d. Study to be *concise* in writing—words that *mean*.

The lady who called on you, was Mrs. Woollaston, wife of a gentleman here, a Surgeon, & a friend. She has told us of her interviews with you.

You must give us timely notice of your coming. "Oh Yes!"—doubt not of the love of all of us.

Your ever affectionate Father
William Hone

NOTES

NOTES TO INTRODUCTION

1. This phrase is taken from an earlier letter: John Childs to William Hone, 15 March 1819, British Library, Add. MS. 40120, f. 118.

2. British Library, Add. MS. 40120, f. 382.

3. John Childs to William Hone, 28 January 1818, British Library, Add. MS. 40120, f. 113.

4. E. P. Thompson, *The Making of the English Working Class* (New York: Vintage, 1963), 721.

5. Editorial, the *Times* (London), 22 December 1817.

6. The transcript of the trials printed in the *Times* and that printed by Hone are very close, mostly identical, but there are significant omissions in the newspaper's coverage (for example, Hone's several references to George Canning in *The First Trial*). The precise source of Hone's fuller text has not yet been determined, but shorthand recorders were present in the court, as always. Joss Marsh suggests that Francis Place may have supplied a shorthand writer for Hone's trials; see *Word Crimes: Blasphemy, Culture, and Literature in Nineteenth-Century England* (Chicago: University of Chicago Press, 1998), 332 n. 11.

7. James Routledge, *Chapters in the History of Popular Progress, chiefly in relation to the Freedom of the Press and Trial by Jury 1660–1820* (London: Macmillan, 1876), 450.

8. Harriet Martineau, *The History of England during the Thirty Years' Peace*, 2 vols. (London: Charles Knight, 1850), 1:144.

9. Ted Peterson, "The Fight of William Hone for British Press Freedom," *Journalism Quarterly* 25 (1948): 132.

10. Quoted by Frances Rolleston in *Some Account of the Conver-*

sion from Atheism to Christianity of the Late William Hone, 2d rev. ed. (London: F. and J. Rivington, 1853), 7. For Knight, see n. 80.

11. Books by Olivia Smith (*The Politics of Language,* 1984) and more recently by Marcus Wood (*Radical Satire and Print Culture 1790–1822,* 1994) have singled out Hone for attention. At the same time, Steven Jones (*Shelley's Satire,* 1994), Iain McCalman (*Radical Underworld Prophets, Revolutionaries and Pornographers in London, 1795–1840,* 1988), David Worrall (*Radical Culture: Discourse, Resistance and Surveillance, 1790–1820,* 1992), Gary Dyer (*British Satire and the Politics of Style, 1789–1832,* 1997), and Kevin Gilmartin (*Print Politics: The Press and Radical Opposition in Early Nineteenth-Century England,* 1996) are among those who have helped renew interest in the world of radical politics and popular satire during the post-Napoleonic period. Hone also figures prominently in the first volume of Robert Patten's *George Cruikshank's Life, Times, and Art* (1992). He is the subject of an article by Kyle Grimes in *Romanticism, Radicalism, and the Press* (ed. Stephen Behrendt, 1997), and Grimes has initiated a massive Hone website (http://www.uab.edu/english/hone) besides offering his own annotated version of *The Political House that Jack Built* on the *Romantic Circles* site (http://www.RC.umd.edu).

12. James Epstein, *Radical Expression: Political Language, Ritual and Symbol in England, 1790–1850* (New York: Oxford University Press, 1994), 35.

13. British Library, Add. MS. 38523, Supplement (Correspondence of Leigh Hunt), f. 41.

14. See the summary by Marcus Wood, *Radical Satire and Print Culture 1790–1822* (Oxford: Clarendon Press, 1994), 10. Hone's sympathy with Catholic emancipation is indicated by a petition he drafted, dated 1824 (British Library, Add. MS. 40120, f. 252).

15. See Michael Scrivener, ed. *Poetry and Reform: Periodical Verse from the English Democratic Press 1792–1824* (Detroit: Wayne State University Press, 1992), 13–19. Wood (p. 5) also provides a vivid sense of the heterogeneity of the term "radical," embracing as it did aristocratic Whigs (Sir Francis Burdett), infidel intellectuals (William Godwin and Jeremy Bentham), popular orators (Henry Hunt), religious zealots (Robert Wedderburn), the literati (the Hunts and William Hazlitt), and journalists (William Cobbett and Thomas Wooler), among others.

16. See Iain McCalman, *Radical Underworld Prophets, Revolutionaries and Pornographers in London, 1795–1840* (Cambridge: Cambridge

University Press, 1988), 26; Wood, *Radical Satire*, 88, 64. For Hone's knowledge of Spence, see his letter to Place (1830) printed below and Olivia Smith, *The Politics of Language 1791–1819* (Oxford: Oxford University Press, 1984), 100, 109. There are also connections with Horne Tooke (see Smith, p. 123, on Tooke's ideas about the law, for example). Hone advertised a reprinting of one of Tooke's works (*Proceedings in an Action*); see Ann Bowden, "William Hone's Political Journalism, 1815–1821," Ph.D. diss., University of Texas at Austin, 1975, 1:229–30.

17. Wood, *Radical Satire*, 89–92. Smith (*Politics of Language*, 86–90) cites Eaton as crucial to the emergence of an authentic radical voice.

18. See McCalman (*Radical Underworld Prophets*, 117, 122) on Spencean tavern entertainment. He suggests that Hone's *Political Litany*, for example, would probably have been dramatized in a tavern; the questions would have been read out and the responses chanted back by the patrons.

19. Kyle Grimes, "Spreading the Radical Word: The Circulation of William Hone's 1817 Liturgical Parodies," in *Radicalism and Revolution in Britain, 1775–1848: Essays in Honour of Malcolm I. Thomis*, ed. Michael T. Davis (London: Macmillan, 2000), 155.

20. Hone describes these aspects of his early life in the "Autograph Notes for Autobiography," British Library, Add. MS. 40121 (Hone Papers, vol. 14), f. 9 and f. 18. The earliest account of Hone is by Frances Rolleston (see note 10 above), and the meeting with Wesley is described on pp. 8–10 of *Some Account*. The only biography of Hone is the early work by Frederick William Hackwood, *William Hone: His Life and Times* (1912; reprint, New York: Augustus M. Kelley, 1970). Biographical sketches of Hone's career are also available in Wood, *Radical Satire*, 6–10; Jonathan Hill, "William Hone," in *British Romantic Prose Writers, 1789–1832*, second series, ed. John R. Greenfield, vol. 110 of *Dictionary of Literary Biography* (Detroit: Gale, 1991, 126–38; and Kyle Grimes, "William Hone," in *British Reform Writers*, ed. Gary Kelly and Edd Applegate, vol. 158 of *Dictionary of Literary Biography* (Detroit: Gale, 1996), 158–68.

21. See Hackwood, "William Hone," 30 and Wood, *Radical Satire*, 6.

22. British Library, Add. MS. 40121, f. 70.

23. Wood states that reading Lilburne "marked the birth of his [Hone's] political consciousness" (*Radical Satire*, 7).

24. British Library, Add. MS. 40121, f. 50.

25. See Hackwood, *William Hone*, 53–56.

26. Ibid., 64ff. The number of children Hone had varies from nine to twelve, depending on the authority.

27. See J. Anne Hone, *For the Cause of Truth: Radicalism in London 1796–1821* (Oxford: Clarendon Press, 1982), 238; J. Anne Hone, "William Hone (1780–1842), Publisher and Bookseller: An Approach to Early Nineteenth Century London Radicalism," *Historical Studies* 16 (April 1974–October 1975): 57; and Hackwood, *William Hone*, 74.

28. J. Anne Hone, *For the Cause of Truth*, 170–71, and "William Hone," 57.

29. Quoted in J. Anne Hone, "William Hone," 64.

30. Edward Wakefield to William Hone, British Library, Add. MS. 40120, f. 20.

31. See Hackwood, *William Hone*, 92–95, and Robert L. Patten, *George Cruikshank's Life, Times, and Art*, vol. 1, *1792–1835* (New Brunswick, N.J.: Rutgers University Press, 1992), 123–24. Hone may have also met George Cruikshank at this time (Hackwood, *William Hone*, 92); it was Cruikshank who made the engraving of William Norris, a patient in Bethlem Hospital who, though "currently sane" when the committee visited him, was nevertheless "completely chained" (J. Anne Hone, "William Hone," 64).

32. See Bowden, "Hone's Political Journalism," 1:30–39; Hackwood, *William Hone*, 98ff.; and J. Anne Hone, "William Hone," 65, and *For the Cause of Truth*, 246–49. How Hone became involved with the Eliza Fenning case is related in Rolleston, *Some Account*, 29–31.

33. Hill, "William Hone," 129.

34. J. Anne Hone, "William Hone," 59–60, and Bowden, "Hone's Political Journalism," 1:7–9. Wood (*Radical Satire*, 3) estimates the number of Hone's publications between 1815 and 1821 as 175 and emphasizes their roots in eighteenth-century satiric forms (chapbooks, children's literature, songs, almanacs, nursery rhymes, and so on).

35. Bowden, "Hone's Political Journalism," 1:50, 54.

36. Edgell Rickword, *Radical Squibs & Royal Ripostes* (Bath, Somerset: Adams & Dart, 1971), 13. Hone also parodied Southey's *Vision of Judgement* in his "A New Vision" (1821). Southey's animosity toward Hone relented through the mediation of Lamb and Hone's move to the more politically neutral ground of antiquarian writing and editing. In a letter of 10 May 1830, Southey told Hone that he "desired to

remember nothing more of his earlier life than the ability & presence of mind which he displayed upon his trial" (British Library, Add MS 40856, f.37).

37. See Bowden, "Hone's Political Journalism," 1:67–68. Hone's alterations to Byron's *Corsair* indicate Hone's conventional morality, according to Marina Vitale, "The Domesticated Heroine in Byron's *Corsair* and William Hone's Prose Adaptation," *Literature and History* 10, no. 1 (spring 1984): 84–89. Hone wrote a letter of protest to Francis Jeffrey of the *Edinburgh Review* after a contributor linked Hone with William Benbow as pirates of Byron's work; Jeffrey eventually secured an apology for Hone (British Library, Add. MS. 40120, f. 200). In a letter to Matthew Hill (15 November 1823), Hone, in reference to a pirated version of Moore's *Melodies*, declares himself "a hater of this species of robbery" (British Library, Add. MS. 41071, f. 10).

38. Bowden ("Hone's Political Journalism," 1:123–24) suggests Place's role and notes that Place may have written most, if not all, of the first five issues. Hone's periodical "appeared on 18 January 1817 as *Hone's Weekly Commentary,* then as *Hone's Reformists' Register and Weekly Commentary* from 1 February to 25 October 1817" (J. Anne Hone, "William Hone," 59n. 31). For the nature and characteristics of the radical weekly, see Kevin Gilmartin, "Radical Print Culture in Periodical Form," in *Romanticism, History, and the Possibilities of Genre: Reforming Literature 1789–1837*, ed. Tilottama Rajan and Julia Wright (Cambridge: Cambridge University Press, 1998), 40ff. For an overview of newspapers and changing technology, distribution methods, ownership patterns, costs, and government control, see Ivon Asquith, "The Structure, Ownership and Control of the Press, 1780–1855," *Newspaper History from the Seventeenth Century to the Present Day*, ed. George Boyce, James Curran, and Pauline Wingate (London: Constable, 1978), 98–116.

39. See Scrivener, *Poetry and Reform,* 22, Bowden; "Hone's Political Journalism," 1:25; Olivia Smith, *Politics of Language,* 160; and A. Aspinall, *Politics and the Press 1780–1850* (London: Home & Van Thal, 1949), 51. Circulation figures are given by Marsh (*Word Crimes,* 337 n.64) and by Scrivener, (*Poetry and Reform,* 23). Hone saw Cobbett on 15 March 1817, before he left for America, and may have agreed to use his *Political Register* to further the cause Cobbett advocated; he may also have expected Cobbett's readers to become his readers (the perspective of Routledge, *History of Popular Progress,*

325). Cobbett and his printer and bookseller had been convicted of seditious libel in 1810 (the judge was Ellenborough); he spent two years in Newgate and paid a one hundred pound fine (Hone, *For the Cause of Freedom*, 147).

40. This order of publication is given by Bowden ("Hone's Political Journalism," 1:103), based on internal evidence (182 n. 4), though the last publication is the one on which Hone was first tried. As Marcus Wood has shown, the text of *The Late John Wilkes's Catechism* is based on a reworked original manuscript by Wilkes (see Wood's detailed account and analysis, *Radical Satire*, 114–21; see also Rolleston, *Some Account*, 41–42). In fact, the text for *The Political Litany* is the result of a similar process of adaptation. Among the British Library's Hone manuscripts is a copy of Hone's revisions to *A Political Litany*, originally published by J. Slater in Sheffield (no date is indicated). The changes are less extensive than in the case of the Wilkes manuscript, but Hone does delete an epigraph, alter the refrain, elaborate the closing prayers, and add a collect (British Library, Add. MS. 40108, vol. 1, f. 172–f. 179).

41. Hone's father may have played some role in the suppression of the parodies; see Rolleston, *Some Account*, 78.

42. Grimes, "William Hone," 164.

43. Routledge, *History of Popular Progress*, 300; Aspinall, *Politics and the Press*, 49; and J. Anne Hone, *For the Cause of Truth*, 271. Hone's first two trials were on charges of both blasphemy and seditious libel, the third on blasphemous libel (Wood, *Radical Satire*, 100).

44. Hackwood, *William Hone*, 121.

45. J. Anne Hone, *For the Cause of Truth*, 195.

46. Aspinall, *Politics and the Press*, 40.

47. J. Anne Hone, *For the Cause of Truth*, 333. Sir Richard Phillips (1767–1840) had a varied career as an author, bookseller, and publisher. He held radical political views and strong humanitarian sympathies, established the *Monthly Magazine* in 1796, and was elected a sheriff of London in 1807. He had unusual ideas (he did not believe the theory of gravitation had any foundation) and practiced strict vegetarianism. Among his publications was *Treatise on the Powers and Duties of Juries and on the Criminal Laws of England* (1811).

48. Sir Richard Phillips to Francis Place, 7 May 1817, British Library, Add. MS. 40120, f. 56, f. 57.

49. Hackwood, *William Hone*, 132–53. Hone and Wooler were two

of sixteen people prosecuted for libel in 1817. After both were victorious in the courts, there were no prosecutions during 1818 (Olivia Smith, *Politics of Language*, 164).

50. Epstein, *Radical Expression*, 39. Hone's account of the attempts to entrap him are also given in British Library, Add. MS., f. 74–f. 79. Marsh (*Word Crimes*, 22) notes that in 1817 there were over twenty prosecutions of radical pressmen and others who were imprisoned without trial. Olivia Smith (*Politics of Language*, 164) notes: "Up to seven years could pass between the indictment and the trial."

51. Epstein, *Radical Expression*, 39, 57–58. The report demonstrated that there were only 485 names available, and that 226 of these were not living in the City; eight men had been summoned forty or more times, and there was one man who had served fifty-five times in one term.

52. British Library, Add. MS. 40120, f. 69.

53. In a letter to his brother Leigh, John describes Hone as "what is understood by the phrase, 'a coarse man,' and will, they say, do things in his trade of bookselling, which are not thought respectable. But then he is poor. I understand that he is honest and consistent. . . ." Hunt is evidently referring to Hone's occasional piratical practices. Hunt also notes the following: "It seems that his immediate friends have tendered bail—but why he has not used it, I cannot learn" (British Library, Add. MS. 38523, f. 41 [Correspondence of L. Hunt]).

54. British Library, Add. MS. 40120, f. 131. Hunt may have been associated with Hone as early as 1816 (see Bowden, "Hone's Political Journalism," 1:49). By 1822, in a review of Hazlitt's *Table Talk*, Hone is linked with Hunt and Hazlitt as "asses" identified with "the Radical School" (*Quarterly Review*, 26 [October 1822], 103, 104).

55. Patten, *Cruikshank's Life*, 132. Hone's letter (together with other letters of thanks after the trials) is printed in R. Brook Aspland, *Memoir of the Life, Works and Correspondence of the Rev. Robert Aspland* (London: Whittfield, 1850). Aspland was concerned with blasphemy, since, as a Unitarian minister, he was also subject to government prosecution (he was, for example, the author of "Inquiry into the Nature of the Sin of Blasphemy, and into the Propriety of Regarding It as a Civil Offence" [see *Memoir*, 380ff]).

56. Epstein, *Radical Expression*, 187 n. 148; Patten, *Cruikshank's Life*, 130–1.

57. See the letter to Samuel Parr of 31 March 1819, British Li-

brary, Add. MS. 40108, vol. 1, f. 7. For Hone's subscription, see page 305 of *The Polemical Magazine; or, Theological Inquirer.* Numbers 7 to 10 of this freethinking periodical print extracts from Hone's *The Apocryphal New Testament.* These issues, together with the proceedings of the Davison trial, were published in London by R. Helder in 1820.

58. Hone contributed some of the most effective portions of Carlile's defense. In 1819 Carlile read Paine's *Age of Reason* aloud to the jury as part of his defense at his trial for blasphemous libel; thus, his wife later could legally issue the offending book since it was literally part of the verbatim report of the trial (Marsh, *Word Crimes,* 65, 69). Hone and other radicals had earlier adopted this technique of deviously publishing banned texts. Carlile had been imprisoned in August 1817 after reprinting Hone's parodies, but he was released after Hone's third acquittal. Between 1817 and 1834 Carlile spent some ten years in prison (Bowden, "Hone's Political Journalism," 1:116). See McCalman, *Radical Underworld Prophets,* 185, for details of Carlile's continuing work while in prison.

59. British Library, Add. MS. 40120, f. 76. Scrivener notes that at least one historian believes that the government had made a similar error in the 1794 treason trials (*Poetry and Reform,* 13).

60. Routledge, *History of Popular Progress,* 366, and Wood, *Radical Satire,* 105, 138. Radicals who republished Paine's *Age of Reason,* for example, were usually prosecuted successfully under the blasphemy charge. For a summary of the evolution of blasphemy from the status of sin to that of crime, see Marsh, *Word Crimes,* 18ff.

61. Olivia Smith, *Politics of Language,* 196. Parallels between Hone's trials and Lilburne's are described on pages 197–98. See also Patten, *Cruikshank's Life,* 137–38 and Wood, *Radical Satire,* 7. An especially valuable account of this entire question of the Protestant martyr persona in terms of Lilburne's precedent is found in Wood, *Radical Satire,* 121–33.

62. Epstein (*Radical Expression,* 33) describes the "ritual spectacle" of trials in this period. See also Olivia Smith, *Politics of Language,* 178, 189, and Wood, *Radical Satire,* 141–42. The latter also notes that the 1794 state trials showed "what stagecraft and rhetorical experimentation could achieve within the court-room" (132). Fox's Libel Act of 1792 restored to juries the right to judge libel cases. Prior to that, convictions could follow simply from proving publication of the offensive material.

63. Thomas Sadler, ed., *Diary, Reminiscences, and Correspondence of Henry Crabb Robinson* (London: Macmillan, 1869), 2:74, 77. Robinson later met Hone at Lamb's in 1825 and 1828: "The conversation of Hone, or rather his manners, pleased me. He is a modest, unassuming man" (Sadler, *Diary*, 2:299). In 1841 Robinson gave money for Hone to Joseph Parkes (Edith J. Morley, ed., *Henry Crabb Robinson on Books and Their Writers* [1938; reprint, New York: AMS Press, 1967], 1:357, 2:590).

64. Routledge, *History of Popular Progress*, 350, 395.

65. Patten, *Cruikshank's Life*, 136. In *Radical Culture: Discourse, Resistance and Surveillance, 1790–1820,* David Worrall (quoting on page 110 from a Home Office file dated 30 June 1817) makes this intriguing observation: "In June 1817 a spy claimed that he [Ellenborough] was on a list of prominent people on the Spenceans' assassination list and that the publisher William Hone 'had been heard to say "it was a Pity no bold fellow could be found to murder Lord Ellenborough."'"

66. Olivia Smith, *Politics of Language*, 180.

67. Wood, *Radical Satire*, 105–6.

68. The following note occurs in Hone's manuscripts: "Travesty is ridicule of the original." British Library, Add MS. 40108, vol. 1, f. 62.

69. Marsh, *Word Crimes*, 32–33, and Wood, *Radical Satire*, 113.

70. Patten, *Cruikshank's Life*, 138.

71. Ibid., 140. At a meeting held on 29 December 1817 at the City of London Tavern, radical leaders and sympathizers initiated a subscription to help Hone. The proceedings of this meeting were published by Hone as an addendum to his trials. Typical of the heartfelt eloquence of the proceedings are the tributes by Sir Francis Burdett to Hone's courage and resolve: "For oppression and undue advantage against a meritorious but defenseless man, this prosecution on the part of his Majesty's Ministers was without a parallel. Indeed, it would be almost impossible to pick out an instance in which injustice and oppression had been so decidedly marked, even if they were to look to the volume of State Trials, which had been called a libel on the judges of England. Few men in the country could have fought their way with such manly intrepidity, and at the same time with such elasticity of moral and intellectual vigor. He believed the country was quite alive on the subject to which he now called their attention [trial by jury and freedom of the press]—and, if they were so, to whom was it owing? Certainly to

Mr. Hone—who, at the peril of his life—at the expense of the destruction of his fortune—and, finally, when the annihilation of all his future views was threatened—stood forward, undismayed, and dauntlessly dared the worst his adversaries could do" ("Trial by Jury and Liberty of the Press" in *The Three Trials of William Hone* [London: Thomas Tegg, 1876], 204–5).

72. 5 January 1818 in Mary Moorman and Alan G. Hill, eds., *The Letters of William and Dorothy Wordsworth: The Middle Years, Part 2, 1812–1820*, 2d ed. (Oxford: Clarendon Press, 1970), 410. William Wordsworth's feelings about the Hone victory are similarly hostile. See his letter of 31 December 1819 to Viscount Lowther (Ibid., 574). Bowden ("Hone's Political Journalism," 1:171ff.) and Herschel M. Sikes ("William Hone: Regency Patriot, Parodist, and Pamphleteer," *Newberry Library Bulletin* 5 [1961]: 289–90) discuss the published responses to Hone's trials.

73. 21 December 1817 in Hyder Rollins, ed., *Letters of John Keats* (Cambridge, Mass: Harvard University Press, 1958), 1:191. For Robinson on Coleridge, see Sadler, *Diary*, 2:80.

74. The letter from Samuel Parr to William Hone of 13 April 1819 also requests that Hone avoid "all ludicrous representations of the Trinity" (British Library, Add. MS. 40108, vol. 1, f. 9), reflecting the persistent unease with Hone's treatment of religion in his writings. As J. Anne Hone observes (*For the Cause of Truth*, 336), Burdett and Waithman supported Hone only "after his acquittal." Bowden ("Hone's Political Journalism," 1:167) notes the bibliographically complex nature of the printing history of the trials and the public meeting following them. Because the trials were issued separately, buyers could have them bound together, but the process was arbitrary, so any particular edition might contain different printings of each trial.

75. Patten, *Cruikshank's Life*, 153–54.

76. Bowden ("Hone's Political Journalism") gives details about the printing history (1:244) and the sales (1:203) of *The Political House*. Grimes gives the collective figure of 250,000 copies sold for pamphlets relating to both Peterloo and the Caroline affair ("William Hone," 163).

77. Patten, *Cruikshank's Life*, 144; Patricia Anderson, *The Printed Image and the Transformation of Popular Culture 1790–1860* (Oxford: Clarendon Press, 1990), 36.

78. Wood, *Radical Satire*, 258–59. For a list of imitations, see

Bowden, "Hone's Political Journalism," 1:257–76, 2:451–73, and in her bibliography 2:540–55.

79. See Rolleston, *Some Account*, 41.

80. Wood, *Radical Satire*, 216, 224; Bowden, "Hone's Political Journalism," 1:240, 2:431. One description of the Hone/Cruikshank collaborative process is given in Charles Knight, *Passages of a Working Life* (1864–65; reprint, Shannon, Ireland: Irish University Press, 1971), 1:245–46. The dispute over who originated the *Bank Restriction Thermometer* is described by Hackwood, *William Hone*, 198ff.

81. Patten, *Cruikshank's Life*, 1:118, 131, 99, and 269.

82. When Cruikshank visited the dying Hone on 6 October 1842, he brought Charles Dickens with him. Dickens also went to Hone's funeral. His description of this event, related in a letter to C. C. Felton dated 2 March 1843, provoked a lengthy controversy after it was published in Forster's biography of Dickens in 1872. For a summary of the arguments, see Madeline House, Graham Storey, and Kathleen Tillotson, eds., *The Letters of Charles Dickens*, vol. 3, *1842–1843* (Oxford: Clarendon Press, 1974), 454–55 n. 4. Dickens was part of a committee that successfully sought financial help for Mrs. Hone and her children (see ibid., 366). Marsh (*Word Crimes*, 51–56) speculates on the literary debt Dickens may have owed Hone.

83. Olivia Smith, *Politics of Language*, 165, and Wood, *Radical Satire*, 218–25. For a comprehensive list of precedents, see Wood, *Radical Satire*, 229–31 and 233–34. See also Olivia Smith, *Politics of Language*, 166 and J. Anne Hone, *For the Cause of Truth*, 183. Bowden's candidate is a contribution to Wooler's *Black Dwarf* in October 1819 ("Hone's Political Journalism," 1:242–43).

84. Michael Scrivener, *Radical Shelley* (Princeton, N.J.: Princeton University Press, 1982), 200; Patten, *Cruikshank's Life*, 165. The phrase "moderately reformist position" should not imply restrained expression. The representations of the victims of Peterloo and the clerical magistrate are among other powerful and haunting images in this satire. Also, the image of the Regent was so successful in damaging his reputation that in 1820 Carlton House paid seventy pounds for copyright to it (Patten, *Cruikshank's Life*, 164). Wood (*Radical Satire*, 14) summarizes the many ways in which Cruikshank's prints represent the prince.

85. Wood, *Radical Satire*, 247–48.

86. Kyle Grimes, "William Hone," 166. Wood (*Radical Satire*, 167–68) discusses the ways in which Hone and Cruikshank borrowed

techniques of writing and iconography from contemporary advertising.

87. McCalman (*Radical Underworld Prophets*, 165ff) reviews the ballad sheets, chapbooks, and pornographic and other scurrilous productions called forth by the Caroline affair, many of them exploiting "the theme of Caroline as a wronged mother exiled from her child in 1814" (165).

88. Wood (*Radical Satire*) describes the graphic traditions behind the *Ladder* (253). He also remarks on the "technical mastery" of several of the wood engravings (177). See also Patten, *Cruikshank's Life*, 177–78.

89. Anna Clark, "Queen Caroline and the Sexual Politics of Popular Culture in London, 1820," *Representations* 31 (summer 1990): 47. Mobilizing the population for political reform required elements of "plebeian pageantry" and a national consciousness of social and political issues: "the transformation of popular literature into overt political language made the mass mobilization possible" (51).

90. Roger Sales, *English Literature in History: 1780–1830, Pastoral and Politics* (London: Hutchinson, 1983), 181–82.

91. Patten, *Cruikshank's Life*, 180; Bowden, "Hone's Political Journalism," 2:326. Hone and Hazlitt began their friendship after meeting at John Hunt's home in early 1819. They shared an interest in Defoe; Hazlitt wrote the "Prospectus" for Hone's *History of Parody;* and Hone published Hazlitt's *Political Essays* (P. P. Howe, *The Life of William Hazlitt*, 2d ed. [New York: George H. Doran, 1923], 276–77). In "Mr. Canning," Hazlitt asserts "that Mr. Hone is a very good-natured man, that he is mild and inoffensive in his manners, that he is utterly void of guile, with a great deal of sincere piety, and that his greatest virtue is that he is fond of a joke, and given to black-letter writing." Note in P. P. Howe, ed., *The Complete Works of William Hazlitt*, 21 vols. (London: J. M. Dent, 1932), 11:158–59.

92. Thompson, *English Working Class*, 723. He mentions the pamphlets of Hone and Cruikshank as the most notable.

93. McCalman, *Radical Underworld Prophets*, 176.

94. Wood, *Radical Satire*, 182. Bowden ("Hone's Political Journalism," 1:146) notes that the method of *The Political Showman* was anticipated by a remark Hone made in his earlier *Official Account. Bartholomew Fair Insurrection.* There he imagined the kidnapping of government ministers, "to exhibit them about the country in caravans, as a collection of living animals."

95. Louis James, "An Artist in Time: George Cruikshank in Three Eras," in *George Cruikshank: A Revaluation*, ed. Robert L. Patten (Princeton, N.J.: Princeton University Press, 1974), 160.

96. Scrivener (*Poetry and Reform*, 25) notes that "Repression provoked a wide range of poetic responses from Aesopian allegory— the animal fables in *Politics for the People*—to revolutionary defiance in the some of the post-Peterloo poems."

97. For evidence of Hone's continuing antiquarian interests, see Bowden, "Hone's Political Journalism," 1:153. For the *Apocryphal New Testament*, see ibid., 2:310–11. After caustic reviews by conservative critics, Hone issued a revised edition in 1821.

98. Marsh, *Word Crimes*, 47. See also Olivia Smith, *Politics of Language*, 173. J. W. Robinson, "Regency Radicalism and Antiquarianism: William Hone's *Ancient Mysteries Described* (1823)," *Leeds Studies in English* 10 (1978): 127, notes that Hone's book "looks rather aggressively like an edition of the authorized Version, and a weapon, like his earlier creed, catechism and litany, with their ecclesiastical title-pages, in the battle for the intellectual and political emancipation of the people of England." Robinson also asserts (132) that Hone's work "constituted a giant leap forward in scholarship," though the world was not ready for what he said.

99. *Ancient Mysteries Described* (London, 1823), ii. Robinson also interprets this volume as an example of Hone's continuing radicalism, in that it shows "the pernicious effects of institutional religion and at the same time the quality of the popular mind which succumbed unharmed to its delusive charms, and adopted them as its own" ("Hone's *Ancient Mysteries Described*," 136).

100. William Hone, *Aspersions Answered: An Explanatory Statement Addressed to the Public at Large, and to Every Reader of the Quarterly Review in Particular* (London: William Hone, 1824), 5.

101. Marsh, *Word Crimes*, 51.

102. Richard M. Dorson, *The British Folklorists: A History* (London: Routledge & Kegan Paul, 1968), 36.

103. J. Anne Hone, *For the Cause of Truth*, 359, and J. R. Dinwiddy, *From Luddism to the First Reform Bill* (Oxford: Blackwell, 1986), 38. McCalman observes: "The execution of the Cato Street conspirators in 1820 and the death of Queen Caroline in 1821 are seen as having marked the end, respectively, of the old Jacobin-style conspiratorial coup d'état and of the old ribald satirical culture asso-

ciated with Regency popular radicalism" (*Radical Underworld Prophets*, 181).

104. Hill, "William Hone," 136.

105. Patten, *Cruikshank's Life*, 123. The memoranda of his daughter, Mrs. Burns, give details of Hone's illnesses in the period 1809–21 (Hackwood, *William Hone*, 206–7), including rheumatic fever (1809), quinsy attack (1814), first apoplectic fit (1815), and hallucinations (1821). Hone's financial situation is aptly summed up in Kyle Grimes's phrase "perpetually impecunious." See "William Hone, John Murray, and the Uses of Byron" in *Romanticism, Radicalism, and the Press*, ed. Stephen Behrendt (Detroit: Wayne State University Press, 1997), 195.

106. British Library, Add MS. 40120, f. 26.

107. Patten, *Cruikshank's Life*, 268–69.

108. British Library, Add. MS. 40120, f. 291, f. 304, and f. 339. Hone had conceived of his major project on the history of parody while researching materials for his court defense; he returned to reading in the British Museum in the years immediately following his trials. Among the British Library's manuscripts relating to Hone's history of parody is a list of the 845 books and pamphlets Hone had collected, as well as draft title pages, table of contents, and introduction; see Add. MS. 40108, vol. 1, f. 15 and following.

109. See letters of Thomas Teggs to Hone of 31 August 1830 and 6 January 1832 in the British Library, Add. MS. 41071 (Hone Papers), f.28, and Add. MS. 49856, f. 44.

110. British Library, Add. MS. 40120, f.390. The *Patriot* supported the movement to abolish church rates (a tax that went only to the established church), an issue Hone's friend John Childs was also active in promoting (see Hackwood, *William Hone*, 327, 329–30, and 332–33).

111. Hone's friendship with Lamb apparently began after Hone sent Lamb a copy of *Ancient Mysteries;* there are some twenty-six extant letters of Lamb to Hone, according to Hackwood (*William Hone*, 268).

112. After his death, Mrs. Hone and the children received a grant of fifty pounds sterling. See House, Storey, and Tillotson, *Letters of Charles Dickens*, 3:366. Dickens was a member of the committee that applied to the General Committee of the Literary Fund for this aid.

113. J. Anne Hone, "William Hone," 66. However, "Aspersions Answered" (1824) contains a strong statement of his Christian belief (66–67).

114. Hackwood, *William Hone*, 304, 317–18. Olivia Smith (*Politics of Language*, 174–75) quotes a poem by Hone in which he surrenders to God (cited by Hackwood, *William Hone*, 343).

115. Letter from Wilson to Hone in British Library, Add. MS. 40120, f. 16, and letter from Hone to John Childs of 23 February 1835, f. 401. Childs was still politically active a year later, since a letter to Hone of 9 April 1836 suggests that he had been jailed for demonstrating against the church rates (f. 429).

116. Binney to Hone in British Library, Add. MS. 40120, f. 412. On the other side of the question, when Hone proposed a publication to be titled *Hone's Almanac*, his political friends agreed to "forsake him 'because he has become a Methodist'" (apparently quoting Binney). See letter of C. H. Gregory to Binney, in British Library, Add MS. 40120, f. 405.

117. Rolleston (*Some Account*, 31) singled out Hone's "self-sacrificing sympathy with the sufferings of others" as the defining quality of his personality.

118. The anecdote is related in Hill, "William Hone," 137.

119. The phrase is in Rolleston, *Some Account*, 7.

NOTES TO "THE BULLET TE DEUM" AND "THE CANTICLE OF THE STONE"

1. On 28 January 1817 a window of the Prince Regent's coach was broken by a stone thrown at it as he returned from the opening of Parliament. The parodies suggest that the government took the opportunity of this attack to transform the stone into a bullet and thereby justify harsh, repressive legislation. The first excerpt from the *Reformists' Register* in this text gives additional treatment of this incident. For a similar incident involving George III on his way to opening Parliament on 29 October 1795, see Antonia Fraser, *George III: A Personal History* (London: Penguin, 1999), 227–28.

2. *Courier:* a Tory evening newspaper, founded in 1792, to which Coleridge, Wordsworth, Southey, and Lamb occasionally contributed.

3. In 1802 the Prince of Wales installed a Chinese Gallery in Brighton Pavilion, and he continued to elaborate the Oriental aspects of the Pavilion thereafter.

4. *Stannaries:* tin mines of Cornwall and Devon, the revenues from which were the privilege of the Prince of Wales.

5. *Hertford:* Isabella, Marchioness of Hertford (1760–1834), with whom the Prince of Wales became infatuated in 1807. *Jersey:* Frances, Countess of Jersey (1753–1821), with whom he fell in love in 1793. *St. Ursula:* fourth-century virgin martyr of Cologne; the companions murdered with her were sometimes said to have numbered eleven thousand.

6. *George Canning* (1770–1827): Tory foreign minister, 1807–9 and 1822–27, and briefly prime minister (1827).

7. The Bank of England.

8. *Louis Phillipe:* Louis XVIII (1755–1824). Very popular with the public during his exile in England from 1807 to 1814. Before his return to France in April 1814, he made the Prince Regent a Chevalier du Saint Esprit, and the Prince Regent made Louis a Knight of the Garter. He always claimed that "la nation toute entière" desired his restoration, which finally took place after Napoleon's abdication on 22 June 1815. *Ferdinand VII:* King of Spain briefly in 1808 before being deposed by Napoleon, but restored to the throne in 1814.

9. *Lord Ellenborough:* Edward Law, first Baron Ellenborough (1750–1818), Lord Chief Justice of England, 1802–18. See note 49 to *Second Trial. Sir John Silvester* (1745–1822) was chosen common sergeant by the corporation of London (1790) and succeeded Sir John William Rose as recorder in 1803. *Mr. Justice Hicks*: a magistrate at Bow Street Court. With Robert Gifford, he examined Thomas Scott, who was charged with being "a party to the outrageous attack made on his Royal Highness . . . ." See the *Times* (London) for Thursday, 30 January 1817.

NOTES TO *REFORMISTS' REGISTER*

1. *Lord James Murray* (1782–1837): the second son of the fourth Duke of Atholl, he was in the carriage with the Prince Regent when stones were thrown at it. Lord James alleged a pistol had been fired, but no bullet was found.

2. *Sir B. Hobhouse*: Right Hon. Henry Hobhouse (1776–1854) was under-secretary of state for the Home Office from 1817 to 1827.

3. *C. W. Wynne*: Right Hon. Charles Watkyn Williams Wym (1775–1850) entered Parliament in 1796 and represented Montgomery

from 1797 until his death. In 1830–31 he was secretary for war under Lord Grey and was also a metropolitan commissioner of lunacy.

4. *Henry Brougham* (1779–1868): lawyer and Whig M.P., he supported legal reforms and public education.

5. *Duke of Montrose*: James Graham, third Duke of Montrose (1755–1836), held many government positions over a long career beginning in 1783, including Master of the Horse (1807–30).

6. *Lord Cochrane* (1775–1860): played an independent, radical role in Parliament and often attacked the admiralty administration. Expelled from Parliament after being unjustly accused of a stock-exchange fraud, he was reinstated as a rear admiral in the British navy in 1832.

7. *Lord Milton*: Charles William Wentworth, third Earl Fitzwilliam (1786–1857), Viscount Milton until the death of his father in 1833. Sympathetic to reform, he was at this time (1817) M.P. for Yorkshire, which he represented in five successive Parliaments.

8. *Sir Robert Heron* (1765–1854) was Whig M.P. for Grimsby and later for Peterborough (1819–47).

9. *Duchess of Cumberland*: wife of Ernest Augustus, Duke of Cumberland and King of Hanover (1771–1851), the fifth son of George III and Queen Charlotte. She bore only one son, later George IV of Hanover, who was blind. She died in 1841.

10. See above note 2 to "The Bullet Te Deum."

11. *tocsin*: a signal bell.

12. *Green Bag*: the traditional color of bags used by lawyers for carrying documents and papers. Hone is referring to the allegedly seditious contents of a green bag brought before Parliament by Lord Sidmouth in February 1817. The phrase came to imply the threat of charges, even persecution. Such bags are now blue. In the same month, Sidmouth introduced a bill suspending habeas corpus, the first of several repressive measures.

13. *John Bowles* (1751–1819): anti-Jacobin publicist. Among his publications were *A protest against T. Paine's 'Rights of man'* (1792) and *Thoughts on the late General Election, as demonstrative of the Progress of Jacobinism* (2d ed. 1802). *John Reeves* (1752?–1829): lawyer, appointed king's printer in 1800 by Pitt. He organized the "Association for Preserving Liberty and Property against Levellers and Republicans" in 1793 after becoming alarmed by the growth of revolutionary sentiments in England. Reeves printed several editions

of the Bible and Prayer Book. In 1796 he was tried and acquitted on a charge of libel for a pamphlet in which he argued that Parliament and juries were "adjunct . . . subsidiary and occasional" to the real source of government, the king.

14. Cf. Gen. 3:14, Exod. 8:16, and Ps. 72:9.

15. *Enghien, Palm, and Wright*: three victims of Napoleon's scheming. Louis, duc d'Enghien (1772–1804), a Bourbon and heir to the Condés, was arrested by Napoleon's soldiers (who crossed illegally into Germany) and was tried and executed on 20 March 1804 for allegedly conspiring with other royalists to assassinate Napoleon. Outrage at his death was a factor in the formation of the Third Coalition against France. Palm was a German bookseller who distributed nationalistic tracts. By Napoleon's direct order, and as a show of force, he was kidnapped from Braunau, tried, and shot in 1806. Captain Wright, an English naval officer, brought royalist conspirators to France on three occasions (1803–5). Captured after a shipwreck, Wright was later found dead in his prison cell (October 1805), supposedly the result of suicide.

16. *cara sposa*: dear wife.

17. *Fontainbleau* is a French royal palace thirty-seven miles southeast of Paris.

18. *James Richardson*: the shop of Richardson the printseller, bookseller, and stationer was at No. 31, Strand (the N.W. corner of Villiers Street).

19. *Buonaparte-phobia, or Cursing Made Easy to the Meanest Capacity:—A Dialogue between the Editor of "the Times,"—Doctor Slop, My Uncle Toby, & My Father* was published by Hone in 1815 and attacks the intemperate language of John Stoddart (1776–1856) in his role as editor of the *Times*. After being dismissed from this position in 1816, with government support he founded the rival *New Times. Crane Court*, mentioned below, was known as a location just off Fleet Street where unstamped, reformist newspapers were printed and where government officers stood ready to seize them.

20. Ernulf (1040–1124) was bishop of Rochester in the twelfth century and author of the *Textus Roffensis*, a collection of curses. The text was printed in the *Harleian Miscellany* 6.493 (London, 1745). The text of his excommunication appears in *Tristam Shandy* (3.9) as an antipapist joke.

21. *Secret Committee*: this committee met in February to decide on

appropriate legislation to deal with the current unrest. After Sidmouth received the committee's report (24 February 1817), he sent his circular letter. The legislation suspending habeas corpus passed on 3 March.

22. *Wooler, Butt, Watson*: Thomas Wooler (1786–1853), publisher of *The Black Dwarf*, a radical weekly (1817–24), was found not guilty on one count of libel on 5 June 1817. A new trial was held on a second count, Woller defended himself, and he was acquitted. Richard Gathorne Butt was tried for libels on Ellenborough and Castlereagh on 24 May 1817. James Watson (1766–1838), a Spencean radical, was tried for high treason in June 1817 in connection with events the previous December. However, as the government's case was based on the testimony of the informer Castle (shown to be a forger, pimp, adulterer, and thief), the jury acquitted Watson.

23. *Sidmouth*: Henry Addington, first Viscount Sidmouth (1757–1844), then secretary of state for home affairs. See also note 23 to *First Trial*.

24. *Guardian*: an evening paper founded by the Whigs, it was published briefly during 1817.

25. No. 5 (22 February), 144.

26. *Sir William Manners* (1766–1833): inherited the bulk of his father's estate and arrogantly began trying to purchase political influence and offices (including an Irish peerage). He "acquired Ilchester" by purchasing the electors in time for the 1802 general election but was defeated in 1807 and never reentered Parliament. He was also never able to collect on the promise of a peerage by the Prince Regent (originally made to his father, John Manners, in 1784). *Sir Mark Wood* (1747–1829): English politician and writer on India, where he spent his early career. In 1802 he was returned for the pocket borough of Gatton, Surrey, and represented it until 1818, when he was succeeded by his son Mark. "Gatton was one of the rottenest of the rotten boroughs swept away by the Reform Act. It had returned two members since 1450, and in one year both were elected by one man." (Arthur Mee, *Surrey* [London: Hodder & Stoughton, 1966], 110).

27. *Scot and lot*: the equivalent to modern rates or real estate taxes.

28. *Maidstone*: the county town of Kent, about forty miles southeast of London.

29. *tantivy*: riding at full gallop, historically applied to High Church Tories of the Restoration period.

30. *Rev. James Murray* (1732–82): his satirical work, *Sermons to Asses,* was first published in 1768. For his influence on Thomas Spence, see Wood, *Radical Satire,* 65. *Mr. Curran*: John Philpot Curran (1750–1817), a brilliant orator, was renowned as a defense attorney in state trials during the 1790s, often on charges of seditious libel.

31. "From grave to gay, from lively to severe" is from Pope, *An Essay on Man,* 4.380.

32. "For his chaste muse employ'd her heav'n-taught lyre / None but the noblest passions to inspire, / Not one immoral, one corrupted thought, / One line, which dying he would wish to blot." Lines 21–24 of Lord Lyttelton's Prologue to *Coriolanus* (1749) by James Thomson, who had died the previous August. George, first Baron Lyttleton (1709–73), also a friend of Pope, became patron to Thomson (1700–1748), who inscribed a copy of *The Seasons* to him. In 1750 Lyttleton published Thomson's collected writings, very freely revised.

NOTES TO *THE FIRST TRIAL*

1. *Guildhall*: the center of civic government, where lord mayors and sheriffs were elected and meetings of the Court of Common Council held. Notable state trials held here include the Earl of Surrey (1547), Lady Jane Grey (1554), and Dr. Garnet (1606), Jesuit superior in England accused of complicity in the Gunpowder Plot.

2. *Charles Abbott*: first Lord Tenterden (1762–1832), Lord Chief Justice, 1818–32. Anti-reform law lord. "In no sense or capacity was Lord Tenterden great" (from the *Dictionary of National Biography,* hereafter cited as *D.N.B.*). His last words (4 November 1832) were, "Gentlemen, you are all dismissed."

3. *information*: complaint or charge against an individual to initiate criminal proceedings without a formal indictment.

4. *Sir Samuel Shepherd* (1760–1840): attorney-general (although very deaf), 1817–19. He lived in Edinburgh, 1819–30, and was a close friend of Sir Walter Scott.

5. *Sir Matthew Hale* (1609–76): lawyer, judge, latterly chief justice of the King's Bench (1671–75), known for his integrity and great authority. He wrote many treatises on law and religion.

6. *John Wilkes* (1727–97): journalist who began the *North Briton* in 1762 and who supported popular causes, including parliamentary

reform. With respect to the subtitle of this "Catechism," Wilkes wanted to introduce a bill into Parliament specifically to get rid of "placemen."

7. *Sureties*: sponsors, backers.

8. John Nash, with the prince's approval, in 1810 proposed a "New Street" that would join Marylebone Park (now Regent's Park) to the Regent's residence, Carlton House, reducing the traveling time to central London and improving the architectural appearance of the capital, thought to be somewhat provincial in comparison with European capitals. The construction of Regent Street, begun in 1813, greatly disrupted the entire area. *Knights of the Bath*: a medieval order of merit revived in 1725 and expanded significantly in 1815 from 35 Companions to 72 Knights Grand Cross, 180 Knight Commanders, and an unspecified number of Companions.

9. *Charles James Fox* (1749–1806): staunch Whig and parliamentary proponent of such reforms as the abolition of slavery.

10. *Lord James Murray* (1782–1837): see note 1 above to *Reformists' Register*. *Betty Martin*: "All my eye and Betty Martin"—slang phrase repudiating as nonsense any attempt to impose a deception.

11. *divide*: the House of Commons "divides" to vote for or against a motion.

12. *Chilterns*: the stewardship of the Chiltern Hundreds, a kind of fictitious public office, was a device to enable an M.P. to give up his seat in the House of Commons. Here, of course, the minister threatens expulsion from the House.

13. *Levee*: from French *lever*, to rise. A reception or assembly held by a monarch during the morning or early afternoon. Under Louis XIV the stages of the ceremonial reception coincided with the stages of the king's rising, ablutions, and dressing, culminating in the donning of his wig. Hone means that government ministers demand the fawning subservience formerly accorded absolute monarchs.

14. *Sir William Turtle*: In *A Slap at Slop* (p. 26), Turtle is described as "the patron of knavish-traders, biscuit bakers, contractors, loanjobbers, and other third-rate thieves" [William Hone, *Facetiae and Miscellanies* (London: Hunt & Clarke, 1827)]. *Sinking Fund*: funds specifically directed to the extinction of a debt, especially a national debt. The British national debt consisted in large part of "floating debts"—very short-term treasury bills—an expensive mode of state borrrowing that the "sinking funds" were intended to eliminate.

15. *Lord Castlereagh* (1769–1822): Robert Stewart, Viscount

Castlereagh, was British foreign secretary from 1812 to 1822. *Sir Matthew Wood* (1768–1843): a radical who was alderman in 1807, sheriff in 1809, and lord mayor of London in 1815 and 1816, the first such reelection in hundreds of years. *Sir John Silvester*: see note 9 above to "The Bullet Te Deum." *Mr. John Langley*: not traced.

16. *Sir William Garrow* (1760–1840): attorney-general in 1813.

17. *tipstaff*: sheriff's officer, constable.

18. *Westminster-hall*: the only surviving part of the Palace of Westminster, built in 1097. For six centuries, until 1882, the building housed the Law Courts (Common Pleas, King's Bench, Chancery, etc.). It was the site of many state trials: William Wallace (1305), Sir Thomas More (1535), Charles I (1649), and Warren Hastings (1788–95).

19. The hall is 238 feet long.

20. *William Dowdeswell* (1721–75): M.P. for Tewkesbury. He urged (in 1771) the necessity of passing a bill to explain the power of juries in prosecution for libels, but his motion was condemned by Lord Chatham and rejected. *Edmund Burke* (1729–97): advocated the political rights of the people, and so in 1771 he supported a motion on the law of libel to protect individuals who criticized the government. He also argued for the right of the press to publish parliamentary proceedings.

21. *Star-chamber*: a court that became, during the reigns of James I and Charles I, notorious for arbitrary trial and sentence.

22. Fox's Libel Act (introduced in 1791) transferred from judges to juries the power of pronouncing verdict in certain cases of libel.

23. *Henry Addington, first Viscount Sidmouth* (1757–1844): son of Dr. Anthony Addington (1713–90), who attended in their illnesses both Chatham (1767) and George III (1788). As home secretary, 1812–21, he "ruled with unwavering sternness." He suspended the Habeas Corpus Act and rigorously enforced laws restraining press and other publications. After the Manchester massacre (16 August 1819) he "hastened to express the thanks of the government to the magistrates and to the troops" *(D.N.B)*.

24. Omitted are passages in which Hone describes and criticizes the prevailing method of "striking juries" by the Master of the Crown Office.

25. The famous satire on Edinburgh notables took the form of a supposed "Chaldee MS" and appeared in the October 1817 issue.

26. *William Blackwood* (1776–1834) founded *Blackwood's Edin-*

burgh Magazine; its first issue (as *Edinburgh Monthly Magazine*) was 1 April 1817. The two editors were William Cleghorn (1778–1838) and Thomas Pringle (1789–1834). *Archibald Constable* (1774–1827) founded and published the *Edinburgh Review* (begun October 1802).

27. *Dr. Lettsom:* John Coakley Lettsom (1744–1815), very successful Quaker physician and philanthropist, one of the founders of the Medical Society of London. One of his many subjects was the effects of alcoholic excess on women, published in a pamphlet *On the Effects of Hard Drinking* (1791).

28. *Jortin:* John Jortin (1698–1770), *The Life of Erasmus*, 2 vols. (London, 1758–60 and reprinted several times in the early nineteenth century). *Sacramentarians:* the name Luther gave to theologians who maintained that the Bread and Wine of the Eucharist were the Body and Blood of Christ only in a metaphorical sense. The word in the sixteenth century was applied to those who denied the doctrine of the Real Presence. *Zwinglians:* Ulrich Zwingli (1484–1531), a Swiss reformer. In 1518 he was elected People's Preacher at the Old Minster in Zurich, where he remained the rest of his life. He believed the sole basis of truth was the Gospel, and he developed a purely symbolic view of the Eucharist. *Zurichers: Consensus Tigurnis* (the "Zurich Agreement," 1549) set forth a doctrine of the Eucharist which conformed with Calvinist principles and which was free of the objections that attached to consubstantiation.

29. *Dr. John Boys* (1571–1625): Dean of Canterbury, an uncompromising Anglican who criticized both Puritans and Roman Catholics.

30. Omitted are Hone's extensive quotations from the following sources: sermons by Bishop Hugh Latimer (1485?–1555) in which he told his hearers allegorically how to win salvation by playing trumps in a game of cards; an article in the second volume of the Harleian Miscellany that parodies prayers for the sick to political purposes (the books, manuscripts, pictures, and medals collected by Robert and Edward Harley, the first and second Earls of Oxford, were sold to the British Parliament in 1753); a biblical parody from the tracts of Lord Somers (1651–1716), Lord Chancellor; satirical verse about Scripture and Thomas Burnet (1635?–1715) from the continuation by Mark Noble (1754–1827) of the *Biographical History of England* (1769) by James Granger (1723–76); a parody of the catechism by François de la Chaise (1624–1709), father confessor of Louis XIV; a scriptural parody published in *The Champion* (1741); scriptural parody from the

Foundling Hospital for Wit; a parody of the catechism ("The British Freeholder's Political Creed") in papers published by the Association for Preserving Liberty and Property against Republicans and Levellers, founded by John Reeves (1752?–1829); scriptural parody from a volume of papers relating to the Westminster election of 1784; passages of parody from *The Chronicle of the Kings of England. Written in the manner of the ancient Jewish historians* (London, 1740), ascribed both to Lord Chesterfield (1694–1773) and to Robert Dodsley (1703–64); an excerpt from *The Rolliad: Criticisms on the Rolliad* (1784), a mock commentary on a fictitious epic about the exploits of the ancestor of John Rolle, Conservative M.P. for Devonshire (the satire is directed at William Pitt and his followers, and the authors included Whigs George Ellis, French Laurence, and Lord John Townshend); a parody of the Lord's Prayer published in *The Oracle* (1807); and a parody on the *Te Deum* attacking Napoleon, as well as two short parodies using the form of a playbill and of a recruiting bill.

31. *Mr. Gilray:* James Gillray (1757–1815) executed 1500 caricatures between 1780 and 1811, almost all on political themes, sometimes on behalf of the opposition, at other times at Canning's direction, since Gillray had also accepted a government pension.

32. *Lepaux:* Louis Marie de la Révellière-Lépeaux (1753–1824), French revolutionary hostile to Christianity (which he hoped to replace by theophilanthropy, a religion invented by English deist David Williams). *Earl Grey:* Charles Grey, second Earl Grey (1764–1845), Whig nobleman devoted to individual liberty and the constitution. In 1817 he condemned the suspension of the Habeas Corpus Act and similar measures, including Lord Sidmouth's circular of 27 March recommending the arrest of those who published or sold seditious libels.

33. *Robert Harding Evans* (1778–1857): bookseller and auctioneer. "A fervid politician, and took a great interest in the history of the Whig party" *(D.N.B.)*.

34. *Mirabeau*: Honoré Gabriel Riqueti, Comte de Mirabeau (1749–91), leader of the National Assembly in the French Revolution. *Voltaire* (1694–1778): famous atheist and sceptic, he was threatened with arrest for *Lettres philosophiques sur les anglais* (1733), essays praising English institutions. *Marat*: Jean Paul Marat (1743–93), was a well-known French revolutionary who was associated with the Reign of Terror, during which 2,596 victims were guillotined in Paris. A

painful skin disease meant he spent hours each day in a warm bath, where, of course, he was murdered in July 1793.

35. *Priestley, Wakefield, Thelwall:* Joseph Priestley (1733–1804) was a scientist, theologian, historian, social reformer, and supporter of the French revolution. Gilbert Wakefield (1756–1801) was a classical scholar at Cambridge. He was imprisoned in 1799 for seditious libel; he had argued in print that a French invasion would be to the advantage of the English poor and labourers. John Thelwall (1764–1834) bought *The Champion* in 1818 to advocate parliamentary reform, a cause to which (together with elocution) he devoted most of his life.

36. *Williams:* John Williams (1761–1818) was a satirist prosecuted several times for his writings. *Holcroft*: Thomas Holcroft (1745–1809), friend of Paine and Godwin, was a novelist and playwright.

37. *Coke:* Thomas William Coke (1752–1842) was a staunch Whig M.P. for Norfolk and supporter of Fox. He was also a pioneer in the agricultural revolution (his innovations included the regular manuring of the soil). *Colquhoun:* Patrick Colquhoun (1745–1820) was a metropolitan police magistrate and a proponent of schemes for educating the laboring class, for a national savings bank, for a national poor rate, and so on. In 1795 he helped to establish a soup kitchen in Spitalfields, the first of its kind. *Anson:* possibly the nephew (b. 1766?) of Lord Anson (1697–1762), the circumnavigator. *Whitbread:* Samuel Whitbread (1758–1815), only son of Samuel Whitbread (d. 1796), the well-known brewer and close adherent of Fox. He proposed a Poor Law (1807) and a scheme for distinguishing between the deserving and undeserving poor by means of badges. From 1809 until cutting his throat in 1815, he was a frequent speaker in the Commons. *The Duke of Bedford:* Francis Russell, fifth Duke of Bedford (1765–1802). Adherent of Fox, in support of whom he often spoke in the House of Lords, once he had overcome a very defective education. He opposed the granting of a pension to Burke. Burke published (1796) "Letter to a Noble Lord," comparing his own pension with the huge grants to the house of Russell. "The duke is the leviathan among the creatures of the crown. . . . Huge as he is he is still a creature. His ribs, his fins, his whalebone, his blubber, the very spiracles through which he spouts a torrent of brine against his origin, and covers me all over with the spray—everything of him and about him is from the throne." *The Anti-Jacobin* versified Burke's attack in this parody.

38. *Mr Tierney:* George Tierney (1761–1830) opposed Pitt and once fought a duel with him. He later became treasurer of the navy (1802) and held other offices.

39. *Rowland Hill* (1744–1833): preacher at Surrey Chapel, London, from 1783.

40. *Dr. Isaac Watts* (1674–1748): famous hymn writer. *John Rippon* (1751–1836): Baptist divine, later best known as compiler of *Selection of Hymns from the Best Authors* (1827).

41. *Montague Philip Corri* (1784–1849): music publisher and composer. Member of a large musical family whose father, Domenico Corri, moved from Rome to Edinburgh in 1771.

42. See "Sweet William's Farewell to Black-ey'd Susan," *The Poetical Works of John Gay*, ed. G. C. Faber (1926; reprint, New York: Russell & Russell, 1969), 181–82.

43. *Downs:* famous rendezvous for ships off the east coast of Kent.

44. *Curtis:* Sir William Curtis (1752–1829), Tory M.P. for London, lord mayor 1795–96, the subject of much ridicule during his lifetime.

45. *Fuseli:* Henry Fuseli (1741–1825) exhibited "The Nightmare" at the Royal Academy in 1782.

46. *Sheridan:* Richard Brinsley Sheridan (1751–1816), dramatist and parliamentarian, supporting Fox. *Burdett:* Sir Francis Burdett (1770–1844), well-known advocate for parliamentary reform and M.P. for Westminster, 1807–37. *Sixteen-string Jack:* John Rann, executed for highway robbery at Tyburn on 30 November 1774, was known as "sixteen-string Jack" because he habitually wore breeches with eight strings at each knee.

47. *Moira:* Francis Rawdon Hastings (1754–1826), first Marquis of Hastings and second Earl of Moira, friend and confidant of the Prince of Wales. Army commander-in-chief and administrator in India, he left directions that after his death his right hand should be cut off and preserved until it could be buried in his wife's coffin.

48. "The Reconciliation" (1804) refers to the meeting at Kew between George III and his son, George, Prince of Wales, on 12 November 1804. The Gillray engraving (20 November 1804) includes the figures of Pitt and Lord Moira, who had promoted the meeting. The "reconciliation" did not long survive the rooted antagonism between father and son. See Christopher Hibbert, *George IV, Prince of Wales 1762–1811* (London: Longman, 1972), 197–200. Hone then presents two more prints by Gillray, the "Apotheosis of Hoche" (French general who died

in 1797 at age thirty-one; see note 110 to *Third Trial*) and a parody on the taking up of Elijah, before summing up his defense. Four depositions by witnesses for the defense follow before the attorney-general reiterates the government's case and Mr. Justice Abbott charges the jury.

NOTES TO *THE SECOND TRIAL*

49. *Lord Ellenborough:* Edward Law, first Baron Ellenborough (1750–1818), lord chief justice of England. As counsel for the crown, Law assisted at the trials of such reformers as Thomas Hardy (1794) and John Reeves (1796). Appointed attorney-general in 1801 and then lord chief justice in 1802, he later presided at the trials of Colonel Despard for high treason and of the two Hunts (proprietors of the *Examiner*) for an article on flogging in the navy and for libelling the Prince Regent. Overbearing and biased, he habitually browbeat juries and opposed any amelioration of the criminal code. He experienced signs of deteriorating health early in 1816 and, after his deep annoyance at Hone's acquittals, he announced his intention to resign to Lord Sidmouth on 21 December 1817. He died a year later.

50. *Nisi Prius:* opening words of a writ directed to a sheriff and commanding him to provide a jury.

51. *tales:* a procedure for appointing substitute jurors drawn from those present in the courtroom.

52. *Blackstone:* Sir William Blackstone (1723–80). At Oxford he was the first to teach English, as opposed to Roman, law. The collection referred to is Blackstone's *Commentaries on the laws of England, in four books*, 12th ed., with notes and additions by Edward Christian (d. 1823), first published in London in 1793–95.

53. Hone vigorously complains to the court about the oppressive use of ex-officio informations against powerless persons. Ellenborough tries to repudiate Hone's charges and set the trial back on course.

54. *special jury:* a jury consisting of persons on the jurors' book who are of a certain station or who occupy premises of a certain notable value.

55. *gravamina:* grievances.

56. *Doctor Slop:* Sir John Stoddart (1773–1856), editor of the *New Times*.

57. As in the first trial, the central part of Hone's self-defense in-

volved quoting from and commenting on numerous examples of historical parodies, almost all repeated from the opening trial: Dr. Lettsom's thermometer, Luther, Boys, the Harleian Miscellany, Somers, Noble, the *Te Deum* parodies, *The History of the Westminster Election*, John Reeves's parody, Bishop Latimer, parodies of the Lord's Prayer and those parts of the Book of Common Prayer for which he was being charged (several examples from the seventeenth-century Cavaliers, especially on the Litany), and Canning's parody from the *Anti-Jacobin.*

58. *Sully:* Maximilian, Duc de Sully (1560–1641), who was superintendent of finances for France, 1598–1611.

59. In 1814 Canning planned to travel with his son (who was ill) to Portugal. The Ministry persuaded him to become ambassador extraordinary and to welcome the Prince Regent at Lisbon on his return from Brazil (the trip was deferred, so there was no meeting). The Whigs attacked the Ministry for extravagance in Canning's appointment (at a much higher salary than his predecessor, who was deprived of his position). Canning's defense of himself in the House was so brilliantly made that no further debate ensued.

60. Cf. *Julius Caesar* 1.2.194.

61. *Mr. Wooler:* Thomas Jonathan Wooler (1786–1853) was tried in June 1817 before Justice Abbott and a special jury on two charges of libel for an article published in *The Black Dwarf.* He was found innocent of one charge but guilty of another. When the unanimity of the verdict was questioned, a new trial was permitted, at which Wooler successfully persuaded the jury that he could not be described as having *written* an article that he set up in type without a manuscript.

62. *King Lear* 3.1.49.

63. *Othello* 4.2.143.

64. The four depositions, the attorney-general's summation, and Lord Ellenborough's charge then follow.

65. *Common Hall:* one of the institutions of London's civic government, the Court of Common Hall was the city's largest assembly. It met to elect City officials, really to confirm nominations by the aldermen, once a year to put forward two candidates for lord mayor, and to participate in electing sheriffs and M.P.'s.

NOTES TO *THE THIRD TRIAL*

66. Joseph Hone, William's younger brother, was a barrister who emigrated to Tasmania in 1824. See note 80 to *Letters*.

67. *Quicunque vult:* "Whosoever will [be saved]" are the opening words of the Athanasian creed.

68. *Old bags:* John Scott (1751–1838), first Earl of Eldon, Lord Chancellor (1801–6 and 1807–27). He was notorious for his opposition to all change and reform. *Derry Down Triangle:* Robert Stewart, Viscount Castlereagh (1769–1822). The most common method of extracting information and intimidating the populace was indiscriminate flogging. As acting chief secretary for Ireland, he suppressed the French-aided rebellion of 1798. The triangle refers to the tripod to which prisoners being flogged were bound. *The Doctor:* Henry Addington, first Viscount Sidmouth (1757–1844), whose father was a doctor. As home secretary, he was responsible for internal security. See also note 23 to *First Trial*.

69. John Entick (1705?–78), *A Compendious dictionary of the English and Latin tongues* (London: Dilly, 1786).

70. *Queue:* pigtail, an appendage. Castlereagh was appointed Chief Secretary for Ireland in 1799 by "the great man" William Pitt (1759–1806); he also helped the prime minister to bring about the union of England, Scotland, and Ireland in 1801.

71. Castlereagh fought a duel with Canning in 1809.

72. As foreign secretary, Castlereagh was perceived to have yielded British interests to French during the negotiations in 1814–15 with Talleyrand (1754–1838), French statesman, following Napoleon's defeat. He introduced the bill for suspending habeas corpus in February 1817.

73. *Reading Easy:* a child's first reading-book, an elementary primer. To match the infernal trinity of government ministers, Hone introduces a trinity of what he perceives as establishment poets seeking the approval of Castlereagh and the Prince Regent *(Hum)*.

74. *Mr. Fox's Libel Bill:* The Libel Act (introduced in 1791) was declaratory (i.e., it explains or declares what the existing law is); it gave juries instead of judges the right to render verdicts in particular cases of libel.

75. *Vinerian Professor of Law:* refers to the holder of the Chair of English Common Law at Oxford, endowed by Charles Viner

(1678–1756), English jurist. *Edward Christian* (d. 1823): law professor at Cambridge whose final preferment was Chief Justiceship of the Isle of Ely. See note 52 to the *Second Trial*.

76. Two old women were indicted for witchcraft before Hale in March 1661–62. In directing the jury, Hale did not comment on the evidence but affirmed the existence of witches by authority of Scripture, general consent, and acts of Parliament. He wrote a preface to *A Collection of modern relations of fact concerning Witches and Witchcraft upon the Persons of the People* (London, 1693).

77. For Wilkes's manuscript with Hone's deletions and additions, see the appendix to Marcus Wood, *Radical Satire*, 272–90.

78. *tyrant of Syracuse:* probably Dionysius the Elder, who established a tyranny at Syracuse in Sicily in 405 B.C. When he died in 367 B.C., he was succeeded by his son (Dionysius the Younger), who held power for ten years before he was driven out of Sicily.

79. Cf. 1 Sam. 20:17: "And Jonathan caused David to swear again, because he loved him: for he loved him as he loved his own soul."

80. Cf. Matt. 8:9 (or *Luke* 7:8).

81. Cf. John 8:7–11.

82. Cf. Matt. 7:12.

83. Cf. Job 2:4.

84. John Dunning, first Baron Ashburton (1731–83), was a lawyer, M.P., and powerful orator. He is supposed to have been the author of the pamphlet "Inquiry into the Doctrines lately promulgated concerning Juries, libels, etc., upon the principles of the Law and the Constitution" (1764).

85. *Rev. Mr. Toplady:* Augustus Montague Toplady (1740–78), author of the hymn "Rock of ages." Described by Wesley (whom he attacked ferociously) as a "chimney-sweeper." The *D.N.B.* characterizes his writings as "acute, incisive and brilliant."

86. Philip Dormer Stanhope, fourth Earl of Chesterfield (1694–1773), began a series of instructive letters to his illegitimate son Philip when the boy was five (1737) and continued until Philip died in 1768. These letters were published by his son's widow in 1774 and were long regarded as a guide to etiquette and social skills.

87. For John Reeves, see note 13 to *Reformists' Register*.

88. *Collyer:* William Bengo Collyer (1782–1854), minister of the Congregational Church and religious writer: *Hymns designed as a Sup-*

plement to Dr. Watts (1812). *Lady Huntingdon:* Selina Hastings, Countess of Huntingdon (1707–91), founded a sect of Calvinistic Methodists known as the Countess of Huntingdon's Connexion. Very rich, she built sixty-four chapels in various parts of England, appointed chaplains to them from a seminary she established in Wales, and superintended them all, autocratically.

89. In 1811 Lord Sidmouth introduced a bill that required all dissenting ministers to be licensed and that restrained unlicensed preachers. An outcry was raised, and on second reading the bill was thrown out by the Lords.

90. *Lord Grenville:* William Wyndham Grenville (1759–1834) was foreign secretary, 1791–1801.

91. John Herriott (1760–1833) wrote for the *Oracle* newspaper for a time, before moving to the *World,* and later to the editorship of both the *Sun* (first issue 1 October 1793) and the *True Briton.* In 1806 he accepted a clerkship in the lottery office.

92. *Desunt pauca:* a few bits are missing. *Desunt plurima:* more bits are missing. *Desunt nonnulla:* enormous bits are missing.

93. *The wonderful magazine or marvellous chronicle* appeared in two volumes between 1764 and 1766. It was revived in 1793–94.

94. William Pitt, first Earl of Chatham (1708–78).

95. Charles Townshend (1725–67), chancellor of the Exchequer, 1766–67; Henry Seymour Conway (1719–95), secretary of state, 1765–68; third Duke of Grafton (1735–1811), First Lord of the Treasury, 1766–70.

96. *patent places:* positions where appointees can profit from their offices.

97. *trimmer:* time-server, a person who associates himself or herself with currently prevailing views, especially for personal advancement.

98. The first "Tales" were published in 1816; they were published in four series over fifteen years and included *Old Mortality* (1816) and *The Heart of Midlothian* (1818).

99. *The Hypocrite* by Isaac Bickerstaffe (1735–1812) was first performed at Drury Lane Theatre in November 1768.

100. *Mr. Whitfield* (1714–70): George Whitefield was an evangelist and leader of Calvinistic Methodists. He joined Wesley and the Methodists in 1735 and became an extraordinarily popular preacher. He started open-air preaching at Rose Green on Kingswood Hill near Bristol in February 1739.

101. *Kingswood colliers:* longshoremen in a small town outside Bristol. It was here that in March 1740 Whitefield laid the first stone of a school for the colliers.

102. *Samuel Foote* (1720–77): English actor and dramatist. His *The Minor* opened at the Haymarket Theatre in November 1759 and is a satire on Whitefield and the Methodists.

103. In *The Minor* Mother Cole, a bawd, acts as an enthusiastic convert to Methodism while tempting the play's young hero with one of her girls. She represented Mother Jennie Douglas, a notorious London procuress.

104. *The Weathercock* by Theodosius Forrest ran for three nights at Covent Garden in October 1775.

105. *Chalmers' Poets:* Alexander Chalmers (1759–1834), prolific editor, whose publications included an enlarged edition of Johnson's *Collection of the English Poets, with some additional lives* (21 vols., 1810).

106. *History of the Westminster Election* (published 1784) describes the election of 1784, in which William Pitt defeated a coalition of Whigs, including Charles James Fox. Caricatures were included in the *History. Lord J. Townshend* (1757–1833): friend of Fox who was eventually elected M.P. for Knaresborough in 1793.

107. *Fuseli:* see note 45 to *First Trial. Wood:* see note 15 to *First Trial*.

108. *Curtis:* see note 44 to *First Trial*.

109. *John Horne Tooke* (1736–1812): politician and philologist, supporter and later enemy of Wilkes. Originally John Horne, he adopted the surname Tooke at the request of a wealthy friend, William Tooke, owner of a large estate at Purley (near Croydon), hence the title *The Diversions of Purley* (vol. 1, 1786).

110. For Gillray, see note 31 to *First Trial. Hoche:* Lazare Hoche, French general, died at thirty-one (19 September 1797). As early as 1793 he wanted to attack Britain, and in 1796–97 he commanded the abortive invasion of Ireland. In the engraving Hoche ascends into a sansculotte paradise strumming on a small guillotine. The ascent of Pitt, titled "Disciples Clutching the Mantle," was published 28 June 1808.

111. *Lord Somers* (1651–1716): Lord Chancellor in 1697. His library formed the basis of the collection known as the "Somers Tracts," published between 1748 and 1752 and later edited by Sir Walter Scott.

112. In 1817 Hone published Southey's *Wat Tyler: A Dramatic Poem* (written in 1794 and full of republican enthusiasm) to embarrass the now conservatively-minded Poet Laureate. Although he later wrote a parody of Southey's *A Vision of Judgement,* "A New Vision" (both 1821), Hone and Southey made peace a decade later and exchanged several polite letters.

113. *The Stuart Papers:* When Prince Regent, George IV was passionately interested in the House of Stewart, and arranged for a large quantity of papers left by Charles the Young Pretender to be transferred from the Vatican to his own library. One of the last acts of his life was to invite Sir Walter Scott to supervise the editing of these papers.

114. *Reeves:* see note 13 to *Reformists' Register.*

115. *Grenville:* see note 90 to *Third Trial.*

116. *Edmund Gibbon* (1737–94). *Athanasius* (296–373): Bishop of Alexandria, known as the "Father of Orthodoxy." The Athanasian Creed is the third principal creed of the Christian church.

117. *Vigilius* (fl. 480): of Thapsus, author of many theological works and supporter of Athanasius, though no longer believed to be the author of *De Trinitate* or so distant in time from Athanasius as "four centuries."

118. *Warburton:* William Warburton (1698–1779), bishop of Gloucester, prolific writer on controversial theological questions. *Waterland:* Daniel Waterland (1683–1740), Oxford theologian. *Archbishop Tillotson:* John Tillotson (1630–94), archbishop of Canterbury, 1690–94, who made these remarks in one of the last letters he wrote. *Dr. Porteus:* Bailley Porteus (1731–1808). As bishop of London, 1787–1808, he was notable for his opposition to slavery and to secular activities on Sunday. *his Lordship's father:* Edmund Law (1703–87), bishop of Carlisle, 1768–87, and described by William Paley as "A man of great softness of manners, and of the mildest and most tranquil disposition."

119. *Act of Uniformity:* the first Act of Uniformity (1549) made the first Prayer-Book of Edward VI the only legal form of public worship in England. The second Act of Uniformity (1552) enforced the second, revised version of the Prayer Book. The Elizabethan Act of Uniformity (1559) revived the second Prayer Book (suppressed under "Bloody" Mary) and imposed a fine of one shilling for each offense on all who failed to attend church on Sundays and holy days. The Caroline Act of Uniformity (1662) established the further revised Prayer Book, incor-

porating some six hundred alterations, "most of them unpalatable to Puritans." [M. W. Patterson, *A History of the Church of England* (London: Longmans, 1929), 359].

120. The bishop of Clogher in Co. Tyrone, Ireland, from 1797 until his death in 1819 was John Porter.

121. *Mr. West:* Benjamin West (1738–1820), historical painter. Toward the end of his life he began to paint a series of scriptural subjects on a large scale. One of these, "Death on the Pale Horse," was exhibited at his own gallery in 1817.

122. *Woolston:* Thomas Woolston (1670–1733), free thinker, indicted for blasphemy after publishing in 1728 the fourth edition of *Discourse on the Miracles of Our Saviour* (1727). He was tried in 1729, sentenced to one year's imprisonment, and fined £100. He died a few years later, never having paid the fine. *Paine:* Thomas Paine (1737–1809), notorious freethinker whose *Age of Reason* (1793) defended Deism. He fled to France to escape prosecution.

123. *Chief Justice Eyre:* Sir Robert Eyre (1666–1735) became lord chief justice of the Common Pleas in 1725.

NOTES TO *THE POLITICAL HOUSE THAT JACK BUILT*

1. The quotation is from the antiquarian and historian John Selden (1584–1654), *Table-Talk: Being the Discourses of John Selden, Esq . . . .* (1689), 31, in a passage on the subject of libels. Dorothy George describes the title page illustration in part as follows: "Wellington stands by a pair of scales, throwing his sword into a scale heaped with three large documents. . . . These are outweighed by a single (feather) pen" (*Catalogue of Political and Personal Satires*, vols. 9–10, ed. M. Dorothy George [London: British Museum, 1938–54], 9:945). Although Wellington gave up command of the army of occupation in November 1818, he was named to the cabinet in December after his return to England, a development Hone and other reformists would have understood as part of the government's repressive measures. Kyle Grimes has noted the following about the illustration: "The sword has not yet landed, and it thus remains to be seen whether or not the pen will continue to outweigh the combined force of legal and military repression. Given this historical context, it is plausible that *The Political House that Jack Built* was intended to test the powers (and the limits) of the post-

Peterloo free press. Such a reading would help to explain the title-page epigraph. . ." (*Romantic Circles* Website: http://www.RC.umd.edu).

2. William Cowper, *The Task* 5.522–28.

3. *Doctor Slop*: Dr. John Stoddart (1773–1856), first attacked by Hone (as his note indicates) in *Buonaparte-phobia, or Cursing made Easy* (1815) where Stoddart is portrayed as Dr. Slop, Sterne's caricature of an obstetrician in *Tristam Shandy*, and where he is ridiculed for his intemperate attacks on Napoleon while writing for the *Times* in 1814 and 1815. See Stanley Jones, *Hazlitt: A Life* (Oxford: Oxford University Press, 1991), 13–15, for details of Stoddart's apostasy. The word "slop" refers to a chamber pot (slop-pail) but can also suggest speaking or acting without restraint, associations Hone would think appropriate to Stoddart.

4. *The Task* 5.535. "The Temple of the Constitution is a dome supported on three columns: *Commons, King, Lords*, and surmounted by a figure of Liberty holding a cap of Liberty on a staff" (George, *Catalogue*, 9:946).

5. *The Task* 6.50–53. The real treasures of the British Constitution—Magna Charta, habeas corpus, and the Bill of Rights (1689)—lie ransacked or abandoned in favor of profit-making (coins, moneybags, and a ledger). Among other provisions, the Bill of Rights restricted the size of the standing army in peacetime.

6. *The Task* 2.826–32. "A group of state parasites" (George, *Catalogue*, 9:946). The figures (l. to r.) are an imperious court official, a swaggering Hussar officer, a clerical magistrate with one hand clasping a Bible and the other clenched on a truncheon (for the clerical magistrate, see note 21 in this section), a vicious tax collector, and a lawyer holding an indictment. In the background is a wispy military officer, more uniform than man.

7. *The Task* 5.477, 491–92. The "Thing" (line 2) is the printing press. The "new Acts" (line 3) refer to the Six Acts of 1819 which followed the "Peterloo massacre" (see note 13 in this section) and which related to procedures for bringing cases to trial, prohibitions against meetings for military exercises, the issue of warrants in the search for arms, regulating public meetings, seizure of blasphemous and seditious literature by magistrates, and the extension of the Stamp Act to a much wider range of papers and pamphlets.

8. *The Task* 4.59–60, 657. The illustration shows a lawyer, malignant and crazed, initiating a prosecution against publishers and

printers. George (*Catalogue*, 9:946) identifies him as Sir Robert Gifford, the attorney-general. He carries numerous "*ex-officio* informations" (see note 3 to *First Trial*).

9. *The Task* 4.568 and 2.322. Pictured in this illustration is the basis of "lawless power," described by George (*Catalogue*, 9:947) in this way: "A jailor holding keys and shackles stands beside a cannon, with its artilleryman holding a match, a grenadier with his bayonet ready for attack, and a mounted Life Guard, sabre in hand."

10. *The Task* 4.788–89. The Prince Regent makes a preposterous figure as commander-in-chief: choked by his collar, squeezed by his corset, spurred, booted, peacock-feather-hatted, and holding his sword in the wrong hand.

11. The Prince Regent enjoyed traveling by sea, but the pointed reference in the phrase "sails about at his pleasure" is to the fact that while the Peterloo massacre was taking place he was aboard the *Royal George* on his first visit to the Regatta at Cowes. Two years later, on his fifty-ninth birthday (12 August 1821), having just heard of the queen's death, he sailed to Ireland and landed at Howth "dead drunk" (see Christopher Hibbert, *George IV, Regent and King, 1811–1830* [London: Allen Lane, 1973], 129, 208–9). The reference to "Friends of his youth" is to the prominent Whigs with whom he had long been friends and who felt betrayed early in 1812 when he proposed they form a coalition with the existing Tory administration instead of offering them outright power.

12. *The Task* 2.58; 2.26–28; 3.217–19; 4.508.

13. On 16 August 1819, in St. Peter's Fields, Manchester, sixty thousand people met to hear radical orator Henry Hunt and to demonstrate in favor of parliamentary reform. Several hundred people were injured and eleven killed (including two women) when cavalry and a company of hussars were ordered to disperse the crowd. The Regent wrote a letter (at Lord Sidmouth's urging) that endorsed the action of the Manchester magistrates in summoning the cavalry and congratulated the commander on his restraint. The illustration depicts the victims of Peterloo.

14. *The Task* 3.807; 4.26; 3.88–89; 4.77; 1.769; 1.570–73; 3.127–29. The "guilty trio" consists of Sidmouth (1757–1844), Castlereagh (1769–1822), and Canning (1770–1827). George's description reads in part as follows: "Sidmouth, holding a clyster-pipe and a constable's staff, Castlereagh holding a scourge, and Canning,

stand together. The first is senile, the second bland and dandified, the third aggressive" (*Catalogue,* 9:947). As home secretary, Sidmouth wrote a "circular" letter (see line 2 of text) to the Lords-Lieutenant in March 1817, following the suspension of habeas corpus, and encouraged them to prosecute those who had allegedly committed blasphemous or seditious libel.

15. An allusion to the duel between Castlereagh and Canning in 1809. Earlier in his career, Canning had mocked Sidmouth and "dubb'd *him*" with the nickname, the Doctor. "Moderate Men and Moderate Measures" and "Ode to the 'Doctor'" are two poems attacking Sidmouth. See *The Poetical Works of the Right Honourable George Canning* (London: Jones & Co., 1827), 43–44 and 45–46. See also note 69 to *The Political Showman* below.

16. *Jack-pudding*: buffoon, especially one attending on a mountebank.

17. *Flash*-man: companion of thieves. *Bravo*: hired assassin.

18. *The Task* 4.672–75; 5.371–73; 6.477–79.

19. "'Waterloo-Man' was the title of a song bitterly attacking Wellington and the war in the *Black Dwarf,* 18 June 1817" (George, *Catalogue,* 9:948).

20. Norfolk, Bedford, Fitzwilliam, Grosvenor, and Albermarle were regarded as an anti-government, Whiggish group in favor of reform.

21. George's description of this illustration is typically acute: "A parson (Ethelston) with two heads and two pairs of arms, emerges Janus-like from a double rostrum, one half pulpit, the other a magistrate's seat. One profile is bland, the other savage; both are drink-blotched. One (l.) holds up a cross, the other (r.) a miniature gallows. The latter also holds blunderbuss, scourge, and shackles" (*Catalogue,* 9:948). Regarding Ethelston, Bowden ("Hone's Political Journalism," 1:257) observes: "after signing the warrant [for the arrests] and reading the Riot Act, he is reputed to have mounted his pulpit in Manchester and told the congregation that the massacre was the will of God."

22. *The Task* 2.332–36; 2.408.

23. *Quorum*: i.e., the judiciary.

24. Since the first English Poor Laws, dating from the reign of Henry VIII, assistance to the poor was organized on a parish basis and funded by compulsory rates, locally assessed and collected. So much destitution resulted from wars and agrarian and industrial changes in the period

1790–1815 that the poor law authorities resorted to a form of out-relief which was, in effect, a subsidizing of farmer-employers by the ratepayers. Mounting protests about this financial burden (the poor rates) at last forced Parliament to introduce the Poor Law Amendment Act in 1834, the first attempt to improve the English Poor Laws since 1601.

25. *sec. Stat.*: according to (by) the Statute.

26. *The Task* 6.446–48.

NOTES TO *THE QUEEN'S MATRIMONIAL LADDER*

1. Before and during her trial Caroline received many addresses of loyalty from various cities as well as groups (seventy-eight by September 1820). These were printed, together with the Queen's replies, and widely disseminated. See Flora Fraser, *The Unruly Queen: The Life of Queen Caroline* (New York: Alfred A. Knopf, 1996), 431–32. For examples, see E. A. Smith, *A Queen on Trial: The Affair of Queen Caroline* (Stroud, Gloucestershire: Allan Sutton, 1993), 106–7, 112–13, 148–49.

2. 3.2.42.

3. See Chapter 4, "The King's Great Matter" (the divorce from Catherine of Aragon to marry Anne Boleyn) in *George Cavendish, Thomas Wolsey, late Cardinal, his Life and Death,* ed. Roger Lockyer (London: Folio Society, 1962), 111–12.

4. Proverbs 31.3. George notes that the illustration is an "adaptation" of Gillray's "A Voluptuary under the horrors of Digestion" (*Catalogue,* 10:78).

5. *The Task* 3.811–13, 795–96.

6. The Prince of Wales was induced to marry Princess Caroline of Brunswick in 1795 by the king's promise to pay his outstanding debts (over £600,000) and to increase his annual allowance from the Civil List by £40,000 to £100,000.

7. Charles Phillips (1787?–1859), *The Lament of the Emerald Isle,* 2d ed. (London: W. Hone, 1817), 19. In the illustration, the prince and Pitt (with bags of money in each hand) are surrounded by a crowd of creditors pouring through an arch marked by the Prince's crest.

8. *The Lament of the Emerald Isle,* "Dedication" and p. 15 (reworded).

9. Not traced in *The Lament of the Emerald Isle.* In the illustration the prince points accusingly at Caroline. He is prompted by Sir

John and Lady Douglas, formerly intimate friends of Caroline but the first witnesses against her in the "Delicate Investigation" (1806). This commission of cabinet ministers investigated Caroline's conduct and her supposed second pregnancy. Cleared of the charge of adultery, she was nevertheless reprimanded for her "unseemly" behavior, and the king continued to refuse to see her. Spencer Perceval and Lord Eldon helped her compose "The Book," a long letter to the king answering the charges against her. It was published in 1807 but quickly withdrawn from circulation by royal command at a cost of £10,000. See Thea Holme, *Caroline: A Biography of Caroline of Brunswick* (London: Hamish Hamilton, 1979), 42–84 *passim*. George notes: "The King sits in a hooded chair like the night-constable in a watch-house, looking up at her from the open pages of *The Book*" (*Catalogue*, 10:79).

10. 5.1.140. The prince (with *The Book* attached to him by a rope) is shown fleeing into Carlton House with the Douglases, while George III is represented as supporting Caroline. In fact, after the Delicate Investigation, she was no longer regarded as an intimate of the family.

11. *The Lament of the Emerald Isle*, 19. "The Princess runs weeping to the shore, waving farewell to Princess Charlotte who leans from the window of a small building where she is imprisoned" (George, *Catalogue*, 10:79). John Fisher (1748–1825), bishop of Salisbury, was appointed Charlotte's superintendent of education in 1804, but here he is pictured as her jailer. By 1812, Caroline's weekly visits with her daughter had been reduced to fortnightly, and in 1814 Caroline left England for six years.

12. 2.1.183. Caroline landed at Dover on 5 June 1820 after crossing the channel from Calais on the ordinary packet. In the illustration she steers her small craft through the combined opposition of the elements and of Sidmouth (lower left), Liverpool (lower right, attempting to scuttle the boat with an extremely protruding nose), Castlereagh, and Eldon (upper right). George IV, shown as a spouting whale, sprays clouds of water at her.

13. "St. Romuald," line 35, in *The Poetical Works of Robert Southey*, 10 vols. (London: Longman, 1838), 6:94. In the illustration Sidmouth desperately applies a clyster pipe (used for administering enemas) to the unconscious George as Caroline approaches. "Essence Bergam" on the pipe refers to bergami, a citrous extract used in perfumes but here as smelling salts, but it also puns on Pergami, her Italian lover. A coin inscribed 2/6 (punning on "half a crown") dangles above the king's head, while in the tapestry behind, "a she-lion roars

toward an ass (George IV) and stags in full flight" (George, *Catalogue*, 10:80). Before Caroline's trial, George ordered her name and title removed from the Church of England's liturgical prayers.

14. 2.4.146 and 3.2.4–6. George IV stands outside the "'House of Incurables'" (Houses of Parliament) as a night watchman ("OLD CHARLEY"), the leech in his lantern referring to Vice-Chancellor Sir John Leach (1760–1834). Reports about Caroline's misconduct abroad were presented to both houses of parliament prior to her trial. The queen, shown with her defense lawyers Henry Brougham and Thomas Denman, sets fire to the bag of accusations, in effect ridiculing the report (in her other hand is a reticule, a handbag here with a mocking face). The words inscribed on the bag suggest the house is a brothel.

15. "Marchionessing" alludes to the string of mistresses with which the king had consorted over many years. "Doctors Commons" refers to the college of doctors of law where legal business relating to wills, marriage licenses, and divorce was transacted.

16. Of the speeches of Richard Brinsley Sheridan (1751–1816), a Whig betrayed by the Regent, 460 were published in three octavo volumes (up to June 1808), but he continued to address the Commons until 21 July 1812, the date of his final speech. This quotation is from a speech of 1810: "Give me the liberty of the Press, and I will give the Minister a venal House of Peers, I will give him a corrupt and servile House of Commons . . . armed with the liberty of the Press, I will go forth to meet him undismayed." The king's plot to "blow up his wife" was exposed by the investigative journalists of the day, or so Hone suggests. In the illustration the obese, ludicrous Guy Fawkes figure is led by a syphilitic and impotent Cupid, all the time watched by the presiding eye of the press and Caroline, unafraid. The fire insurance plaque above the door suggests that his scheming, while endangering the nation and the monarchy, is in vain (Albion Life Assurance was a company founded in 1805 [George, *Catalogue*, 10:80]).

17. *Cooke:* William Cooke (1757–1832) was one of three men chosen for the Milan Commission (1818), the inquiry into the princess's behavior overseas.

18. 5.3.128. In the illustration the nation (the lion) angrily repudiates the charges brought against Caroline. The king cowers.

19. See John 8:7.

20. *'sloe'*: blue-black fruit of the blackthorn. *'whiter than snow'*: see Ps. 51:7.

21. *Spanish:* "ready money" (*Dictionary of the Vulgar Tongue,* 1811).

22. "The King wishes it." Sir William Blackstone (1723–80): the first volume of his *Commentaries on the Laws of England* (4 vols.) was published in 1765. In the illustration, George, holding a hatchet (with coiled leech) rather than a sceptre, is crowned with a large (green) bag by Castlereagh (l.) and Liverpool (r.). Sidmouth provides musical accompaniment on his clyster pipe while Eldon struggles to produce trumpet notes on a primitive horn. The Parson's prayer book evidently omits prayers for Caroline, as the king had directed.

23. "It is the curse of kings to be attended / By slaves that take their humours for a warrant / To break within the bloody house of life. . . ." (*King John* 4.2.208–10).

24. A prediction that George's courtiers and sycophants will eventually abandon him.

25. *The Curse of Minerva* 207. In the first illustration, George IV, crestfallen and defeated, stands on the stool of penance and is berated by the preacher and ridiculed by the congregation. The Seventh, Ninth, and Tenth Commandments are highlighted in the background. Looking up at the king on the right is a cat in coat and breeches, fulfilling the old adage "a cat may look at a king." This saying, signifying the mighty brought low, was the title of a political pamphlet published in 1652. The equation of cat and king is extended to the second illustration, in which the king has become "Cats' Meat" carried off in a wheelbarrow and followed by three hungry, stray crowned cats. The barrow is being pushed by a brawny Cupid crying his wares.

26. See "Fum and Hum, the Two Birds of Royalty," a satiric fragment published in the *Morning Chronicle.* Like Cruikshank's drawing, this fragment ridicules the Prince Regent, Brighton Pavilion, and the fad for Chinoiserie. *prime:* excellent, but also sexually excited. *spooney:* foolish, silly, sentimental. *Joss:* Chinese figure of a god or idol. The Byron quotation is from "Farewell to Malta," 49.

27. See note 11 to *The Political House that Jack Built.*

28. *Rape of the Lock* 4.49–50. The final illustration is full of fantastic details: "George IV as a teapot . . . stands astride on an ornate barge, formed of a monster with the scales of a dragon, an ass's head (as figurehead) and three large peacock's feathers as tail which curve over the teapot King. There is a sail supported on a mast up which coils a leech. A little Chinese Cupid seated on the feathers plies a pair of bellows, so filling the sail" (George, *Catalogue,* 10:82).

NOTES TO *"NON MI RICORDO!"*

1. 2.2.35. The title ("I do not remember") refers to the confused, evasive replies of Theodore Majocchi, Italian servant of Princess Caroline, the first witness cross-examined during the public hearings in the House of Lords which lasted from August to November 1820. Prompted by Brougham (see note 2 below), Majocchi used this phrase more than eighty times. George describes (*Catalogue*, 10:92) the woodcut on the title page as follows: "George IV, a seedy and bloated dandy, stands at the bar, saying, with melancholy anger, *Non mi Ricordo!* in answer to the question printed below the design: 'Who are you?'"

2. *besom:* broom, a pun on Henry Brougham (1778–1868), the brilliant lawyer who defended Princess Caroline in the public inquiry.

3. Hone plays with legal terms and titles throughout this passage as he mocks the terminological wrangling often characterizing legal procedures. The Turnstile General, or attorney-general, who led the prosecution was Sir Robert Gifford (1779–1826). The Lord Precedent Furthermore probably refers to the lord chancellor, Lord Eldon (1751–1838). The Twister General who appears later is the solicitor-general, Sir John Copley (1772–1863). *Erminians:* ermine was the fur used to trim the gowns of judges and peers.

4. This passage is full of bawdy double entendres. For example, "goose" is a tailor's smoothing iron but also means to tickle or poke, especially between the buttocks, and "tools" refer to a man's private parts (*Dictionary of the Vulgar Tongue,* 1811). Being raised to be "A Cabinet maker" identifies the defendant as the future George IV.

5. *Juryman:* Thomas Denman (1779–1854), the queen's solicitor-general who supported Brougham in defending Caroline. His speech of summation for Caroline on 24 and 25 October lasted ten hours. Generally pro-Reform, Denman had defended radical leader Jerry Brandreth at Derby in 1816.

6. *Muddlepool:* Robert Jenkinson, second Earl of Liverpool (1770–1828).

7. *Veils:* vails were bribes, gifts, gratuities. As Prince of Wales, of course, George *waited* many years to succeed his father. *Crown Inn:* see note 34 in this section.

8. The Prince Regent entertained various fantasies about his military prowess. In one version he had delusions about having led the army to victory at the Battle of Waterloo. Another fantasy was that he

had led the Germans' charge at Salamanca "disguised as General Bock. 'Was not that so?' he would shout to the Duke [of Wellington] down the dinner-table. 'I have often heard Your Majesty say so,' his Grace would reply." Quoted in Elizabeth Longford, *Wellington: Pillar of State* (New York: Harper & Row, 1972), 79. The Battle of Salamanca, however, occurred in the Peninsular War (1812) and marked an important victory by Wellington over the French.

    9. See note 6 to *The Queen's Matrimonial Ladder.*

    10. *fanfaron:* braggart.

    11. *letter of license:* "an instrument or writing granted to a debtor by his creditors, giving him respite and time for payment of his debts" (*Oxford English Dictionary,* hereafter cited as *O.E.D.*).

    12. *Jersey:* Lady Jersey (1785–1867). *Manchester Square:* location of Hertford House, residence of Lady Hertford (1760–1836), for whom the Prince Regent discarded Lady Jersey and Mrs. Fitzherbert (1756–1837).

    13. "Every afternoon his yellow chariot [the Prince Regent's] was to be seen driving through London with the purple blinds drawn, towards Hertford House in Manchester Square. . . ." Stella Margetson, *Regency London* (New York: Praeger, 1971), 36.

    14. *Marquis of C.*: Henry, first Marquess of Conyngham (1766–1832), husband of Elizabeth, the Marchioness (?1766–1861) with whom the Prince Regent became infatuated in 1820.

    15. Matt. 5:32: "But I say unto you, that whosoever shall put away his wife, saving for the cause of fornication, causeth her to commit adultery: and whosoever shall marry her that is divorced committeth adultery."

    16. *False Keys:* a skeleton key giving access everywhere.

    17. While living at Clapham, 1795–1808, William Wilberforce (1759–1833) founded an Evangelical sect dedicated to morality. They had already persuaded the king to issue in 1787 a proclamation condemning Sabbath-breaking, blasphemy, drunkenness, obscene literature, and immoral amusements. They founded a society for the enforcement of this proclamation, which in 1802 reorganized itself as the Society for the Suppression of Vice. It included "the entire bench of bishops, members of both houses, and wealthy merchants." It "carried on a vigorous warfare against blasphemous or obscene publications, brothels and fortune-tellers. But its principal object was the observance of the Sunday rest." Elie Halévy, *England in 1815* (London: Benn, 1960), 452.

18. See note 17 to *The Queen's Matrimonial Ladder.*

19. In 1817, along with other repressive measures, Lord Sidmouth restricted the liberty of the press by issuing a circular to the lords lieutenant of counties to enforce rigorously the laws against blasphemous or seditious libel.

20. *Bathos:* Lord Bathurst (1762–1834), a long-standing member of the Tory cabinet and secretary for the colonies.

21. *prigged:* stolen.

22. *Ratstail:* Lord John Russell (1792–1878), who addressed the Prince Regent in an open letter to the *Times,* urging him to intervene in person and stop the proceedings. *Boudoir:* perhaps a joke about such ranks as "Master of the King's Bedchamber." Lord Jersey was descended from George Villiers, first Duke of Buckingham, favourite of James I, who made him "Gentleman of the Bedchamber." *Black stick:* Gentleman Usher of the Black Rod, so called from his symbol of office. He was assistant to the lord chamberlain as usher to the House of Lords.

23. Brighton Pavilion was a favorite haunt of the Prince Regent's and one of the more obvious symbols of his self-indulgence. See the description in J. B. Priestley, *The Prince of Pleasure and His Regency 1811–20* (New York: Harper & Row, 1969), 249–55.

24. The Marchioness of Conyngham. See note 14 above.

25. Colonel Thomas Henry Browne (1768–1851) was, with William Cooke and John Alan Powell, a member of the Milan Commission. Majocchi was questioned by Brougham about Colonel Browne.

26. *Curaçao:* liqueur flavored with orange peel, named after the Dutch island in the Caribbean. George IV was a notoriously heavy drinker. By January 1821, for example, his gout had become very bad: "He could scarcely manage to walk to the dining-room table; and when he did get there he ate very little, and could eat nothing without previously imbibing cherry brandy in quantities 'not to be believed.'" Christopher Hibbert, *George IV, Regent and King 1811–1830,* 238.

27. *cat:* suggests prostitute and drunken vomiting (*Dictionary of the Vulgar Tongue,* 1811).

28. *Trifle:* flirting. *Bagatelle:* a pun on the game and on its meaning as trifle. The "C" simultaneously refers to Lady Conyngham and conveys an apposite obscene reference.

29. A series of bawdy puns. Doll refers to a "tawdry over-dressed woman" (*Dictionary of the Vulgar Tongue,* 1811), and the import of the

rest of the sentence is simply "I have loose women all over the place." *horn-boys:* adulterers. *flashmen:* whore's bullies.

30. *scarlet fever:* a passion for soldiers. *putrid fever:* typhus fever (corruption).

31. *green bag:* contained the most important papers from the Milan Commission. After having been studied by a secret committee of the House of Lords, these documents established the need for an inquiry into Caroline's bahavior.

32. See note 8 above. "[Wellington was] continually provoked by the military airs the king gave himself and his tendency to dogmatize, over the dinner-table, on tactics and drill." Leonard Cooper, *The Age of Wellington* (New York: Dodd, Mead and Co., 1963), 268. George IV liked "devising new fancy dresses for the army," had a remarkable knowledge of uniforms, and "ordered at least eight field-marshal's full-dress uniforms" after becoming king. See Sir John Fortescue, *Wellington* (London: Ernest Benn, 1960), 232; and Hibbert, *George IV, Regent and King, 1811–1830,* 249 and n.

33. Canova (1757–1822) visited London in 1815 to receive British commissions and to see the Elgin Marbles (he helped to persuade the government to purchase them from Lord Elgin). Like Castlereagh, Wellington, and others, the Prince Regent commissioned sculptures from Canova, which were delivered over the next two years. There are three in the Royal Collection in Buckingham Palace. According to *L'Opera Completa del Canova* (Milan: Giuseppe Pavanello, 1976), they were initially placed in Carlton House.

34. George (*Catalogue,* 10:93) suggests that Hone's allegory of John Bull and the Crown Inn derives from John Arbuthnot (1667–1735), *Law is a Bottomless Pit; or the History of John Bull* (1712), ascribed to Arbuthnot by Swift (*Journal to Stella,* 12 December 1712).

NOTES TO *THE POLITICAL SHOWMAN—AT HOME!*

1. Bunyan's *Pilgrim's Progress* begins, "As I walked through the wilderness of this world, I lighted on a certain place where was a den, and laid me down in that place to sleep; and as I slept, I dreamed a dream."

2. *Mr. Lambton:* John George Lambton, first Earl of Durham (1792–1840), brought forward an advanced scheme for parliamentary

reform in 1821 and was one of four persons who drew up the Reform Bill a decade later. George describes the title page's woodcut as follows: "A monster with seven hydra-heads, webbed wings, stands erect on the splayed legs of a bird of prey. The heads are those of sovereigns of Europe, crowned, and with the addition of birds' beaks. They are: the Pope, tonsure downwards, his tiara falling; Ferdinand VII, crown downwards, choked by bulky papers inscribed *Constitution;* Louis XVIII, looking up, a tricolour cockade in his beak; Alexander, at the apex, swallowing an orb; Frederick William III with a paper, *Promised Constitution,* in his beak; Ferdinand of Naples, head downwards, his gaping beak receiving the impact of an eruption from Vesuvius. On the monster's chest hang emblems of the Saint Esprit" (*Catalogue,* 10:207).

3. Andrew Marvell, *"The Rehearsal Transpros'd" and "The Rehearsal Transpros'd, The Second Part,"* ed. D. I. B. Smith (Oxford: Clarendon Press, 1971), 4–5. Hone has altered several words and slightly shortened the passage in Marvell. The subtitle for *A Whip for the Devil* (London: Thomas Malthas, 1683) is as follows: *or, the Roman conjurer, discovering the intolerable folly, profaneness and superstition of the Papists, in endeavouring to cast the Devil out of the bodies of men and women by him possest.*

4. *turnery:* wood decoration.

5. The transparency shows "an irradiated Liberty, holding a laurel-framed portrait of the queen, standing before a printing press, dispelling by her light the bodiless heads (no-bodys) of the King and his supporters" (Robert L. Patten, *George Cruikshank's Life, Times, and Art* [New Brunswick, N.J.: Rutgers University Press, 1992], 183).

6. Slightly misquoted from Southey's *Joan of Arc* (1796 edition), 10.200–01 and 208–12.

7. *Dialogues of Creatures Moralysed* (translated from Latin and published in Antwerp, 1535) was reprinted in 1816 (London: Robert-Triphook), edited by Joseph Haslewood, and subtitled *Applicable and edifying to every merry and jocund matter, and right profitable to the governance of men.*

8. Recently pardoned from prison, bankrupt, and with a wife and large family, Daniel Defoe was induced by Robert Harley to start a newspaper that would speak for the government. The quotation is from the statement of editorial aims for *A Weekly Review of the Affairs of France.* . . . Begun in February 1704, it ceased publication in 1713.

9. See Cowper's *The Task* 2.668–71, 673–74.

10. *Juglator Regis:* cutthroat of the king. *Joseph Strutt* (1749–1802) was an English antiquarian, engraver, and miscellaneous writer. His *Glig-Gamena Angel Dead, or the Sports and Pastimes of the People of England* (London: J. White, 1801) was published in a new edition by Hone in 1830. George's description of the accompanying illustration reads as follows: "Eldon's face, rectangular between two pendent bags representing his wig, is supported on a body formed by the Purse of the Great Seal" (*Catalogue,* 10:207).

11. Richard Corbett (1582–1635) was an anti-Puritan divine who became Dean of Christ Church at the age of 37 in 1620. The *D.N.B.* entry describes his poems as "for the most part in a rollicking satiric vein."

12. Henry Maddock (?–1824) published *A Treatise on the Principles and Practice of the High Court of Chancery* in 1815. He had earlier written *A Vindication of the Privileges of the House of Commons* (1810).

13. *The Retrospective Review,* a quarterly founded by Henry Southern (1799–1853) and published from 1820 to 1828, aimed to revive interest in earlier literature, particularly that of the sixteenth and seventeenth centuries.

14. *King John* 4.3.107; *Richard III* 1.3.352.

15. Gifford's translation of Juvenal appeared in 1802. The passage from which the quotation is drawn is from a section condemning avarice and miserliness: "But why this dire avidity of gain? / This mass collected with such toil and pain? / Since 'tis the veriest madness, to live poor, / And die with bags and coffers running o'er" (ll.189–92 in *Satire* XIV).

16. See Cowper's *Conversation,* 119–34.

17. The quotation is from *The Character of a London-Diurnall* (first published 1644) by John Cleveland (1613–58). A diurnal is a kind of early newspaper that kept Englishmen informed of international events. Cleveland's poem satirizes Parliament and Puritan diurnals, and the passage quoted singles out Thomas, Lord Grey of Groby (1623?–57), one of Charles I's judges and a signatory of his death warrant.

18. Possibly a translation of *Kalendrier des Bergers,* a popular publication of the sixteenth century combining almanac, scientific information of the day, and devotional exercises. George (*Catalogue,* 10:204) suggests that the weeping crocodile represents Sir John Leach

(1760–1834), a supporter of the Prince Regent who was appointed vice-chancellor of England in 1818 after ten years in the House of Commons, 1806–16.

19. From "Cupid's Cryer," ll.59–62, Crashaw's translation of a poem by Moschus.

20. *Linnaeus:* Carolus Linnaeus (1707–78) devised the system for naming plants and animals using one Latin word for the genus and another for the species. *An history of the earth, and animated nature* by Oliver Goldsmith (1728–74) was published in eight volumes (London: J. Nourse, 1774) and reprinted many times over the next century.

21. Cowper's "The Jack Daw" (1782), ll.7–10, translated from the Latin of Vincent Bourne's "Cornicula." George (*Catalogue*, 10:208) describes the illustration as follows: "A face covered by a black mask, supported on clerical bands, one inscribed 41 [?1641], the other 39 [Articles]. It is framed by a bushy episcopal wig, and supports a mitre on which are crossed cannons. This is topped by a weathercock on which sceptre and crown are poised. The Archbishop of Canterbury." It was in 1641 that the movement to abolish bishops, deans, and chapters (the "Episcopacy Controversy") began. Charles Manner Sutton (1755–1828) was archbishop of Canterbury at the time of Hone's publication.

22. Robert South (1634–1716), English divine and controversialist, was famous for his "graphic humour" *(D.N.B.)*. His collected sermons were published over a period of a century and a half (six volumes, 1679–1715, a seventh in 1717, and five more in 1844), but a *Select Sermons* appeared in 1819. The asterisk points to Hone's annotation where he notes the fortuitous linking of imposture and clerical wigs.

23. *Incrustation:* a scab. *Relique:* remains, left over.

24. The first three lines are from *Conversation*, 297–99, the final line from *The Task* 4.292.

25. From *Tirocinium; or, Review of Schools* (1784), ll. 412–19, 425, a satirical attack on public schools, arguing that private education at home is better. Hone omits line 420: "Behold your bishop!"

26. *Nos numerus sumus et fruges consumere nati* (Horace, *Epistles* 1.2.27): "we are but ciphers, born to consume earth's fruits." In the illustration, "A scaly and fantastic locust wearing coronet and mitre represents the bishops" (George, *Catalogue*, 10:208).

27. The *Essais* (1580) of Michel de Montaigne (1533–92) was first translated into English by John Florio (1553?–1626) in 1603. The quo-

tation is actually from chapter 12 of volume 3, where Montaigne is writing about war: "Monstrueuse guerre: les autres agissent au delors; cette-cy encore contre soy se ronge et se desfaict par son propre venin. Elle est de nature si maligne et ruineuse qu'elle se ruine quand et quand le reste, et se deschire et desmembre de rage." Hone seems to have made his own translation; in any case, it is not Florio's. George (*Catalogue*, 10:208) gives the following description of the illustration: "A scorpion with the (ferocious) profile of Wellington wearing a cocked hat. Its tail is a chain terminating in a sabre."

28. Pierre Louis Moreau de Maupertuis (1698–1759) was a French mathematician and astronomer who visited London in 1728 and was elected a fellow of the Royal Society.

29. Guillaume de Salluste Du Bartas (1544–90) was a French poet whose best known work was the creation epic *La Semaine*. *Lobster* is a contemptuous name for the red-coated British soldier.

30. Several publications involving religious controversy and having Tom of Bedlam in the title appeared in the later seventeenth and early eighteenth centuries, including *New Mad Tom of Bedlam* (1670?) and *Tom of Bedlam's Answer to his brother Ben Headly, St. Peter's-Poor Parson . . .* (1709), as well as *Tom of Bedlam: or, a mad poem, writ by a mad Author* (1704). In the illustration the head of Robert Banks Jenkinson, second Earl of Liverpool (1770–1828), sits on a crutch breaking from the weight of a bag (containing the "huge fat places" of the first quotation) attached to his wig. He was prime minister from 1815 to 1827.

31. Not traced.

32. *The Task* 5.250–54 ("they" has been changed to "he").

33. Sir Thomas Charles Morgan (1783–1843) was a surgeon and philosophical and miscellaneous writer. His *Sketches of the philosophy of life* (London: H. Colbourn, 1818) was attacked by critics for its materialism.

34. I.e., the House of Lords.

35. The "wondrous Lad" is William Pitt (whom Liverpool is criticized for imitating) and the classical reference is to Phaeton. Ephesus was the scene of important labors of St. Paul (see Acts 18, 19), who lived there for three years. Cf. "But now they desire a better [country]" (Heb. 11:16). *The Purple Island* (1633), an allegory of the human body and mind, was written by Phineas Fletcher (1582–1650). The quotation is from canto 8, stanza 41, with the first and seventh lines altered.

36. John Asgill (1659–1738) was charged with blasphemy for a book (published 1700) arguing that "death was not obligatory upon Christians." The book was ordered to be burned in 1707. *Mr. Asgill's Defence upon his Expulsion from the House of Commons of Great Britain in 1707* was published in 1712. Asgill died in debtors' prison after a lifetime of dubious legal and financial entanglements.

37. John G. Stedman (1744–97) condemned the cruelties of slavery in *Narrative of a five years expedition against the revolted Negroes of Surinam . . . from the year 1772 to 1777 . . . .*, 2 vols. (London: J. Johnson, 1796). George Shaw (1751–1813) was an English naturalist who helped found the Linnean Society of London in 1788 and became Fellow of the Royal Society in 1789. His *General Zoology, or Systematic Natural History* appeared in fourteen volumes between 1800 and 1826, Shaw writing vols. 1–8 (1800–1812) and J. F. Stephens vols. 9–14.

38. Thomas Frognall Dibdin (1776–1847) helped to excite an interest in rare books and early editions with *Bibliomania* (1809; 2d ed. 1811). Dibdin was the originator of the Roxborough Club (prototype of later publishing societies), and his most amusing and successful work was *Bibliographical Decameron* (1817).

39. The passage from Jonson attacks flatterers and sycophants. See *Timber, or, Discoveries* in *Ben Jonson,* ed. Ian Donaldson (Oxford: Oxford University Press, 1985), 564.

40. The lines praise a cat's triumph in the mock heroic "Monody on The Death of Dick, An Academical Cat": "What congregated rats his valour quells! / What mice descended, at each direful blow, / To nibble brimstone in the realms below!—" In *Salmagundi: A miscellaneous combination of original poetry,* ed. George Huddesford [1749–1809] (London: T. Bensley, 1791; 2d ed. 1793), 139.

41. Sir Joseph Sydney Yorke (1768–1831) was a naval commander (admiral and lord of the Admiralty) and member for Reigate, 1790–1806 and 1818–31.

42. The first part of this quotation is from a passage that contemptuously describes the influx of effeminate Greeks into Rome; the second part is from a passage condemning the corrupt conditions in Rome (see l.118 and ll.50–51, Satire III, of Gifford's translation, as in note 15 above).

43. From chapter 1 of *The Compleat Angler* (first published 1653). "Venator" has suggested that anglers are usually "more patient and more simple men" than "Piscator" appears. "Piscator" replies that an-

glers are patient and simple in the best, old-fashioned sense: "if you mean such simple men as lived in those times when there were fewer Lawyers?"

44. *The Praise of Folly* (1511) by Erasmus was a satire suggested by Thomas More and principally directed against theologians and church dignitaries.

45. *Gaudentio Di Lucca. The Memoirs of Sig^r Gaudentio Di Lucca: taken from his confession and examination before the Fathers of the Inquisition at Bologna in Italy* (London: T. Cooper, 1737). Translated from Italian by E. T. Gent. The *NUC-pre 1956* notes "rather written originally in English by S. Berington." It was reprinted many times in the remaining years of the eighteenth century.

46. Chapters 11–15 of *Gargantua* (1534) by Rabelais attack lawyers and the legal profession.

47. *White*: Gilbert White (1720–93), a naturalist whose *Natural History and Antiquities of Selborne* (1789) has long been an English classic. *Letters from Bodleian Library: Letters written by eminent persons in the seventeenth and eighteenth centuries . . .* , 2 vols. (London: Longman, 1813).

48. *Amoretti* 41.10.

49. *Pierce Egan* (1772–1849): author of *Life in London,* a very successful monthly that began in 1820. Illustrated by George and Robert Cruikshank, it describes the activities of a man-about-town and introduces many slang phrases. George describes the illustration as follows: "The head of the Duke of Clarence is supported on a broken anchor round which twines a serpent inscribed *Evil be to him who thinks evil;* from its mouth issue clouds of smoke" (*Catalogue,* 10:208). The Duke of Clarence (1765–1837) was put into the navy as a boy, and the Prince Regent made him admiral of the fleet in 1811. He succeeded his brother as William IV in 1830 and died seven years later.

50. Cowper's *Expostulation* 164 and *Conversation* 141–42.

51. Daniel Pell, *An improvement of the sea, upon the nine nautical verses in the 107 Psalm. . . .* (London: L. Chapman, 1659).

52. *Cadge* is a pun on Kedge, the third size of anchor (the Duke of Clarence was the third brother in the royal family) and the smallest on a ship. All the brothers, in Hone's view, were drags on the ship of state. *Remora* is a leech. Clarence was £56,000 in debt when he began a protracted search for a rich wife, eventually marrying the German Princess Adelaide in 1818.

53. *The Tempest* 2.2.24–31; 2.2.91–92; 5.1.291; 4.1.191–92.

54. *Paradise Lost* 7.388. In the illustration the new king, George IV, emerges from "*stagnant* waters" looking forward to the benefits of his new status as monarch.

55. *libellula:* genus of neuropterous insects (e.g., dragon-fly).

56. *an useless generation:* possibly an echo of the prophetic condemnations in Luke, Mark, and Matthew when Christ describes the unresponsive people variously as "faithless and perverse generation" (Luke 9:41), "evil generation" (Luke 11:29), a "generation of vipers" (Luke 3:7), "adulterous and sinful generation" (Mark 8:38), or "wicked generation" (Matt. 12:45).

57. See Bacon's essay "Of Seditions and Troubles": "To give moderate Liberty, for Griefes, and *Discontentments* to evaporate, (so he that turneth the Humors backe; and maketh the Wound bleed inwards), endangereth maligne Ulcers and pernicious Impostumations." In *The Essayes,* ed. Michael Kiernan (Cambridge, Mass.: Harvard University Press, 1985), 48. The remedies for sedition in the body politic include removing want and poverty, developing good policy, and making some political concessions. George (*Catalogue,* 10:209) describes the illustration as follows: "The head of Castlereagh . . . rests on a dagger, whose hilt forms his extended arms, the blade, dripping blood, his body. On the r. hand is a scourge, in the l. a bleeding shamrock."

58. Cowper, *Table Talk* 476–77.

59. *Character of the Murderer of the Marrs:* A Mr. Marr, his wife, and infant son were murdered and disfigured at their home in London on 7 December 1811, apparently by robbers. This unsolved crime resulted in numerous pamphlets, lurid accounts, sermons, and elegies.

60. "Letter to [John Murray], Esquire, on The Rev. W. L. Bowles's Strictures on the Life and Writings of Pope" (published March 1821). See Lord Byron, *Selected Prose,* ed. Peter Gunn (Harmondsworth, Middlesex: Penguin, 1972), 392.

61. *Woodward:* John Woodward (1665–1728), English physician and geologist who recognized the existence of various strata in the earth's crust. The first result of his interest in fossils was *An essay toward a Natural History of the Earth* (1695), but Hone's reference is probably to either *Fossils of all kinds, digested into a method . . .* (1728) or *An attempt towards a natural history of the fossils of England . . .* (2 vols., 1728–29).

62. Daniel Defoe (1660–1731) published *Colonel Jack* in 1722.

The hero's extraordinary adventures—he is abandoned by his parents, enlists in the army, deserts, is kidnapped and sold to a planter in Virginia, becomes a planter and acquires wealth—end in prosperity and repentance. The quotation occurs in the second to last paragraph of the novel as he reflects on his life and experiences a strong sense of penitence. That he had temporarily been a pickpocket when young picks up the reference in the quotation from Byron earlier on the same page.

63. *Richard III* 5.3.247. George (*Catalogue*, 10:209) describes the illustration as follows: "A dog with spiked collar tears at the fettered and prostrate Erin, her broken harp and cap of Liberty beside her. A shackle is inscribed *Union*. In the background are a wheel (instrument of torture), two gibbets, and a man tied to a triangle." The Act of Union (1801) forcibly united the parliaments of Great Britain and Ireland. It was imposed on the reluctant Irish as a result of the 1798 rebellion and the threat of French invasion.

64. *Ban Dog:* fierce mastiff, according to the *Dictionary of the Vulgar Tongue* (1811).

65. *Edwards:* Bryan Edwards (1743–1800), English historian, traveller, and politician whose chief work was *The History of the British Colonies in the West Indies* (1793). *Rainsford:* Marcus Rainsford (1750–c.1805), author and soldier who—after being arrested, condemned to death, but then reprieved and set free—published *A Memoir of Transactions that took place in St. Domingo in the Spring of 1799* (1802). *Scott:* John Scott (1774–1827), well-known engraver of animals, as in *The Sportsman's Repository; comprising a series of . . . engravings representing the horse and the dog in all their varieties* (1820).

66. *Romeo and Juliet* 5.1.37; *The Taming of the Shrew* 4.1.26. In the illustration Sidmouth's head "rests on a clysterpipe, whose inflated bag forms his body" (George, *Catalogue*, 10:209). A clysterpipe is an instrument for administering an enema. The tag attached to his hair reads, "When taken To Be well Shaken."

67. Cowper, *The Task* 5.268.

68. *Swift: Memoirs of P. P., Clerk of this Parish,* included in *The Works of Jonathan Swift,* ed. Thomas Roscoe (1850) but not in the modern edition of Davis and Ehrenpreis (Oxford: Blackwell, 1965–68). The passage reads as follows: "Shoes, saith he, did I make (and, if entreated mend) with good approbation; faces also did I shave, and I clipped the hair. Chirurgery I also practised in the worming of dogs; but to bleed adventured I not, except the poor."

69. From Canning's parody of a speech (beginning "My name is Norval: on the Grampian hills / My father feeds his flocks") in *Douglas* (2.1.44–75), a play (1756) by John Home (1722–1808). The attack on Sidmouth in this parody was used to embarrass Canning when Hone reprinted it in 1820 together with *The Man in the Moon*. The speech from *Douglas* was still recognizable to theatre audiences in 1899 when the first line was quoted in G. B. Shaw's *You Never Can Tell.*

70. Untraced.

71. Hazlitt's Essay XV, "On Paradox and Common-place" in which he attacks Canning's opposition to change. See P. P. Howe, ed., *The Complete Works of William Hazlitt,* 21 vols. (London: J. M. Dent, 1932) 8:153.

72. John Lilburne (1614?–57) was tried first in 1637 for printing and circulating unlicensed books, including John Bastwick's *Litany* (a satire against the ecclesiastical authorities). A difficult, uncompromising man continually entangled in political and legal quarrels, Lilburne was tried in 1649 for sedition; on that occasion he refused to plead, challenged the court's authority, and was acquitted by the jury. Hone quotes from a pamphlet Bastwick wrote in 1645 when the two men were on different sides *(A Just Defence . . . against the Calumnies of John Lilburne).* However, as Pauline Gregg observes, "Lilburne could not be dismissed as easily as that. . . ." See *Free-Born John: A Biography of John Lilburne* (London: George G. Harrap, 1961), 125.

73. *The Merry Wives of Windsor* 3.1.102–3; *Romeo and Juliet* 5.1.57.

74. *Dejection:* medical term for fecal discharge.

75. See p. 395 in Byron's *Selected Prose* (note 60 above).

76. *Caetera desunt:* the rest is missing.

77. *Elias Ashmole* (1617–92): antiquarian and astrologer who, in 1682, presented his collection of curiosities to Oxford, founding the Ashmolean Museum. His *Memoirs* (1774) were published as a diary in 1817, and Hone quotes extracts from different days.

78. *Twelfth Night* 5.1.343–44. Both *geck* and *gull* mean fool or dupe. George describes the illustration as follows: "A quasi-gull with bag-like body and bag-wig for tail. He is a stupid placeman and borough-member" *(Catalogue,* 10:209).

79. *Booby:* a dunce and a species of gannet (large sea fowl resembling a goose).

80. *Noddy:* nitwit.

81. *Twopenny Flat:* worthless simpleton.

82. James Smith, "The Theatre by Rev. G. C." (George Crabbe), ll.2–4, in *Rejected Addresses* (1812). "Cobb" has been substituted for the lamplighter because a cobbler is described as working in his stall by candlelight, but also because "cobb" is yet another pun on a species of gull (the Greater Black-backed Gull).

83. *Mother Carey's Chickens:* sailors' name for the Stormy Petrel, a sea-bird.

84. *Martyn:* Thomas Martyn (1735–1825), author of *Elements of Natural History* (Cambridge, 1775). *Bewick*: Thomas Bewick (1753–1828), wood engraver whose publications included *History of Quadrupeds* (1790) and *History of British Birds* (1797 and 1804).

85. "Epistle to Dr. Arbuthnot," l.92. "Stoddart, 'Dr. Slop,' empties a huge *Slop Pail* into a large overturned crown; a (tricolour) cockade floats in the contents" (George, *Catalogue*, 10:209). George identifies the pail as the *New Times*.

86. *kicked down:* sold out.

87. *The Jacobite Relics of Scotland; being the Songs, Airs, and Legends of the Adherents to the House of Stuart,* ed. James Hogg (Edinburgh: Blackwood, 1819) was a project, Hogg notes in his introduction, encouraged by "the royal family" (x). Hone parodies the second to last verse paragraph of Hogg's fifty-six-line preface praising the Stuarts and their cause—for Hone a retrograde cause. Here are Hogg's lines:

Ah! Wo to the nation, its honours fall low,
When mendicant meddlers dare Majesty brow,
And turn up the snout of derision and scorn
At those who to honour or titles are born!
All beggarly power is the bane of mankind:
'It leads to bewilder, and dazzles to blind.'

88. The boots represent George IV. *welted:* bound with strips of leather. *vamped:* "to put new feet to old boots" (*Dictionary of the Vulgar Tongue,* 1811), i.e., re-sole.

89. Hone disparages Southey, Poet Laureate, for his loyalist poems and pictures him as simply a boy who shines the boots of the establishment.

90. See *Othello* 3.3.23: "I'll watch him tame." "A giant eye, the pupil containing a tiny printing-press . . . looks down upon characters represented in other illustrations of the satire, who lie in a confused heap, revengeful or despairing, while the 'Great Boots,' representing

George IV . . . are in wild flight to the l. Wellington with his sword, and Castlereagh with dagger and scourge, attempt retaliation. The others are the Duke of York, Eldon, Liverpool, Sidmouth, the Archbishop, the Law Officers, and Clarence" (George, *Catalogue*, 10:209).

91. This attack on legitimacy occurs in Hazlitt's scathing review of Southey's *Carmen Nuptiale*, "The Lay of the Laureate," first published on 7 July 1816 in the *Examiner* (see Howe, *Complete Works*, 7:93). Typical of Hazlitt's tone is the following: "The poetry of the Lay is beneath criticism . . . a Methodist sermon turned into doggrel [*sic*] verse."

92. *ferruginous:* ironlike.

93. From The Litany, *Book of Common Prayer.*

94. Carol von Linne (1707–78): see note 20 above. Leopold Gmelin (1788–1853). *Art. Boa Constrictor* is apparently part of the later volumes (9–14) of Shaw's *General Zoology* (see note 37 above), as continued by J. F. Stephens.

95. John Macleod (1777?–1820), a naval surgeon appointed in 1815 to the frigate *Alceste* going to China. The ship was wrecked in 1817. En route home he wrote *Narrative of a Voyage in His Majesty's late Ship Alceste to the Yellow Sea . . .* (1817).

96. *cranches:* crunches cruelly.

97. See Rev. 13:1 and 17:3.

98. This passage from Southey's *Joan of Arc* (published 1796) was suppressed in the collected works (1840). The opening two lines in Hone's rendering actually appear at the end of the passage:

"Th' imperishable seed," soon to become
That Tree, beneath whose vast and mighty shade
The sons of men shall pitch their tents in peace,
And in the unity of love preserve
The bond of love.

In the 1796 edition, the section opens with Southey's prophetic glance forward: "And one day doomed to know the damning guilt / Of Brissot. . . ." See 3.71–80. *Brissot:* Jacques Pierre Brissot (1754–93), a Girondist (moderate republican), was guillotined during the Reign of Terror. *Roland:* Madame Roland (1754–93), supporter of the Girondin Party, is supposed to have said on the scaffold, "O liberty, what crimes are committed in thy name."

99. The opening phrase is from Letter VII, the rest from Letter IV of Moore's *The Fudge Family in Paris* (1818). The word "Beast" has been substituted by Hone for the word "flock." George describes the

vampire as a "scaly serpentine monster with huge fanged jaw, a crown of spikes, webbed wings, barbed tail, and spouting like a whale," as it "swallows a heap of tiny men and women, and crushes others." It satirizes "autocratic monarchy and the Holy Alliance" (*Catalogue,* 10:209).

100. *Philostratus:* the name of three or four sophists of the Roman imperial period, the most likely reference being to Philostratus "the Athenian," author of *Life of Apollonius Tyana* and *Lives of the Sophists.*

NOTES TO *THE EVERY-DAY BOOK*

1. Probably Hone's poetry. The verses that close this article are attributed to Hone by John Wardroper, ed. *The World of William Hone* (London: Shelfmark Books, 1997), 171.

2. *Sir Walter Raleigh* (1552?–1618): Elizabethan soldier, explorer, courtier, and man of letters.

3. Geoffrey Crayon was the pen name of a character invented by American writer Washington Irving (1783–1859) in "The Poor Devil Author," part 2 of *Tales of a Traveller,* composed in Paris and published in 1824.

4. See chapter 24 of Washington Irving, *Life of Oliver Goldsmith* (1849): "His summer retreat for the present year, 1768, was a little cottage with a garden, pleasantly situated about eight miles from town on the Edgware road . . . Much of *[The Deserted Village]* we are told, was composed this summer, in the course of solitary strolls about the green lanes and beautifully rural scenes of the neighborhood."

5. *Vattell:* Emmerich de Vattell (1714–67), whose *The Law of Nations* (1758) modernized the law of nations and became recognized as a classic work. *Martens:* Gereng Friedrich von Martens (1756–1821), German jurist and diplomatist.

6. *Behnes:* William Behnes (1795–1864), sculptor whose best known bust is of Sir Francis Chantrey. Although appointed Sculptor in Ordinary to Victoria, he died in poverty.

7. *Lord Northampton:* Spencer Joshua Alwyne Compton, second Marquis of Northampton (1790–1851). Resided for several years in Italy. Unlike all his high Tory family, he was a political independent, supported criminal law reform and the abolition of slavery, had strong literary and scientific interests, and wrote poetry.

8. Perhaps a mélange of "Far from the madding crowd's ignoble strife" (Gray, *Elegy*, 1.19); "the busy hum of men" (Milton, *L'Allegro*, 1.148); and Felicia Dorothea Hemans (1793–1835), "In the busy haunts of men" ("Tale of the Secret Tribunal," part 1, 1.203).

9. *Thomas Cromwell* (1485?–1540): secretary to Henry VIII and the king's principal adviser and agent. After falling from favor, he was beheaded (with exceptional clumsiness) on 28 July 1540. Canonbury Tower was built c.1530 as a country house of the priors of St. Bartholomew's. Home to Sir John Spencer, lord mayor of London 1594–95, the buildings were let as lodgings in the eighteenth century. Hone's friend Charles Lamb was fond of exploring the tower (*Muirhead's London,* ed. Findley Muirhead [London: Macmillan, 1927], 276–77).

10. John Nelson, *The history and antiquities of the parish of Islington* (London: J. Nichols and Son, 1811).

11. *Blackheath hill:* Blackheath is a common of 267 acres south of Greenwich Park. Once the haunt of highwaymen (and the gathering place of Wat Tyler's rebels in 1381 and of Jack Cade's in 1450), it was also the site of Blackheath Golf Club (founded 1608), the first in the world.

12. *Princess Sophia of Gloucester* (1773–1844): unmarried sister of Prince William, Duke of Gloucester (1776–1854), "Silly Billy." When the Duke of Clarence (later William IV) was searching for a wife, he turned his attention to Sophia but "that match was ruled out" (Hibbert, *George IV: Regent and King, 1811–1830*, 113).

13. *Benvenuto Cellini* (1500–1571): Italian sculptor and goldsmith. The quotation is untraced.

14. *Sot's hole:* the resort of drinkers (an alehouse). *corporal refection:* bodily refreshment by food and drink. *Lord Chesterfield:* Philip Dormer Stanhope, fourth Earl of Chesterfield (1694–1773), is best known for *Letters to His Son* and *Letters to His Godson,* practical advice for getting on in the world.

15. St. Anne's, a parish church designed by Nicholas Hawksmoor, pupil of Christopher Wren. Near the East London docks, Limehouse was a prosperous middle-class community in the first half of the nineteenth century.

16. *Lollard:* in England the term applied to fourteenth-century disciples of John Wycliffe (c.1330–84) who opposed worldliness and foreign domination of the church as well as many of the Catholic ac-

coutrements (e.g., pilgrimages, crosses, priestly confession). The Lollard power was broken by persecution after Parliament in 1401 passed the first English act for burning heretics. *Thomas Delaune* (d. 1685), author of *Plea for the Non conformists,* was arrested for libel and imprisoned at Newgate. Found guilty and unable to pay the fine, he remained (now with wife and children) in Newgate. The entire family died within fifteen months. In the preface to a later edition of the *Plea,* Defoe criticizes the parsimony of the dissenters. *Prynne:* William Prynne (1600–1669) was an ardent Puritan who attacked Archbishop Laud's ceremonialism. In 1634 he was sentenced to the pillory and having his ears cut off; he was freed from prison in 1640. *Laud:* William Laud (1573–1645), archbishop of Canterbury and chief adviser to Charles I. After the Puritans gained control of Parliament, he was imprisoned and later beheaded in January 1645.

17. *Angelica:* Guido Di Pietro (called Fra) Angelico (1387–1455), Italian painter subsequently rediscovered by the Pre-Raphaelites in mid nineteenth-century England.

18. *G. R.:* Georgius Rex (King George).

19. *Der Freischütz:* "The Marksman," an opera by Carl Maria von Weber (1786–1826) first produced in London at the Lyceum on 22 July 1824.

20. Izaak Walton (1593–1683) wrote three versions of *The Compleat Angler* (1653, 1655, and 1676), each an expansion of the one before.

21. From Thomas Gray (1716–71), "Elegy Written in a Country Churchyard" (1750), l.32.

22. "An Act for the following of Hue and Cry" was passed in the Fifth Parliament of Elizabeth I, 1584–85, and was directed against local authorities who were negligent in prosecuting thieves.

23. 1 Kings 19:22. This poem is attributed to Hone by John Wardroper, *The World of William Hone,* 237.

24. Hone's friendship with Charles Lamb (1775–1834) seems to have begun after Hone sent Lamb a copy of *Ancient Mysteries* in 1823. Lamb later helped Hone with advice and contributions when *The Every-Day Book* began. Lamb was also among the friends who tried to help Hone into the coffeehouse business and, when that did not prosper, with a public subscription which did not raise enough money (E. V. Lucas, ed., *Letters of Charles Lamb* [London: Methuen, 1921] 2:152, 224).

25. *Quatorzains* (not quatorzians) are poems of fourteen lines.

26. Cf. Cowper, *The Task* 3.108.

27. *As You Like It* 2.1.17.

28. St. Dunstan's Church in Fleet Street dates from the twelfth century. According to legend, the saint held the devil captive with red-hot pincers applied to his nose.

29. *Baptiste:* John Gaspars Baptist (d. 1691), artist who worked for Sir Godfrey Kneller (1646–1723) and painted a portrait of Charles II. His correct name was apparently Jean-Baptiste Gaspars.

30. Cf. Matt. 6:28–29.

31. A discussion of England's patron saint, St. George, in Russian history then follows.

32. George Cruikshank (1792–1878), whose *Phrenological Illustrations* (1826) illustrates the thirty-three human characteristics phrenologists believed they could deduce from examining the surface of the cranium.

33. *praetorium:* headquarters of the commanding general (or the governor of a Roman province). *Boadicea:* British warrior queen in first century A.D. In the absence of the provincial governor Suetonius Paulinus, she led a revolt against Rome, capturing Londinium (London) and Verulamium (St. Alban's). Suetonius later defeated the Britons, and Boadicea (or Boudicca) died. The tradition is that she took poison to avoid capture and slavery in Rome. Her burial place is unknown; one candidate is Platform 8 of King's Cross railway station (see Antonia Fraser, *Boadicea's Chariot* [London: Weidenfeld and Nicolson, 1988], 100).

34. William Huntingdon, S. S. (1745–1813): eccentric preacher. "After acquiring the barest rudiments of knowledge at the Cranbrook grammar school, he went into service as an errand-boy, and was afterwards successively gentleman's servant, gunmaker's apprentice, sawyer's pitman, coachman, hearse-driver, tramp, gardener, coalheaver, and popular preacher" *(D.N.B.).* As a young man he had impregnated a woman and abandoned her and the child. Following his conversion (S. S. means "sinner saved") he went to London in 1782 and later built Providence Chapel in Titchfield Street, Oxford Market. After it burned down in 1810, New Providence Chapel was erected in Gray's Inn Lane and Huntingdon preached there until his death in 1813.

35. *pop:* any effervescing beverage such as ginger-beer (called pop because of the sound made when the cork is drawn from the bottle).

36. *skittle-playing:* ninepins.

37. *brick clamps:* compact stacks for burning.

NOTES TO *THE TABLE BOOK*

These selections are reprinted from *The Table Book* (1827; reprint, London: William Tegg and Co., 1878): "My Table Book" (2, 14), "The Newsman" (31–34), and "West Wickham Church" (406–7).

1. *Merchant of Venice* 1.1.116.

2. An illustration of hyperbole in Alexander Pope, *Martin Scriblerus . . . or, of the Art of Sinking in Poetry* in *The Prose Works of Alexander Pope,* ed. Rosemary Cowler (Oxford: Blackwell, 1986), vol. 2, *The Major Works,* 1725–1744, ch. 11, p. 211: "Ye Gods! annihilate but Space and Time / And make two lovers happy."

3. *Richard III* 4.2.115.

4. *Antony and Cleopatra* 2.5.67.

5. The above extracts from Cowper's *The Task* are from Book 4 as follows: 50–57, 16–17, 30–33, 73–97, 1–15, and 36–41.

6. *Merchant of Venice* 3.1.61.

7. *Gilbert West* (1703–56): *Observations on the history and evidences of the resurrection of Jesus Christ* (1747) and *Odes of Pindar* (1749).

8. *Lord Lyttelton:* George Lyttelton, first Baron Lyttelton (1709–73) was connected by marriage to William Pitt, first Earl of Chatham (1708–78), and with him formed a small, powerful party first known as the "Cobhamites" and later the "cousinhood." Lyttelton's *Observations on the conversion and apostleship of St. Paul* (1747) was reprinted into the nineteenth century.

9. *Paley:* William Paley (1743–1805), author of *"Horae Paulina": or, The truth of the Scripture history of St. Paul evinced* (1790) and *Evidences of Christianity* (1794).

10. Decimus Magnus Ausonius (c.310–c.395 A.D.).

11. *Edward Hasted* (1732–1812): *The history and topographical survey of the county of Kent,* 4 vols. (Canterbury: Simmons and Kirkby, 1778–99).

12. *lich-gate:* roofed gate in a churchyard under which a bier rests during the initial part of the burial service.

13. *trivet:* a tripod with short legs (e.g., to hold a kettle near a fire).

14. Hone's eldest son, William, died in October 1827, though the parents did not find out from the Navy until December. See the letter to John Childs, quoted in Hackwood, *William Hone,* 260–61.

NOTES TO *THE YEAR BOOK*

1. Cf. William Wordsworth, *The Excursion* (1850), 4.274–75.

2. Hone here prints extracts from *The Excursion* (1850) 4.1204–17, 4.1230–75.

3. Not exactly what Alfred wrote in his will: "The councillors of the West Saxons pronounced it right for me that I could leave them free or servile, whichever I should choose. But I desire for the love of God and the needs of my soul that they be entitled to their freedom and their free choice." See *Alfred the Great: Asser's 'Life of King Alfred' and other contemporary sources,* trans. Simon Keynes and Michael Lapidge (Harmondsworth, Middlesex: Penguin, 1983), 678.

4. Probably not "one of his laws," but an extract from the long preface, in which Alfred explains that his list of "dooms" is based on the Bible, including the Ten Commandments, and the already established (but not codified) laws of Mercia, Kent, and Wessex.

5. Ps. 111:10.

6. *Upas-heap:* the Upas is a poisonous Japanese tree believed to destroy all animal life nearby, a metaphor for the destructive effects of materialism on English society.

7. Here Hone prints an extract from *The Excursion* 4.611–30.

8. *The Heart of Midlothian* was published in 1818 as the second series of "Tales of My Landlord."

9. From John Clare, "A Cottage Evening" (ll.231–67), the second part of *January* in *The Shepherd's Calendar* (1827). Hone omits ll.249–50.

10. Coleridge, "The Rime of the Ancient Mariner," l.372.

11. This poem was composed in 1796, published in 1797 (in Coleridge's *Poems*), and included in *Works of Charles Lamb* (1818).

12. *Thyrsus:* staff or spear tipped with an ornament, twined with ivy and borne by Bacchus.

13. *Eblis:* in Moslem demonology, the chief of the jinns (an order of spirits lower than angels); Satan.

NOTES TO *LETTERS*

To John Hunt: British Library [Add. MS. 38108, f. 189]

1. *John Hunt:* see below note 17.

2. *Thieves' Vinegar:* an infusion of herbs and vinegar to combat the plague.

3. *Fenning:* Elizabeth (elsewhere referred to as Eliza) Fenning (1792–1815) was a domestic servant and cook to the family of Orlibar Turner. She was tried and executed for attempting to poison the family by lacing dumplings with arsenic. The evidence against her was circumstantial, and there was much public sentiment for her innocence. Hone capitalized on the situation and issued several publications related to the case.

To Francis Place: British Library [Add. MS. 37949, f. 46]

4. *Francis Place* (1771–1854): radical reformer and political organizer. Place's large collection of documents in the British Library is a principal resource in the study of early nineteenth-century radicalism.

5. *T. J. Wooler* (1786–1853): editor of the *Black Dwarf,* a radical weekly. An article in the tenth number, "Past, Present and Future," led to two prosecutions for libel. See note 61 to the *Second Trial.*

To Sir Samuel Shepherd: British Library [Add. MS. 40120, f. 73]

6. *Sir Samuel Shepherd* (1760–1840): solicitor-general (1813), attorney-general (1817), and M.P. for Dorchester (1813–19). He prosecuted James Watson (1766–1838) for high treason in 1817, and in 1818 successfully prosecuted Richard Carlile (1790–1843) for reprinting Paine's *Age of Reason* (1818). Deafness prevented his accepting further judicial appointments. This letter to Shepherd is in draft form and may never have been sent.

To William Upcott: John Rylands University Library of Manchester [MS. 725, vol. 4]

7. *William Upcott* (1779–1845): an antiquarian and autograph collector who suggested the founding of the Guildhall Library.

To John Childs: British Library [Add. MS. 40120, f. 109]

8. *John Childs* (1783–1853): printer at Bungay from 1806 to his death, a staunch dissenter, and a pioneer in the movement to provide good literature cheaply to the mass public.

9. *Alderman in chains:* "A roasted turkey garnished with sausages; the latter are supposed to represent the gold chain worn by those magistrates" (*Dictionary of the Vulgar Tongue*, 1811).

To Matthew Hill: Pembroke College, Oxford [63/12/3/89]
10. *Matthew Davenport Hill* (1763–1851) defended Richard Carlile on the charge of selling a libel (1820), was a leading counsellor for the Nottingham rioters (1831), and was M.P. for Hull (1832–35).
11. *powder of projection:* in alchemy, the casting of the powder of the philosopher's stone would transmute base metals into gold. Hone has overdosed on this nonexistent medicine for poverty.

To John Childs: British Library [Add. MS. 40120, f. 150]
12. *'pint stoup':* beaker or tankard containing one pint (in quotation marks because archaic and a convivial-sounding phrase).
13. *groat:* silver coin worth four pennies (issued 1351 to 1662).
14. Thomas Gray, *The Bard* 3.1.
15. *jugged:* boiled or stewed, originally in a jug or jar, almost always applied to hare, occasionally to rabbits.
16. *vitrifies:* hardens into glass.

To Francis Place: British Library [Add. MS. 37949, f. 92]
17. *John Hunt* (1775–1848): elder brother of Leigh, he was tried in King's Bench on 21 February 1821 for a libel on the House of Commons regarding the Queen Caroline affair. In preparing his defense, Hunt wrote Hone on 19 December 1820, to thank him for books and to request any additional help and advice Hone could offer. Hunt was found guilty and sentenced to a year in prison. In March 1821, Hone published *Report of the Trial of the King v. John Hunt . . .* with Hunt's speeches recorded verbatim. Hunt (together with his brother) had earlier been fined and imprisoned for two years (1813–14) for libelling the Prince Regent, and in 1822 he was fined for seditious libel on the late George III by virtue of being the publisher of Byron's *Vision of Judgment*. Byron's executors intervened and paid the fine of one hundred pounds.

To John Childs: British Library [Add. MS. 41071, f. 3]
18. *The Right Divine of Kings to Govern Wrong: Dedicated to the Holy Alliance* (1821) is a revised version of Daniel Defoe's satiric *Jure Divino*

(1706). *The Spirit of Despotism: Dedicated to Lord Castlereagh* (1821) is a shortened version of the text by Vicesimus Knox originally published in 1795. See Bowden, "Hone's Political Journalism," 2:366–77.

19. *stultus:* stupid man.

To Mrs. Cruikshank: Berg Collection of English and American Literature, The New York Public Library, Astor, Lenox and Tilden Foundations

20. Mary Cruikshank is characterized by Robert Patten as "strong willed, disciplined, thrifty, and hot tempered" (*Cruikshank's Life*, 23). She was a pious Christian who endured her husband Isaac's drinking and his lively companions. Mary's relationship with her son George was "severely strained" by 1819, as he also drank freely and ran up debts (Patten, *Cruikshank's Life*, 212).

To Mr. Rhodes: Bath Central Library [AL 1948]

21. *watergruel:* a thin gruel made with meal and water instead of milk; anything insipid or poverty-stricken.

22. *St. Dunstan* (924 or 925–988): English archbishop, chief minister, and trusted advisor of King Edgar.

23. *Tarquin* (d. 498 B.C.): the seventh and last king of Rome, a murderous despot. In legend, he repeatedly refused to buy the Sibylline books (which contained details of ceremonies to avert catastrophes). After six of the nine books had been burned by the Cumean Sybil, Tarquin capitulated and agreed to the demanded price. He is therefore synonymous with someone who has no understanding of the value of books.

To Walter Wilson: National Library of Scotland [MS. 1706, f. 57]

24. *Walter Wilson* (1781–1847): initially a bookseller, he went on to write a life of Defoe and four volumes of *The History and antiquities of Dissenting churches and Meeting Houses in London, Westminster, and Southwark* (1808–14). He bequeathed his manuscript collection on the history of dissent to Dr. Williams's Library (see below, note 31).

25. *Macbeth* 5.3.22–23.

26. Benjamin Franklin, *Poor Richard's Almanac* (June 1746).

27. *Ancient Mysteries Described, especially the English Miracle Plays, including Notices of Ecclesiastical Shows, Festivals of Fools and Asses, etc.* was published in May 1823.

28. Cf. Heb. 1:3: "by the word of his power."

29. Not traced. Hone uses the same quotation in a letter to Francis Jeffrey of 9 December 1823 [British Library, Add. MS. 40120, f. 203].

30. Not traced.

31. *Sion College Library:* founded in 1632, Sion College was a guild for the clergy of London and the suburbs, with an almshouse for ten poor men and ten women. The mainly theological library was added later. *Dr. Williams's Library* was founded in 1720 in Cripplegate under the will of Dr. Daniel Williams (c. 1643–1716); it was originally restricted to dissenters (in 1841 it was opened to everyone).

32. G. Chalmers published the first biography of Defoe in 1785. Wilson's *Memoirs of the Life and Times of Daniel Defoe* came out in three volumes in 1830.

33. *The Review*: started in 1704 by Defoe, who wrote most of it himself, it came out three times weekly until 1713.

To Francis Place: British Library [Add. MS 37949, f. 144]

34. *Cholera-morbus*: the disease cholera (*morbus*: Latin for disease).

35. *Another Article for the 'Quarterly Review'* (1824): Hone's spirited answer to a reviewer's response (August 1824) to his *Aspersions Answered: An Explanatory Statement addressed to the Public at large* . . . (1824), itself a belated reply to a critical attack in the *Quarterly* (October 1821) on Hone's *The Apocryphal New Testament* (1820).

36. *James Mill* (1773–1836): Utilitarian philosopher, born near Montrose in Scotland, moved to London in 1802.

37. *Morning Chronicle:* Whig journal founded by William Woodfall (1746–1803) in 1769. Contributors included James and J. S. Mill and Charles Dickens. The editor at this time (1824) was John Black (1783–1855).

To James Montgomery: Guildhall Library, London [MS. 14592]

38. *James Montgomery* (1771–1854): philanthropic and anti-slavery poet. His compilation, *The Chimney Sweepers' Friend and Climbing Boys' Album,* was published in 1824. See "Chimney Sweepers on Mayday" in *The Every-Day Book* (1826), volume 1 for May 1.

To Robert Childs: British Library [Add. MS. 40856, f. 19]

39. *Robert Childs* (d. 1837): partner to his brother John in a printing business. He committed suicide by jumping out of an upper window of his house in Bungay.

40. See "Hannah Want" in *The Every-Day Book* (1826), volume 1 for October 2.

41. *amativeness:* propensity to love. *PhiloproJenny:* (philoprogeny) fondness for having children. *Jackeytiveness*: meaning she liked having both daughters (Jennies) and sons (Jackeys), combined into one compound word ending in the typically phrenological "-tiveness."

42. See "Cottage formerly in Hagbush-lane" in *The Every-Day Book* (1826), volume 1 for June 26, and included in our selection above.

43. By the Congress of Vienna (1815) Poland was divided between Prussia, Austria, and Russia. A military revolt in 1830 led to a war in 1831 that was suppressed by Russia, at which time Poland was reduced to a province of Russia.

To John Childs: British Library [Add. MS. 40856, f. 25]

44. Hone was confined to the King's Bench in April 1826. He was released in September 1828, bankrupt. Six months later his publishers, Hunt and Clarke, also went bankrupt.

To Robert Southey: National Library of Scotland [MS. 2528, f. 71]

45. *Robert Southey* (1774–1843): the poet laureate and Hone put aside past bitterness and exchanged a number of friendly letters. Lamb had encouraged this reconciliation. (See Hackwood, *William Hone,* 276–77.) In the reply to this letter, Southey sympathizes with Hone's troubles: "It is the want of charity which makes men unjust in their judgements of each other." He hopes Hone can "resume a pen which has of late years been so meritoriously employed" [British Library, Add. MS. 40120, f. 345].

46. Southey's biography of Bunyan appeared in an edition of *The Pilgrim's Progress* published by John Murray in 1830.

47. With Hone's financial problems persisting, some of his friends tried to set him up as the keeper of a coffeehouse (known as the Grasshopper Hotel) in Gracechurch Street. A subsequent public appeal helped the Hone family for a few years. (See Hackwood, *William Hone,* 276, 296–97.)

To Walter Wilson: Bodleian Library, Oxford [MS. Montagu d. 21, f. 140]

48. Hazlitt's review of Wilson's biography of Defoe was published in *Edinburgh Review* 50 (1830) and is reprinted in Hazlitt's *Complete Works,* ed. P. P. Howe, 16:364–93.

49. *Tantalus:* mythical Phrygian king condemned in the after life to stand up to his chin in water which receded when he tried to drink and under branches of fruit which drew back when he tried to eat.

50. *Joseph Birch* (1755–1833): Whig M.P. for Nottingham (1802–16, 1818–30) and Ludgershall (1812–18), he married the daughter of Benjamin Heywood (1793–1865), Liverpool banker interested in the welfare and education of the working classes; *Charles Blundell* (d. 1837): son of Henry Blundell (1724–1810), art collector; *Arthur Heywood:* Heywood's Bank was located on Bold Street, Liverpool; *William Rathbone* (1787–1868): advocate of parliamentary and municipal reform and mayor of Liverpool in 1837; *Rev. William Shepherd*: Unitarian minister and one of the principal writers for the Whigs of witty verses during parliamentary elections; *Earl of Sefton:* William Philip Molyneux (1772–1838), a respected liberal in politics and made a peer in 1831; *Mr. Behnes:* William Behnes (d. 1864) whose reputation as a sculptor was highest between 1820 and 1840, when he executed several important public works (e.g. a bust of Disraeli). He died a bankrupt; *T. M. Alsager* (1779–1846): musician and music critic who wrote for the *Times; Joseph Parkes* (1796–1865): Birmingham solicitor who became politically active at the introduction of the Reform Bill. He was in correspondence with London radicals like Francis Place and was, for a time, preparing for an armed rebellion. He drafted resolutions for the Birmingham Political Union and became a member in 1832. Latterly, he was successful as a parliamentary solicitor and his home was a meeting place for Whig parliamentarians.

To Francis Place: British Library [Add. MS. 27808, f. 314]

51. *Spence* (1750–1814): bookseller and advocate of a scheme of land nationalization as well as a new phonetic system. In 1775 he published a new alphabet consisting of forty characters, each of which represents a different sound of the voice. The following is a specimen of his mode of spelling: "It ma hile perpleks a karlis redir ov nu Kariktirz, too disifir thi troo sens tharov; tho it shud be eze inuf to no it bi a litil aplikashin and praktis.—Ensiklopedea Britianika." Spence was tried for seditious libel in 1801 and imprisoned for twelve months.

52. *Annals: Full Annals of the Revolution in France* (1830). See Hackwood, *William Hone,* 365.

53. *Newcastle:* Hone sent Place the memoir of Spence in a letter of 18 October 1830; it formed a section of Eneas Mackenzie's *History*

of Newcastle (Newcastle, 1827). Place's unfinished biography of Spence occuoies folios 138 to 330 of Add. MS. 27808 in the British Library.

54. *Entick:* see note 69 to the *Third Trial.*

55. *Cullendered:* with holes like a sieve.

56. *Thomas Hardy* (1752–1832): the radical who helped to found the London Corresponding Society in 1792. He was arrested on 12 May 1794 on a charge of high treason. On 5 November the jury returned a verdict of not guilty, and Hardy's coach was drawn in triumph by the crowd through London's main streets. Hone had joined the London Corresponding Society when he was sixteeen (see Hackwood, *William Hone,* 53–54).

To Robert Southey: British Library [RP5191 (iv)]

57. *Juggernaut:* the statue of the Hindu god Krishna carried in a gigantic car.

58. Eccles. 7.29.

59. In the *Times* for Tuesday, 25 November 1830, is an account of "the petition of the labourers of Ringmer" [in East Sussex] for higher wages to Lord Gage, who was reported to have said "there is no man that would less permit his labourers to be paid in any part by the parish than myself. . . ."

60. *François René, Viscomte de Chateaubriand* (1768–1848): French author who fought for the royalists 1791–92, lived in exile in England until 1800, and later held diplomatic appointments under Louis XVIII.

To Robert Childs: British Library [Add. MS. 40120, f. 353]

61. *craters:* creatures (affecting lower-class speech).

62. *head-hitter:* word play on "editor."

63. *rapper:* door knocker.

64. *"Informer pauper us":* one of a series of legal expressions used here in mock threat. *action in trover:* legal action to recover the value of stolen property. *bill of discovery:* compulsory disclosure of essential evidence. *interlocutory judgement:* provisional or interim judgment. *informer pauper us:* pun on "forma pauperis," a provision enabling a poor person to bring a legal action without payment.

65. *"Come at he":* word play on "committee."

66. George III was born on 4 June 1738.

To Robert Childs: British Library [Add. MS. 40120, f. 355]

67. Robert Mackenzie Beverley published "A Letter to his Grace the Archbishop of York, on the present corrupt state of the Church of England . . ." in 1831. It went through twelve printings in one year and provoked numerous responses. A "Second Letter" appeared in 1832, and in 1833 he turned his attention elsewhere with "A Letter to His Royal Highness the Duke of Gloucester, Chancellor, on the present corrupt state of the University of Cambridge."

68. See 3.10 of Thomas Fuller, *The Holy State* (1642), vol. 2 of *The Holy State and the Profane State* (New York: Columbia University Press, 1838), 174.

To Charles Sturgeon: Bath Central Library [AL 1949]

69. *matrice* (matrix): piece of metal, usually copper, by means of which the face of a type is cast.

To Charles Mott: British Library [Add. MS. 40120, f. 365]

70. *Charles Mott* (d. 1851): assistant poor law commissioner, manager of lunatic asylum at Haydock Lodge, and auditor of the South Lancashire poor law to his death. In 1838 he published "Report from the poor law commissioners relative to statements concerning management of the workhouse at Eye, Suffolk."

71. *Wharncliffe:* James A. S. W. Mackenzie, First Baron Wharncliffe (1776–1845) was a moderate Tory who changed his mind about reform.

72. Riots broke out in Derby on 8 October 1831, the night the Reform Bill was defeated in the House of Lords, and the houses of anti-reformers were attacked. The burning of Nottingham Castle (the property of the reactionary Duke of Newcastle) followed the next day. A new, modified bill was introduced two months later and eventually passed in June 1832.

73. *Mr. Parkes:* see n. 50 above.

74. Richard Guest, *A compendious history of the cotton-manufacture* (Manchester, 1823); John Clare (1793–1864), *Poems, descriptive of Rural Life and Scenery* (1821).

To John Childs: British Library [Add. MS. 40120, f. 369]

75. Both Apollyon and Belial were synonymous with Satan or the devil.

76. A common phrase, conflating such prophetic texts as Rev. 14:7 and Luke 22:53.

To Matthew Hill: Somerville College, Oxford [Amelia B. Edwards Archive 72]
77. *William Young Ottley* (1771–1836): appointed keeper of the prints in the British Museum in 1833, serving three years before his death.
78. *Chalcography:* the art of engraving on copper. Ottley had published *Inquiry into the Origin and Early History of Engraving on Copper and Wood* (1816) and *Notices of Engravers and their Works* (1831), among other books.
79. In some boroughs the bridgemaster was also a member of the Corporation.

To Joseph Hone: British Library [Add. MS. 40120, f. 387]
80. *Joseph Hone* (1784–1861): lawyer and civil servant. He emigrated with his wife and three daughters to Hobart in 1824 and held a variety of positions for the Crown over a period of thirty years, including master of the Tasmanian Supreme Court. Joseph Hone was "'little removed from an idiot' according to objective observers, drew large crowds (or at least numerous observers) to the court to watch his antics, which included pulling grotesque faces before proceeding to judgement and waggling his fingers in the air" (*The Diaries and Letters of G. T. W. B. Boyes,* ed. Peter Chapman, vol. 1, 1820–1832 [Melbourne: Oxford University Press, 1985], 22).
81. *Henry Scougal* (1650–78): son of the bishop of Aberdeen, Patrick Scougal (1607–82), Henry was reckoned one of the saints in the Scottish church. His *Life of God in the Soul of Man* was published by Gilbert Burnet in 1677. *Remains of the Rev. Richard Cecil* [1748–1810], the 4th edition appearing in 1813.
82. *Mr. Binney:* Reverend Thomas Binney (1798–1874) was a distinguished nonconformist clergyman in charge of the Weigh House church in London from 1829 until 1869. He was well known for his pulpit oratory, and later he published widely on controversial subjects as well as devotional poetry.

To John Childs: British Library [Add. MS. 40120, f. 481]
83. *Cruden:* Alexander Cruden (1701–70), whose *Complete con-*

cordance to the Bible first appeared in 1737. *Adams:* possibly Thomas Adams (?1633–70), one of the ejected divines of 1662 who wrote *Protestant Union, or Principles of Religion wherein the Dissenters agree with the Church of England* (1675) and *The Main Principles of Christian Religion* (1677).

84. *postillers:* a postil is an annotation on a text, especially Scripture.

85. The New Metropolitan Police Act was introduced in 1829 by Sir Robert Peel (1788–1850).

To Alice Hone: British Library [Add. MS. 40856, f. 50]
86. *Alice Hone*: youngest daughter (b. 1825) of William and Sarah Hone.

SELECTED BIBLIOGRAPHY

Anderson, Patricia. *The Printed Image and the Transformation of Popular Culture 1790–1860.* Oxford: Clarendon Press, 1990.

Aspinall, A. *Politics and the Press, 1780–1850.* London: Home & Van Thal, 1949.

Asquith, Ivon. "The Structure, Ownership and Control of the Press, 1780–1855." In *Newspaper History from the Seventeenth Century to the Present Day,* edited by George Boyce, James Curran, and Pauline Wingate, 98–116. London: Constable, 1978.

Bowden, Ann. "William Hone's Political Journalism, 1815–1821." 2 vols. Ph.D. diss., University of Texas at Austin, 1975.

Clark, Anna. "Queen Caroline and the Sexual Politics of Popular Culture in London, 1820." *Representations* 31 (summer 1990): 47–68.

Dinwiddy, J. R. *From Luddism to the First Reform Bill.* Oxford: Blackwell, 1986.

Dorson, Richard. *The British Folklorists: A History.* London: Routledge & Kegan Paul, 1968.

Dyer, Gary. *British Satire and the Politics of Style, 1789–1832.* Cambridge: Cambridge University Press, 1997.

Epstein, James. *Radical Expression: Political Language, Ritual and Symbol in England, 1790–1850.* New York: Oxford University Press, 1994.

Fraser, Flora. *The Unruly Queen: The Life of Queen Caroline.* New York: Alfred A. Knopf, 1996.

Freshwater, Peter B. "Thomas Sharp, William Hone, and Hearne's Hell-Mouth." *Library* 5, no. 3 (September 1983): 263–67.

George, M. Dorothy, ed. *Catalogue of Political and Personal Satires,* vols. 9 and 10. London: British Museum, 1938–54.

Gilmartin, Kevin. *Print Politics: The Press and Radical Opposition in Early Nineteenth-CenturyEngland.* 1996, Cambridge University Press.

———. "Radical Print Culture in Periodical Form." In *Romanticism, History and the Possibilities of Genre: Reforming Literature 1789–1837,* edited by Tilottama Rajan and Julia Wright, 39–63. Cambridge: Cambridge University Press, 1998.

Grimes, Kyle. "William Hone." In *British Reform Writers,* edited by Gary Kelly and Edd Applegate, 158–68. Vol. 158 of *Dictionary of Literary Biography.* Detroit: Gale, 1996.

———. "William Hone, John Murray, and the Uses of Byron." In *Romanticism, Radicalism, and the Press,* edited by Stephen Behrendt, 192–202. Detroit: Wayne State University Press, 1997.

———. "Spreading the Radical Word: The Circulation of William Hone's 1817 Liturgical Parodies." In *Radicalism and Revolution in Britain, 1775–1848: Essays in Honour of Malcolm I. Thomis,* edited by Michael T. Davis, 143–55. London: Macmillan, 2000.

Hackwood, Frederick William. *William Hone: His Life and Times.* 1912. Reprint, New York: Augustus M. Kelley, 1970.

Hibbert, Christopher. *George IV, Prince of Wales 1762–1811.* London: Longman, 1972.

———. *George IV, Regent and King, 1811–1830.* London: Allen Lane, 1973.

Hill, Jonathan. "William Hone." In *British Romantic Prose Writers, 1789–1832.* 2d ser. Edited by John R. Greenfield, 126–38. Vol. 110 of *Dictionary of Literary Biography.* Detroit: Gale, 1991.

Holme, Thea. *Caroline: A Biography of Caroline of Brunswick.* London: Hamish Hamilton, 1979.

Hone, J. Anne. "William Hone (1780–1842), Publisher and Bookseller: An Approach to Early Nineteenth-Century London Radicalism." *Historical Studies* 16 (April 1974–October 1975): 55–70.

———. *For the Cause of Truth: Radicalism in London 1796–1821.* Oxford: Clarendon Press, 1982.

James, Louis. "An Artist in Time: George Cruikshank in Three Eras." In *George Cruikshank: A Revaluation,* edited by Robert L. Patten, 157–68. Princeton, N.J.: Princeton University Press, 1974.

Jones, Steven E. *Shelley's Satire.* Dekalb, Ill.: Northern Illinois University Press, 1994.

———. *Satire and Romanticism.* New York: St. Martin's Press, 2000.

Marsh, Joss. *Word Crimes: Blasphemy, Culture, and Literature in Nineteenth-Century England.* Chicago: University of Chicago Press, 1998.

Martineau, Harriet. *The History of England during the Thirty Years' Peace.* 2 vols. London: Charles Knight, 1850.

McCalman, Iain. *Radical Underworld: Prophets, Revolutionaries and Pornographers in London, 1795–1840.* Cambridge: Cambridge University Press, 1988.

Neuburg, Victor E. *Popular Literature: A History and Guide.* Harmondsworth, Middlesex: Penguin, 1977.

Patten, Robert L. *George Cruikshank's Life, Times, and Art.* Vol. 1, *1792–1835.* New Brunswick, N.J.: Rutgers University Press, 1992.

Peterson, Ted. "The Fight of Willliam Hone for British Press Freedom." *Journalism Quarterly* 25 (1948): 132–38.

Rickword, Edgell. *Radical Squibs & Royal Ripostes.* Bath, Somerset: Adams & Dart, 1971.

Robinson, J. W. "Regency Radicalism and Antiquarianism: William Hone's *Ancient Mysteries Described* (1823)." *Leeds Studies in English* 10 (1978): 121–44.

Rolleston, Frances. *Some Account of the Conversion from Atheism to Christianity of the Late William Hone.* 2d rev. ed. London: Francis and John Rivington, 1853.

Routledge, James. *Chapters in the History of Popular Progress, chiefly in relation to the Freedom of the Press and Trial by Jury, 1660–1820.* London: Macmillan, 1876.

Sales, Roger. *English Literature in History: 1780–1830, Pastoral and Politics.* London: Hutchinson, 1983.

Scrivener, Michael. *Radical Shelley.* Princeton, N.J.: Princeton University Press, 1982.

———, ed. *Poetry and Reform: Periodical Verse from the English Democratic Press 1792–1824.* Detroit: Wayne State University Press, 1992.

Sikes, Herschel M. "William Hone: Regency Patriot, Parodist, and Pamphleteer." *Newberry Library Bulletin* 5 (1961): 281–94.

Smith, E. A. *A Queen on Trial: The Affair of Queen Caroline.* Stroud, Gloucestershire: Allan Sutton, 1993.

Smith, Olivia. *The Politics of Language.* Oxford: Oxford University Press, 1984.

Sutton, David C., ed. *Location Register of English Literary Manu-*

scripts and Letters: Eighteenth and Nineteenth Centuries. Vol. 1. London: British Library, 1995.

Thompson, E. P. *The Making of the English Working Class.* New York: Vintage, 1963.

Vitale, Marina. "The Domesticated Heroine in Byron's *Corsair* and William Hone's Prose Adaptation." *Literature and History* 10, no. 1 (spring 1984): 72–94.

Wardroper, John, ed. *The World of William Hone.* London: Shelfmark Books, 1997.

Wood, Marcus. *Radical Satire and Print Culture 1790–1822.* Oxford: Clarendon Press, 1994.

Worrall, David. *Radical Culture: Discourse, Resistance and Surveillance, 1790–1820.* London: Harvester Wheatsheaf, 1992.